JOE CELKO'S
SQL FOR SMARTIES:
ADVANCED SQL PROGRAMMING

Second Edition

The Morgan Kaufmann Series in Data Management Systems
Series Editor, Jim Gray

JOE CELKO'S
SQL FOR SMARTIES:
ADVANCED SQL PROGRAMMING

Second Edition

Joe Celko

MORGAN KAUFMANN PUBLISHERS

AN IMPRINT OF ACADEMIC PRESS
A Harcourt Science and Technology Company
SAN FRANCISCO   SAN DIEGO   NEW YORK   BOSTON
LONDON   SYDNEY   TOKYO

Senior Editor	Diane D. Cerra
Senior Production Editor	Elisabeth Beller
Cover Design	Canary Design/Side by Side Studios
Text Design	Canary Design
Copyeditor	Steve Hiatt
Proofreader	Ken DellaPenta
Composition	Nancy Logan
Illustration	Cherie Plumlee
Indexer	Steve Rath
Printer	Courier Corporation

ACADEMIC PRESS
A Harcourt Science and Technology Company
525 B Street, Suite 1900, San Diego, CA 92101-4495, USA
http://www.academicpress.com

Academic Press
Harcourt Place, 32 Jamestown Road, London NW1 7BY, United Kingdom
http://www.academicpress.com

Morgan Kaufmann Publishers
340 Pine Street, Sixth Floor, San Francisco, CA 94104-3205, USA
http://www.mkp.com

04   03   02   01   6   5   4   3

Library of Congress Cataloging-in-Publication Data
Celko, Joe.
    [SQL for smarties]
    Joe Celko's SQL for smarties: advanced SQL programming/
    Joe Celko—2nd ed.
        p. cm.
    Includes bibliographical references and index.
    ISBN 1-55860-576-2
    1. SQL (Computer program language) I. Title: SQL for smarties. II.
    Title.
QA76.73.S67 C44 1999
005.13'3—dc21   99-046068

This book has been printed on acid-free paper.

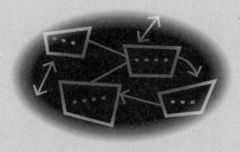

To Ann and Jackers

C O N T E N T S

README_2.JOE

I have been quite happy with the success of *SQL for Smarties* and have
enjoyed all the feedback readers have given me since its publication.
The success of the book even prompted *DBMS Magazine* to change the
name of my column, the "SQL Explorer," to "SQL for Smarties."

I am also very happy with the new programming tricks that readers
have been sending me to include in this second edition. This saves me
a lot of work while still allowing me to take the royalty money in
exchange for giving them the glory.

I have reorganized this book quite a bit since the first edition. Many
of the previous sections have been moved to new locations and expanded. I have also dropped a lot of the more theoretical material in favor of
more programming methods. Don't worry; the theory stuff has been
moved to the next book in this series, *Data and Databases*.

What I first called the edge and visitation model for trees in SQL has
been changed to the adjacency list and nested set model, respectively. I
have also added more material on trees than I had in the first edition.

Organization of the Book

The book is still organized into nested, numbered sections arranged by
topic. If you have a problem and want to look up a possible solution
now, you can go to the index or table of contents and thumb to the
right section. Feel free to highlight the parts you need and to write
notes in the margins.

I kept the casual conversational style of the first edition and the
practice of discussing why a particular trick works since I got very
positive feedback from readers.

Chapter 1 starts with the first step in building a database, namely
how to set up tables in the schema. I cover the details of using constraints and discuss some of the practical problems of normalization in
Chapter 2. You might be surprised by how much work the database can
do for you even before you put any data in it.

Entering data into tables is the next step, so Chapters 3, 4, and 5 discuss SQL datatypes—a topic I have not seen covered in detail in any
other book. Chapter 6 is devoted to NULLs, which are the trickiest part

of SQL. Chapter 7 discusses expressions, and Chapter 8 deals with other schema objects.

Chapter 9 assumes that we now have tables and want to do operations on them, such as INSERT INTO, DELETE FROM, and UPDATE.

In Chapters 10 to 16, I deal with the predicates and logical operators of SQL. SQL is based on logic, so you have to learn logic before you can ask a query.

I do not show you the SELECT statement until Chapter 17. Most other SQL books would have tried to discuss it as soon as possible, but I think that you need some background before you do queries. I discuss all the flavors of JOINs I can think of—left, right, full, outer, inner, self, natural, T-, and exotic.

Chapter 18 deals with VIEWs, which can be much handier than you would think.

Chapters 19 to 30 cover all kinds of complicated queries. In particular, look at the representations of trees in SQL in Chapters 28 and 29. Yes, it takes that long to get to the good stuff in SQL.

Chapter 31 offers tips for optimizing queries. Again, these are general tricks that may not apply to a particular SQL product, so beware.

Corrections and Future Editions

I will be glad to receive corrections, new tricks and techniques, and other suggestions for future editions of this book. Send your ideas to

Joe Celko
235 Carter Avenue
Atlanta, GA 30317-3303
    email: *71062.1056@compuserve.com*
    website: *www.celko.com*

or contact me through the publisher, Morgan Kaufmann (*www.mkp.com*). You could see your name in print!

Acknowledgments

The first group of people to thank are the crew at Morgan Kaufmann: Diane Cerra, Mike Morgan, Elisabeth Beller, Belinda Breyer, Bruce Spatz (formerly at Morgan Kaufmann, who first nagged me into writing a book for them), and Masayuki Akita (my Japanese edition translator).

The next group are the crew at Miller-Freeman Publications, where I have done most of my work: David Kalman of *DBMS Magazine,* David Stodder of *Database Programming & Design,* Maurice Frank (my editor at *DBMS Magazine*), Phil Chapnik, Teresa Rigney, and Kathleen O'Connor.

In no particular order, I also got help from the following people: Alan Flancman, Bill Gettys of DEC, Cary Harwin at Logic Gem, Dave Roberts of George Washington University, David Fyffe at Microsoft, Doug Hubbard, George Schusell of Digital Consulting Inc., Graeme Birchall, Jane S. Roseen at *Powerbuilder Developer Journal,* Jeff Jacobs on the CompuServe Oracle forum, Jeff Winchell, Jeffrey R. Garbus at Northern Lights Consulting, Jim Panttaja, Johannes Becher, John Paulson at Ensodex, Ken North, Lee Fesperman at FFE Software, Leo Tohill, Rudy Limeback of New York Life (Toronto), Rud Merriam, Mike Ault, Pamela Miller at the SQL Pro web site, Ralph Kimball, Rich Cohen, Richard Finkelstein, Richard Romley at Smith-Barney, Rob Mattison, Rory Murchison of the Aetna Institute, Simon Griffiths, Steve Roti, Susan Vombreck at Loral, Tanj Bennett at Microsoft, Tom Bragg, Tom Kregel of Intuitive Software Developers, and Tom Ochs. Other people are mentioned by name in the text with the problems or solutions they submitted.

And of course, I thank all the members of the ANSI X3H2 Database Standards Committee, past and present.

Introduction

THIS BOOK, LIKE the first edition, is for the working SQL programmer who wants to pick up some advanced programming tips and techniques. It assumes that the reader is an SQL programmer with a year of actual experience.

I was a bit surprised at the success of the first edition, which has become a minor classic among working SQL programmers. I received a lot of feedback over the years since the first edition appeared and have incorporated those ideas into the second edition.

The SQL code is now very portable because vendors have converged to ANSI/ISO Standard SQL-92 (see *Understanding the New SQL* by Jim Melton and Alan R. Simon [1993]) in their products. Other related standards that were first developed by other groups, such as the SQL/CLI for embedded SQL and the SQL/PSM (see *Understanding SQL's Stored Procedures* by Jim Melton [1998]) for procedural code, are now ISO standards. But, even with the move to the ISO standard, existing implementations will still use their own proprietary syntax in many places.

Sadly, for political reasons NIST (the National Institute for Standards and Technology) no longer issues FIPS-127 conformance test certifications. However, the NIST test suite is available to the public on request.

X/Open and SQL Access merged in 1995. Not too surprisingly, the same vendors (and even the same people representing the vendors) are members of the consortia and on the ANSI X3H2 Database Standards Committee. When the first edition of this book was written, the "language de jour" was

ADA. Today, ADA is gone completely as of 1999, and other consortia have come into place for SQLJ and JDBC to put SQL into Java.

I have had lots of readers correct the code and use my email address to tell about everything that was wrong, could be done differently, or could be done better. Special thanks to Masayuki Akita, my Japanese translator, who tested everything in the book and made me clear up my English in the way that only comes when you do a translation to a totally different language; and to Richard Romley, who loves to cook every puzzle I write.

I have added new techniques and improved the old ones. I also decided to drop some of the theory from this book and move it to my *Data & Databases*. My three volumes for Morgan Kaufmann have some rhyme and reason to them. All of them are intended for a working programmer with some experience, but

1. *SQL for Smarties* is a collection of practical techniques; it assumes you know SQL and how to program in it. You need enough experience to know that you have problems.

2. *Data and Databases* (Celko 1999) is an explanation of why you use those techniques, how different vendors implement things, and so forth. This information will guide you in moving the techniques from one product to another.

3. *SQL Puzzles and Answers* (Celko 1997) is your chance to prove you learned something from the first two books. It is also a demonstration and explanation in detail of multiple ways to solve the same problem.

The Nature of the SQL Language

SQL-92 has three levels: entry, intermediate, and full. It will be many years before most vendors have a full implementation, but all products are moving toward that goal. I have tried to stick to the SQL-89 standard and to use only the SQL-92 features that are already used in existing implementations. These features might be present with a different syntax in a particular product, however, so programmers will have to adjust their code to match products. Readers should also be aware of other standards bodies besides ANSI and ISO that deal with SQL.

A procedural language is a detailed description of how a task is accomplished, and it operates on one record or one unit of data at a time. Such languages are also called 3GL (third-generation languages) and are familiar

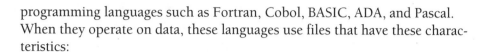
programming languages such as Fortran, Cobol, BASIC, ADA, and Pascal. When they operate on data, these languages use files that have these characteristics:

1. Data is stored in files of records. The programmer must know the physical location, logical location, and structure of a file to use it.

2. The program has the information needed to read a file and accesses it one record at a time.

3. The structure of the records is defined within each program.

4. The order of the records within a file is important.

5. The order of the data within a record is important.

6. Records can be complex data structures.

In contrast, a nonprocedural language is a description of what you want; the system figures out how to get it. SQL is such a language. SQL is not considered an end-user language; it has no input and output statements, so it has to be used with a host language that can handle those functions. When SQL operates on data, it models the world with tables that have these characteristics:

1. Data is stored in a database made up of tables; the tables can be real or virtual. Users are connected to the whole database, not to individual tables.

2. The program asks SQL to return data to it, without any concern as to the physical structure or location of the data.

3. The structure of the tables is defined within the database, not within each program.

4. The order of the tables within the database is not important. They are identified by name.

5. The order of the columns within a table is not important. They are identified by name or a combination of table name and column name.

6. The order of the rows within a table is not important. They are identified by unique values within their columns (keys).

7. The data is always presented as a table to the user, no matter what internal structure is used by the database.

SQL often presents a problem for an experienced programmer who has to unlearn old habits developed while using 3GLs. But think of this process as similar to learning recursion in a 3GL. At first, it is impossible to see things recursively; then suddenly it all makes sense, and you write your first recursive program. In SQL, complex queries look impossible until the day you can think in sets and formal logic, and then you simply write the query.

I have tried to provide comments with the solutions, to explain why they work. I hope this will help the reader see underlying principles that can be used in other situations.

Programming Tips

Pete Jensen of Georgia Tech used to tell a story about doing a programming project with an accountant. The programmer did not understand accounting, and the accountant did not understand programming. At one point, the programmer was having a hard time understanding what the accountant wanted the program to do, and they were beating their heads together. The breakthrough came when the accountant said, "If you can't think of it as a ratio, then think of it as a percentage!" and the programmer suddenly got the idea.

Never mind that a ratio and a percentage are the same thing mathematically; the change in the mental model made the difference.

In SQL, there are a series of mental models you can use to help you write a query. These tips cannot be formalized, but they do seem to help.

1. Start with the SELECT clause, and write a list of what you want to see in the result set. This gives you a goal and something to show to the user.

2. Put all the tables containing the columns needed to complete the SELECT list into the FROM clause. You can remove the extras later. All the work is in the WHERE clause.

3. Think about how to word the problem solution with sets instead of individual instances. The best example of this trick is to use nested sets to represent trees instead of modeling them as individual nodes and edges.

4. Sometimes reversing the wording of the problem helps. Instead of saying "Give me all the cars that are red," say "Red is the color of all the cars I want," which lets you see the underlying logic.

5. Sometimes negating the wording of the problem helps. Instead of saying "Give me the cars that met all the test criteria," say "Don't give me any car that failed one of the test criteria" instead. It is often easier to find what you do not want than what you do want.

This is method is especially helpful when you use the NOT EXISTS predicate, but beware of NULLs and empty tables when you try this.

6. Nesting functions inside each other is a handy way of doing many things in one pass. In particular, learn to use the new CASE expression and aggregate functions.

7. Watch your logic! It is very easy to make mistakes in long logical expressions. Procedural languages allow the programmer to write programs that filter the data to a result set in a series of simple steps; SQL requires that all the work be done in a single expression, which can be complex. I recommend that you use a tool like LOGIC GEM (Logic Technologies; Yucca Valley, CA), a decision-table generator, for complex expressions.

8. Remember to allow for NULLs creating UNKNOWN logical values. Always test your code with NULLs in all possible places.

9. Remember to allow for empty tables and to test for them. Try to design test data that covers all cases. This is why I like to use a decision-table generator, which will validate your logic and ensure that everything has been handled.

Database Design

THIS CHAPTER DISCUSSES the DDL (Data Definition Language), which is used to create a database schema, and it is related to the next chapter on the theory of database normalization.

SQL has spawned a whole branch of the CASE (computer-aided software engineering) industry devoted to designing its schemas and tables. This is impressive because nobody ever developed a tool to validate the design of a file. Most of these tools use a graphic or text description of the rules and the constraints on the data to produce a schema declaration statement that can be used directly in a particular SQL product.

1.1 Schema and Table Creation

One of the initial problems in learning SQL is that programmers are used to thinking in terms of files rather than tables. Programming languages are usually based on some underlying model; if you understand the model, the language makes more sense. For example, Fortran is based on algebra. This does not mean that Fortran is exactly like algebra. But if you know algebra, Fortran does not look that strange to you. You can write an expression in an assignment statement or make a good guess as to the names of library functions you have never seen before.

The model for SQL is *data kept in sets,* not in physical files. Programmers are used to working with files in almost every other language, so they have to unlearn that model.

A sequential file consists of records that are ordered sequentially within the file. You find a first record when you open a file, a series of next records as you use the data, and a last record to raise the end-of-file condition. You navigate among these records and perform actions one record at a time. Files model the way people handle paper forms.

On the other hand, sets are those mathematical abstractions you studied in school. Sets are not ordered, and the members of a set are all of the same type. When you do an operation on a set, the action happens all at once to the entire membership. That is, if I ask for the subset of odd numbers from the set of positive integers, I get all of them back as a set. I do not build the set of odd numbers one element at a time. I define odd numbers with a rule—"If the remainder is 1 when you divide the number by 2, it's odd" —that could test any integer and classify it.

SQL is not a perfect set language any more than Fortran is a perfect algebraic language, as we will see. But when in doubt about something in SQL, ask yourself how you would specify it in terms of sets and you will probably get the right answer.

1.1.1 Schemas

A schema is the skeleton of an SQL database; it defines the structures of the objects and the rules under which they operate. The only data structure in SQL is the table. Tables can be permanent (base tables), used for working storage (temporary tables), or virtual (VIEWs); SQL-92 also allows you to have temporary, global, and shared tables, but we will not discuss them here since most products have not implemented them yet.

The advantage of having only one data structure is that the results of all operations are also tables—you never have to convert structures, write special operators, or deal with any irregularity in the language.

Conceptually, a table is a set of zero or more rows, and a row is a set of one or more columns. Each column has a specific datatype. The way a table is physically implemented does not matter because you access it only with SQL. The database engine handles all the details for you and you never worry about the internals, as you would with a physical file.

In fact, almost no two SQL products use the same internal structures.

Two common conceptual errors are made by programmers who are accustomed to file systems or PCs. The first is thinking that a table is a file; the second is thinking that a table is a spreadsheet. Tables do not behave like either one of these, and you will get surprises if you do not understand the basic concepts.

It is easy to imagine that a table is a file, a row is a record, and a column is a field because this model works almost all the time. The big differences between working with a file system and working with SQL are in the way SQL fits into a host program. Using a file system, your programs must open and close files individually; using SQL, the whole schema is connected to or disconnected from the program in one step and brings all the authorized tables with it.

Fields within a file are defined by the program, whereas SQL defines its columns in the schema. Fortran uses the FORMAT and READ statements to get data from a file. Likewise, a Cobol program uses a Data Division to define the fields and a READ to fetch it. And so on for every 3GL's programming; the concept is the same, though the syntax and options vary.

A file system lets you reference the same data by a different name in each program. If a file's layout changes, you must rewrite all the programs that use that file. When a file is empty, it looks exactly like all other empty files. When you try to read an empty file, the EOF (end of file) flag pops up and the program takes some action. Column names and datatypes in a table are defined within the database schema. Within reasonable limits, the tables can be changed without the knowledge of the host program.

The host program worries only about transferring the values to its own variables from the database. Remember the empty set from your high school math class? It is still a valid set. When a table is empty, it still has columns, but has zero rows. There is no EOF flag to signal an exception.

Another major difference is that tables and columns can have constraints attached to them. A constraint is a rule that defines what must be true about the database after each transaction. In this sense, a database is more like a collection of objects than a traditional passive file system.

A table is not a spreadsheet, even though they look very much alike when you view them on a screen or in a printout. In a spreadsheet you can access a row, a column, a cell, or a collection of cells by navigating with a cursor. A table has no concept of navigation. Cells in a spreadsheet can store instructions and not just data. There is no real difference between a row and column in a spreadsheet; you could flip them around completely and still get valid results. This is not true for an SQL table.

1.1.2 Manipulating Tables

The three basic table statements in the SQL DDL are CREATE TABLE, DROP TABLE, and ALTER TABLE. They pretty much do what you would think they do from their names. We will explain them in detail shortly, but they bring a table into existence in the database, remove a table from the database, and change the structure of an existing table, respectively.

The table name must be unique in the schema, and the column names must be unique within a table. The names in SQL can consist of letters, underscores, and digits, and vendors commonly allow other printing characters. However, it is a good idea to avoid using anything except letters and digits. Special characters are not portable and will not sort the same way in different products. The underscore is often hard to read and to print clearly. SQL-92 allows you to use spaces, reserved words, and special characters in a name if you enclose them in double quotation marks, but this should be avoided as much as possible. Otherwise, you will just confuse yourself. For example, PRIMARY is a reserved word, 'PRIMARY' is a character string, and "PRIMARY" is a name. Do you think you can tell them apart when you are trying to debug a program and you haven't had any sleep? A table must have at least one column. SQL can handle a table and a column with the same name, but it is a good practice to name tables differently from their columns. I happen to use plural or collective nouns for table names and use singular attribute names for columns, but you will see other authors who use singular nouns for table names. I feel the use of the plural helps you think of tables as sets. For example, do not name a table "Employee"; use something like "Personnel," or even "Employees," for the table name. It is also a good idea to use the same name for the same attribute or thing in different tables. For example, do not name a column in one table "sex" and a column in another table "gender" when they refer to the same property. Though it is not required, it is also a good idea to place related columns in their conventional order in the table. By default, the columns will print out in the order in which they appear in the table. For example, put name, address, city, state, and ZIP code in that order, so that you can read them easily in a display.

I have also introduced, in the database magazines in which I have had regular columns, the convention that keywords are in uppercase, table names are capitalized, and column names are in lowercase. I feel this makes the code easier to read. I also use capital letter(s) followed by digit(s) for correlation names (e.g., the table Personnel would have correlation names P0, P1, ..., Pn), where the digit shows the depth of nesting in the query.

DROP TABLE

The DROP TABLE statement removes a table from the database. This is *not* the same as making the table an empty table. When a schema object is dropped, it is gone forever. The syntax of the statement is

```
<drop table statement> ::= DROP TABLE <table name>
<drop behavior> ::= RESTRICT | CASCADE
```

The <drop behavior> clause is new to SQL-92. If RESTRICT is specified, the table cannot be referenced in the query expression of any view or the search condition of any constraint. This is supposed to prevent the unpleasant surprise of having other things fail because they depended on this particular table for their own definitions. If CASCADE is specified, then such referencing objects will also be dropped along with the table.

The SQL-89 standard was silent as to what would happen when you dropped a table. Either the particular SQL product would post an error message, and in effect do a RESTRICT, or you would find out about any dependencies by having your database blow up when it ran into constructs that needed the missing table.

The DROP keyword and <drop behavior> clause are also used in other statements that remove schema objects, such as DROP VIEW, DROP SCHEMA, DROP CONSTRAINT, and so forth.

This is usually a "DBA-only" statement that, for obvious reasons, programmers are not usually allowed to use.

ALTER TABLE

The ALTER TABLE statement adds, removes, or changes columns within a table. This statement was not part of the SQL-89 standard, but it is in SQL-92 and it existed in most SQL implementations before it was standardized. It is still implemented in many different ways, so you should see your product documentation for details. This is also a statement that your DBA will not want you to use without permission. The SQL-92 syntax looks like this:

```
ALTER TABLE <table name> <alter table action>

<alter table action> ::=
  ADD [COLUMN] <column definition>
    | ALTER [COLUMN] <column name> <alter column action>
    | DROP [COLUMN] <column name> <drop behavior>
    | ADD <table constraint definition>
    | DROP CONSTRAINT <constraint name> <drop behavior>
```

As you would expect, the ADD COLUMN clause extends the existing table by putting another column on it. The new column must have a name that is unique within the table and follow the other rules for a valid column declaration.

The ALTER COLUMN clause can change a column and its definition. Exactly what is allowed will vary from product to product, but usually the datatype can be changed to a compatible datatype (e.g., you can make a CHAR() column longer, but not shorter; change an INTEGER to a REAL; and so forth). You can often add DEFAULT and CHECK() clauses.

The DROP COLUMN clause removes the column from the table. SQL-92 gives you the option of setting the drop behavior, which most current products do not. The two options are RESTRICT and CASCADE. RESTRICT will not allow the column to disappear if it is referenced in another schema object. CASCADE will also delete any schema object that references the dropped column.

When this statement is available in your SQL product, I strongly advise that you first use the RESTRICT option to see if there are references before you use the CASCADE option.

The ADD <table constraint definition> clause lets you put a constraint on a table. Many current versions of SQL, such as DB2 and Oracle, require that you use the ALTER statement to add referential integrity constraints to a table rather than allowing you to declare the constraints at schema creation time.

The DROP CONSTRAINT clause requires that the constraint be given a name, so this is a good habit to get into. If the constraint to be dropped was given no name, you will have to find what name was assigned to it by the system in the schema tables and use that name. The standard does not say how such names are to be constructed, only that they are unique within a table. Actual products will usually pick a long random string of digits and preface it with some letters to make a valid name that is so absurd that no human being would think of it. A constraint name will also appear in warnings and error messages, making debugging much easier. The <drop behavior> option behaves as it did for the DROP COLUMN clause.

CREATE TABLE

The CREATE TABLE statement does all the hard work. The basic syntax looks like this:

```
CREATE TABLE <table name> (<table element list>)

<table element list> ::=
  <table element> | <table element>, <table element list>

<table element> ::=
  <column definition> | <table constraint definition>
```

The table definition includes data in the column definitions and rules for handling that data in the table constraint definitions. This means that a table acts more like an object (with its data and methods) than just a simple, passive file.

1.1.3 Column Definitions

Beginning SQL programmers often fail to take full advantage of the options available to them, and they pay for it with errors or extra work in their applications. Saving yourself time and trouble begins with column definition, using the following syntax:

```
<column definition> ::=
  <column name> <data type>
  [<default clause>]
  [<column constraint>...]

<column constraint> ::= NOT NULL
        | <check constraint definition>
        | <unique specification>
        | <references specification>
```

The first important thing to notice here is that each column must have a datatype, which it keeps unless you ALTER the table. The SQL standard offers many datatypes because SQL must work with many different host languages. The datatypes fall into four major categories: numerics, character strings, temporal, and bit datatypes. We will discuss the datatypes and their rules of operation in other sections; they are fairly obvious, so not knowing the details will not prevent you from understanding the examples that follow.

DEFAULT Clause

The DEFAULT clause is an underused feature; its syntax is

```
<default clause> ::=
  [CONSTRAINT <constraint name>] DEFAULT <default option>

<default option> ::= <literal> | <system value> | NULL
```

Whenever the system does not have an explicit value to put into this column, it will look for its DEFAULT clause and insert that value. The default option can be a literal value of the relevant datatype, or something provided by the system, such as the current timestamp, current date, current user identifier, and so forth. If you do not provide a DEFAULT clause, the column definition acts as if you had declared it DEFAULT NULL.

Using a DEFAULT clause is a good way to make the database do a lot of work that you would otherwise have to code into all the application programs. The most common tricks are to use a zero in numeric columns, a string to encode a missing value ('unknown') or true default ('same address') in character columns, and the system timestamp to mark transactions.

Column Constraints

Column constraints are rules that are attached to a table. All the rows in the table are validated against them. File systems have nothing like this, since validation is done in the application programs. They are also one of the most underused features of SQL, so you can look like a real wizard if you can master them.

NOT NULL Constraint

The most important column constraint is the NOT NULL, which forbids the use of NULLs in a column. Use this constraint automatically, then remove it only when you have good reason. It will help you avoid the complications of NULL values when you make queries against the data.

The NULL is a special value in SQL that belongs to all datatypes. SQL is the only language that has such a creature; if you can understand how it works, you will have a good grasp of SQL. A NULL means that we have a missing, unknown, miscellaneous, or inapplicable value in the data.

The problem is that exactly which of these four possibilities the NULL indicates depends on how it is used. For example, imagine that I am looking at a carton of Easter eggs and I want to know their colors. If I see an empty hole, I have a *missing* egg, which I hope will be provided later. If I see a foil-wrapped egg, I have an *unknown* color value in my set. If I see a multicolored egg, I have a *miscellaneous* value in my set. If I see a cue ball, I have an *inapplicable* value in my set. The way you handle each situation is a little different.

When you use NULLs in math calculations, they propagate in the results so that the answer is another NULL. When you use them in logical expressions or comparisons, they return a logical value of UNKNOWN and give SQL its strange three-valued logic. They sort either high or low in the collation sequence. They group together for some operations but not for others. In short, NULLs cause a lot of irregular features in SQL, which we will discuss later. Your best bet is just to memorize the situations and the rules for NULLs when you cannot avoid them.

CHECK() Constraint

The CHECK constraint is underused by even experienced SQL programmers. It tests the rows of the table against a logical expression, which SQL calls a search condition, and rejects rows whose search condition returns FALSE. However, the constraint accepts rows when the search condition returns TRUE or UNKNOWN. The UNKNOWN is a "benefit-of-the-doubt" feature that even experienced programmers forget. The syntax is

```
<check constraint definition> ::=
    [CONSTRAINT <constraint name>] CHECK (<search condition>)
```

The usual technique is to do simple range checking, such as CHECK (rating BETWEEN 1 AND 10), or to verify that a column's value is in an enumerated set, such as CHECK (sex IN ('M', 'F')), with this constraint. Remember that the sex column could also be set to NULL, unless a NOT NULL constraint is also added to the column's declaration. While it is optional, it is a really good idea to use a constraint name. Without it, most SQL implementations will create a huge, ugly, unreadable random string for the name since they need to have one in the schema tables. If you provide your own, you can drop the constraint more easily and understand the error messages when the constraint is violated.

The real power of the CHECK() clause comes from writing complex expressions that verify relationships with other rows, with other tables, or with constants.

For example, you can use a single CHECK clause to enforce the rule that a firm does not hire anyone under 21 years of age for a job that requires serving liquor by checking the birth date and hire date. However, you cannot put the current system date into the CHECK() clause logic for the obvious reason—that it is always changing.

As an example of how complex things can get, consider a database of movies for which you want to enforce a rule that you cannot export a movie to its own country of origin.

```
CREATE TABLE Exports
(movie_id INTEGER NOT NULL,
 country_id CHAR(2) NOT NULL,    -- use 2-letter ISO  nation codes
 sales DECIMAL (12,2) NOT NULL,
```

```
PRIMARY KEY (movie_id, country_id),
CONSTRAINT Foreign_film
CHECK (NOT EXISTS
        (SELECT *
          FROM Movies AS M1
          WHERE M1.movie_id = Exports.movie_id
            AND M1.country_of_origin = Exports.country_id)));
```

SQL is weak on string expressions that could be used to enforce patterns in strings, along the lines of grep() in UNIX systems and the Cobol PICTURE specifications. This just means that the programmer has to get clever. For example, to assure that a VARCHAR column has only a single string made up of only alphabetic characters, you can write this constraint:

```
CREATE TABLE Foobar
 (roman_letters VARCHAR(6) NOT NULL
    CONSTRAINT alpha_only
    CHECK ((TRIM BOTH FROM (UPPER(roman_letters)) || 'AAAAA')
            BETWEEN 'AAAAAA' AND 'ZZZZZZ'
      AND (TRIM BOTH FROM (LOWER (roman_letters)) || 'aaaaa')
            BETWEEN 'aaaaaa' AND 'zzzzzz'),
 . . .
 );
```

The TRIM() function will remove only leading and trailing blanks, so any embedded blanks will put the uppercase string out of the range given in the BETWEEN predicate. Likewise, using a string of only five alphabetic characters ('AAAAA') will result in a final trailing blank after the concatenation, which will fall outside the range if a blank or empty string is entered into the column.

UNIQUE and PRIMARY KEY Constraints

The UNIQUE constraint says that no duplicate values are allowed in the column. The SQL-92 syntax is

```
<unique specification> ::= UNIQUE | PRIMARY KEY
```

File system programmers understand the concept of a PRIMARY KEY, but for the wrong reasons. They are used to a file, which can have only one key because that key is used to determine the physical order of the records within the file. There is no order in a table; the term PRIMARY KEY in SQL has to do with defaults in referential actions, which we will discuss later.

There are some subtle differences between UNIQUE and PRIMARY KEY. There can be only one PRIMARY KEY per table but many UNIQUE columns. A PRIMARY KEY is automatically declared to have a NOT NULL constraint on it, but a UNIQUE column can have multiple NULLs in a row unless you explicitly add a NOT NULL constraint to each column. Adding the NOT NULL whenever possible is a good idea.

There is also a multiple-column form of the <unique specification>, which is usually written at the end of the column declarations. It is a list of columns in parentheses after the proper keyword and means that the combination of those columns is unique. For example, I might declare PRIMARY KEY (city, department) so I can be sure that though I have offices in many cities and many identical departments in those offices, there is only one personnel department in Chicago.

REFERENCES Clause

The REFERENCES specification is the simplest version of a referential constraint definition, which can be quite tricky. For now, let us just consider the simplest case:

```
<references specification> ::=
 [CONSTRAINT <constraint name>]
  REFERENCES <referenced table name>[(<reference column>)]
```

This relates two tables together, so it is different from the other options we have discussed so far. It says that the value in this column of the referencing table must appear somewhere in the referenced table's column that is named in the constraint. Furthermore, the referenced column must have UNIQUE constraint. For example, you can set up a rule that the Orders table will have orders only for goods that appear in the Inventory table.

If no <reference column> is given, then the PRIMARY KEY column of the referenced table is assumed to be the target. This is one of those places where the PRIMARY KEY is important, but you can always play it safe and explicitly name a column. There is no rule to prevent several columns from referencing the same target column. For example, we might have a table of flight crews that has pilot and copilot columns that both reference a table of certified pilots.

Notice that if an item is dropped from the referenced table, rows in the referencing table will be made invalid. The constraint would not allow this to happen and will raise an error condition.

The more complex versions of this clause defined in SQL-92 will allow the database to take appropriate actions automatically, without programmer intervention. Vendors are starting to add parts of this referential integrity to their products, but we will ignore it for now. There is a multicolumn form of this clause, which we will also ignore.

1.1.4 A Remark on Duplicate Rows

Dr. E. F. Codd's two relational models do not allow duplicate rows, and they are based on a set theoretical model; SQL has always allowed duplicate rows and is based on a multiset, or bag, model.

When the question came up in the SQL standards committee, we decided to leave duplicates in the standard. The example we used internally, and which Len Gallagher used in a reply letter to *Database Programming & Design* magazine (Gallagher 1993) and David Beech used in a letter to *Datamation* (Beech 1989), was a cash register receipt with multiple occurrences of cans of cat food on it. That is how this came to be called the "cat food problem" in the literature.

The fundamental question is, What are you modeling in a table? Both Codd and Date take the position that a table is a collection of facts (Codd 1990; Date 1995a). Codd pointed out that, once one states that a fact is true, it serves no useful purpose to state it again.

The other position is that a table can represent an entity, a class, or a relationship among entities. With that approach, a duplicate row means more than one occurrence of an entity. This leads to a more object-oriented view of data where I have to deal with different fundamental relationships among "duplicates," such as

Identity = "Clark Kent is Superman!" We really have only one entity, but multiple expressions of it. These expressions are not substitutable (Clark Kent does not fly until he changes into Superman).

Equality = "Two plus two is four." We really have only one entity with multiple expressions that are always substitutable.

Equivalency = "You use only half as much Concentrated Sudso as your old detergent to get the same cleaning power!" We have two distinct entities, substitutable both ways under all conditions.

Substitutability = "We are out of wine; would you like a vodka?" We have two distinct entities, whose replacement for each other is not always in both directions or under all conditions. You might be willing to accept a glass of vodka when there is no wine, but you cannot make a wine sauce with a cup of vodka.

Codd later added a "degree of duplication" operator to his model as a way of handling duplicates when he realized that there is information in duplication that has to be handled (Codd 1990). The degree of duplication is not exactly a COUNT(*) or a quantity column in the relation. It does not behave like a numeric column. For example, given table A (with "dod" meaning the degree of duplication operator for each row)

A

x	y
1	a
2	b
3	b

when I do a projection on them, I eliminate duplicates rows in Codd's model, but I can reconstruct the original table from the dod function.

A   **A**

y		y	dod
a		a	1
b		b	2

See the difference? It is an operator, not a value.

Having said all of this, I try to use duplicate rows only for loading data into an SQL database from legacy sources. This is a frequent problem when you get data from the real world—like cash register tapes.

Otherwise, I might leave duplicates in results because using a SELECT DISTINCT to remove them will (1) cost too much sorting time, and (2) sorting will force an ordering in the working table that will result in a bad performance hit later.

Codd mentions this example in his book, *The Relational Model for Database Management: Version 2* (1990, sec. 23.2.5, 378, 379) as "The Supermarket Check-Out Problem." He critiques the problem and credits it to David Beech in a later piece (Codd 1989).

1.1.5 A Remark on UNIQUE Constraints versus Unique Indexes

The UNIQUE constraints are not the same thing as unique indexes. Technically speaking, indexes do not exist in standard SQL because they were considered too physical to be part of a logical model of a language. In practice, virtually all products have some form of "access enhancement" for the DBA to use, and it is most often an index.

The column referenced by a FOREIGN KEY has to be either a PRIMARY KEY or a column with a UNIQUE constraint; a unique index on the same set of columns cannot be referenced since the index is on one table and not a relationship between two tables.

There is no order to a constraint, but an index is ordered, so the unique index might be an aid for sorting. Some products construct special index structures for the declarative referential integrity constraints, which in effect "pre-JOIN" the referenced and referencing tables.

In SQL-92, all the constraints can be defined as equivalent to some CHECK constraint, for example:

```
PRIMARY KEY = CHECK (UNIQUE (SELECT <key columns> FROM <table>)
             AND (<key columns>) IS NOT NULL)

UNIQUE = CHECK (UNIQUE (SELECT <key columns> FROM <table>))

NOT NULL = CHECK (<column> IS NOT NULL)
```

These predicates can be reworded in terms of other predicates and subquery expressions and then passed on to the optimizer.

1.2 Generating Sequential Numbers

Some method of generating a sequence of integers to use as primary keys is a common vendor extension. These are very nonrelational extensions, are highly proprietary, and have major disadvantages.

The exact method used varies from product to product. But the results of using them are all the same—their behavior is unpredictable.

Oracle has the ability to expose the physical address of a row on the hard drive as a special variable called ROWID. This is the fastest way to locate a row in a table, since the read-write head is positioned to the row immediately. This exposure of the underlying physical storage at the logical level commits Oracle to using contiguous storage for the rows of a table. This means that they cannot use hashing, distributed databases, dynamic bit vectors, or any of several newer techniques for VLDB. When the database is moved or reorganized for any reason, the ROWID is changed.

SQL Anywhere has a special function, NUMBER(*), which produces the next value in the sequence starting at 1. The difference between this and a "regular" function is that it produces a new number for every row in the result set in which it is used.

You should not use the NUMBER(*) function anywhere but in a SELECT clause list because the behavior is not reliable in several circumstances. For example, including the function in a WHERE clause or a HAVING clause produces unpredictable results, and you should not include NUMBER(*) in a UNION operation.

In Embedded SQL, you should exercise care when seeking a cursor that references a query containing a NUMBER(*) function. In particular, this function returns negative numbers when a database cursor is positioned relative to the end of the file (an absolute seek with a negative offset).

The Sybase family allows you to declare an exact numeric column with the property IDENTITY in Sybase or AUTOINCREMENT in SQL Anywhere attached to it. This column will autoincrement with every row that is inserted into the table. The numbering is totally dependent on the order in which the rows were inserted into the table, even if they came into the table as a single statement (i.e., INSERT INTO Foobar SELECT . . . ;).

The AUTOINCREMENT column constraint should be used only on PRIMARY KEY or UNIQUE constrained columns. Without an index on the column, each row is constructed using a full table search of the column to find the current highest value in it. However, if the column has an index on it, then an AUTOINCREMENT does not adversely affect performance.

If the next value to be used causes an overflow, you may get a wraparound to negative values. This occurs with numbers larger than $(2**31 - 1)$ in SQL Anywhere, while Sybase allows the user to set a NUMERIC(p, 0) column to any desired size.

The proper way to do this operation is one row at a time, using this SQL-92 statement:

```
INSERT INTO Foobar (keycol, ...)
VALUES (COALESCE((SELECT MAX(keycol) FROM Foobar), 0) + 1, ..);
```

Notice the use of the COALESCE() function to handle the empty table and to get the numbering started with 1. This generalizes from a row insertion to a table insertion:

```
INSERT INTO Foobar (keycol, ...)
VALUES (COALESCE((SELECT MAX(keycol) FROM Foobar), 0) + 1, ..),
       (COALESCE((SELECT MAX(keycol) FROM Foobar), 0) + 2, ..),
       . . .
       (COALESCE((SELECT MAX(keycol) FROM Foobar), 0) + n, ..);
```

Another valid approach is to put a TRIGGER on the table. Here is the code for an SQL-92 trigger; actual products may have a slightly different syntax.

```
CREATE TRIGGER Autoincrement
BEFORE INSERT ON Foobar
REFERENCING NEW AS N1
SET N1.keycol = (SELECT COALESCE(MAX(keycol), 0) + 1
                   FROM Foobar)
FOR EACH ROW;
```

Notice the use of the COALESCE() function to handle the first row inserted into an empty table.

Normalization

T HE RELATIONAL MODEL and the normal forms of the relational model were first defined by Dr. E. F. Codd (Codd 1970), then extended by other writers after him. He invented the term *normalized relations* by borrowing from the political jargon of the day. A branch of mathematics called relations deals with mappings among sets defined by predicate calculus from formal logic. Just as in an algebraic equation, there are many forms of the same relational statement, but the "normal forms" of relations are certain formally defined desirable constructions. The goal of normal forms is to avoid certain data anomalies that can occur in unnormalized tables. Data anomalies are easier to explain with an example, but first please be patient while I define some terms. A predicate is a statement of the form A(X), which means that X has the property A. For example, "John is from Indiana" is a predicate statement; here, "John" is the subject and "is from Indiana" is the predicate. A relation is a predicate with two or more subjects. "John and Bob are brothers" is an example of a relation. The common way of visualizing a set of relational statements is as a table where the columns are attributes of the relation and each row is a specific relational statement. When Codd defined the relational model, he gave 13 rules for the visualization of the relation as a table:

  0. (Yes, there is a rule zero.) For a system to qualify as a relational database management system, that system must use its relational facilities (exclusively) to manage the database. SQL is not so pure on this rule, since you can often do procedural things to the data.

1. The information rule: This simply requires all information in the database to be represented in one and only one way, namely, by values in column positions within rows of tables. SQL is good here.

2. The guaranteed access rule: This rule is essentially a restatement of the fundamental requirement for primary keys. It states that every individual scalar value in the database must be logically addressable by specifying the name of the containing table, the name of the containing column, and the primary key value of the containing row. SQL follows this rule for tables that have a primary key, but does not require a table to have a key at all.

3. Systematic treatment of NULL values: The DBMS is required to support a representation of missing information and inapplicable information that is systematic, distinct from all regular values, and independent of datatype. It is also implied that such representations must be manipulated by the DBMS in a systematic way. SQL has a NULL that is used for both missing information and inapplicable information, rather than having two separate tokens as Codd wished.

4. Active online catalog based on the relational model: The system is required to support an online, inline, relational catalog that is accessible to authorized users by means of their regular query language. SQL does this.

5. The comprehensive data sublanguage rule: The system must support at least one relational language that (a) has a linear syntax; (b) can be used both interactively and within application programs; and (c) supports data definition operations (including view definitions), data manipulation operations (update as well as retrieval), security and integrity constraints, and transaction management operations (begin, commit, and rollback). SQL is pretty good on this point since all of the operations Codd defined can be written in DML (Data Manipulation Language).

6. The view updating rule: All views that are theoretically updatable must be updatable by the system. SQL is weak here and has elected to standardize on the safest case. View updatability is a very complex problem.

7. High-level insert, update, and delete: The system must support set-at-a-time `INSERT`, `UPDATE`, and `DELETE` operators. SQL does this.

8. Physical data independence: This is self-explanatory. Any real product is going to have some physical dependence, but SQL is better than most programming languages on this point.

9. Logical data independence: This is self-explanatory. SQL is quite good about this point.

10. Integrity independence: Integrity constraints must be specified separately from application programs and stored in the catalog. It must be possible to change such constraints as and when appropriate without unnecessarily affecting existing applications. SQL-92 has this.

11. Distribution independence: Existing applications should continue to operate successfully (a) when a distributed version of the DBMS is first introduced and (b) when existing distributed data is redistributed around the system. We are just starting to get distributed versions of SQL, so it is a little early to say whether SQL will meet this criterion or not.

12. The nonsubversion rule: If the system provides a low-level (record-at-a-time) interface, that interface cannot be used to subvert the system (e.g., bypassing a relational security or integrity constraint). SQL-92 is good about this one.

Codd also specified 9 structural features, 3 integrity features, and 18 manipulative features, all of which are required as well. He later extended the list from 13 rules to 333 in the second version of the relational model. However, this section is getting too long as it is, and you can look Codd's rules up for yourself.

Normal forms are an attempt to make sure that you do not destroy true data or create false data in your database. One of the ways of avoiding errors is to represent a fact only once in the database, since if a fact appears more than once, one of the instances of it is likely to be in error—a man with two watches can never be sure what time it is.

This process of table design is called *normalization*. It is not mysterious, but it can get complex. You can buy CASE tools to help you do it, but you should know a bit about the theory before you use such a tool.

2.1 Functional and Multivalued Dependencies

A normal form is a way of classifying a table based on the functional dependencies (FDs for short) in it. A functional dependency means that if I know the value of one attribute, I can always determine the value of another. The notation used in relational theory is an arrow between the two attributes, for example, A → B, which can be read in English as "A determines B." If I know your employee number, I can determine your name; if I know a part number, I can determine the weight and color of the part; and so forth.

A multivalued dependency means that if I know the value of one attribute, I can always determine the values of a set of another attribute. The notation used in relational theory is a double-headed arrow between the two attributes, for instance, A ↠ B, which can be read in English as "A determines many Bs." If I know a teacher's name, I can determine a list of her students; if I know a part number, I can determine the part numbers of its components; and so forth.

2.2 First Normal Form (1NF)

Consider a requirement to maintain data about class schedules. We are required to keep the course, section, department, time, room, professor, student, major, and grade. Suppose that we initially set up a Pascal file with records that look like this:

```
Classes = RECORD
         course: ARRAY [1:7] OF CHAR;
        section: CHAR;
           time: INTEGER;
           room: INTEGER;
       roomsize: INTEGER;
      professor: ARRAY [1:25] OF CHAR;
     department: ARRAY [1:10] OF CHAR;
       Students: ARRAY [1:classsize]
                 OF RECORD
                     student ARRAY [1:25] OF CHAR;
                     major ARRAY [1:10] OF CHAR;
                     grade CHAR;
                     END;
        END;
```

This table is not in the most basic normal form of relational databases. First Normal Form (1NF) means that the table has no repeating groups. That is, every column is a scalar (or atomic) value, not an array or a list or anything with its own structure. In SQL, it is impossible not to be in 1NF unless the vendor has added array or other extensions to the language. The Pascal record could be "flattened out" in SQL to look like this:

```
CREATE TABLE Classes
(course CHAR(7) NOT NULL,
 section CHAR(1) NOT NULL,
 time INTEGER NOT NULL,
 room INTEGER NOT NULL,
 roomsize INTEGER NOT NULL,
 professor CHAR(25) NOT NULL,
 department CHAR(10) NOT NULL,
 student CHAR(25) NOT NULL,
 major CHAR(10) NOT NULL,
 grade CHAR(1) NOT NULL);
```

This table is acceptable to SQL. In fact, we can locate a row in the table with a combination of (course, section, student), so we have a key. But what we are doing is hiding the Students record array, which has not changed its nature by being flattened. This leads to problems.

If Professor Jones of the math department dies, we delete all his rows from the Classes table. This also deletes the information that all his students were taking a math class, and maybe not all of them wanted to drop out of the class just yet. I am deleting more than one fact from the database. This is called a *deletion anomaly*.

If student Wilson decides to change one of his math classes, formerly taught by Professor Jones, to English, we will show Professor Jones as an instructor in both the math and English departments. I could not change a simple fact by itself. This creates false information and is called an *update anomaly*.

If the school decides to start a new department, which has no students yet, we cannot put in the data about the professors we just hired until we have classroom and student data to fill out a row. I cannot insert a simple fact by itself. This is called an *insertion anomaly*.

There are more problems in this table, but you see the point. Yes, there are some ways to get around these problems without changing the tables. We could permit NULLs in the table. We could write routines to check the table for false data. These are tricks that will only get worse as the data and the relationships become more complex. The solution is to break the table up into other tables, each of which represents one relationship or simple fact.

2.2.1 Note on Repeated Groups

The definition of 1NF is that the table has no repeating groups and that all columns are scalar. This means no arrays, linked lists, tables within tables, or record structures, like those you would find in other programming languages. As I have already said, this is very easy to avoid in SQL since arrays and structured data are simply not supported.

The way you "fake it" in SQL is to use a group of columns in which all the members of the group have the same semantic value; that is, they represent the same attribute in the table. Consider the table of an employee and her children:

```
CREATE TABLE Employees
(empno INTEGER NOT NULL,
 empname CHAR(30) NOT NULL,
 . . .
 child1 CHAR(30), birthday1 DATE, sex1 CHAR(1),
 child2 CHAR(30), birthday2 DATE, sex2 CHAR(1),
 child3 CHAR(30), birthday3 DATE, sex3 CHAR(1),
 child4 CHAR(30), birthday4 DATE, sex4 CHAR(1));
```

This looks like the layouts of many existing file system records in Cobol and other 3GL languages. The birthday and sex information for each child is part of a repeated group and therefore violates 1NF. This is faking a four-element array in SQL! Most books simply stop at this point and never bother to explain why this is good or bad; we will go into detail in Chapter 25, "Array Structures in SQL."

Suppose I have a table with the quantity of a product sold in each month of a particular year and I originally built the table to look like this:

```
CREATE TABLE Abnormal
(product CHAR(10) NOT NULL PRIMARY KEY,
 bin_01 INTEGER,
 bin_02 INTEGER,
 . . .
 bin_12 INTEGER);
```

Now suppose I want to flatten it out into a more normalized form, like this:

```
CREATE TABLE Normal
(product CHAR(10) NOT NULL,
```

```
bin_nbr INTEGER NOT NULL,
qty INTEGER NOT NULL,
PRIMARY KEY (product, bin_nbr));
```

I can use the statement

```
INSERT INTO Normal
SELECT product, 1, bin_01
  FROM Abnormal
 WHERE bin_01 IS NOT NULL
UNION ALL
SELECT product, 2, bin_02
  FROM Abnormal
 WHERE bin_02 IS NOT NULL

UNION ALL
SELECT product, 12, bin_12
  FROM Abnormal
 WHERE bin_12 IS NOT NULL;
```

While a UNION ALL query is usually slow, this has to be run only once to load the normalized table, and then the original table can be dropped.

2.3 Second Normal Form (2NF)

A table is in Second Normal Form (2NF) if it has no *partial key* dependencies. That is, if X and Y are columns and X is a key, then for any Z that is a proper subset of X, it cannot be the case that $Z \rightarrow Y$. Informally, the table is in 1NF, and it has a key that determines all non-key attributes in the table.

In the example, our users tell us that knowing the student and course is sufficient to determine the section (since students cannot sign up for more than one section of the same course) and the grade. This is the same as saying that (student, course) $\rightarrow$ (section, grade).

After more analysis, we also discover from our users that (student $\rightarrow$ major)—students have only one major. Since student is part of the (student, course) key, we have a partial key dependency! This leads us to the following decomposition:

```
CREATE TABLE Classes (course, section, room, roomsize, time,
professor, PRIMARY KEY (course, section));
```

```
CREATE TABLE Enrollment (student, course, section, grade)
PRIMARY KEY (student, course));

CREATE TABLE Students (student, major) PRIMARY KEY (student));
```

At this point, we are in 2NF. Every attribute depends on the entire key in its table. Now if a student changes majors, the update can be done in one place. Furthermore, a student cannot sign up for different sections of the same class because we have changed the key of Enrollment. Unfortunately, we still have problems.

Notice that while roomsize depends on the entire key of Classes, it also depends on room. If the room is changed for a course and section, we may also have to change the roomsize, and if the room is modified (we knock down a wall), we may have to change roomsize in several rows in Classes for that room.

2.4 Third Normal Form (3NF)

Another normal form can address these problems. A table is in Third Normal Form (3NF) if for all X → Y, where X and Y are columns of a table, X is a key or Y is part of a *candidate key*. (A candidate key is a unique set of columns that identify each row in a table; you cannot remove a column from the candidate key without destroying its uniqueness.) This implies that the table is in 2NF, since a partial key dependency is a type of transitive dependency. Informally, all the non-key columns are determined by the key, the whole key, and nothing but the key.

The usual way that 3NF is explained is that there are no transitive dependencies. A transitive dependency is a situation where we have a table with columns (A, B, C) and (A → B) and (B → C), so we know that (A → C). In our case, the situation is that (course, section) → room and room → roomsize. This is not a simple transitive dependency, since only part of a key is involved, but the principle still holds. To get our example into 3NF and fix the problem with the roomsize column, we make the following decomposition:

```
CREATE TABLE Rooms (room, roomsize, PRIMARY KEY (room));

CREATE TABLE Classes (course, section, room, time,
PRIMARY KEY (course, section));

CREATE TABLE Enrollment (student, course, section, grade,
PRIMARY KEY (student, course));
```

```
CREATE TABLE Students (student, major, PRIMARY KEY (student));
```

A common misunderstanding about relational theory is that 3NF has no transitive dependencies. As indicated above, if $X \rightarrow Y$, X does not have to be a key if Y is part of a candidate key. We still have a transitive dependency in the example—(room, time) $\rightarrow$ (course, section)—but since the right side of the dependency is a key, it is technically in 3NF. The unreasonable behavior that this table structure still has is that several courses can be assigned to the same room at the same time.

2.5 Case Tools for Normalization

Third Normal Form is very popular with CASE tools, and most of them can generate a schema where all of the tables are in 3NF. They obtain the FDs from an E-R (entity-relationship) diagram or from a statistical analysis of the existing data, then put them together into tables and check for normal forms. It is often possible to derive more than one 3NF schema from a set of FDs. A good CASE tool will find more than one of them, and ideally will find the highest possible normal form schemas too. Yes, there are still more normal forms we have not mentioned yet. (Nobody said this would be easy.) Some people will argue that it is all right to "denormalize" a schema for reasons of efficiency. For example, to get a list of all the students and their majors in a given class, we must JOIN Enrollment and Students. The case for leaving the solution normalized is based on reducing the programming requirement. If we denormalize, either we are not enforcing some of the user-required constraints or we have to write additional code to enforce the constraints.

Not enforcing all the rules is obviously bad. If we choose to write additional code, we have to be sure to duplicate it in all of the programs that work with the DBMS. Normalization reduces programming.

2.6 Boyce-Codd Normal Form (BCNF)

A table is in BCNF when for all nontrivial FDs $(X \rightarrow A)$, X is a superkey for the whole schema. A *superkey* is a unique set of columns that identifies each row in a table, but you can remove some columns from it and it will still be a key. Informally, a superkey is carrying extra weight.

BCNF is the normal form that actually removes all transitive dependencies. A table is in BCNF if for all $(X \rightarrow Y)$, X is a key—period. We can go to this normal form just by adding another key with a UNIQUE (room, time) constraint clause to the table Classes. There are some other interesting and useful "higher" normal forms, but they are outside the scope of this discussion. In our example, we have removed all of the important anomalies with BCNF.

Third Normal Form was concerned with the relationship between key and non-key columns. However, a column can often play both roles. Consider a table for computing salesmen's bonus gifts that has for each salesman his base salary, the number of sales points he has won in a contest, and the bonus gift awarded for that combination of salary range and points. For example, we might give a fountain pen to a beginning salesman with a base pay rate somewhere between $15,000 and $20,000 and 100 sales points, but give a car to a master salesman, whose salary is between $30,000 and $60,000 and who has 200 points. The functional dependencies are, therefore,

```
(paystep, points) → gift
gift → points
```

Let's start with a table that has all the data in it and normalize it.

Gifts

salary	points	gift
$15,000	100	Pencil
$17,000	100	Pen
$30,000	200	Car
$31,000	200	Car
$32,000	200	Car

This schema is in 3NF, but it has problems. You cannot insert a new gift into our offerings and points unless we have a salary to go with it. If you remove any sales points, you lose information about the gifts and salaries (e.g., only people in the $30,000 range can win a car). And, finally, a change in the gifts for a particular point score would have to affect all the rows within the same pay step. This table needs to be broken apart into two tables:

PayGifts

salary	gift
$15,000	Pencil
$17,000	Pen
$30,000	Car
$31,000	Car
$32,000	Car

GiftsPoints

gift	points
Pencil	100
Pen	100
Car	200

2.7 Fourth Normal Form (4NF)

Fourth Normal Form (4NF) makes use of multivalued dependencies (MVDs). The problem it solves is that the table has too many of them. For example, consider a table of departments, their projects, and the parts they stock. The MVDs in the table would be

```
department  →→ projects

department  →→ parts
```

Assume that department d1 works on jobs j1 and j2 with parts p1 and p2; that department d2 works on jobs j3, j4, and j5 with parts p2 and p4; and that department d3 works on only job j2 with parts p5 and p6. The table would look like this:

department	job	part
d1	j1	p1
d1	j1	p2
d1	j2	p1
d1	j2	p2
d2	j3	p2
d2	j3	p4
d2	j4	p2
d2	j4	p4
d2	j5	p2
d2	j5	p4
d3	j2	p5
d3	j2	p6

If you want to add a part to a department, you must create more than one new row. Likewise, removing a part or a job from a row can destroy information. Updating a part or job name will also require multiple rows to be changed.

The solution is to split this table into two tables, one with (department, projects) in it and one with (department, parts) in it. The definition of 4NF is that we have no more than one MVD in a table. If a table is in 4NF, it is also in BCNF.

2.8 Fifth Normal Form (5NF)

Fifth Normal Form (5NF), also called the Join-Projection Normal Form or the Projection-Join Normal Form, is based on the idea of a lossless join or the lack of a join-projection anomaly. This problem occurs when you have an n-way relationship, where $n > 2$. A quick check for 5NF is to see if the table is in 3NF and all the candidate keys are single columns.

As an example of the problems solved by 5NF, consider a table of house notes that records the buyer, the seller, and the lender:

HouseNotes

buyer	seller	lender
Smith	Jones	National Bank
Smith	Wilson	Home Bank
Nelson	Jones	Home Bank

This table is a three-way relationship, but because many CASE tools allow only binary relationships, it might have to be expressed in an E-R diagram as three binary relationships, which would generate CREATE TABLE statements leading to these tables:

BuyerLender

buyer	lender
Smith	National Bank
Smith	Home Bank
Nelson	Home Bank

SellerLender

seller	lender
Jones	National Bank
Wilson	Home Bank
Jones	Home Bank

BuyerSeller

buyer	seller
Smith	Jones
Smith	Wilson
Nelson	Jones

The trouble is that when you try to assemble the original information by joining pairs of these three tables together thus:

```
SELECT BS.buyer, SL.seller, BL.lender
  FROM BuyerLender AS BL,
       SellerLender AS SL,
       BuyerSeller AS BS
 WHERE BL.buyer = BS.buyer
   AND BL.lender = SL.lender
   AND SL.seller = BS.seller;
```

you will recreate all the valid rows in the original table, such as ('Smith', 'Jones', 'National Bank'), but there will also be false rows, such as ('Smith', 'Jones', 'Home Bank'), which were not part of the original table. This is called a *join-projection anomaly.*

There are also strong JPNF and overstrong JPNF, which make use of join dependencies (JD for short). Unfortunately, there is no systematic way to find a JPNF or 4NF schema because the problem is known to be NP complete.

2.9 Domain-Key Normal Form (DKNF)

A functional dependency has a defined system of axioms that can be used in normalization problems. These six axioms, known as Armstrong's axioms, are given below:

Reflexive: $X \rightarrow X$
Augmentation: if $X \rightarrow Y$ then $XZ \rightarrow Y$
Union: if ($X \rightarrow Y$ and $X \rightarrow Z$) then $X \rightarrow YZ$
Decomposition: if $X \rightarrow Y$ and Z a subset of Y, then $X \rightarrow Z$
Transitivity: if ($X \rightarrow Y$ and $Y \rightarrow Z$) then $X \rightarrow Z$
Pseudotransitivity: if ($X \rightarrow Y$ and $YZ \rightarrow W$) then $XZ \rightarrow W$

They make good sense if you just look at them, which is something we like in a set of axioms. In the real world, the FDs are the business rules we are trying to model.

In the normalization algorithm for 3NF developed by P. A. Bernstein (Bernstein 1976), we use the axioms to get rid of redundant FDs. For example, if we are given

A → B
A → C
B → C
DB → E
DAF → E

A → C is redundant because it can be derived from A → B and B → C with transitivity. DAF → E is also redundant because it can be derived from DB → E and A → B with pseudotransitivity (which gives us DA → E) and augmentation (which then allows DAF → E). What we would like to find is the smallest set of FDs from which we can generate all of the given rules. This is called a *nonredundant cover.* For the FDs above, one cover would be

A → B
B → C
DB → E

Once we do this, Bernstein shows that we can just create a table for each of the FDs where A, B, and DB are the respective keys. We have taken it easy so far, but now it's time for a challenge.

As an example of a schema with more than one Third Normal Form, here is a problem that was used in a demonstration by DBStar Corporation (San Francisco, CA). The company uses it as an example in a demonstration that comes with its CASE tool.

We are given an imaginary and simplified airline that has a database for scheduling flights and pilots. Most of the relationships are obvious things. Flights have only one departure time and one destination. They can get a different pilot and can be assigned to a different gate each day of the week. The functional dependencies for the database are given below:

1. flight → destination
2. flight → hour
3. (day, flight) → gate
4. (day, flight) → pilot
5. (day, hour, pilot) → gate
6. (day, hour, pilot) → flight

7. (day, hour, pilot) → destination
8. (day, hour, gate) → pilot
9. (day, hour, gate) → flight
10. (day, hour, gate) → destination

Your problem is to find 3NF database schemas in these FDs. You have to be careful! You have to have all of the columns, obviously, but your answer could be in 3NF and still ignore some of the FDs. For example, this will not work:

```
CREATE TABLE PlannedSchedule
(flight, destination, hour, PRIMARY KEY (flight));

CREATE TABLE ActualSchedule
(day, flight, gate, pilot, PRIMARY KEY (day, flight));
```

If we apply the Union axiom to some of the FDs, we get

```
(day, hour, gate) → (destination, flight, pilot)
(day, hour, pilot) → (destination, flight, gate)
```

This says that the user has required that if we are given a day, an hour, and a gate, we should be able to determine a unique flight for that day, hour, and gate. We should also be able to determine a unique flight given a day, hour, and pilot.

Given the PlannedSchedule and ActualSchedule tables, you cannot produce views where either of the two constraints we just mentioned are enforced. If the query "What flight does pilot X have on day Y and hour Z?" gives you more than one answer, it violates the FDs. Here is an example that is allowable in this proposed schema but that is undesirable given our constraints:

TABLE PlannedSchedule

flight	hour	destination
118	17:00	Dallas
123	13:00	Omaha
155	17:00	Los Angeles
171	13:00	New York
666	13:00	Hades

TABLE ActualSchedule

day	flight	pilot	gate
Wed	118	Tom	12A
Wed	155	Tom	13B
Wed	171	Tom	12A
Thu	123	John	12A
Thu	155	John	12A
Thu	171	John	13B

The constraints mean that we should be able to find a unique answer to each the following questions and not lose any information when inserting and deleting data.

1. Which flight is leaving from gate 12A on Thursdays at 13:00 Hrs? This looks fine until you realize that you don't know about flight 666, which was not required to have anything about its day or pilot in the ActualSchedule table. And likewise, I can add a flight to the ActualSchedule table that has no information in the PlannedSchedule table.

2. Which pilot is assigned to the flight that leaves gate 12A on Thursdays at 13:00 Hrs? This has the same problem as before.

3. What is the destination of the flight in query 1 and 2? This has the same problem as before.

4. What gate is John leaving from on Thursdays at 13:00 Hrs?

5. Where is Tom flying to on Wednesdays at 17:00 Hrs?

6. What flight is assigned to Tom on Wednesdays at 17:00 Hrs?

It might help if we gave an example of how one of the FDs in the problem can be derived using the axioms of FD calculus, just as you would do a geometry proof:

Given

1. (day, hour, gate) → pilot
2. (day, hour, pilot) → flight

prove that
(day, hour, gate) → flight.

3. (day, hour) → (day, hour);   Reflexive
4. (day, hour, gate) → (day, hour);   Augmentation on 3
5. (day, hour, gate) → (day, hour, pilot);   Union 1 & 4
6. (day, hour, gate) → flight;   Transitive 2 and 5
    Q.E.D.

The answer is to start by attempting to derive each of the functional dependencies from the rest of the set. What we get is several short proofs, each requiring different "given" functional dependencies in order to get to the derived FD.

Here is a list of each of the proofs used to derive the 10 fragmented FDs in the problem. With each derivation we include every derivation step and the legal FD calculus operation that allows us to make that step. An additional operation that we include here is left reduction, which was not included in the axioms listed earlier. Left reduction says that if XX → Y then X → Y. It was not included because this is actually a theorem and not one of the basic axioms (side problem: can you derive left reduction?).

Prove (day, hour, pilot) → gate
a. day → day;   Reflexive
b. (day, hour, pilot) → day;   Augmentation (a)
c. (day, hour, pilot) → (day, flight);   Union (6, b)
d. (day, hour, pilot) → gate;   Transitive (c, 3)
    Q.E.D.

Prove (day, hour, gate) → pilot
a. day → day;   Reflexive
b. day, hour, gate → day;   Augmentation (a)
c. day, hour, gate → (day, flight);   Union (9, b)
d. day, hour, gate → pilot;   Transitive (c, 4)
    Q.E.D.

Prove (day, flight) → gate
a. (day, flight, pilot) → gate;   Pseudotransitivity (2, 5)
b. (day, flight, day, flight) →gate;   Pseudotransitivity (a, 4)
c. (day, flight) → gate;   Left reduction (b)
    Q.E.D.

Prove (day, flight) → pilot
a. (day, flight, gate) → pilot;   Pseudotransitivity (2, 8)
b. (day, flight, day, flight) → pilot;   Pseudotransitivity (a, 3)

c. (day, flight) → pilot;   Left reduction (b)
    Q.E.D.

Prove (day, hour, gate) → flight
a. (day, hour) → (day, hour);   Reflexivity
b. (day, hour, gate) → (day, hour);   Augmentation (a)
c. (day, hour, gate) → (day, hour, pilot);   Union (b, 8)
d. (day, hour, gate) → flight;   Transitivity (c, 6)
    Q.E.D.

Prove (day, hour, pilot) → flight
a. (day, hour) → (day, hour);   Reflexivity
b. (day, hour, pilot) → (day, hour);   Augmentation (a)
c. (day, hour, pilot) → day, hour, gate;   Union (b, 5)
d. (day, hour, pilot) → flight;   Transitivity (c, 9)
    Q.E.D.

Prove (day, hour, gate) → destination
a. (day, hour, gate) → destination;   Transitivity (9, 1)
    Q.E.D.

Prove (day, hour, pilot) → destination
a. (day, hour, pilot) → destination;   Transitivity (6, 1)
    Q.E.D.

Now that we've shown you how to derive 8 of the 10 FDs from other FDs, you can try mixing and matching the FDs into sets so that each set meets the following criteria:

1. Each attribute must be represented on either the left or right side of at least one FD in the set.

2. If a given FD is included in the set, not all the FDs needed to derive it can be included.

3. If a given FD is excluded from the set, the FDs used to derive it must be included.

This produces a set of *nonredundant covers,* which can be found with trial and error and common sense. For example, if we excluded (day, hour, gate) → flight, we must then include (day, hour, gate) → pilot, and vice versa, because each is used in the other's derivation. If you want to be sure your search is exhaustive, however, you may want to apply a more mechanical method, which is what the CASE tools do for you.

The algorithm for accomplishing this task is basically to generate all the combinations of sets of the FDs. (flight $\rightarrow$ destination) and (flight $\rightarrow$ hour) are excluded in the combination generation because they cannot be derived. This gives us (2^8), or 256, combinations of FDs. Each combination is then tested against the criteria.

Fortunately, a simple spreadsheet does all the tedious work. In this problem, criterion 1 eliminates only 15 sets. Criterion 2 eliminates 152 sets, and criterion 3 drops another 67. This leaves us with 22 possible covers, 5 of which are the answers we are looking for (we will explain the other 17 later). These 5 nonredundant covers are

Set I:
flight $\rightarrow$ destination
flight $\rightarrow$ hour
(day, hour, gate) $\rightarrow$ flight
(day, hour, gate) $\rightarrow$ pilot
(day, hour, pilot) $\rightarrow$ gate

Set II
flight $\rightarrow$ destination
flight $\rightarrow$ hour
(day, hour, gate) $\rightarrow$ pilot
(day, hour, pilot) $\rightarrow$ flight
(day, hour, pilot) $\rightarrow$ gate

Set III
flight $\rightarrow$ destination
flight $\rightarrow$ hour
(day, flight) $\rightarrow$ gate
(day, flight) $\rightarrow$ pilot
(day, hour, gate) $\rightarrow$ flight

Set IV
flight $\rightarrow$ destination
flight $\rightarrow$ hour
(day, flight) $\rightarrow$ gate
(day, hour, gate) $\rightarrow$ pilot
(day, hour, pilot) $\rightarrow$ flight

Set V
flight → destination
flight → hour
(day, flight) → pilot
(day, hour, gate) → flight
(day, hour, pilot) → gate
(day, hour, pilot) → flight

At this point we perform unions on FDs with the same left-hand side and make tables for each grouping with the left-hand side as a key. We can also eliminate symmetrical FDs (defined as X → Y and Y → X, and written with a two-headed arrow, X ↔ Y) by collapsing them into the same table.

These five nonredundant covers convert into the following five sets of 3NF relational schemas. They are given in a shorthand SQL DDL (Data Declaration Language) without datatype declarations.

Solution 1

```
CREATE TABLE R1 (flight, destination, hour,
  PRIMARY KEY (flight));
CREATE TABLE R2 (day, hour, gate, flight, pilot,
  PRIMARY KEY (day, hour, gate));
```

Solution 2

```
CREATE TABLE R1 (flight, destination, hour,
  PRIMARY KEY (flight));
CREATE TABLE R2 (day, hour, gate, flight, pilot,
  PRIMARY KEY (day, hour, pilot));
```

Solution 3

```
CREATE TABLE R1 (flight, destination, hour, PRIMARY KEY (flight));
CREATE TABLE R2 (day, flight, gate, pilot,
  PRIMARY KEY (day, flight));
CREATE TABLE R3 (day, hour, gate, flight,
  PRIMARY KEY (day, hour, gate));
CREATE TABLE R4 (day, hour, pilot, flight,
  PRIMARY KEY (day, hour, pilot));
```

Solution 4

```
CREATE TABLE R1 (flight, destination, hour,
  PRIMARY KEY (flight));
```

```
CREATE TABLE R2 (day, flight, gate, PRIMARY KEY (day, flight));
CREATE TABLE R3 (day, hour, gate, pilot,
  PRIMARY KEY (day, hour, gate));
CREATE TABLE R4 (day, hour, pilot, flight,
  PRIMARY KEY (day, hour, pilot));
```

Solution 5

```
CREATE TABLE R1 (flight, destination, hour,
  PRIMARY KEY (flight));
CREATE TABLE R2 (day, flight, pilot, PRIMARY KEY (day, flight));
CREATE TABLE R3 (day, hour, gate, flight,
  PRIMARY KEY (day, hour, gate));
CREATE TABLE R4 (day, hour, pilot, gate,
  PRIMARY KEY (day, hour, pilot));
```

Once you match up these solutions with the minimal covers that generated them, you will probably notice that the first two solutions have transitive dependencies. But they are still 3NF! This is a point not well understood by most analysts. A relation is in 3NF if for each FD X → Y, X is a superkey *or* Y is part of a candidate key. The first two solutions meet this criterion.

You may also notice that no additional candidate keys are defined in any of the tables. This would make sense in the first two solutions but was not done (this is why they are in 3NF and not BCNF). You will find this algorithm used in CASE tool software because SQL-89 only allowed you to define PRIMARY KEY constraints. SQL-92 allows you to define a UNIQUE constraint on one or more columns in addition. Most implementations of SQL also allow the user to define unique indexes on a subset of the columns.

All of the five solutions are 3NF, but the first two solutions leave out two FDs. It appears that solutions without all the constraints are considered valid by this particular automated normalizer. These tables could have defined the required candidate keys with UNIQUE constraints, however. The normalizer used to get these solutions may leave out some of the constraints but still generate 3NF schemas. Watch out! The normalizer is assuming that you can handle this outside the schema or are willing to convert the FDs to some sort of constraints.

If we are allowed to drop FDs (as this particular normalizer does), there are actually 22 solutions (most of which are not generated by this normalizer). These solutions can be found by dropping attributes or whole tables from the solutions above (note that each attribute must still be represented in at least one table). Some of the other 17 solutions can be generated by

1. Dropping either or both of the last two tables in the last three solutions

2. Dropping combinations of gate, flight, and pilot where they are not keys (remember to keep at least one non-key in each table and make sure if an attribute is dropped from one table it is still represented somewhere else)

3. Adding UNIQUE constraints or indexes to the first two solutions

Did you notice that the last three of the five given solutions to the problem still allow some anomalous states? Consider this: In solution 3 the last two tables could have day and flight combinations that are not part of the valid day and flight list as defined in the second table. The other solutions also have similar integrity problems.

There is a normal form that fixes this for us: Domain/Key Normal Form (DKNF), defined by Ronald Fagin (1981). As yet there is no general algorithm that will always generate the DKNF solution given a set of constraints. We can, however, determine DKNF in many special cases. Here is our DKNF solution to the problem:

Solution 6

```
CREATE TABLE R1 (flight, hour, destination,
  UNIQUE (flight, hour, destination),
  UNIQUE (flight, hour),
  UNIQUE (flight));

CREATE TABLE R2 (day, flight, hour, gate, pilot,
  UNIQUE (day, flight, hour, gate, pilot),
  UNIQUE (day, flight, pilot),
  UNIQUE (day, flight, gate),
  FOREIGN KEY (flight, hour) REFERENCES R1(flight, hour));
```

Notice that this is a case of normalization by dropping a table and adding UNIQUE constraints. The candidate key (flight, hour) may not seem necessary with flight also defined as a candidate key in R1. This is done so that the FOR-EIGN KEY in R2 carries the (flight, hour) combination and not just flight. This way, the second relation cannot contain an invalid (flight, hour) combination.

Once we add in the FOREIGN KEYs to solutions 3, 4, and 5, are all of the anomalies removed? No, not entirely. The only solution that removes all anomalies is still the DKNF solution. The best way to enforce these constraints is to collapse all but the first table into one. This way inconsistent gate, pilot, day, hour, and flight combinations cannot exist. This is because

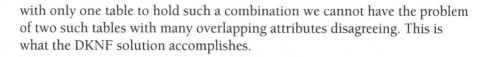

with only one table to hold such a combination we cannot have the problem of two such tables with many overlapping attributes disagreeing. This is what the DKNF solution accomplishes.

2.10 Practical Hints for Normalization

CASE tools implement formal methods for doing normalization. In particular, E-R diagrams are very useful for this purpose. However, a few informal hints can help speed up the process and give you a good start.

Broadly speaking, tables represent either entities or relationships, which is why E-R diagrams work so well as a design tool. The tables that represent entities should have a simple, immediate name suggested by their contents—a table named Students should have student data in it, not student data and bowling scores. It is also a good idea to use plural or collective nouns as the names of such tables to remind you that a table is a set of entities, and that the rows are the single instances of them.

Tables that represent many-to-many relationships should be named by their contents and should be as minimal as possible. For example, Students are related to Classes by a third (relationship) table for their attendance. These tables might represent a pure relationship or they might contain attributes that exist within the relationship, such as a grade for the class attended. Since the only way to get a grade is to attend the class, the relationship will have a column for it named ReportCards or Grades.

Avoid NULLs whenever possible. If a table has too many NULLable columns, it is probably not normalized properly. Try to use a NULL only for a value that is missing now, but that will be resolved later. Even better, put missing values into the encoding schemes for that column, as discussed in the section of this book on encoding schemes.

A normalized database will tend to have a lot of tables with a small number of columns per table. Don't panic when you see that happen. People who first worked with file systems (particularly on computers that used magnetic tape) tend to design one monster file for an application and do all the work against those records. This made sense in the old days since there was no reasonable way to join a number of small files together without having the computer operator mount and dismount lots of different tapes. The habit of designing this way carried over to disk systems since the procedural programming languages were still the same.

The presence of the same non-key attribute in more than one table is probably a normalization problem. This is not a certainty, just a guideline.

The key that determines that attribute should be in only one table, and therefore the attribute should be with it.

As a practical matter, you are apt to see the same attribute under different names and need to make the names uniform in the entire database. The columns date_of_birth, birthdate, birthday, and dob are very likely the same attribute of an employee.

2.11 Practical Hints for Denormalization

Mentioning denormalization is a great way to start religious wars. At one extreme, you will find relational purists who think that the idea of not carrying a database design to at least 3NF is a crime against nature. At the other extreme, you will find people who simply add and move columns all over the database with ALTER statements, never keeping the schema stable.

The reason for denormalization is performance. A fully normalized database requires a lot of JOINs to construct common VIEWs of data from its components. JOINs are very costly in terms of time and computer resources, so "pre-constructing" the JOIN in a denormalized table can save quite a bit.

Consider this actual problem, which appeared on CompuServe's Oracle forum. A pharmaceutical company has an inventory table and a table of price changes, which look like this:

```
CREATE TABLE Drugs
(drugno INTEGER PRIMARY KEY,
 drugname CHAR(30) NOT NULL,
 quantity INTEGER NOT NULL
         CONSTRAINT positive_quantity
         CHECK(quantity > 0),
 . . .);

CREATE TABLE Prices
(drugno INTEGER NOT NULL,
 startdate DATE NOT NULL,
 enddate DATE NOT NULL
         CONSTRAINT started_before_ended
         CHECK(startdate <= enddate),
 price DECIMAL(8,2) NOT NULL,
 PRIMARY KEY (drugno, startdate));
```

Every order has to use the order date to find what the selling price was when the order was placed. The current price will have a value of 'eternity' (a dummy date set so high that it will not be reached, like '9999-12-31'). The (enddate + INTERVAL1 DAY) of one price will be equal to the startdate of the next price for the same drug.

Although this schema is normalized, performance will stink. Every report, invoice, or query will have a JOIN between Drugs and Prices. The trick here is to add more columns to Drugs, like this:

```
CREATE TABLE Drugs
(drugno INTEGER PRIMARY KEY,
 drugname CHAR(30) NOT NULL,
 quantity INTEGER NOT NULL
         CONSTRAINT positive_quantity
         CHECK(quantity > 0),
 currentstartdate DATE NOT NULL,
 currentenddate DATE NOT NULL,
 CONSTRAINT current_start_before_ended
 CHECK(currentstartdate <= currentenddate),
 currentprice DECIMAL(8,2) NOT NULL,
 priorstartdate DATE NOT NULL,
 priorenddate DATE NOT NULL,
 CONSTRAINT prior_start_before_ended
 CHECK(priorstartdate <= priorenddate),
        AND (currentstartdate = priorenddate + INTERVAL1 DAY),
 priorprice DECIMAL(8,2) NOT NULL,
 . . .);
```

This covered over 95% of the orders in the actual company because very few orders are held up through more than two price changes. The odd exception was trapped by a procedural routine.

Another good trick is to preserve the constraints that were implied by the original tables and move them into CHECK() clauses. Consider two of the tables from the examples used at the start of this chapter:

```
CREATE TABLE Enrollment (student, course, section, grade,
  PRIMARY KEY (student, course));

CREATE TABLE Students (student, major, PRIMARY KEY (student));
```

If we want to combine them into a single denormalized table, we might start with

```
CREATE TABLE StudentEnrollment
(student, major, course, section, grade);
```

then add a constraint to ensure that every student has exactly one major:

```
CHECK (NOT EXISTS (SELECT student, COUNT(DISTINCT major)
                   FROM StudentEnrollment
                   GROUP BY student
                   HAVING COUNT(DISTINCT major) <> 1);
```

and then more constraints to ensure that a student is not signed up for the same course twice, and so forth. Yes, insertions will take time because of the extra checking that will be done, but this is the price you pay for speed in doing queries.

Numeric Data in SQL

SQL IS A DATABASE language and not a calculational or procedural language, so the arithmetic capability of SQL is weaker than that of any other language you have ever used. But there are some tricks that you need to know when working with numbers in SQL and when passing them to a host program. Much of the arithmetic and the functions are implementation-defined, so you should experiment with your particular product and make notes on the defaults, precision, and tools in the math library of your database.

You should also look at Chapter 21, which deals with the related topic of aggregate functions. This section deals with the arithmetic that you would use *across a row* instead of *down a column*; they are not quite the same.

3.1 Numeric Types

The SQL standard has a very wide range of numeric types. The idea is that any host language can find an SQL numeric type that matches one of its own. You will also find some vendor extensions in the datatypes, the most common of which is MONEY. This is really a DECIMAL or NUMERIC datatype that also accepts and displays currency symbols in input and output.

Numbers in SQL are classified as either exact or approximate numerics. An exact numeric value has a precision, P, and a scale, S. The precision is a positive integer that determines the number of significant digits in a particular *radix* (formerly called a base of a number system). The standard says the radix can be either binary or decimal, so you need to know what your implementation does. The scale is a nonnegative integer that tells you how many decimal places the number has. An integer has a scale of zero.

The datatypes NUMERIC, DECIMAL, INTEGER, and SMALLINT are exact numeric types. DECIMAL(P,S) can also be written DEC(P,S), and INTEGER can be abbreviated INT. For example, DECIMAL(8,2) could be used to hold the number 123456.78, which has eight significant digits and two decimal places.

The difference between NUMERIC and DECIMAL is subtle. NUMERIC specifies the exact precision and scale to be used. DECIMAL specifies the exact scale, but the precision is implementation-defined to be equal to or greater than the specified value.

Mainframe Cobol programmers can think of NUMERIC as a Cobol picture numeric type, whereas DECIMAL is like a BCD. Personal-computer programmers these days probably have not seen anything like this. You may find that many small-machine SQLs do not support NUMERIC or DECIMAL because the programmers do not want to have to have Cobol-style math routines that operate on character strings or an internal decimal representation.

An approximate numeric value consists of a mantissa and an exponent. The mantissa is a signed numeric value; the exponent is a signed integer that specifies the magnitude of the mantissa. An approximate numeric value has a precision. The precision is a positive integer that specifies the number of significant binary digits in the mantissa. The value of an approximate numeric value is the mantissa multiplied by 10 to the exponent. FLOAT(P), REAL, and DOUBLE PRECISION are the approximate numeric types. There is a subtle difference between FLOAT(P), which has a binary precision equal to or greater than the value given, and REAL, which has an implementation-defined precision.

Most SQL implementations use the floating-point hardware in their machines rather than trying to provide a special floating-point package for approximate numeric datatypes.

In recent years, IEEE has introduced a floating-point hardware standard that can work quite well with SQL. As more vendors adopt it, query results will become more uniform across platforms. The IEEE floating-point standard also has certain bit configurations, called NaNs (Not a Number), to represent overflow, underflow, errors, and missing values; these provide a way to implement NULLs as well as to capture errors.

3.2 Numeric Type Conversion

You may encounter a few surprises in converting from one numeric type to another. The SQL standard left it up to the implementation to answer a lot of basic questions, so the programmer has to know his package.

3.2.1 Rounding and Truncating

When an exact or approximate numeric value is assigned to an exact numeric column, it may not fit. SQL says that the database engine will use an approximation that preserves leading significant digits of the original number after rounding or truncating. The choice of whether to truncate or round is implementation-defined, however. This can lead to some surprises when you have to shift data among SQL implementations, or storage values from a host language program into an SQL table. It is probably a good idea to create the columns with more decimal places than you think you need.

Truncation is defined as truncation toward zero; this means that 1.5 would truncate to 1, and –1.5 would truncate to –1. This is not true for all programming languages; everyone agrees on truncation toward zero for the positive numbers, but you will find that negative numbers may truncate away from zero (i.e., –1.5 would truncate to –2).

SQL is also indecisive about rounding, leaving the implementation free to determine its method. There are two major types of rounding in programming.

The *scientific method* looks at the digit to be removed. If this digit is 0, 1, 2, 3, or 4, you drop it and leave the higher-order digit to its left unchanged. If the digit is 5, 6, 7, 8, or 9, you drop it and increment the digit to its left. This method works with a small set of numbers and was popular with Fortran programmers because it is what engineers use.

The *commercial method* looks at the digit to be removed. If this digit is 0, 1, 2, 3, or 4, you drop it and leave the digit to its left unchanged. If the digit is 6, 7, 8, or 9, you drop it and increment the digit to its left. However, when the digit is 5, you want to have a rule that will round up about half the time. One rule is to look at the digit to the left: If it is odd, then leave it unchanged; if it is even, increment it. There are other versions of the decision rule, but they all try to make the rounding error as small as possible. This method works with a large set of numbers and is popular with bankers because it reduces the total rounding error in the system.

Here is your first programming exercise for the notes you are making on your SQL. Generate a table of 5,000 random numbers, both positive and negative, with four decimal places. Round the test data to two decimal places and total them using both methods.

Notice the difference and save those results. Now load those same numbers into a table in your SQL, like this:

```
CREATE TABLE RoundTest
(original DECIMAL(10, 4) NOT NULL,
 rounded DECIMAL(10, 2) NOT NULL);

-- insert the test data
INSERT INTO RoundTest VALUES (2134.5678, 0.00);
 etc.
UPDATE RoundTest SET rounded = original;

-- write a program to use both rounding methods
-- compare those results to this query

SELECT SUM(original), SUM(rounded)
  FROM RoundTest;
```

Compare these results to those from the other two tests. Now you know what your particular SQL is doing. If you got a third answer, there might be other things going on, which we will deal with in Chapter 21, on aggregate functions. We will postpone discussion here, but the order of the rows in a SUM() function can make a difference in accumulated floating-point rounding error.

3.2.2 CAST() Function

SQL-92 defines the general CAST(<cast operand> AS <datatype>) function for all datatype conversions, but most implementations use several specific functions of their own for the conversions they support. The SQL-92 CAST() function is not only more general, but it also allows the <cast operand> to be either a <column name>, a <value expression>, or a NULL.

For numeric-to-numeric conversion, you can do anything you wish, but you have to watch for the rounding errors. The comparison predicates can hide automatic type conversions, so be careful. SQL implementations will also have formatting options in their conversion functions that are not part of the standard. These functions either use a picture string, like Cobol or some versions of BASIC, or return their results in a format set in an environment variable. This is very implementation-dependent.

3.3 Four-Function Arithmetic

SQL is weaker than a pocket calculator. The dyadic arithmetic operators +, –, *, and / stand for addition, subtraction, multiplication, and division, respectively. The multiplication and division operators are of equal precedence and are performed before the dyadic plus and minus operators.

In algebra and in some programming languages, the precedence of arithmetic operators is more restricted. They use the "My Dear Aunt Sally" rule; that is, multiplication is done before division, which is done before addition, which is done before subtraction. This can lead to subtle errors.

For example, consider (largenum + largenum – largenum), where largenum is the maximum value that can be represented in its numeric datatype. If you group the expression from left to right, you get ((largenum + largenum) – largenum) = overflow error! However, if you group the expression from right to left, you get (largenum + (largenum – largenum)) = largenum.

Because of these differences, an expression that worked one way in the host language may get different results in SQL and vice versa. SQL could reorder the expressions to optimize them, but in practice, you will find that many implementations will simply parse the expressions from left to right. The best way to be safe is always to make extensive use of parentheses in all expressions, whether they are in the host language or in your SQL.

The monadic plus and minus signs are allowed, and you can string as many of them in front of a numeric value of variables as you like. The bad news about this decision is that SQL also uses ADA-style comments, which put the text of a comment line between a double dash and a new line-character. This means that the parser has to figure out whether "--" is two minus signs or the start of a comment. Most versions of SQL also support C-style comment brackets (i.e., /* comment text */). Such brackets have been proposed in the SQL3 discussion papers because some international data transmission standards do not recognize a new line in a transmission and the double-dash convention will not work.

If both operands are exact numeric, the datatype of the result is exact numeric, as you would expect. Likewise, an approximate numeric in a calculation will cast the results to approximate numeric. The kicker is in how the results are assigned in precision and scale.

Let S1 and S2 be the scale of the first and second operands, respectively. The precision of the result of addition and subtraction is implementation-defined, and the scale is the maximum of S1 and S2. The precision of the result of multiplication is implementation-defined, and the scale is (S1 + S2).

The precision and scale of the result of division are implementation-defined, and so are some decisions about rounding or truncating results.

The ANSI X3H2 committee debated whether to require precision and scales in the standard and finally gave up. This means I can start losing high-order digits, especially with a division operation, where it is perfectly legal to make all results single-digit integers.

Nobody does anything that stupid in practice. In the real world, some vendors allow you to adjust the number of decimal places as a system parameter, some default to a few decimal places, and some display as many decimal places as they can so that you can round off to what you want. You will simply have to learn what your implementation does by experimenting with it.

Most vendors have extended this set of operators with other common mathematical functions. The most common additional functions are modulus, absolute value, power, and square root. But it is also possible to find logarithms to different bases, and to perform exponential, trigonometric, and other scientific, statistical, and mathematical functions. Precision and scale are implementation-defined for these functions, of course, but they tend to follow the same design decisions as the arithmetic did. The reason is obvious: They are using the same library routines under the covers as the math package in the database engine.

3.4 Arithmetic and NULLs

Missing values are probably one of the most formidable database concepts for the beginner. Chapter 6 is devoted to a detailed study of how NULLs work in SQL, but this section is concerned with how they act in arithmetic expressions.

The NULL in SQL is only one way of handling missing values. The usual description of NULLs is that they represent currently unknown values that might be replaced later with real values when we know something. This actually covers a lot of territory. *The Interim Report 75-02-08 to the ANSI X3* (SPARC Study Group 1975) showed 14 different kinds of incomplete data that could appear as the results of operations or as attribute values. They included such things as arithmetic underflow and overflow, division by zero, string truncation, raising zero to the zeroth power, and other computational errors, as well as missing or unknown values.

The NULL is a global creature, not belonging to any particular datatype but able to replace any of their values. This makes arithmetic a bit easier to define. You have to specifically forbid NULLs in a column by declaring the column with a NOT NULL constraint. But in SQL-92 you can use the CAST function to declare a specific datatype for a NULL, such as CAST (NULL AS INTEGER). One reason for this convention is completeness; another is to let you pass information about how to create a column to the database engine.

The basic rule for math with NULLs is that they propagate. An arithmetic operation with a NULL will return a NULL. That makes sense; if a NULL is a missing value, then you cannot determine the results of a calculation with it. However, the expression (NULL / 0) is not consistent in SQL implementations. The first thought is that a division by zero should return an error; if NULL is a true missing value, there is no value to which it can resolve and make that expression valid. However, almost all SQL implementations propagate the NULL and do not even issue a warning about division by zero when it appears as a constant in an expression. A non-NULL value divided by zero will cause a runtime error, however.

I asked people on CompuServe to try a short series of SQL commands on different products for me. The DDL was very simple:

```
CREATE TABLE GotNull (test INTEGER);
INSERT INTO GotNull VALUES (NULL);

CREATE TABLE GotOne (test INTEGER);
INSERT INTO GotOne VALUES (1);

CREATE TABLE GotZero (test INTEGER);
INSERT INTO GotZero VALUES (0);
```

They sent me the results of three queries that had explicit divisions by zero in them. This is as opposed to a runtime division by zero.

```
SELECT test / 0 FROM GotNull;
SELECT test / 0 FROM GotOne;
SELECT test / 0 FROM GotZero;
```

The results are shown below.

product	Null/0	one/zero	zero/zero
Ingres 6.4/03	NULL	float point err, no data	float point err, no data
Oracle 6.0	NULL	divide by 0 err, no data	divide by 0 err, no data
Progress 6.2	NULL	NULL	NULL
R:Base 4.0a	NULL	divide by 0 err, no data	divide by 0 err, no data

(cont.)	product	Null/0	one/zero	zero/zero
	Rdb	truncation at runtime divide by 0	truncation at runtime divide by 0	truncation at runtime divide by 0
	SQL Server 4.2	NULL	NULL & error	NULL & error
	SQLBase 5.1	NULL	plus infinity	plus infinity
	Sybase 4.9	NULL	NULL & error	NULL & error
	WATCOM SQL	NULL	NULL	NULL
	XDB 2.41	NULL	divide by 0 err, no data	divide by 0 err, no data

Everyone agrees that NULLs always propagate, but everyone has another opinion on division by zero. Getting a floating-point error from integer math is a violation of the standard, as is not giving a division-by-zero error. The positive infinity in SQLBase is also a floating-point number that is all nines. Other products return NULLs for all three cases, but with and without error messages.

3.5 Converting Values to and from NULL

Since host languages do not support NULLs, the programmer can elect either to replace them with another value that is expressible in the host language or to use indicator variables to signal the host program to take special actions for them.

3.5.1 NULLIF() Function

SQL-92 specifies two functions, NULLIF() and the related COALESCE(), that can be used to replace expressions with NULL and vice versa. These functions are not yet present in most SQL implementations, but you will often find something like them. The NULLIF(V1, V2) function has two parameters. It is equivalent to the following CASE expression:

```
NULLIF(V1, V2) := CASE
                  WHEN (V1 = V2)
                  THEN NULL
                  ELSE V1 END;
```

That is, when the first parameter is equal to the second, the function returns a NULL; otherwise, it returns the first parameter's value. The properties of this function allow you to use it for many purposes. The important properties are these:

1. NULLIF(x, x) will return NULL for all values of x. This includes NULL, since (NULL = NULL) is UNKNOWN, not TRUE.

2. NULLIF(0, (x − x)) will convert all non-NULL values of x into NULL. But it will convert x NULL into x zero, since (NULL − NULL) is NULL and the equality test will fail.

3. NULLIF(1, (x − x + 1)) will convert all non-NULL values of x into NULL. But it will convert a NULL into a 1. This can be generalized for all numeric datatypes and values.

3.5.2 COALESCE() Function

The COALESCE(<value expression>, . . . , <value expression>) function scans the list of <value expression>s from left to right and returns the first non-NULL value in the list. If all the <value expression>s are NULL, the result is NULL. This is the same function, under a new name, as the VALUE(<value expression>, . . . , <value expression>) in DB2 and other SQL implementations based on DB2.

The most common use of this function is in a SELECT list where columns must be added, but one can be a NULL. For example, to create a report of the total pay for each employee, you might write this query:

```
SELECT empno, empname, (salary + commission) AS totalpay
 FROM Employees;
```

But salesmen may work on commission only or on a mix of salary and commission. The office staff is on salary only. This means an employee could have NULLs in his salary or commission column, which would propagate in the addition and produce a NULL result. A better solution would be

```
SELECT empno, empname,
       (COALESCE(salary, 0.00) + COALESCE(commission, 0.00)) AS total-
pay
 FROM Employees;
```

A more elaborate use for this function is with aggregate functions. Consider a table of customers' purchases with a category code and the amount of each purchase. You are to construct a query that will have one row, with one column for each category and one column for the grand total of all customer purchases. The table is declared like this:

```
CREATE TABLE Customers
(custno INTEGER NOT NULL,
 purchaseno INTEGER NOT NULL,
 category CHAR(1)
         CONSTRAINT proper_category
         CHECK(category IN ('A', 'B', 'C'),
 amt DECIMAL(8,2) NOT NULL,
 ... PRIMARY KEY (custno, purchaseno));
```

The query could be done with VIEWs, but you can also write this:

```
SELECT SUM(amt),
    (SUM(amt) - SUM(CASE
                      WHEN category = 'A'
                      THEN NULL
                      ELSE amt END)) AS CatA,
    (SUM(amt) - SUM(CASE
                      WHEN category = 'B'
                      THEN NULL
                      ELSE amt END)) AS CatB,
    (SUM(amt) - SUM(CASE
                      WHEN category = 'C'
                      THEN NULL
                      ELSE amt END)) AS CatC
    FROM Customers;
```

This query works by computing the grand total of all purchases with SUM(amt), then computing the total purchases without category A rows, without category B rows, and without category C rows. To find the total for category A rows, subtract the non-A rows from the total, and so forth. The SUM() function will drop all NULLs before adding the amounts. If you use this trick in a table that has no occurrences of one category, don't worry. The SUM() of an empty table is always NULL and not zero, which is a meaningful result.

As another example of the use of COALESCE(), create a table of payments made for each month of a single year. (Yes, this could be done with a column for the months, but bear with me.)

```
CREATE TABLE Payments
(custno INTEGER NOT NULL,
 jan DECIMAL(8,2),
 feb DECIMAL(8,2),
 mar DECIMAL(8,2),
 apr DECIMAL(8,2),
 may DECIMAL(8,2),
 jun DECIMAL(8,2),
 jul DECIMAL(8,2),
 aug DECIMAL(8,2),
 sep DECIMAL(8,2),
 oct DECIMAL(8,2),
 nov DECIMAL(8,2),
 "dec" DECIMAL(8,2),
 PRIMARY KEY custno);
```

The problem is to write a query that returns the customer and the amount of the last payment he made. Unpaid months are shown with a NULL in them. We could use a COALESCE function like this:

```
SELECT custno,
       COALESCE("dec", nov, oct, sep,
                aug, jul, jun, may, apr, mar, feb, jan)
   FROM Customers;
```

Of course this query is a bit incomplete, since it does not tell you in what month this last payment was made. This can be done with the rather ugly-looking expression that will turn a month's non-NULL payment into a character string with the name of the month. The general case for a column called "mon," which holds the number of a month within the year, is NULLIF (COALESCE(NULLIF (0, mon - mon), 'Month'), 0) where 'Month' is replaced by the string for the actual name of the particular month. A list of these statements in month order in a COALESCE will give us the name of the last month with a payment. The way this expression works is worth examining in detail.

Case 1: mon is a numeric value

```
NULLIF(COALESCE(NULLIF(0, mon - mon), 'Month'), 0)
NULLIF(COALESCE(NULLIF(0, 0), 'Month'), 0)
NULLIF(COALESCE(NULL, 'Month'), 0)
```

```
NULLIF('Month', 0)
('Month')
```

Case 2: mon is NULL

```
NULLIF(COALESCE(NULLIF(0, mon - mon), 'Month'), 0)
NULLIF(COALESCE(NULLIF(0, NULL - NULL), 'Month'), 0)
NULLIF(COALESCE(NULLIF(0, NULL), 'Month'), 0)
NULLIF(COALESCE(0, 'Month'), 0)
NULLIF(0, 0)
(NULL)
```

Many versions of SQL have vendor extensions that will allow you to do this sort of conversion; they will probably be faster as well as easier to read. The CASE expression is another way to do this.

3.6 Vendor Math Functions

All other math functions are vendor extensions, but you can plan on several common ones in most SQL implementations. They are implemented under assorted names, and often with slightly different functionality.

3.6.1 Number Theory Operators

(x MOD m) or MOD(x, m) = Perform modulo or remainder arithmetic. This is tricky when the values of x and m are not cardinals (i.e., positive, nonzero integers). Experiment and find out how your package handles negative numbers and decimal places.

Len Gallagher proposed an amendment for the MOD function in SQL3 (Gallagher 1996). Originally, the working draft defined MOD(x, m) only for positive values of both m and x, leaving the result to be implementation-dependent when either of m or x is negative.

Negative values of x have no required mathematical meaning, and many implementations of MOD either don't define it at all, or give some result that is the easiest to calculate on a given hardware platform. However, negative values for m do have a very nice mathematical interpretation that we wanted to see preserved in the SQL definition of MOD. Gallagher proposed the following:

1. If x is positive, then the result is the unique nonnegative exact numeric quantity r with scale 0 such that r is less than x and $x = (m * k) + r$ for some exact numeric quantity k with scale 0.

2. Otherwise, the result is an implementation-defined exact numeric quantity r with scale 0, which satisfies the requirements that r is strictly between x and $(-x)$ and that $x = (m * k) + r$ for some exact numeric quantity k with scale 0, and a completion condition is raised: warning—implementation-defined result.

This definition guarantees that the MOD function, for a given positive value of x, will be a homomorphism under addition from the mathematical group of all integers, under integer addition, to the modular group of integers {0, 1, . . . , $m - 1$} under modular addition. This mapping then preserves the following group properties:

1. The additive identity is preserved: `MOD(0, m) = 0`

2. Additive inverse is preserved in the modular group defined by `MOD(-MOD(x, m), m) = m - MOD(x, m)`:

   `MOD(-x, m) = - MOD(x, m)`

3. The addition property is preserved where "$\oplus$" is a modular addition defined by `MOD((MOD(m, m) + MOD(x, m)), m)`:

   `MOD((m + x), m) = MOD(m, m) $\oplus$ MOD(x, m)`

4. Subtraction is preserved under modular subtraction, which is defined as `MOD((MOD(m, m) $\ominus$ MOD(x, m)), m)`:

   `MOD(m-x, m) = MOD(m, m) $\ominus$ MOD(x, m)`

From this definition, we would get the following:

```
MOD(12, 5) = 2
MOD(-12, 5) = 3
```

There are some applications where the "best" result to `MOD(-12, 5)` might "–2" or "–3" rather than "3", and that is probably why various implementations of the MOD function differ. But the advantages of being able to rely on the above mathematical properties outweigh any other considerations. If a user knows what the SQL result will be, it is easy to modify the expressions of a particular application to get the desired application result. Here is a chart of the differences in SQL implementations, with the SQL3 results included:

test	n	m	Type A mod(n, m)	Type B mod(n, m)	Type C mod(n, m)	Gallagher Proposal mod(n, m)
a	12	5	2	2	2	2
b	−12	5	−2	−2	−2	3
c	12	−5	−2	−2	−2	3
d	12	−5	2	2	2	2
e	NULL	5	NULL	NULL	NULL	NULL
f	NULL	NULL	NULL	NULL	NULL	NULL
g	12	NULL	NULL	NULL	NULL	NULL
h	12	0	12	NULL	err	12
i	−12	0	−2	NULL	err	−12
j	0	5	0	0	0	0
k	0	−5	0	0	0	0

Type A:
   Oracle 7.0

Type B:
   DataFlex - ODBC
   SQL Server 6.5, SP2
   SQLBase Version 6.1 PTF level 4
   Xbase

Type C:
   DB2/400, V3r2
   DB2/6000 V2.1.1
   Sybase SQL Anywhere 5.5
   Sybase System 11

<datatype>(x) = Convert the number x into the <datatype>. This is the most common form of a conversion function and it is not as general as the standard CAST().

ABS(x) = Return the absolute value of x.

SIGN(x) = Returns −1 if x is negative, 0 if x is zero, and +1 if x is positive.

3.6.2 Exponential Functions

POWER(x, n) = Raise the number x to the nth power.

SQRT(x) = Return the square root of x.

LOG10(x) = Return the base 10 logarithm of x. See remarks about LN(x).

LN(x) or LOG(x) = Return the natural logarithm of x. The problem is that logarithms are undefined when $(x \leftarrow 0)$. Some SQL implementations return an error message, others return a NULL, and DB2/400 Version 3 Release 1 returned "*NEGINF" (short for "negative infinity") as its result.

EXP(x) = Returns e to the x power; the inverse of a natural log.

3.6.3 Scaling Functions

ROUND(x, p) = Round the number x to p decimal places.

TRUNCATE(x, p) = Truncate the number x to p decimal places.

FLOOR(x) = The largest integer less than or equal to x.

CEILING(x) = The smallest integer greater than or equal to x.

3.6.4 Generator Functions

COUNTER(*), NUMBER(), IDENTITY = Return a new incremented value each time this function is used in an expression. This is a way to generate unique identifiers. This can be either a function call or a column property, depending on the product. This is also a horrible, nonstandard, nonrelational proprietary extension that should be avoided whenever possible.

Many implementations also allow for the use of external functions written in other programming languages. The SQL3 proposal currently has a definition for such calls, which also requires that the programmer use explicit code to handle NULLs or do datatype conversions.

Temporal Datatypes in SQL

LEAP YEARS DID not exist in solar calendars, such as the Roman or Egyptian calendars, prior to 708 AUC. Political and religious calendars before this time had drifted with respect to the sun by approximately one day every four years. The Egyptian calendar drifted completely around approximately every 1,461 years. As a result, it was useless for agriculture; the Egyptians relied on the stars to predict the flooding of the Nile. Sosigenes, who was from Alexandria, knew that the calendar had drifted completely around more than twice since it was first introduced.

To realign the calendar with the seasons, Julius Caesar decreed that the year 708 *ab urbe condita* (from the founding of the city of Rome)—the year 46 BCE to us today—would have 445 days. Caesar, on the advice of Sosigenes, also introduced leap years (known as bissextile years) at this time. Many Romans simply referred to 708 AUC as the "year of confusion."

The "old style," or Julian, calendar, with a leap year every four years, was reasonably accurate in the short or medium range, but it drifted by approximately three days every 400 years. It had gotten 10 days out of step with the seasons by 1582. (A calendar without a leap year would have drifted completely around slightly more than once between 708 AUC and 2335 AUC [that is, 1582 CE].) The summer solstice, so important to planting crops, had no relationship to 21 June. Scientists finally convinced Pope Gregory to lower the boom, so almost two weeks were chopped from the month of October in 1582. (Note that the "primitive" Aztecs and Mayas had figured this out a thousand years earlier; they knew the number of days in a solar year to three decimals.)

The years 800 and 1200 were leap years anywhere that they were called AD 800 and AD 1200, that is, anywhere in the Christian world. But whether AD 1600 was a leap year did indeed depend on where you lived:

◆ Spain and Portugal (at that time under the same king, Felipe II) including their colonies: 4 October 1582 was followed by 15 October 1582.

◆ Italian duchies and kingdoms and the Catholic parts of Switzerland: 4 October 1582 was followed by 15 October 1582.

◆ France (including its colonies): 9 December 1582 was followed by 20 December 1582.

◆ Poland: 4 October 1582 was followed by 15 October 1582.

◆ Possessions of the Holy Roman Emperor (the Habsburgs in Austria): in 1583.

◆ German duchies (Catholic states): in 1583.

◆ German duchies (Protestant states): 18 February 1700 was followed by 1 March 1700.

◆ The Netherlands converted in 1700.

◆ The Protestant parts of Switzerland converted in 1701.

◆ Denmark and Norway: 18 February 1700 was followed by 1 March 1700.

◆ Sweden and Finland: 17 February 1753 was followed by 1 March 1753, but one day apart from the old calendar between 1700 and 1712! That is, 28 February 1700 was followed by 1 March 1700 and then 29 February 1712 was followed by 30 February 1712, which was followed by 1
March 1712.

◆ Russia and the former Soviet Union: 18 January 1918 was followed by 1 February 1918 (therefore the October Revolution took place 7 November 1917 in the Gregorian calendar).

◆ The Balkan nations: between 1918 and 1924.

The calendar corrections had economic and social ramifications. In Great Britain and its colonies, 2 September 1752 was followed by 14 September 1752. The calendar reform bill of 1751, 24 Geo. #2 c. 23, "An Act for regulating the commencement of the Year, and for correcting the Calendar now in use," included provisions to adjust the amount of money owed or collected by means of rents, leases, mortgages, and similar legal arrangements whereby money owed is calculated according to the passage of time, so that rents and so forth were prorated by the number of actual elapsed days in the time period affected by the calendar change. Nobody had to pay the full monthly rate for the short month of September 1752, and nobody had to pay the full yearly rate for the short year.

The rioting (which was serious, widespread, and persistent) was mostly due to the belief (common in those days and not unheard of today) that each person's days were "numbered," that each individual was preordained to be born and die at a divinely ordained time that no human agency could alter in any way. Thus the removal of 11 days from the month of September brought nearer by 11 days the death of every person, shortening their lives by 11 days. And there was also the matter of the missing 83 days due to the change of the New Year's Day from 25 March to 1 January, which was believed to have a similar effect. Today, some of us might scoff at such nonsense, but there are many who still take such matters very seriously. For example, there are regions where many people get upset about the yearly one-hour clock adjustments for daylight saving time—imagine how they would react to a proposal to cut several days or weeks out of the calendar, no matter what scientific arguments might be advanced.

To complicate matters, the beginning of the year also varied from country to country. Great Britain preferred to begin the year on 25 March, while other countries began at Easter, 25 December, 1 March, and 1 January—all important details for historians to keep in mind.

In Great Britain and its colonies, the calendar year 1750 began on 25 March and ended on 24 March—that is, the day after 24 March 1750 was 25 March 1751. The leap year day was added to the end of the last full month in the year, which was then February. The extra leap year day comes at the end of February, since this part of the calendar structure was not changed.

In Latin, "septem" means seventh, from which we derived September. Likewise, "octem" means eighth, "novem" means ninth, and "decem" means tenth. Thus, September should be the seventh month, October should be the eighth, November should be the ninth, and December should be the tenth.

So, how come September is the ninth month? September was the seventh month until 1752 when the new year was changed from 25 March to 1 January.

Until fairly recently, nobody agreed on the proper display format for dates. Every nation seems to have its own commercial conventions. Most of us know that Americans put the month before the day and the British do the reverse, but do you know any other national conventions? National date formats may be confusing when used in an international environment. When it was 12/16/95 in Boston, it was 16/12/95 in London, 16.12.95 in Berlin, and 95-12-16 in Stockholm. Then there are conventions within industries within each country that complicate matters further.

Faced with all of the possibilities, software vendors came up with various general ways of formatting dates for display. The usual ones are some mixture of a two- or four-digit year, a three-letter or two-digit month, and a two-digit day within the month. The three fields can be separated by slashes, dashes, or spaces.

At one time, NATO tried to use Roman numerals for the month to avoid language problems among treaty members. The United States Army did a study and found that the two-digit day, three-letter month, and four-digit year format was the least likely to be missorted, misread, or miswritten by English speakers. That is also the reason for "24 hour" or "military" time.

Today, you want to set up a program to convert your data to conform to ISO 8601:1988 "Data elements and interchange formats—Information interchange—Representation of dates and times" as a corporate standard and EDIFACT for EDI messages. This is the *yyyy-mm-dd* format. It is already a part of the SQL-92 standards and will become part of other standard programming languages as they add temporal datatypes.

The full ISO 8601 timestamp can be either a local time or UTC/GMT time. UTC is the code for "Universal Coordinated Time," which replaced the older GMT, which was the code for "Greenwich Mean Time" (if you listen to CNN, you are used to hearing the term UTC, but if you listen to BBC radio, you are used to the term GMT).

In 1970 the Coordinated Universal Time system was devised by an international advisory group of technical experts within the International Telecommunication Union (ITU). The ITU felt it was best to designate a single abbreviation for use in all languages in order to minimize confusion. The two alternative original abbreviation proposals for the "Universal Coordinated Time" were CUT (English: Coordinated Universal Time) and TUC (French: *temps universel coördiné*), but UTC was selected both as a compromise between the French and English proposals and because the C at the end looks more like an index in UT0, UT1, UT2, and a mathematical-style notation is always the most international approach.

Technically, Universal Coordinated Time is not quite the same thing as Greenwich Mean Time. GMT is a 24-hour astronomical time system based on the local time at Greenwich, England. GMT can be considered equivalent to Universal Coordinated Time when fractions of a second are not important. However, by international agreement, the term UTC is recommended for all general timekeeping applications, and use of the term GMT is discouraged.

Another problem in the United States is that besides having four time zones, we also have "lawful time" to worry about. This is the technical term for time required by law for commerce. Usually, this means whether or not you use daylight saving time.

The need for UTC time in the database and lawful time for display and input has not been generally handled yet. EDI and replicated databases must use UTC time to compare timestamps. A date without a time zone is ambiguous in a distributed system. A transaction created 1995-12-17 in London may be younger than a transaction created 1995-12-16 in Boston.

SQL-92 has a very complete description of its temporal datatypes. There are rules for converting from numeric and character strings into these datatypes, and there is a schema table for global time-zone information that is used to make sure that all temporal datatypes are synchronized. It is so complete and elaborate that nobody has implemented it yet. And it will take them years to do so! As an international standard, SQL-92 has to handle time for the whole world, and most of us work with only local time. If you have ever tried to figure out the time in a foreign city to place a telephone call, you have some idea of what is involved.

The common terms and conventions related to time are also confusing. We talk about "an hour" and use the term to mean a particular point within the cycle of a day ("The train arrives at 13:00 Hrs") or to mean an interval of time not connected to another unit of measurement ("The train takes three hours to get there"); the number of days in a month is not uniform; the number of days in a year is not uniform; weeks are not related to months; and so on.

All SQL implementations have a DATE datatype; most have a TIME and a TIMESTAMP datatype. These values are drawn from the system clock and are therefore local to the host machine. They are based on what is now called the Common Era calendar, which many people would still call the Gregorian or Christian calendar.

The SQL-92 standard has a set of date and time (DATE, TIME, and TIME-STAMP) and INTERVALs (DAY, HOUR, MINUTE, and SECOND with decimal fraction) datatypes. Both of these groups are temporal datatypes, but datetimes represent points in the time line, while the interval datatypes are durations of time. SQL-92 also has a full set of operators for these datatypes. The full syntax and functionality have not been implemented in any SQL product yet, but you can use some of the vendor extensions to get around a lot of problems in most existing SQL implementations today.

4.1 Tips for Handling Dates, Timestamps, and Times

The syntax and power of date, timestamp, and time features vary so much from product to product that it is impossible to give anything but general advice. This chapter will assume that you have simple date arithmetic in your SQL, but you might find that some library functions will let you do a better job than what you see here. Please continue to check your manuals until the SQL-92 standards are implemented.

4.1.1 Date Format Standards

The ISO ordinal date formats are described in ISO-2711-1973. Their format is a four-digit year, followed by a digit day within the year (001–366). The year can be truncated to the year within the century. The ANSI date formats are described in ANSI X3.30-1971. Their formats include the ISO standard, but add a four-digit year, followed by the two-digit month (01–12), followed by the two-digit day within month (01–31). This option is called the *calendar date format*. The SQL-92 standard uses this all-numeric *yyyy-mm-dd* format to conform to ISO 8601, which had to avoid language-dependent abbreviations. It is fairly easy to write code to handle either format. The ordinal format is better for date arithmetic; the calendar format is better for display purposes.

The Defense Department has now switched to the year, three-letter month, and day format so that documents can be easily sorted by hand or by machine. This is the format I would recommend using for output on reports to be read by people, for just those reasons; otherwise, use the standard calendar format for transmissions.

Many programs still use a year-in-century date format of some kind. This was supposed to save space in the old days when that sort of thing mattered (i.e., when punch cards had only 80 columns). Programmers assumed that they would not need to tell the difference between the years 1900 and 2000 because they were too far apart. Old Cobol programs that did date arithmetic on these formats are already returning erroneous negative results. If Cobol had a DATE datatype, instead of making the programmers write their own

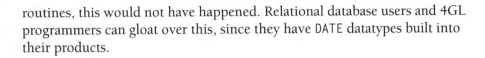

routines, this would not have happened. Relational database users and 4GL programmers can gloat over this, since they have DATE datatypes built into their products.

4.1.2 Handling Timestamps

TIMESTAMP(n) is defined as a timestamp to *n* decimal places (e.g., TIME-STAMP(9) is nanosecond precision), where the precision is hardware-dependent. The FIPS-127 standard requires at least five decimal places after the second.

TIMESTAMPs usually serve two purposes. They can be used as a true time-stamp to mark an event connected to the row in which they appear. Or they can be used as a sequential number for building a unique key that is not temporal in nature. For example, the date and time when a payment is made on an account are important, and a true timestamp is required for legal reasons. The account number just has to be different from all other account numbers, so we need a unique number and TIMESTAMP is a quick way of getting one.

Remember that a TIMESTAMP will read the system clock once and use that same time on all the items involved in a transaction. It does not matter if the actual time it took to complete the transaction was days; a transaction in SQL is done as a whole unit or is not done at all. This is not usually a problem for small transactions, but it can be in large batched ones where very complex updates have to be done.

TIMESTAMP as a source of unique identifiers is fine in most single-user systems, since all transactions are serialized and of short enough duration that the clock will change between transactions—peripherals are slower than CPUs. But in a client/server system, two transactions can occur at the same time on different local workstations. Using the local client machine clock can create duplicates and adds the problem of coordinating all the clients. The coordination problem has two parts:

1. How do you get the clocks to start at the same time? I do not mean just the technical problem of synchronizing multiple machines to the microsecond but also the one or two clients who forgot about daylight saving time.

2. How do you make sure the clocks stay the same? Using the server clock to send a timestamp back to the client increases network traffic yet does not always solve the problem.

Many operating systems, such as those made by Digital Equipment Corporation, represent the system time as a very long integer based on a count of machine cycles since a starting date. One trick is to pull off the least significant digits of this number and use them as a key. But this will not work as transaction volume increases. Adding more decimal places to the time-stamp is not a solution either. The real problem lies in statistics.

Open a telephone book (white pages) at random. Mark the last two digits of any 13 consecutive numbers, which will give you a sample of numbers between 00 and 99. What are the odds that you will have a pair of identical numbers? It is not 1 in 100, as you might first think. Start with one number and add a second number to the set; the odds that the second number does *not* match the first are 99/100. Add a third number to the set; the odds that it matches neither the first nor the second number are 98/100. Continue this line of reasoning, and compute $(0.99 * 0.98 * \ldots * 0.88) = 0.4427$ as the odds of *not* finding a pair. Therefore, the odds that you will find a pair are 0.5572, a bit better than even. By the time you get to 20 numbers, the odds of a match are about 87%; at 30 numbers, the odds exceed a 99% probability of one match. You might want to carry out this model for finding a pair in three-digit numbers and see when you pass the 50% mark.

A good key generator needs to eliminate (or at least minimize) identical keys and give a statistical distribution that is fairly uniform to avoid excessive index reorganization problems. Most key-generator algorithms are designed to use the system clock on particular hardware or a particular operating system and depend on features with a "near key" field, such as employee name, to create a unique identifier.

The mathematics of such algorithms is much like that of a hashing algorithm. Hashing algorithms also try to obtain a uniform distribution of unique values. The difference is that a hashing algorithm must ensure that a hash result is both unique (after collision resolution) and repeatable, so that it can find the stored data. A key generator needs only to ensure that the resulting key is unique in the database, which is why it can use the system clock and a hashing algorithm cannot.

You can often use a random-number generator in the host language to create pseudorandom numbers to insert into the database for these purposes. Most pseudorandom number generators will start with an initial value, called a *seed*, then use it to create a sequence of numbers. Each call will return the next value in the sequence to the calling program. The sequence will have some of the statistical properties of a real random sequence, but the same seed will produce the same sequence each time, which is why the numbers are called pseudorandom numbers. This also means that if the sequence ever repeats a number, it will begin to cycle. (This is not usually a problem, since the size of the cycle can be hundreds of thousands or even millions of numbers.)

4.1.3 Handling Times

Most databases live and work in one time zone. If you have a database that covers more than one time zone, you might consider storing time in UTC and adding a numeric column to hold the local time-zone offset. The time zones start at UTC, which has an offset of zero. This is how the system-level time-zone table in SQL-92 is defined. There are also ISO standard three-letter codes for the time zones of the world, such as EST, for Eastern Standard Time, in the United States. The offset is usually a positive or negative number of hours, but there were some odd zones that differed by 15 minutes from the expected pattern, which were removed in 1998.

You should use a 24-hour time format, which is less prone to errors than 12-hour (AM/PM) time, since it is less likely to be misread or miswritten. This format can be manually sorted more easily and is less prone to computational errors. Americans use a colon as a field separator between hours, minutes, and seconds; Europeans use a period. (This is not a problem for them, since they also use a comma for a decimal point.) Most databases give you these display options.

One of the major problems with time is that there are three kinds: fixed events ("He arrives at 13:00 Hrs"), durations ("The trip takes three hours"), and intervals ("The train leaves at 10:00 Hrs and arrives at 13:00 Hrs")— which are all interrelated. SQL-92 introduces an INTERVAL datatype that does not explicitly exist in most current implementations (Rdb, from Oracle Corporation, is an exception). An INTERVAL is a unit of duration of time rather than a fixed point in time—days, hours, minutes, seconds.

There are two classes of intervals. One class, called *year-month intervals,* has an express or implied precision that includes no fields other than YEAR and MONTH, though it is not necessary to use both. The other class, called *day-time intervals,* has an express or implied interval precision that can include any fields other than YEAR or MONTH—that is, DAY, HOUR, MINUTE, and SECOND (with decimal places).

4.2 Queries with Dates

Almost every SQL implementation has a DATE datatype, but the functions available for them vary quite a bit. The most common ones are a constructor that builds a date from integers or strings; extractors to pull out the month, day, or year; and some display options to format output.

You can assume that your SQL implementation has simple date arithmetic functions, although with different syntax from product to product, such as

1. A date plus or minus a number of days yields a new date.

2. A date minus a second date yields an integer number of days.

Here is a table of the valid combinations of `<datetime>` and `<interval>` datatypes in the SQL-92 standard:

```
<datetime> - <datetime> = <interval>
<datetime> ± <interval> = <datetime>
<interval> (* or /) <numeric> = <interval>
<interval> + <datetime> = <datetime>
<interval> ± <interval> = <interval>
<numeric> * <interval> = <interval>
```

There are other rules, which deal with time zones and the relative precision of the two operands, that are intuitively obvious.

There should also be a function that returns the current date from the system clock. This function has a different name with each vendor: `TODAY`, `SYSDATE`, `CURRENT DATE`, and `getdate()` are some examples. There may also be a function to return the day of the week from a date, which is sometimes called `DOW()` or `WEEKDAY()`. The SQL-92 standard provides for `CURRENT_DATE`, `CURRENT_TIME [(<time precision>)]`, and `CURRENT_TIMESTAMP [(<timestamp precision>)]` functions, which are self-explanatory.

4.3 Personal Calendars

One of the most common applications of dates is to build calendars that list upcoming events or actions to be taken by their user. People have no trouble with using a paper calendar to trigger their own actions, but the idea of having an internal calendar as a table in their database is somehow strange. Programmers seem to prefer to write a function that calculates the date and matches it to events.

It is easier to create a table for cyclic data than people first think. There is a trick that comes from the fact that every 28 years, the months and days of the week within a year repeat themselves in a cycle. A table of just over 10,000 rows can hold a complete cycle. The cycle has to repeat itself every

400 years, so today is on the same day of the week that it was on 400 years ago. The first cycle was completed in 1982, and it will be broken in 2100.

As an example, consider the rule that a stockbroker must settle a transaction within three business days after a trade (this is a change that was made in 1995; the old rule was five business days). Business days are defined as excluding Saturdays, Sundays, and certain holidays. The holidays are determined at the start of the year by the New York Stock Exchange, but this can be changed by an act of Congress or presidential decree. The problem is how to write an SQL query that will return the proper settlement date when it is given a trade date.

There are several tricks in this problem. The real trick is to decide what you want, not to be fooled by what you have. You have a list of holidays, but you want a list of settlement days. Let's start with a table of the given holidays and their names:

```
CREATE TABLE Holidays -- Insert holiday list into this table
(holidate DATE NOT NULL PRIMARY KEY,
 holiname CHAR(20) NOT NULL);
```

The next step is to build a table of trade and settlement dates for the whole year. Building the INSERT INTO statements to load the second table is easily done with a spreadsheet; these always have good date functions.

The trick is to notice a few things about the calendar. If we had no holidays, the trade date and the settlement date would always be exactly three days apart (CURRENT_DATE + INTERVAL 3 DAYS). One trick to save typing is to build a two column spreadsheet with the trade dates in one column and (tradedate + 3 days) in the other. The spreadsheet can be saved as ASCII text and loaded into the table, whose declaration looks like this:

```
CREATE TABLE Settles
(tradedate DATE NOT NULL PRIMARY KEY,
 settledate DATE NOT NULL);

-- sample month, February 1992, built with spreadsheet
-- Saturday
INSERT INTO Settles VALUES ('1992-02-01', '1992-02-04');

-- Sunday
INSERT INTO Settles VALUES ('1992-02-02', '1992-02-05');
```

```
-- Monday
INSERT INTO Settles VALUES ('1992-02-03', '1992-02-06');

etc.
```

Now the table is populated as if we had no holidays or weekends. We now have to update it so that the settlement days are in the right locations. Start with the holidays from the list:

```
UPDATE Settles -- Holidays move forward one day
 SET settledate = settledate + 1
 WHERE settledate IN (SELECT holidate FROM Holidays);
```

This will move holiday settlements one day forward. In particular, Friday holidays will move to Saturday. Now move the weekend settlement dates to Monday:

```
UPDATE Settles -- Saturdays settle on Monday
 SET settledate = settledate + 2
 WHERE DayOfWeek(settledate) = 'Saturday';

UPDATE Settles -- Sundays settle on Monday
 SET settledate = settledate + 1
 WHERE DayOfWeek(settledate) = 'Sunday';
```

Repeat these three UPDATEs until the system tells you that you have changed zero records. This is important; consider a four-day weekend, starting on Friday. Friday settlement moves to Saturday, Saturday settlement moves to Monday, Sunday settlement moves to Monday, and Monday settlement moves to Tuesday. But Monday was a holiday; they should all settle on Tuesday. The second round will move everything to its proper place.

If you want to shrink your table a bit, notice that all trade dates must be on a weekday, not on a weekend. You can trim the final table by about 100 rows (52 weekends × 2 days) with

```
DELETE FROM Settle
 WHERE DayOfWeek(tradedate) IN ('Saturday', 'Sunday');
```

If you need to know why a settlement date has been moved, you can find the names and dates for the holidays involved with this query:

```
SELECT tradedate, settledate, holidate, holiname
FROM Holidays, Settles
WHERE holidate BETWEEN tradedate AND settledate;
```

The final settlement table will be about 250 rows and only 2 columns wide. This is quite small; it will fit into main storage easily on any machine. Finding the settlement day is a straight simple query; if you had built just the Holiday table, you would have had to provide procedural code.

4.4 Time Series

One of the major problems in the real world is how to handle a series of events that occur in the same time period or in some particular order. The code is tricky and a bit hard to understand, but the basic idea is that you have a table with start and stop times for events and you want to get information about them as a group.

4.4.1 Gaps in a Time Series

The time line can be partitioned into intervals and a set of intervals can be drawn from that partition for reporting. One of the stock questions on an employment form asks the prospective employee to explain any gaps in his record of employment. Most of the time this gap means that you were unemployed. If you are in data processing, you answer that you were consulting, which is a synonym for unemployed.

Given this table, how would you write an SQL query to display the time periods and their durations for each of the candidates? You will have to assume that your version of SQL has DATE functions that can do some simple calendar math.

```
CREATE TABLE JobApps
(candidate CHAR(25) NOT NULL,
 jobtitle CHAR(10) NOT NULL,
 startdate DATE NOT NULL,
 enddate DATE NOT NULL
        CONSTRAINT started_before_ended
        CHECK(startdate <= enddate)
 . . .);
```

Notice that the end date of the current job has to be set to some distant time or you can drop the NOT NULL constraint and use NULL. SQL does not support an 'eternity' or 'end of time' value for temporal datatypes. Use '9999-12-31 23:59:59.999999', which is the highest possible date value that SQL can represent.

It is obvious that this has to be a self-JOIN query, but you have to do some date arithmetic to allow for the fact that the first day of each gap is the last day of an employment period plus 1, and that the last day of each gap is the first day of the next job minus 1. This start-point and end-point problem is the reason that SQL-92 defined the OVERLAPS predicate this way.

Most versions of SQL support dates, and SQL-92 has definitions for DATE datatypes and date arithmetic. Unfortunately, no two implementations look alike, and none look like the ANSI standard. I will be using a readable but nonstandard notation for date math, which you can translate into your target product.

The first attempt at this query is usually something like the following, which will produce the right results, but with a lot of extra rows that are just plain wrong. Assume that if I add a number of days to a date, or subtract a number of days from it, I get a new date.

```
SELECT J1.candidate,
  (J1.enddate + INTERVAL 1 DAY) AS gapstart,
  (J2.startdate - INTERVAL 1 DAY) AS gapend,
  (J2.startdate - J1.enddate) AS gaplength
FROM JobApps AS J1, JobApps AS J2
WHERE (J1.candidate = J2.candidate)
AND (J1.enddate + INTERVAL 1 DAY)
  <= (J2.startdate - INTERVAL 1 DAY);
```

Here is why this does not work. Imagine that we have a table that includes candidate name 'Bill Jones' with the following work history:

candidate	jobtitle	startdate	enddate
'John Smith'	'Vice Pres'	'1989-01-10'	'1989-12-31'
'John Smith'	'President'	'1990-01-12'	'1991-12-31'
'Bill Jones'	'Scut Worker'	'1990-02-24'	'1990-04-21'
'Bill Jones'	'Manager'	'1991-01-01'	'1991-01-05'
'Bill Jones'	'Grand Poobah'	'1991-04-04'	'1991-05-15'

We would get this as a result:

candidate	gapstart	gapend	gaplength
'John Smith'	'1990-01-01'	'1990-01-11'	12
'Bill Jones'	'1990-04-22'	'1990-12-31'	255
'Bill Jones'	'1991-01-06'	'1991-04-03'	89
'Bill Jones'	'1990-04-22'	'1991-04-03'	348 ← false data

The problem is that the 'John Smith' row looks just fine and can fool you into thinking that you are doing fine. He had two jobs; therefore, there was one gap in between. However, 'Bill Jones' cannot be right—only two gaps separate three jobs, yet the query shows three gaps.

The query does its JOIN on all possible combinations of start and end dates in the original table. This gives false data in the results by counting the end of one job, 'Scut Worker', and the start of another, 'Grand Poobah', as a gap. The idea is to use only the most recently ended job for the gap. This can be done with a MAX() function and yet another correlated subquery. The final result is this:

```
SELECT J1.candidate,
    (J1.enddate + INTERVAL 1 DAY) AS gapstart,
    (J2.startdate - INTERVAL 1 DAY) AS gapend,
    (J2.startdate - J1.enddate) AS gaplength
  FROM JobApps AS J1, JobApps AS J2
  WHERE (J1.candidate = J2.candidate)
  AND (J1.enddate + INTERVAL 1 DAY) =
    (SELECT MAX(J3.enddate + INTERVAL 1 DAY)
      FROM JobApps AS J3
    WHERE (J3.candidate = J1.candidate)
      AND (J3.enddate + INTERVAL 1 DAY
        <= J2.startdate - INTERVAL 1 DAY));
```

4.4.2 Continuous Time Periods

Given a series of jobs that can start and stop at any time, how can you be sure that an employee doing all these jobs was really working without any gaps? Let's build a table of timesheets for one employee.

```
CREATE TABLE Timesheets
(job CHAR(5) NOT NULL PRIMARY KEY,
 startdate DATE NOT NULL,
 enddate DATE NOT NULL);
```

```
INSERT INTO Timesheets
VALUES ('J1', '1998-01-01', '1998-01-03'),
       ('J2', '1998-01-06', '1998-01-10'),
       ('J3', '1998-01-05', '1998-01-08'),
       ('J4', '1998-01-20', '1998-01-25'),
       ('J5', '1998-01-18', '1998-01-23'),
       ('J6', '1998-02-01', '1998-02-05'),
       ('J7', '1998-02-03', '1998-02-08'),
       ('J8', '1998-02-07', '1998-02-11');
```

The most immediate answer is to build a search condition for all of the characteristics of a continuous time period.

```
SELECT T1.startdate,
       MAX(T2.enddate) AS finishdate -- end of Continuous period
  FROM Timesheets AS T1, Timesheets AS T2
 WHERE T1.startdate < T2.enddate -- all possible start-end pairs
   AND NOT EXISTS
       (SELECT *
          FROM Timesheets AS T3, Timesheets AS T4
   -- all intervals inside bounds set by T1-T2
         WHERE T3.enddate < T4.startdate
           AND T3.startdate BETWEEN T1.startdate AND T2.enddate
           AND T4.startdate BETWEEN T1.startdate AND T2.enddate
   -- no gaps between T1-T2
           AND NOT EXISTS
               (SELECT *
                  FROM Timesheets AS T5
                 WHERE T5.startdate
                       BETWEEN T3.startdate AND T3.enddate
                   AND T5.enddate
                       BETWEEN T4.startdate AND T4.enddate))
   -- group by startdate, so max() will work
 GROUP BY T1.startdate
HAVING T1.startdate    -- first start point of Continuous period
       = MIN(T2.startdate);
```

Result

startdate	finishdate
1998-01-01	1998-01-03
1998-01-05	1998-01-10
1998-01-18	1998-01-25
1998-02-01	1998-02-11

However, another way of doing this is a query, which will also tell you which jobs bound the Continuous periods.

```
SELECT T2.startdate,
       MAX(T1.enddate) AS finishdate,
       MAX(T1.job || ' to ' || T2.job) AS job_pair
  FROM Timesheets AS T1, Timesheets AS T2
 WHERE T2.job <> T1.job

   AND T1.startdate BETWEEN T2.startdate AND T2.enddate
   AND T2.enddate BETWEEN T1.startdate AND T1.enddate
 GROUP BY T2.startdate;
```

Result

startdate	finishdate	job_pair
1998-01-05	1998-01-10	J2 to J3
1998-01-18	1998-01-25	J4 to J5
1998-02-01	1998-02-08	J7 to J6
1998-02-03	1998-02-11	J8 to J7

If you are using Sybase SQL Anywhere, you can modify this query to take advantage of its LIST( ) aggregate string function (see Section 21.5 for details).

```
SELECT T2.startdate,
       MAX(T1.enddate) AS finishdate,
       LIST(T3.job) AS job_list
  FROM Timesheets AS T1, Timesheets AS T2, Timesheets AS T3
 WHERE T2.job <> T1.job
   AND T1.startdate BETWEEN T2.startdate AND T2.enddate
   AND T2.enddate BETWEEN T1.startdate AND T1.enddate
   AND T3.startdate BETWEEN T2.startdate AND T1.enddate
 GROUP BY T2.startdate;
```

Result

startdate	finishdate	job_list
1998-01-05	1998-01-10	J2, J3
1998-01-18	1998-01-25	J4, J5
1998-02-01	1998-02-08	J6, J7, J8
1998-02-03	1998-02-11	J7, J8

There was some automatic sorting in the LIST() function when it assembled the answers. Notice that the last row is actually a subset of the next-to-last row in the results. It would be possible to use the POSITION() string function to remove all such subsets from the results, if you were willing to store the answer in a table:

```
DELETE FROM Results
  WHERE EXISTS
        (SELECT R1.job_list
           FROM Results AS R1
          WHERE POSITION (Results.job_list IN R1.job_list) > 0);
```

Doing this with just the dates is possible, but quite complex.

4.4.3 Locating Dates

This little problem is sneakier than it sounds. I first saw it in *Explain* magazine, then met the author, Rudy Limeback (of New York Life, Toronto), at the Database World conference in Boston. The problem is to print a list of the employees whose birthdays will occur in the next 45 days. The employee files have each date of birth. The answer will depend on what date functions you have in your implementation of SQL, but Rudy was working with DB2.

What makes this problem interesting is the number of possible false starts. Most versions of SQL also have a library function MAKEDATE(year, month, day) or an equivalent, which will construct a date from three numbers representing a year, month, and day, and extraction functions to disassemble a date into integers representing the month, day, and year. The SQL-92 standard would do this with the general function CAST (<string> AS DATE), but there is no provision in the standard for using integers without first converting them to strings, either explicitly or implicitly. For example,

```
-- direct use of strings to build a date
  CAST ('1999-01-01' AS DATE)
```

```
-- concatenation causes integer to string conversion
CAST (1999 || '-'|| 01 ||'-' || 01 AS DATE)
```

The first "gotcha" in this problem is trying to use the component pieces of the dates in a search condition. If you were looking for birthdays all within the same month, it would be easy:

```
SELECT name, dob, CURRENT_DATE
 FROM Employees
WHERE EXTRACT(MONTH FROM CURRENT_DATE) = EXTRACT(MONTH FROM dob);
```

Attempts to extend this approach fall apart, however, since a 45-day period could extend across three months and possibly into the following year, and might fall in a leap year. Very soon, the number of function calls is too high and the logic is too complex.

The second "gotcha" is trying to write a simple search condition with these functions to construct the birthday in the current year from the date of birth (dob) in the Employee table:

```
SELECT name, dob, CURRENT_DATE
   FROM Employees
 WHERE MAKEDATE(EXTRACT (YEAR FROM CURRENT_DATE),
                EXTRACT (MONTH FROM dob),
                EXTRACT (DAY FROM dob))
        BETWEEN CURRENT_DATE AND (CURRENT_DATE + INTERVAL 45 DAYS);
```

But a leap-year date of birth will cause an exception to be raised on an invalid date if this is not also a leap year. There is also another problem. The third "gotcha" comes when the 45-day period wraps into the next year. For example, if the current month is December 1992, we should include January 1993 birthdays, but they are not constructed by the MAKEDATE() function. At this point, you can build a messy search condition that also goes into the next year when constructing birthdays.

Rory Murchison of the Aetna Institute pointed out that if you are working with DB2 or some other SQL implementations, you will have an AGE(date1 [,date2]) function. This returns the difference in years between date1 and date2. If date2 is missing, it defaults to CURRENT_DATE. The AGE() function can be constructed from other functions in implementations that do not support it. In SQL-92, the expression would be (date2 - date1) YEAR, which would construct an INTERVAL value. That makes the answer quite simple:

```
SELECT name, dob, CURRENT_DATE
  FROM Employees
 WHERE INTERVAL (CURRENT_DATE - birthday) YEAR
     < INTERVAL (CURRENT_DATE - birthday + INTERVAL 45 DAYS) YEAR;
```

In English, this says that if the employee is a year older 45 days from now, he must have had a birthday in the meantime.

4.4.4 First and Last Days of a Month

Dates can be stored in several different ways in a database. Designers of one product might decide that they want to keep things in a Cobol-like field-oriented format, which has a clear, separate area for the year, month, and day of each date. Another product might want to be more UNIX-like and keep the dates as a displacement in some small unit of time from a starting point, then calculate the display format when it is needed. The SQL-92 standard does not say how a date should be stored, but the "Cobol approach" is easier to display, and the "displacement approach" can do calculations easier.

The result is that there is no best way to calculate either the first day of the month or the last day of the month from a given date. In the Cobol method, you can get the first day of the month easily by using extractions from the date to build the date, with a 1 in the day field.

```
SET first_day = MAKEDATE (EXTRACT (YEAR FROM mydate),
                          EXTRACT (MONTH FROM mydate),
                          1);
```

The last day of the month is a bit harder. The Cobol-style products usually have a function that will construct a date from numeric fields for the year, month, and day. Therefore, you would think you can construct the first day of the next month, and then subtract one day from it, like this:

```
SET last_day = MAKEDATE (EXTRACT (YEAR FROM mydate),
                         EXTRACT (MONTH FROM mydate) + 1,
                         1) - 1;
```

But this does not always work! Look at what happens in December, when the month number becomes 13 and you have an invalid date in the calculation. Strangely, SQL Anywhere in the Sybase family will accept this expression and produce the correct answer. For the products that follow standards, the logic used in this approach gets to be fairly complex when you start allowing for leap year.

Here is a little temporal algebra that will return the last day of the month for a given date:

```
SET last_day = (mydate
            + INTERVAL (((32 - EXTRACT (DAY FROM mydate)))
            - (EXTRACT (DAY FROM mydate)
            + (32 - EXTRACT(DAY FROM mydate)) + 1)) DAYS;
```

This will run faster on products that use the displacement approach to dates. The common subexpression is calculated only once, and the INTERVAL calculation is done once. The rest is integer arithmetic. It is easy to calculate the first day:

```
SET first_day
        = (mydate - INTERVAL (EXTRACT (DAY FROM mydate) + 1) DAY;
```

4.5 Julian Dates

All SQL implementations support a DATE datatype, but there is no standard defining how they should support it. Some products represent the year, month, and day as parts of a double-word integer, others use Julianized dates, some use ISO ordinal dates, and some store dates as character strings. The programmer does not care as long as the dates work correctly.

There is a technical difference between a *Julian date* and a *Julianized date*. A Julian date is an astronomer's term that counts the number of days since 1 January 4713 BCE. This count is now well over 2 billion; nobody but astronomers uses it. However, computer companies have corrupted the term to mean a count from some point in time from which they can build a date or time. The fixed point is usually the year 1, or 1900, or the start of the Gregorian calendar.

A Julianized, or ordinal, date is the position of the date within its year, so it falls between 1 and 365 or 366. You will see this number printed on the bottom edges of desk calendar pages. The usual way to find the Julianized day within the current year is to use a simple program that stores the number of days in each month as an array and sums them with the day of the month for the date in question. The only difficult part is remembering to add 1 if the year is a leap year and the month is after February.

Here is a very fast and compact algorithm that computes the Julian date from a Gregorian date and vice versa. These algorithms appeared as Algorithm 199 (ACM 1980) and were first written in ALGOL by Robert Tantzen. Here are SQL translations of the code:

```
FUNCTION Julianize1
  (day INTEGER, month INTEGER, year INTEGER)
  LANGUAGE SQL
  RETURNS INTEGER;
BEGIN
DECLARE century INTEGER, yearincentury INTEGER;
IF (month > 2)
THEN SET month = month - 3
ELSE SET month = month + 9;
    SET year = year - 1
END IF;
SET century = year / 100;
SET yearincentury = year - 100 * century;
RETURN ((146097 * century) / 4
       + (1461 * yearincentury) / 4
       + (153 * month + 2) / 5 + day + 1721119);
END;
```

Remember that the division will be integer division because the variables involved are all integers. Here is another version of the algorithm for the same calculation:

```
FUNCTION Julianize2 (day INTEGER, month INTEGER, year INTEGER)
  LANGUAGE SQL
  RETURNS INTEGER;
BEGIN
DECLARE jul_yr INTEGER, jul_leap INTEGER, jul_month INTEGER;
IF month > 2
THEN SET jul_yr = year;
    SET jul_month = month + 1;
ELSE SET jul_yr = year - 1;
    SET jul_month = month + 13;
ENDIF;
jul_day = CAST ((365.2522 * jul_yr) AS INTEGER)
       + CAST ((30.6001 * jul_month) AS INTEGER)
       + day + 1720995;
IF (day + 31 * (month + 12 * year) >= 588829)
THEN SET jul_leap = CAST ((jul_yr * 0.01) AS INTEGER);
    RETURN (jul_day + 2 - jul_leap
           + CAST ((0.25 * jul_leap) AS INTEGER);
```

```
END IF;
END;
```

This assumes that CAST(x AS INTEGER) will truncate *x* instead of rounding it; check your particular SQL engine's proprietary functions on this point.

Here is a Pascal procedure taken from *Numerical Recipes in Pascal* (Press, Flannery, and Vetterling 1989) for converting a Georgian date to a Julian date.

```
FUNCTION Julianize (VAR year, month, day: INTEGER): INTEGER;

CONST
 gregorian = 588829;

VAR
 jul_yr, jul_leap, jul_month : INTEGER;

BEGIN
IF year = 0
THEN BEGIN
    WriteLn ('error: there was no year 0');
    Halt(1);
    END;
IF year < 0 THEN year := year + 1;

IF month > 2
THEN BEGIN
    jul_yr := year;
    jul_month := month + 1;
    END
ELSE BEGIN
    jul_yr := year - 1;
    jul_month := month + 13;
    END;

jul_day := TRUNC(365.2522 * jul_yr)
         + TRUNC(30.6001 * jul_month)
         + day + 1720995;

IF (day + 31 * (month + 12 * year) >= gregorian)
THEN BEGIN
    jul_leap := TRUNC(jul_yr * 0.01);
    jul_day := jul_day + 2 - jul_leap + TRUNC(0.25 * jul_leap);
```

```
      END;
END;
```

To convert a Julian day number into a Gregorian calender date:

```
PROCEDURE Jdate (IN julian: INTEGER,
OUT year INTEGER, OUT month INTEGER, OUT day INTEGER)
 LANGUAGE SQL
BEGIN
SET julian = julian - 1721119;
SET year = (4 * julian - 1) / 146097;
SET julian = 4 * julian - 1 - 146097 * year;
SET day = julian / 4;
SET julian = (4 * day + 3) / 1461;
SET day = 4 * day + 3 - 1461 * julian;
SET day = (day + 4) / 4;
SET month = (5 * day - 3) / 153 * month;
SET day = 5 * day - 3 - 153 * month;
SET day = (day + 5) / 5;
SET year = 100 * year + julian;
IF month < 10
THEN SET month = month + 3;
ELSE month = month - 9;
     year = year + 1
END IF;
END;
```

There are two problems with these algorithms. First, the Julian day the astronomers use starts at noon. If you think about it, it makes sense because they are doing their work at night. The second problem is that the integers involved get large and you cannot use floating-point numbers to replace them because the rounding errors are too great. You need long integers, ones in the 2.5 million range.

4.6 Date and Time Extraction Functions

No two SQL products agree on the functions that should be available for use with <datetime> datatypes. In keeping with the practice of overloading functions, the SQL3 proposal has a function for extracting components from a datetime or interval value. The syntax looks like this:

```
<extract expression> ::=
 EXTRACT <left paren> <extract field>
    FROM <extract source> <right paren>

<extract field> ::= <datetime field> | <time zone field>

<time zone field> ::= TIMEZONE_HOUR | TIMEZONE_MINUTE

<extract source> ::= <datetime value expression>
        | <interval value expression>
```

The interesting feature is that this function always returns a numeric value. For example, EXTRACT (MONTH FROM birthday) will be an INTEGER between 1 and 12. No vendor has implemented this function yet, so you should look for many separate functions, such as YEAR(<date>), MONTH(<date>), and DAY(<date>), that extract components from a <datetime> datatype. Most versions of SQL also have a library function something like MAKEDATE(<year>, <month>, <day>), DATE(<year>, <month>, <day>), or an equivalent, which will construct a date from three numbers representing a year, month, and day. Standard SQL-92 uses the CAST function, but the details are not pretty since it involves assembling a string in the ISO format, then converting it to a date.

Bill Karwin at the Interbase division of Enprize (nee Borland International) came up with a fairly portable trick for doing extractions in SQL products that don't have this library function. Use the LIKE predicate and CAST() operator (or whatever the product uses for formatting output) to convert the DATE expressions into character string expressions and test them against a template. For example, to find all the rows of data in the month of March:

```
SELECT *
  FROM Table1
 WHERE CAST(datefield AS CHAR(10)) LIKE '%MAR%';
```

Obviously, this technique can be extended to use other string functions to search for parts of a date or time, to look for ranges of dates, and so forth.

The best warning is to read your SQL product manual and see what you can do with its library functions.

4.7 Other Temporal Functions

Another common set of functions, which are not represented in standard SQL, deal with weeks. For example, Sybase's SQL Anywhere (nee WATCOM

SQL) has a DOW(<date>) that returns a number between 1 and 7 to represent the day of the week (1 = Sunday, 2 = Monday, . . . , 7 = Saturday, following an ISO standard convention). You can also find functions that add or subtract weeks from a date, give the number of the date within the year, and so on. The function for finding the day of the week for a date is called Zeller's algorithm:

```
FUNCTION Zeller (year INTEGER, month INTEGER, day INTEGER)
  LANGUAGE SQL
  RETURNS INTEGER;
BEGIN
DECLARE m INTEGER, d INTEGER, y INTEGER;
SET y = year;
SET m = month - 2;
IF (m <= 0)
THEN SET m = m + 12;
     SET y = y - 1;
END IF;
RETURN (MOD((day + (13 * m - 1) / 5
    + 5 * MOD(y, 100) / 4 - 7 * y / 400), 7) + 1);
END;
```

   DB2 and XDB SQL have an AGE(<date1>, <date2>) function, which returns the difference in years between <date1> and <date2>.

   The table on page 167 gives a summary of the valid arithmetic operators involving <datetimes> and <intervals> in SQL-92. Arithmetic operations involving <datetimes> or <intervals> obey the natural rules associated with dates and times and yield valid <datetime> or <interval> results according to the Common Era calendar.

   Operations involving items of type <datetime> require that the <datetime> items be mutually comparable. Operations involving intervals require that the <interval> items be mutually comparable.

   Operations involving a <datetime> and an <interval> preserve the time zone of the <datetime> operand. If the <datetime> operand does not include a time zone part, then the local time zone is used.

   The OVERLAPS predicate determines whether two chronological periods overlap in time (see Section 13.2 for details). A chronological period is specified either as a pair of <datetimes> (starting and ending) or as a starting <datetime> and an <interval>.

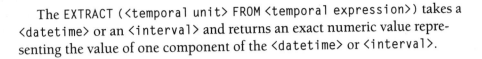

The EXTRACT (`<temporal unit> FROM <temporal expression>`) takes a `<datetime>` or an `<interval>` and returns an exact numeric value representing the value of one component of the `<datetime>` or `<interval>`.

4.8 Problems with the Year 2000

The special problems with the year 2000 have taken on a life of their own in the computer community, so they rate a separate section in this book. The three major problems with representations of the year 2000 in computer systems are

1. The year 2000 has a lot of zeros in it.

2. The year 2000 is a leap year.

3. The year 2000 is a millennium year.

4. Many date fields are not really dates.

4.8.1 The Zeros

I like to call problem 1—the zeros in 2000—the "odometer problem" because it is in the hardware or system level. This is not the same as the millennium problem, where date arithmetic is invalid. If you are using a year-in-century format, the year 2000 is going to "roll over" like a car odometer that has reached its limit and leave a year that is assumed to be 1900 (or something else other than 2000) by the application program.

This problem lives where you cannot see in hardware and operating systems related to the system clock. Information on such problems is very incomplete, so you will need to keep yourself posted as new releases of your particular products come out.

Another subtle form of the zero problem is that some hashing and random number generators use parts of the system date as a parameter. Zero is a perfectly good number until you try to divide by it and your program aborts.

The problem is in mainframes. For example, the Unisys 2200 system was set to fail on the first day of 1996 because the 8th bit of the year field—which is a signed integer—will go to 1. Fortunately, the vendor had some solutions ready. Do you know what other hardware uses this convention? You might want to look.

The real killer will be with Intel-based PCs. When the odometer wraps around, DOS jumps to 1980 most of the time, and sometimes to 1984, depending on your BIOS chip. Windows 3.1 jumps to 1900 most of the time.

Since PCs are now common as stand-alone units and as workstations, you can test this for yourself. Set the date and time to 1999-12-31 at 23:59:30 Hrs and let the clock run. What happens next depends on your BIOS chip and version of DOS.

The results can be that the clock display shows "12:00 AM" and a date display of "01/01/00," so you think you have no problems. However, you will find that you have newly created files dated 1984 or 1980. Surprise!

This problem is passed along to application programs, but not always the way that you would think. Quicken Version 3 for the IBM PC running on MS-DOS 6 is one example. As you expect, directly inputting the date 2000-01-01 results in the year resetting to 1980 or 1984 off the system clock. But strangely enough, if you let the date wrap from 1999-12-31 into the year 2000, Quicken Version 3 interprets the change as 1901-01-01 and not as 1900.

4.8.2 Leap Year

Problem 2 always seems to shock people. You might remember being told in grade school that there are 365.25 days per year and that the accumulation of the fractional day creates a leap year every four years. Once more, your teachers lied to you; there are really 365.2422 days per year, and every 400 years the fraction of the fractional day that was left over from the leap years accumulates enough to create an additional day. Since most of us are not over 400 years old, we have not had to worry about this until now. The correct test for leap years in SQL/PSM is

```
FUNCTION leapyear (year INTEGER)
 RETURNS CHAR(3)
 LANGUAGE SQL
RETURN (IF MOD(year, 400) = 0
        THEN 'Yes'
        ELSE IF MOD(year, 100) = 0
             THEN 'No'
             ELSE IF MOD(year, 4) = 0
                  THEN 'Yes'
                  ELSE 'No'
                  END IF
             END IF
        END IF);
```

Or if you would like a more compact form, you can use this solution from Phil Alexander, which will fit into in-line code as a search expression:

```
(MOD(year, 400) = 0
 OR (MOD(year, 4) = 0 AND NOT (MOD(year, 100) = 0)))
```

Lots of programs were written by people who did not know this algorithm. I do not mean Cobol legacy programs in your organization; I mean packaged programs for which you paid good money. The date functions in the first releases of Lotus, Excel, and Quattro Pro did not handle the day 2000-02-29 correctly. Lotus simply made an error and the others followed suit to maintain "Lotus compatibility" in their products. Currently, Microsoft Excel for Windows Version 4 shows correctly that the next day after 2000-02-28 is 2000-02-29. However, it thinks that the next day after 1900-02-28 is also 29 February instead of 1 March. Microsoft Excel for Macintosh doesn't handle the years 1900–1903.

Have you checked all of your word processors, spreadsheets, desktop databases, appointment calendars, and other off the shelf packages for this problem yet? Just key in the date 2000-02-29, then do some calculations with date arithmetic and see what happens.

With networked systems, this is going to be a real nightmare. All you need is one program on one node in the network to reject leap year day 2000, and the whole network is useless for that day; transactions might not reconcile for some time afterwards. How many nodes do you think there are in the ATM banking networks in North America and Europe?

4.8.3 The Millennium

I saved problem 3 for last because it is the one best known in the popular and computer trade press. We programmers have not been keeping TRUE dates in data fields for a few decades. Instead, we have been using one of several year-in-century formats. These will not work in the last year of this millennium (the first millennium of the Common Era calendar ends in the year 2000 and the second millennium begins on with the year 2001—that is why Arthur C. Clarke used it for the title of his book).

If only we had been good programmers and not tried to save storage space at the expense of accuracy, we would have used ISO standard formats and would not have to deal with these problems today. Since we didn't, programs have been doing arithmetic and comparisons based on the year-in-century and not on the year. A thirty-year mortgage taken out in 1992 will be over in the year 2022, but when you subtract the two year-in-centuries, you get $(22 - 92) = -70$ years. This is a very early payoff of a mortgage!

Inventory retention programs are throwing away good stock, thinking it is outdated—look at the ten-year retention required in the automobile industry. Lifetime product warranties are now being dishonored because the service schedule dates and manufacturing dates cannot be resolved correctly. One hospital has already sent a geriatrics patient to the children's ward because it keeps only two digits of the birth year. Imagine your own horror story.

According to Benny Popek of Coopers & Lybrand LLP (Xenakis 1995), "This problem is so big that we will consider these bugs to be out of the scope of our normal software maintenance contracts. For those clients who insist that we should take responsibility, we'll exercise the cancellation clause and terminate the outsourcing contract."

Popek commented, "We've found that a lot of our clients are in denial. We spoke to one CIO who just refused to deal with the problem, since he's going to retire next year."

But the problem is more subtle than just looking for date data fields. Timestamps are often buried inside encoding schemes. If the year-in-century is used for the high-order digits of a serial numbering system, then any program that depends on increasing serial numbers will fail. Those of you with magnetic tape libraries might want to look at your tape labels now. The five-digit code is used in many mainframe shops for archives, and tape management software also has the convention that if programmers want a tape to be kept indefinitely, they code the label with a retention date of 99365—that is, 1999-12-31—because the routine checks the last three digits to see that they are between 001 and 365. This method will fail at the start of the year 2000 when the retention label has 00001 in it.

4.8.4 Weird Dates in Legacy Data

Some of the problems with dates in legacy data have been discussed in an article by Randall L. Hitchens (Hitchens 1991) and in one by me on the same subject (Celko 1981). The problem is more subtle than Hitchens implied in his article, which dealt with nonstandard date formats. Dates hide in other places, not just in date fields. The most common places are serial numbers and computer-generated identifiers.

In the early 1960s, a small insurance company in Atlanta bought out an even smaller company that sold burial insurance policies to poor people in the Deep South. The burial insurance company used a policy number format

identical to that of the larger company. The numbers began with the two digits of the year-in-century, followed by a dash, followed by an eight-digit
sequential number.

The systems analysts charged with integrating the two files decided that
the easiest way was to add 20 years to the first two digits. Their logic was
that no customer would keep these cheap policies for twenty years—and the
analyst who did this would not be working there in 20 years, so who cared?
As the years passed, the company moved from a simple file system to a hierarchical database and was using the policy numbers for unique record keys.
The system simply generated new policy numbers on demand, using a global
counter in a policy library routine, and no problems occurred for decades.

There were about 100 burial policies left in the database after 20 years.
Nobody had written programs to protect against duplicate keys, since the
problem had never occurred. Then, one day, they created their first duplicate
number. Sometimes the database would crash, but sometimes the child
records would get attached to the wrong parent. This second situation was
worse, since the company started paying and billing the wrong people.

The company was lucky enough to have someone who recognized the old
burial insurance policies when he saw them. It took months to clean up the
problem, because they had to search a warehouse to find the original policy
documents. If the policies were still valid, there were insurance regulation
problems because those policies had been made illegal in the intervening
years.

In this case, the date was being used to generate a unique identifier. But
consider a situation in which this same scheme is used, starting in the year
1999, for a serial number. Once the company goes into the year 2000, you
can no longer select the largest serial number in the database and increment
it to get the next one.

According to a quotation in *CFO* magazine (CFO 1991), ITT Hartford
estimated that adding the century years to the dates in its computer systems
will cost the company up to $20 million—and costs can only have risen
since 1991.

Character Datatypes in SQL

SQL-89 DEFINED A CHARACTER(n) or CHAR(n) datatype, which represents a fixed-length string of *n* printable characters, where *n* is always greater than 0. Some implementations allow the string to contain control characters, but this is not the usual case. The allowable characters are usually drawn from ASCII or EBCDIC character sets and most often use those collation sequences for sorting.

SQL-92 added the VARYING CHARACTER(n) or VARCHAR(n), which was already present in many implementations. A VARCHAR(n) represents a string that varies in length from 1 to *n* printable characters. This is important; SQL-92 does not have a string of zero length.

SQL-92 also added NATIONAL CHARACTER(n) and NATIONAL VARYING CHARACTER(n) datatypes, which are made up of printable characters drawn from ISO-defined foreign-language character sets. SQL-92 also allows the database administrator to define collation sequences and do other things with the character sets. Most products have not implemented these features yet, so they will not be covered in this book, which will assume that you are using ASCII or EBCDIC.

5.1 Problems with SQL Strings

Different programming languages handle strings differently. You simply have to do some unlearning when you get to SQL. Here are the major problem areas for programmers.

In SQL, character strings are printable characters enclosed in single quotation marks. Many older SQL implementations and several programming languages use double quotation marks or make doing so an option so that the single quotation mark can be used as an apostrophe. SQL-92 uses two apostrophes together to represent a single apostrophe in a string literal.

Double quotation marks are reserved for names that have embedded spaces, illegal syntax or characters, or that are also SQL keywords in SQL-92.

5.1.1 Problems of String Equality

No two languages agree on how to compare character strings as equal unless they are identical in length and match position for position, exactly character for character.

The first problem is whether uppercase and lowercase versions of a letter compare as equal to each other. Many programming languages, including all proper SQL implementations, treat them that way within the program text. Though the standard says that the two cases are different, it is very implementation-dependent. Some implementations, such as Sybase, allow the DBA to set uppercase and lowercase matching as a system configuration parameter.

The SQL-92 standard has two functions that change the case of a string: LOWER(<string expression>) shifts all letters in the parameter string to corresponding lowercase letters; UPPER(<string expression>) shifts all letters in the string to uppercase. Most implementations have had these functions (perhaps with different names) as vendor library functions.

Equality between strings of unequal length is calculated by first padding out the shorter string with blanks on the right-hand side until the strings are of the same length. Then they are matched, position for position, for identical values. If one position fails to match, the whole equality fails.

In contrast, the Xbase languages (FoxPro, dBase, and so on) truncate the longer string to the length of the shorter string and then match them position for position. Other programming languages ignore upper- and lowercase differences.

5.1.2 Problems of String Ordering

SQL-89 was silent on the collating sequence to be used in string ordering. In practice, almost all SQL implementations use either ASCII or EBCDIC, which are both Roman I character sets in ISO terminology. A few implementations have a dictionary or library order option (uppercase and lowercase letters mixed together in alphabetic order: *A, a, B, b, C, c, . . .*), and many vendors offer a national-language option that is based on the appropriate ISO standard.

National-language options can be very complicated. The Nordic languages all share a common ISO character set, but they do not sort the same letters in the same position. German is sorted differently in Germany and in Austria. Spain only recently decided to quit sorting *ch* and *ll* as if they were single characters. You really need to look at the ISO Unicode implementation for your particular product.

The SQL-92 standard allows the DBA to define a collating sequence that is used for comparisons. No product has this feature yet, so you have to see what the vendor of your SQL product supports.

5.1.3 Problems of String Grouping

Because the equality test has to pad out the shorter of the two strings, you will often find that a GROUP BY on a VARCHAR(n) has unpredictable results:

```
CREATE TABLE Foobar (x VARCHAR(5) NOT NULL);
INSERT INTO Foobar VALUES ('a');
INSERT INTO Foobar VALUES ('a ');
INSERT INTO Foobar VALUES ('a  ');
INSERT INTO Foobar VALUES ('a   ');
```

Now, execute the query

```
SELECT x, CHAR_LENGTH(x), COUNT(*)
  FROM Foobar
 GROUP BY x;
```

The value for CHAR_LENGTH(x) will vary for different products. The most common answers are 1, 4, or 5 in this example. A length of 1 is returned because it is the length of the shortest string or because it is the length of the first string physically in the table; a length of 4 because it is the length of the longest string in the table; a length of 5 because it is the greatest possible length of a string in the table.

As a suggestion, be sure that the host language application or a TRIGGER on the table trims the trailing blanks to avoid problems.

5.2 Standard String Functions

SQL-92 defines a set of string functions that appear in most products, but with vendor-specific syntax. You will probably find that products will continue to support their own syntax, but will also add the SQL-92 standard syntax in new releases. String concatenation is shown with the || operator, taken from PL/I.

The SUBSTRING(<string> FROM <start> FOR <length>) function uses three arguments: the source string, the starting position of the substring, and the length of the substring to be extracted. Truncation occurs when the implied starting and ending positions are not both within the given string.

The fold functions are a pair of functions for converting all the lowercase characters in a given string to uppercase, UPPER(string>), or all the uppercase ones to lowercase LOWER(<string>).

The TRIM([[<trim specification>] [<trim character>] FROM] <trim source>) produces a result string that is the source string with an unwanted character removed. The <trim source> is the original character value expression. The <trim specification> is either LEADING or TRAILING or BOTH, and the <trim character> is the single character that is to be removed.

The TRIM( ) function removes the leading and/or trailing occurrences of a character from a string. The default character if one is not given is a space. The SQL-92 version is a very general function, but you will find that most SQL implementations have a version that works only with spaces.

A character translation is a function for changing each character of a given string according to some many-to-one or one-to-one mapping between two not necessarily distinct character sets.

The syntax TRANSLATE(<string expression> USING <translation>) assumes that a special schema object, called a translation, has already been created to hold the rules for doing all of this. No product has this feature yet.

CHAR_LENGTH(<string>), also written CHARACTER_LENGTH (<string>), determines the length of a given character string, as an integer, in characters. In most current products, this function is usually expressed as LENGTH( ) and the next two functions do not exist at all; they assume that the database will hold only ASCII or EBCDIC characters.

BIT_LENGTH(<string>) determines the length of a given character string, as an integer, in bits.

OCTET_LENGTH(<string>) determines the length of a given character string, as an integer, in octets. Octets are units of 8 bits that are used by the one and two (Unicode) octet character sets. This is the same as TRUNCATE (BIT_LENGTH (<string>)/8).

The POSITION(<search string> IN <source string>) determines the first position, if any, at which the <search string> occurs within the <source string>. If the <search string> is of length zero, then it occurs at position 1 for any value of the <source string>. If the <search string> does not occur in the <source string>, zero is returned.

5.3 Common Vendor Extensions

The original SQL-89 standard did not define any functions for CHAR(n) datatypes. The SQL-92 standard added the basic functions that have been common to implementations for years. However, there are other common or useful functions, and it is worth knowing how to implement them outside of SQL.

Many vendors also have functions that will format data for display by converting the internal format to a text string. A vendor whose SQL is tied to a 4GL is much more likely to have these extensions simply because the 4GL can use them. The most common one is something to convert a date and time to a national format.

These functions generally use either a Cobol-style picture parameter or a globally set default format. Some of this conversion work is done with the CAST() function in SQL-92, but since SQL does not have any output statements, such things will be vendor extensions for some time to come.

Vendor extensions are varied, but there are some that are worth mentioning. The names will be different in different products, but the functionality will be the same.

REVERSE(<string expression>) reverses the order of the characters in a string to make it easier to search. This function is impossible to write with the standard string operators because it requires either iteration or recursion.

FLIP(<string expression>, <pivot>) will locate the pivot character in the string, then concatenate all the letters to the left of the pivot onto the end of the string and finally erase the pivot character. This is used to change the order of names from "military format" to "civilian format"—for example, FLIP('Smith, John', ',') yields John Smith. However, this function can be written with the standard string functions.

NUMTOWORDS(<numeric expression>) will write out the numeric value as a set of English words to be used on checks or other documents that require both numeric and text versions of the same value.

5.3.1 Phonetic Matching

People's names are a problem for designers of databases. Names are variable in length, can have strange spellings, and are not unique. American names have a diversity of ethnic origins, which give us names pronounced the same way but spelled differently, and vice versa.

In addition to this diversity of names, errors in reading or hearing a name lead to mutations. Anyone who gets junk mail is aware of this; I get mail addressed to "Selco," "Selko," "Celco," as well as "Celko," which are phonetic errors, and also some that result from typing errors, such as "Cellro," "Chelco," and "Chelko." Such errors result in the mailing of multiple copies of the same item to the same address. To solve this problem, we need phonetic algorithms that can find similar sounding names.

Soundex Functions

The Soundex family of algorithms is named after the original algorithm. A Soundex algorithm takes a person's name as input and produces a character string that identifies a set of names that are (roughly) phonetically alike.

A few versions of SQL, such as WATCOM and Oracle, and some other 4GL products have a Soundex algorithm in their library functions. It is also possible to compute a Soundex in SQL using string functions and the CASE expression in the SQL-92 standard, but it is very difficult. Programmers will usually compute the Soundex in a host language outside of the database, then insert it into a column next to the name that it indexes.

The Original Soundex

The original Soundex algorithm was patented by Margaret O'Dell and Robert C. Russell in 1918. The method is based on the phonetic classification of sounds by how they are made.

In case you wanted to know, the six groups are bilabial, labiodental, dental, alveolar, velar, and glottal. The algorithm is fairly straightforward to code and requires no backtracking or multiple passes over the input word. This should not be too surprising since it was in use before computers and had to be done by hand by clerks. Here is the algorithm:

1. Capitalize all letters in the word. Pad the word with rightmost blanks as needed during each procedure step.

2. Retain the first letter of the word.

3. Drop all occurrences of the following letters after the first position: A, E, H, I, O, U, W, Y.

4. Change letters from the following sets into the corresponding digits given:
1 = B, F, P, V
2 = C, G, J, K, Q, S, X, Z
3 = D, T
4 = L
5 = M, N
6 = R

5. Remove all consecutive pairs of duplicate digits from the string that resulted after step 4.

6. Pad the string that resulted from step 5 with trailing zeros and return only the first four positions, which will be of the form `<uppercase letter> <digit> <digit> <digit>`.

An alternative version of the algorithm, due to Russell, changes the letters in step 3 to 9s, retaining them. Then step 5 is replaced by two steps: 5.1, which removes duplicates as before; followed by 5.2, which removes all 9s and closes up the spaces. This allows pairs of duplicate digits to appear in the result string. This version has more granularity and will work better for a larger sample of names.

An Improved Soundex

The improved Soundex algorithm given here is a procedure that will take a name and return a four-letter code. The original Soundex has only (26 * 10 * 10 * 10) = 26,000 code groups; this algorithm has (26 * 26 * 26 * 26) = 456,976 code groups. The higher granularity of the codes tends to separate names that are phonetically close together into smaller groups than the original algorithm. It is not perfect by any means, but does a good job given a large database. Its main advantage is that it considers digrams and trigrams (groups of two and three letters) that can have a different phonetic value in spoken English from their letters when those are taken separately.

I do not know the original source of the algorithm given below, but I tested it against the State of Georgia Motor Vehicles Department database and found it to give good results. My source was the late Gus Baird of Georgia Tech. Here is the algorithm:

1. Capitalize all letters in the word. Pad the word with rightmost blanks as needed during each procedure step.

2. Replace all nonleading vowels with A.

3. Use this table to change prefixes:

Prefix	Transform
MAC	MCC
KN	NN
K	C
PF	FF
SCH	SSS
PH	FF

4. Phonetic changes are made on the part of the word after the first letter, according to these subrules:

   4.1 Transform certain letter combinations:

Text	Transform
DG	GG
CAAN	TAAN
D	T
NST	NSS
AV	AF
Q	G
Z	S
M	N
KN	NN
K	C

   4.2 Replace H with A unless it is preceded and followed by A (that is, AHA).

   4.3 Replace AW with A.

   4.4 Replace PH with FF.

   4.5 Replace SCH with SSS.

5. Perform cleanup functions.

   5.1 Drop all terminal A and S characters. Pad the word with rightmost blanks as needed.

   5.2 Replace terminal NT with TT.

5.3 Strip out all A characters except for the leading A. Pad the word with rightmost blanks as needed.

5.4 Strip all but the first of repeating adjacent character substrings. Pad the word with rightmost blanks as needed.

6. The result is the first four characters of the resulting string.

Metaphone

Metaphone is another improved Soundex that first appeared in *Computer Language* magazine (Philips 1990). A Pascal version written by Terry Smithwick (Smithwick 1991), based on the original C version by Lawrence Philips, is reproduced with permission here:

```
FUNCTION Metaphone (p : STRING) : STRING;
CONST
VowelSet = ['A', 'E', 'I', 'O', 'U'];
FrontVSet = ['E', 'I', 'Y'];
VarSonSet = ['C', 'S', 'T', 'G'];
  { variable sound - modified by following 'h' }
FUNCTION SubStr (A : STRING;
 Start, Len : INTEGER) : STRING;
BEGIN
SubStr := Copy (A, Start, Len) ;
END;
FUNCTION Metaphone (p : STRING) : STRING;
VAR
  i, l, n    : BYTE;
  silent, new  : BOOLEAN;
  last, this, next, nnext : CHAR;
  m, d : STRING;
BEGIN { Metaphone }
IF (p = '')
THEN BEGIN
  Metaphone := '';
  EXIT;
  END;
{ Remove leading spaces }
FOR i := 1 TO Length (p)
DO p[i] := UpCase (p[i]) ;
```

```
{ Assume all alphas }
{ initial preparation of string }
d := SubStr (p, 1, 2) ;
IF d IN ('KN', 'GN', 'PN', 'AE', 'WR')
THEN p := SubStr (p, 2, Length (p) - 1) ;
IF (p[1] = 'X')
THEN p := 'S' + SubStr (p, 2, Length (p) - 1) ;
IF (d = 'WH')
THEN p := 'W' + SubStr (p, 2, Length (p) - 1) ;
{ Set up for Case statement }
l := Length (p) ;
m := '';
     { Initialize the main variable }
new := TRUE;
     { this variable only used next 10 lines!!! }
n := 1;
     { Position counter }
WHILE ((Length (m) < 6) AND (n <> 1) )
DO BEGIN { Set up the 'pointers' for this loop-around }
  IF (n > 1)
  THEN last := p[n-1]
  ELSE last := #0;
  { use a nul terminated string }
  this := p[n];
  IF (n < 1)
  THEN next := p[n+1]
  ELSE next := #0;
  IF ((n+1) < 1)
  THEN nnext := p[n+2]
  ELSE nnext := #0;
  new := (this = 'C') AND (n > 1) AND (last = 'C') ;
  { 'CC' inside word }
  IF (new)
  THEN BEGIN
    IF ((this IN VowelSet) AND (n = 1) )
    THEN m := this;
  CASE this OF
  'B' : IF NOT ((n = 1) AND (last = 'M') )
    THEN m := m + 'B';
  { -mb is silent }
```

```
'C' : BEGIN      { -sce, i, y = silent }
  IF NOT ((last = 'S') AND (next IN FrontVSet) )
  THEN BEGIN
    IF (next = 'i') AND (nnext = 'A')
    THEN m := m + 'X'{ -cia- }
    ELSE IF (next IN FrontVSet)
      THEN m := m + 'S' { -ce, i, y = 'S' }
      ELSE IF (next = 'H') AND (last = 'S')
        THEN m := m + 'K' { -sch- = 'K' }
        ELSE IF (next = 'H')
          THEN IF (n = 1) AND ((n+2) < = 1)
            AND NOT (nnext IN VowelSet)
            THEN m := m + 'K'
            ELSE m := m + 'X';
    END { Else silent }
  END;
 { Case C }
'D' : IF (next = 'G') AND (nnext IN FrontVSet)
    THEN m := m + 'J'
    ELSE m := m + 'T';
'G' : BEGIN
  silent := (next = 'H') AND (nnext IN VowelSet) ;
  IF  (n > 1) AND (((n+1) = 1) OR ((next = 'n') AND
    (nnext = 'E') AND (p[n+3] = 'D') AND ((n+3) = 1) )
{ Terminal -gned }
  AND (last = 'i') AND (next = 'n') )
  THEN silent := TRUE;
 { if not start and near -end or -gned.) }
  IF (n > 1) AND (last = 'D'gnuw) AND (next IN FrontVSet)
  THEN { -dge, i, y }
  silent := TRUE;
  IF NOT silent
  THEN IF (next IN FrontVSet)
    THEN m := m + 'J'
    ELSE m := m + 'K';
  END;
'H' : IF NOT ((n = 1) OR (last IN VarSonSet) ) AND (next IN VowelSet)
    THEN m := m + 'H';
  { else silent (vowel follows) }
'F', 'J', 'L', 'M', 'N', 'R' : m := m + this;
```

```
'K' : IF (last <> 'C')
   THEN m := m + 'K';
'P' : IF (next = 'H')
   THEN BEGIN
      m := m + 'F';
      INC (n) ;

      END  { Skip the 'H' }
   ELSE m := m + 'P';
'Q' : m := m + 'K';
'S' : IF (next = 'H')
   OR ((n > 1) AND (next = 'i') AND (nnext IN ['O', 'A']) )
  THEN m := m + 'X'
  ELSE m := m + 'S';
'T' : IF (n = 1) AND (next = 'H') AND (nnext = 'O')
  THEN m := m + 'T' { Initial Tho- }
  ELSE IF (n > 1) AND (next = 'i') AND (nnext IN ['O', 'A'])
    THEN m := m + 'X'
    ELSE IF (next = 'H')
      THEN m := m + 'O'
      ELSE IF NOT ((next = 'C') AND (nnext = 'H') )
        THEN  m := m + 'T';
 { -tch = silent }
'V' : m := m + 'F';
'W', 'Y' : IF (next IN VowelSet)
   THEN m := m + this;
 { else silent }
'X' : m := m + 'KS';
'Z' : m := m + 'S';
END;
 { Case }
INC (n) ;
END; { While }
END; { Metaphone }
Metaphone := m
END;
```

Other Pattern-Matching Predicates

The most common extension to pattern-matching predicates is a version of
grep(), the general regular expression parser, from the UNIX operating sys-

tem. A version of grep(), <string expression> SIMILAR TO <pattern>, which follows the POSIX model, has been proposed for SQL3. I will say more about grep() in Chapter 12 when I discuss string comparison predicates.

5.4 Cutter Tables

Another encoding scheme for names has been used by libraries for over 100 years. The catalog number of a book often needs to reduce an author's name to a simple fixed-length code. While the results of a Cutter table look much like those of a Soundex, their goal is different. They attempt to preserve the original alphabetical order of the names in the encodings.

But the librarian cannot just attach the author's name to the classification code. Names are not the same length, nor are they unique within their first letters. For example, "Smith, John A." and "Smith, John B." are not unique until the last letter.

Librarians have solved this problem by using Cutter tables to map authors' full names into letter-and-digit codes. There are several versions of the Cutter tables. The older tables tended to use a mix of letters (both upper- and lowercase) followed by digits. The three-figure Cutter-Sanborn table is probably better for computer use, however. It uses a single letter followed by three digits. For example, using that table

"Adams, J" becomes "A214"
"Adams, M" becomes "A215"
"Arnold" becomes "A752"
"Dana" becomes "D168"
"Sherman" becomes "S553"
"Scanlon" becomes "S283"

The distribution of these numbers is based on the actual distribution of names of authors in English-speaking countries. You simply scan down the table until you find the place where your name would fall and use that code.

Cutter tables have two important properties. They preserve the alphabetical ordering of the original name list, which means that you can do a rough sort on them. The second property is that each grouping tends to be of approximately the same size as the set of names gets larger. These properties can be handy for building indexes in a database.

If you would like copies of the Cutter tables, you can get them from Libraries Unlimited, Box 263, Littleton, CO 80160. Unfortunately, Libraries Unlimited does not yet offer the Cutter tables on diskette, so you would have to scan in the text to build your own file.

CHAPTER 6

NULLs—Missing Data in SQL

A DISCUSSION OF HOW to handle missing data enters a sensitive area in relational database circles. Dr. E. F. Codd, creator of the relational model, favors two types of missing-value tokens, one for "unknown" (the eye color of a man wearing sunglasses) and one for "not applicable" (the eye color of an automobile). Chris Date, a leading author on relational databases, advocates not using any general-purpose tokens for missing values at all. To quote David McGoveran and C. J. Date (McGoveran and Date 1992): "It is this writer's opinion that NULLs, at least as currently defined and implemented in SQL, are far more trouble than they are worth and should be avoided; they display very strange and inconsistent behavior and can be a rich source of error and confusion. (Please note that these comments and criticisms apply to any system that supports SQL-style NULLs, not just to SQL Server specifically.)"

SQL takes the middle ground and has a single general-purpose NULL for missing values. Rules for how NULLs are used in particular statements appear in the sections of this book where those statements are discussed; this section will discuss NULLs and missing values in general.

People have trouble with things that are not there. There is no concept of zero in Roman numerals. It was centuries before Hindu-Arabic numerals became popular in Europe. In fact, many early Renaissance accounting firms advertised that they did not use the fancy, newfangled notation and kept records in well-understood Roman numerals instead.

Many of the conceptual problems with zero arose from not knowing the difference between ordinal and cardinal numbers. Ordinal numbers measure position; cardinal numbers measure quantity or magnitude. The argument against the zero was this: If there is no quantity or magnitude there, how can you count or measure it? What does it mean to multiply or divide a number by zero? Likewise, it was a long time before the idea of an empty set found its way into mathematics. The argument was that if there are no elements, how can you have a set of them? Is the empty set a subset of itself? Is the empty set a subset of all other sets? Is there only one universal empty set or one empty set for each type of set?

Computer science now has its own problem with missing data. *The Interim Report 75-02-08 to the ANSI X3* (SPARC Study Group 1975) listed 14 different kinds of incomplete data that could appear as the result of queries or as attribute values. These types included overflows, underflows, errors, and other problems in trying to represent the real world within the limits of a computer.

Instead of discussing the theory for the different models and approaches to missing data, I would rather explain why and how to use NULLs in SQL. In the rest of this book, I will be urging you not to use them, which may seem contradictory, but isn't. Think of a NULL as a drug; use it properly and it works for you, but abuse it and it can ruin everything. Your best policy is to avoid them when you can and use them properly when you have to.

6.1 Empty and Missing Tables

An empty table or view is a different concept from a missing table. An empty table is one that is defined with columns and constraints, but that has zero rows in it. This can happen when a table or view is created for the first time, or when all the rows are deleted from the table. It is a perfectly good table.

A missing table has been removed from the database schema with a DROP TABLE statement, or it never existed at all (you probably typed the name wrong). A missing view is a bit different. It can be absent because of a DROP VIEW statement or a typing error, too. But it can also be absent because a table or view from which it was built has been removed. This means that the view cannot be constructed at runtime and the database reports a failure.

The behavior of an empty table or view will vary with the way it is used. The reader should look at Chapters 14, 15, and 16, which deal with predicates that use a subquery. In general, an empty table can be treated either as a NULL or as an empty set, depending on context.

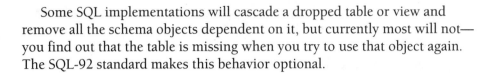

Some SQL implementations will cascade a dropped table or view and remove all the schema objects dependent on it, but currently most will not—you find out that the table is missing when you try to use that object again. The SQL-92 standard makes this behavior optional.

6.2 Missing Values in Columns

The usual description of NULLs is that they represent currently unknown values that may be replaced later with real values when we know something. Actually, the NULL covers a lot of territory, since it is the only way of showing any missing values. Going back to basics for a minute, we can define a row in a database as an entity that has one or more attributes (columns), each of which is drawn from some domain. Let us use the notation $E(A) = V$ to represent the idea that an entity, E, has an attribute, A, which has a value, V. For example, I could write "John(hair) = black" to say that John has black hair.

SQL's general-purpose NULLs do not quite fit this model. If you have defined a domain for hair color and one for car color, then a hair color should not be comparable to a car color because they are drawn from two different domains. You would need to make their domains comparable with an implicit or explicit casting function. This is now being done in SQL-92 and in SQL3, which have a CREATE DOMAIN statement, but most implementations do not have this feature yet. Trying to find out which employees drive cars that match their hair is a bit weird outside of Los Angeles, but in the case of NULLs, do we have a hit when a bald-headed man walks to work? Are no hair and no car somehow equal in color? In SQL-89, we would get an UNKNOWN result, rather than an error, if we compared these two NULLs directly. The domain-specific NULLs are conceptually different from the general NULL because we know what kind of thing is UNKNOWN. This could be shown in our notation as E(A) = NULL to mean that we know the entity, we know the attribute, but we do not know the value.

Another flavor of NULL is Not Applicable (shown as N/A on forms and spreadsheets and called "I-marks" by Codd (Codd 1990), which we have been using on paper forms and in some spreadsheets for years. For example, a bald man's hair-color attribute is a missing-value NULL drawn from the hair-color domain, but his feather-color attribute is a Not Applicable NULL. The attribute itself is missing, not just the value. This missing-attribute NULL could be written as E(NULL) = NULL in the formula notation.

How could an attribute not belonging to an entity show up in a table? Consolidate medical records and put everyone together for statistical purposes. You should not find any male pregnancies in the result table. The programmer has a choice as to how to handle pregnancies. He can have a column in the consolidated table for "number of pregnancies" and put a zero or a NULL in the rows where sex = 'male' and then add some CHECK( ) clauses to make sure that this integrity rule is enforced.

The other way is to have a column for "medical condition" and one for "number of occurrences" beside it. Another CHECK( ) clause would make sure male pregnancies don't appear. But what happens when the sex is unknown and all we have is a name like 'Alex Morgan,' which could belong to either gender? Can we use the presence of one or more pregnancies to determine that Alex is a woman? What if Alex is a woman without children? The case where we have NULL(A) = V is a bit strange. It means that we do not know the entity, but we are looking for a known attribute, A, which has a value of V. This is like asking "What things are colored red?," which is a perfectly good question but is very hard to ask in an SQL database.

If you want to try writing such a query in SQL, you have to get to the system tables to get the table and column names, then join them to the rows in the tables and come back with the PRIMARY KEY of that row.

For completeness, we could play with all eight possible combinations of known and unknown values in the basic $E(A) = V$ formula. But such combinations are of little use or meaning. For example, NULL(NULL) = V would mean that we know a value, but not the entity or the attribute. This is like the running joke from *Hitchhiker's Guide to the Galaxy* (Adams 1979), in which the answer to the question "What is the meaning of life, the universe, and everything?" is 42. Likewise, "total ignorance" NULL, shown as NULL(NULL) = NULL, means that we have no information about the entity, even about its existence, its attributes, or their values.

6.3 Context and Missing Values

Create a domain called Tricolor that is limited to the values 'Red', 'White', and 'Blue' and a column in a table drawn from that domain with a UNIQUE constraint on it. If my table has a 'Red' and two NULL values in that column, I have some information about the two NULLs. I know they are either 'White' and 'Blue' or 'Blue' and 'White'. This is what Chris Date calls a "distinguished NULL," which means we have some information in it.

If my table has a 'Red', a 'White', and a NULL value in that column, can I change the last NULL to 'Blue' because it can only be 'Blue' under the rule? Or do I have to wait until I see an actual value for that row? There is no clear way to handle this in SQL. Multiple values cannot be put in a column, nor can the database automatically change values as part of the column declaration.

This idea can be carried further with marked NULL values. For example, we are given a table of hotel rooms that has columns for check-in date and check-out date. We know the check-in date for each visitor, but we don't know their check-out dates. Instead, we know relationships among the NULLs. We can put them into groups—Mr. and Mrs. X will check out on the same day, members of tour group Y will check out on the same day, and so forth. We can also add conditions on them: Nobody checks out before his check-in date, tour group Y will leave after 7 January 1993, and so forth. Such rules can be put into SQL database schemas, but it is very hard to do. The usual method is to use procedural code in a host language to handle such things.

David McGoveran has proposed that each column that can have missing data should be paired with a column that encodes the reason for the absence of a value (McGoveran 1993, 1994a,b,c). The cost is a bit of extra logic, but the extra column makes it easy to write queries that include or exclude values based on the semantics of the situation.

6.4 Comparing NULLs

The main trouble with NULLs is that it seems unnatural to work with them. The fact that a NULL cannot be compared to another NULL with what Codd called a theta operator and what programmers call a comparison operator (equal, not equal, less than, greater than, and so forth) means that we get three-valued logic instead of two-valued logic. Most programmers don't easily think in three values.

If I execute

```
SELECT * FROM SomeTable WHERE SomeColumn = 2;
```

and then execute

```
SELECT * FROM SomeTable WHERE SomeColumn <> 2;
```

I expect to see all the rows of SomeTable between these two queries. In addition, however, I need to execute

```
SELECT * FROM SomeTable WHERE SomeColumn IS NULL;
```

to do that. The IS [NOT] NULL predicate will return only TRUE or FALSE.

6.5 NULLs and Logic

George Boole developed two-valued logic and attached his name to Boolean algebra forever (Boole 1854). This is not the only possible system, but it is the one that works best with a binary (two-state) computer and with a lot of mathematics. SQL has three-valued logic: TRUE, FALSE, and UNKNOWN. The UNKNOWN value results from using NULLs in comparisons and other predicates, but UNKNOWN is a logical value and not the same as a NULL, which is a data value. That is why you have to say (x IS [NOT] NULL) in SQL and not use (x = NULL) instead. Here are the tables for the three operators that come with SQL:

x	NOT x
TRUE	FALSE
UNK	UNK
FALSE	TRUE

AND	TRUE	UNK	FALSE
TRUE	TRUE	UNK	FALSE
UNK	UNK	UNK	FALSE
FALSE	FALSE	FALSE	FALSE

OR	TRUE	UNK	FALSE
TRUE	TRUE	TRUE	TRUE
UNK	TRUE	UNK	UNK
FALSE	TRUE	UNK	FALSE

All other predicates in SQL resolve themselves to chains of these three operators. But that resolution is not immediately clear in all cases, since it is done at runtime in the case of predicates that use subqueries.

6.5.1 NULLS in Subquery Predicates

People forget that a subquery often hides a comparison with a NULL. Consider these two tables:

```
CREATE TABLE Table1 (col1 INTEGER);
INSERT Table1 (col1) VALUES (1);
INSERT Table1 (col1) VALUES (2);
```

```
CREATE TABLE Table2 (col1 INTEGER);
INSERT Table2 (col1) VALUES (1);
INSERT Table2 (col1) VALUES (2);
INSERT Table2 (col1) VALUES (3);
INSERT Table2 (col1) VALUES (4);
INSERT Table2 (col1) VALUES (5);
```

Notice that the columns are NULL-able. Execute this query:

```
SELECT col1
  FROM Table2 WHERE col1 NOT IN (SELECT col1 FROM Table1);
```

Result

col1
3
4
5

Now insert a NULL and reexecute the same query:

```
INSERT Table1 (col1) VALUES (NULL);
SELECT col1
  FROM Table2
 WHERE col1 NOT IN (SELECT col1 FROM Table1);
```

The result will be empty. This is counterintuitive, but correct. The NOT IN predicate is defined as

```
SELECT col1
  FROM Table2
 WHERE NOT (col1 IN (SELECT col1 FROM Table1));
```

The IN predicate is defined as

```
SELECT col1
  FROM Table2
 WHERE NOT (col1 = ANY (SELECT col1 FROM Table1));
```

which becomes:

```
SELECT col1
  FROM Table2
```

```
WHERE NOT ((col1 = 1)
        OR (col1 = 2)
        OR (col1 = 3)
        OR (col1 = 4)
        OR (col1 = 5)
        OR (col1 = NULL));
```

The last expression is always UNKNOWN, so applying DeMorgan's laws, the query is really

```
SELECT col1
  FROM Table2
 WHERE ((col1 <> 1)
        AND (col1 <> 2)
        AND (col1 <> 3)
        AND (col1 <> 4)
        AND (col1 <> 5)
        AND UNKNOWN);
```

Look at the truth tables and you will see this always reduces to UNKNOWN, and an UNKNOWN is always rejected in a search condition in a WHERE clause.

6.5.2 SQL-92 Solutions

SQL-92 has solved this problem by adding a new predicate of the form

```
<search condition> IS [NOT] TRUE | FALSE | UNKNOWN
```

which will let you map any combination of three-valued logic to two values. For example, ((age < 18) OR (gender = 'Female')) IS NOT FALSE will return TRUE if (age IS NULL) or (gender IS NULL) and the remaining condition does not matter.

6.6 Math and NULLs

NULLs propagate when they appear in arithmetic expressions (+, -, *, /) and return NULL results. See Chapter 3 on numeric datatypes for more details.

6.7 Functions and NULLs

Most vendors propagate NULLs in the functions they offer as extensions of the standard ones required in SQL. For example, the cosine of a NULL will be

NULL. There are two functions, discussed in detail in Section 3.5, that convert NULLs into values.

1. NULLIF (V1, V2) returns a NULL when the first parameter equals the second parameter. The function is equivalent to the following case specification:

    ```
    CASE WHEN (V1 = V2)
        THEN NULL
        ELSE V1 END
    ```

2. COALESCE (V1, V2, V3, . . . , Vn) processes the list from left to right and returns the first parameter that is not NULL. If all the values are NULL, it returns a NULL.

6.8 NULLs and Host Languages

This book will not go into the details of using SQL statements embedded in a particular host language. If you are writing in C, then I would recommend *Optimizing SQL: Embedded SQL in C* (Gulutzan and Pelzer 1994); unfortunately, there are no other trade books aimed at particular host languages, so you will have to depend on vendor manuals for help. However, you should know how NULLs are handled when they have to be passed to a host program. No standard host language for which an embedding is defined supports NULLs, which is another good reason to avoid using them in your database schema.

Roughly speaking, the programmer mixes SQL statements bracketed by EXEC SQL and a language-specific terminator (the semicolon in Pascal and C, END-EXEC in Cobol, and so on) into the host program. This mixed-language program is run through a preprocessor, which converts the SQL into procedure calls that the host language can compile; then the host program is compiled in the usual way.

There is an EXEC SQL BEGIN DECLARE SECTION, EXEC SQL END DECLARE SECTION pair that brackets declarations for the host parameter variables that will get values from the database via CURSORs. This is the "neutral territory" where the host and the database pass information. SQL knows that it is dealing with a host variable because these have a colon prefix added to them when they appear in an SQL statement. A CURSOR is an SQL query statement that executes and creates a structure that looks like a sequential file. The records in the CURSOR are returned, one at a time, to the host program in the BEGIN DECLARE section with the FETCH statement. This avoids the impedance mismatch between record processing in the host language and SQL's set orientation.

NULLs are handled by declaring INDICATOR variables in the host language BEGIN DECLARE section, which are paired with the host variables. An INDI-CATOR is an exact numeric datatype with a scale of zero—that is, some kind of integer in the host language.

The FETCH statement takes one row from the cursor, then converts each SQL datatype into a host-language datatype and puts that result into the appropriate host variable. If the SQL value was a NULL, the INDICATOR is set to −1; if no indicator was specified, an exception condition is raised. As you can see, the host program must be sure to check the INDICATORs because otherwise the value of the parameter will be garbage. If the parameter is passed to the host language without any problems, the INDICATOR is set to zero. If the value being passed to the host program is a non-NULL character string and it has an indicator, the indicator is set to the length of the SQL string and can be used to detect string overflows or to set the length of the parameter.

6.9 Design Advice for NULLs

It is a good idea to declare all your base tables with NOT NULL constraints on all columns whenever possible. NULLs confuse people who do not know SQL, and they are expensive as well. NULLs are usually implemented with an extra bit somewhere in the row where the column appears, rather than in the column itself. They adversely affect storage requirements, indexing, and searching.

NULLs are not permitted in PRIMARY KEY columns. Think about what a PRIMARY KEY that was NULL (or partially NULL) would mean. The SQL model for NULLs has always been based on the idea that the NULLs could be resolved at some future time. A NULL in a key means that the DBMS cannot decide whether the PRIMARY KEY does or does not duplicate a key that is already in the table.

NULLs should be avoided in FOREIGN KEYs. SQL allows this "benefit of the doubt" relationship, but it can cause a loss of information in queries that involve joins. For example, given a part number code in Inventory that is referenced as a FOREIGN KEY by an Orders table, you will have problems getting a listing of the parts that have a NULL.

NULLs should not be allowed in encoding schemes that are known to be complete. For example, employees are people, and people are either male and female. (But even this simple example gets more complicated, as we will see shortly.)

However, you have to use NULLs in date fields when a DEFAULT date does not make sense. For example, if you don't know someone's birthdate, a default date does not make sense; if a warranty has no expiration date, then a NULL can act as an "eternity" symbol.

If you know a default value for quantities, you can use a DEFAULT clause to insert it into the column automatically without changing the structure of the table. Zero is a common default for numeric columns, and blanks for character columns, but you are free to use any legal value you wish.

If you need to show missing values, design your encoding schemes with values for them. For example, the ISO sex codes are 0 = unknown, 1 = male, 2 = female, 9 = not applicable. No, you have not missed a new gender; code 9 is for legal persons, such as corporations. This use of all zeros and all 9s for "Unknown" and "N/A" is quite common in numeric encoding schemes. This convention is a leftover from the old punch-card days, when a missing value was left as a field of blanks (i.e., it had no punches) that could punched into the card later. Likewise, a field of all 9s would sort to the end of the file, and it was easy to hold the 9 key down when the keypunch machine was in numeric shift.

For names, you are probably better off using a special dummy string for unknown values rather than the general NULL. In particular, you can build a list of 'John Doe #1', 'John Doe #2', and so forth to differentiate them; and you cannot do that with a NULL. Quantities have to use a NULL in some cases. There is a difference between an unknown quantity and a zero quantity; it is the difference between an empty gas tank and not having a car at all. Using negative numbers to represent missing quantities does not work because it makes accurate calculations too complex.

Dates and times have to use a NULL in some cases. Unfortunately, you often know relative times, but have no way of expressing them in a database. For example, a pay raise occurs some time after you have been hired, not before. A convict serving on death row should expect a release date resolved by an event: his termination by execution or by natural causes.

When programming languages had no DATE datatypes, this could have been handled with a character string of '9999-99-99 23:59:59.999999' for 'eternity' or 'the end of time'. When 4GL products with a DATE datatype came onto the market, programmers usually inserted the maximum possible date for 'eternity'. But again, this will show up in calculations and in summary statistics. The best trick was to use two fields, one for the date and one for a flag. But this made for fairly complex code in the 4GL.

6.9.1 Avoiding NULLs from the Host Programs

You can avoid putting NULLs into the database from the host programs with some programming discipline.

1. Initialization in the host program: Initialize all the data elements and displays on the input screen of a client program before inserting data into the database. Exactly how you can make sure that all the programs use the same default values is another problem.

2. Automatic defaults: Initialize data elements by storing data to the database, then updating it from the program.

3. Deducing values: Infer the missing data from the given values. For example, a patient who reports a pregnancy is female; if they report prostate cancer, they are male. This technique can also be used to limit choices to valid values for the user.

4. Tracking missing data: Data is tagged as missing, unknown, in error, out of date, or whatever other condition makes it missing. This will involve a companion column with special codes.

5. Determine the impact of missing data on programming and reporting. Reporting format as a list of rows may not be a problem because the keyword NULL will print out in columns. Using statistics in reporting is the problem. McFadden and Hoffer (1994) feel that INTEGER columns with NULLs are the major problem because queries using aggregate functions can provide misleading results.

6. Prevent missing data: Use a batch process to scan and validate data elements before they go into the database.

7. The data types and their NULL-ability constraints have to be consistent across databases (e.g., the chart of account tables should be defined the same in DB2 and Sybase). Data conversion is too confusing and too costly.

6.10 A Note on Multiple NULL Values

In a discussion on CompuServe in July 1996, Carl C. Federl presented an interesting idea for multiple missing value tokens in a database.

If you program in embedded SQL, you are used to having to work with an INDICATOR column. This is used to pass information to the host program, mostly about the NULL or NOT NULL status of the SQL column in the database.

What the host program does with the information is up to the programmer. So why not extend this concept a bit and provide an indicator column? Let's work out a simple example:

```
CREATE TABLE Bob
(keycol INTEGER NOT NULL PRIMARY KEY,
 valcol INTEGER NOT NULL,
 multi_indicator INTEGER NOT NULL
  CHECK (multi_indicator IN (0, -- Known value
                             1, -- Not applicable value
                             2, -- Missing value
                             3  -- Approximate value));
```

Let's set up the rules: When all values are known, we do a regular total. If a value is "not applicable," then the whole total is "not applicable." If we have no "not applicable" values, then "missing value" dominates the total; if we have no "not applicable" and no "missing" values, then we give a warning about approximate values. The general form of the queries will be

```
SELECT SUM (valcol),
       (CASE WHEN NOT EXIST (SELECT multi-indicator
                               FROM Bob
                               WHERE multi-indicator > 0)
             THEN 0
             WHEN EXISTS (SELECT *
                            FROM Bob
                            WHERE multi-indicator = 1)
             THEN 1
             WHEN EXISTS (SELECT *
                            FROM Bob
                            WHERE multi-indicator = 2)
             THEN 2
             WHEN EXISTS (SELECT *
                            FROM Bob
                            WHERE multi-indicator = 3)
             THEN 3
             ELSE NULL END) AS totals_multi-indicator
     FROM Bob;
```

Why would I muck with the valcol total at all? The status is over in the multi-indicator column, just like it was in the original table. Here is an exercise for the reader:

1. Make up a set of rules for multiple missing values and write a query for the SUM( ), AVG( ), MAX( ), MIN( ), and COUNT( ) functions.

2. Set degrees of approximation (plus or minus 5, plus or minus 10, etc.) in the multi-indicator. Assume the valcol is always in the middle. Make the multi-indicator handle the fuzziness of the situation.

```
CREATE TABLE MultiNull
(groupcol INTEGER NOT NULL,
 keycol INTEGER NOT NULL,
 valcol INTEGER NOT NULL CHECK (valcol >= 0),
 valcol_null  INTEGER NOT NULL DEFAULT 0,
  CHECK(valcol_null IN
  (0,    -- Known Value
   1,    -- Not applicable
   2,    -- Missing but applicable
   3,    -- Approximate within 1%
   4,    -- Approximate within 5%
   5,    -- Approximate within 25%
   6     -- Approximate over 25% range)),
 PRIMARY KEY (groupcol, keycol),
   CHECK (valcol = 0 AND valcol_null NOT IN (1,2));
        OR (valcol_null = 0)));

CREATE VIEW Group_MultiNull
(groupcol, sum_valcol, avg_valcol, max_valcol, min_valcol, cnt_rows,
cnt_notnull, cnt_na, cnt_missing, cnt_approximate, cnt_appr_1,
cnt_approx_5, cnt_approx_25, cnt_approx_big)
AS
SELECT groupcol, SUM(valcol), AVG(valcol), MAX(valcol),
       MIN(valcol), COUNT(*),
       SUM (CASE WHEN valcol_null = 0 THEN 1 ELSE 0 END)
         AS cnt_notnull,
       SUM (CASE WHEN valcol_null = 1 THEN 1 ELSE 0 END)
         AS cnt_na,
       SUM (CASE WHEN valcol_null = 2 THEN 1 ELSE 0 END)
         AS cnt_missing,
```

```
        SUM (CASE WHEN valcol_null IN (3,4,5,6) THEN 1 ELSE 0 END)
          AS cnt_approximate,
        SUM (CASE WHEN valcol_null = 3  THEN 1 ELSE 0 END)
          AS cnt_appr_1,
        SUM (CASE WHEN valcol_null = 4  THEN 1 ELSE 0 END)
          AS cnt_approx_5,
        SUM (CASE WHEN valcol_null = 5  THEN 1 ELSE 0 END)
          AS cnt_approx_25,
        SUM (CASE WHEN valcol_null = 6  THEN 1 ELSE 0 END)
          AS cnt_approx_big
   FROM MultiNull
 GROUP BY groupcol;

SELECT groupcol, sum_valcol, avg_valcol, max_valcol, min_valcol,
       (CASE WHEN cnt_rows = cnt_notnull
             THEN 'All are known'
             ELSE 'Not all are known' END) AS WarningMessage,
       cnt_rows, cnt_notnull, cnt_na, cnt_missing, cnt_approximate,
       cnt_appr_1, cnt_approx_5, cnt_approx_25, cnt_approx_big
   FROM Group_MultiNull;
```

CHAPTER 7

Other Expressions

SQL-92 ADDED NEW expressions and extended the rules for old ones to make the language more orthogonal. Basically, anything that looks reasonable is probably legal syntax.

7.1 The CASE Expression

The CASE expression is probably the most useful addition to SQL-92. This is a quick overview of how to use the expression, but you will find other tricks spread throughout the book. In particular, look at Section 9.3, which discusses UPDATE statements.

The CASE expression allows the programmer to pick a value based on a logical expression in his code. ANSI stole the idea and the syntax from the ADA programming language. Here is the BNF for a <case specification>:

```
<case specification> ::= <simple case> | <searched case>

<simple case> ::=
   CASE <case operand>
     <simple when clause>...
     [<else clause>]
   END

<searched case> ::=
   CASE
```

```
    <searched when clause>...
    [<else clause>]
  END

<simple when clause> ::= WHEN <when operand> THEN <result>

<searched when clause> ::= WHEN <search condition> THEN <result>

<else clause> ::= ELSE <result>

<case operand> ::= <value expression>

<when operand> ::= <value expression>

<result> ::= <result expression> | NULL

<result expression> ::= <value expression>
```

The searched CASE expression is probably the most used version of the expression. The WHEN . . . THEN . . . clauses are executed in left-to-right order. The first WHEN clause that tests TRUE returns the value given in its THEN clause. And, yes, you can nest CASE expressions inside each other. If no explicit ELSE clause is given for the CASE expression, then the database will insert a default ELSE NULL clause.

I recommend always giving the ELSE clause, so that you can change it later when you find something explicit to return. I would also recommend that you let a NULL in the CASE expression result in a NULL result, since that is how most SQL functions work.

The <simple case expression> is defined as a searched CASE expression in which all the WHEN clauses are made into equality comparisons against the <case operand>. For example,

```
CASE iso_sex_code
WHEN 0 THEN 'Unknown'
WHEN 1 THEN 'Male'
WHEN 2 THEN 'Female'
WHEN 9 THEN 'N/A'
ELSE NULL END
```

could also be written as

```
CASE
WHEN iso_sex_code = 0 THEN 'Unknown'
WHEN iso_sex_code = 1 THEN 'Male'
```

```
WHEN iso_sex_code = 2 THEN 'Female'
WHEN iso_sex_code = 9 THEN 'N/A'
ELSE NULL END
```

7.1.1 The COALESCE() and NULLIF() Functions

The SQL-92 standard defines other functions in terms of the CASE expression, which makes the language a bit more compact and easier to implement. For example, the COALESCE() function can be defined for one or two expressions by

1. COALESCE (<value exp #1>) is equivalent to (<value exp #1>)

2. COALESCE (<value exp #1>, <value exp #2>) is equivalent to

```
CASE WHEN <value exp #1> IS NOT NULL
    THEN <value exp #1>
    ELSE <value exp #2> END
```

Then we can recursively define it for (n) expressions, where ($n >= 3$), in the list by

```
COALESCE (<value exp #1>, <value exp #2>,  . . . , n),
```

as equivalent to

```
CASE WHEN <value exp #1> IS NOT NULL
    THEN <value exp #1>
    ELSE COALESCE (<value exp #2>, . . ., n)
END
```

Likewise, NULLIF (<value exp #1>, <value exp #2>) is equivalent to

```
CASE WHEN <value exp #1> = <value exp #2>
    THEN NULL
    ELSE <value exp #1> END
```

7.1.2 CASE Expressions with GROUP BY

A CASE expression is very useful with a GROUP BY query. For example, to determine how many employees of each gender by department you have in your personnel table, you can write

```
SELECT dept_nbr,
       SUM(CASE WHEN gender = 'M' THEN 1 ELSE 0) AS males,
       SUM(CASE WHEN gender = 'F' THEN 1 ELSE 0) AS females
  FROM Personnel
 GROUP BY dept_nbr;
```

or

```
SELECT dept_nbr,
       COUNT(CASE WHEN gender = 'M' THEN 1 ELSE NULL) AS males,
       COUNT(CASE WHEN gender = 'F' THEN 1 ELSE NULL) AS females
  FROM Personnel
 GROUP BY dept_nbr;
```

I am not sure if there is any general rule as to which form will run faster.

The previous example shows the CASE expression inside the aggregate function; it is also possible to put aggregate functions inside a CASE expression. For example, assume you are given a table of employees' skills:

```
CREATE TABLE PersonnelSkills
(emp_id CHAR(11) NOT NULL,
 skill_id CHAR(11) NOT NULL,
 primary_skill_ind CHAR(1) NOT NULL
               CONSTRAINT primary_skill_given
               CHECK (primary_skill_ind IN ('Y', 'N'),
 PRIMARY KEY (emp_id, skill_id));
```

Each employee has a row in the table for each of his skills. An employee who has multiple skills will have multiple rows in the table, and the primary skill indicator will be a 'Y' for their main skill. If he only has one skill (which means one row in the table), the value of primary_skill_ind is indeterminate. The problem is to list each employee once along with

    a.   his only skill if he has only one row in the table

or

    b.   his primary skill if he has multiple rows in the table.

```
SELECT emp_id,
       CASE WHEN COUNT(*) = 1
            THEN MAX(skill_id)
            ELSE MAX(CASE WHEN primary_skill_ind = 'Y'
```

```
                       THEN skill_id
                       ELSE NULL END)
          END AS main_skill
  FROM PersonnelSkills
 GROUP BY emp_id;
```

This solution looks at first like a violation of the rule in SQL that prohibits nested aggregate functions, but if you look closely, it is not. The aggregate functions are inside the CASE expression, and the CASE expression is also inside an aggregate function. The reason this works is that every branch of the CASE expression resolves to an aggregate function, MAX(), or a NULL.

7.1.3 CASE, CHECK() Clauses and Logical Implication

Complicated logical predicates can be put into a CASE expression that returns either 1 (TRUE) or 0 (FALSE):

```
CONSTRAINT implication_example
CHECK (CASE WHEN dept_nbr = 'D1'
            THEN CASE WHEN salary < 44000.00
                      THEN 1 ELSE 0 END
            ELSE 1 END = 1)
```

This is a logical implication operator. It is usually written as an arrow with two stems ($\Rightarrow$), and its definition is usually stated as "a true premise cannot imply a false conclusion," or as "If a then b" in English.

In English, this condition says, "If an employee is in department D1, then his salary is less than \$44,000.00," which is not the same as saying, (dept_nbr = 'D1' AND salary < 44000.00) in the constraint.

7.1.4 The Oracle DECODE() Function

Oracle provides the DECODE() function, which is a simple version of the CASE expression:

```
DECODE (<control variable>,
        <value1>, <value2>,
        <value3>, <value4>, ...
        [<last value>])
```

It is equivalent to

```
CASE <control variable>
WHEN <value1> THEN <value2>
WHEN <value3> THEN <value4>
. . .
ELSE <last value> END
```

It is up to the programmer to properly match the pairs of values after the initial <control variable>, and the <last value> is optional.

7.2 Subquery Expressions and Constants

Subquery expressions are SELECT statements inside of parentheses. But there is more to it than that. The four flavors of subquery expressions are tabular, columnar, row, and scalar. As you might guess from the names, the tabular or table subquery returns a table as a result, so it has to appear any place that a table is used in SQL-92, which usually means it is in the FROM clause.

The columnar subquery returns a table with a single column in it. This was the important one in the original SQL-86 and SQL-89 standards because the IN, <comp op> ALL, and <comp op> ANY predicates were based on the ability of the language to convert the column into a list of comparisons connected by ANDs or ORs.

The row subquery returns a single row. It can be used anywhere a row can be used. This sort of query is the basis for the singleton SELECT statement used in embedded SQL. It is not used much right now, but with the extension of theta operators to handle row comparisons, it may become more popular.

The scalar subquery returns a single scalar value. It can be used anywhere a scalar value can be used, which usually means it is in the SELECT or WHERE clauses.

A scalar subquery is better thought of as the SQL version of a subroutine or in-line function. That is, it is a body of code in the native language, available to the program. The use of the scalar subquery will be discussed as needed in the following sections when we get to programming tricks and techniques. I will make the *very* general statement now that the performance of scalar subqueries depends a lot on the architecture of the hardware upon which your SQL is implemented. A massively parallel machine can allocate a processor to each scalar subquery and get drastically improved performance.

A table of any shape can be constructed using the VALUES() expression. This is covered in detail in Section 9.2, which analyzes the INSERT INTO statement, but the idea is that you can build a row as a comma-separated list of scalar expressions, and build a table as a comma-separated list of row constructors.

7.3 Rozenshtein Characteristic Functions

A *characteristic function* converts a logical expression into a one if it is TRUE and into a zero if it is FALSE. This is what we have been doing with some of the CASE expressions shown here, but not under that name. The literature uses a lowercase delta (δ) or a capital chi (X) as the symbol for this operator. The name comes from the fact that it is used to define a set by giving a rule for membership in the set.

David Rozenshtein found ways of implementing characteristic functions with algebraic expression on numeric columns in the Sybase T-SQL language (Rozenshtein 1995) before Sybase added a CASE expression to its product. Without going into the details, I will borrow Rozenshtein's notation and list the major formulas for converting numeric comparisons into a computed characteristic function:

$\delta(a = b)$	becomes	`(1 - ABS(SIGN(a - b)))`
$\delta(a <> b)$	becomes	`(ABS(SIGN(a - b)))`
$\delta(a < b)$	becomes	`(1 - SIGN(1 + SIGN(a - b)))`
$\delta(a <= b)$	becomes	`(SIGN(1 - SIGN(a - b)))`
$\delta(a > b)$	becomes	`(1 - SIGN(1 - SIGN(a - b)))`
$\delta(a >= b)$	becomes	`(SIGN(1 + SIGN(a - b)))`

The basic logical operators can also be put into computed characteristic functions:

NOT $\delta(a)$ becomes $(1 - \delta(a))$
$(\delta(a) \text{ AND } \delta(b))$ becomes $(\delta(a) * \delta(b))$
$(\delta(a) \text{ OR } \delta(b))$ becomes $(\delta(a) + \delta(b))$

If you remember George Boole's original notation for Boolean algebra, this will look very familiar. But be aware that if *a* or *b* is a NULL, then the results will be a NULL and not a one or zero—something that Boole never thought about.

Character strings can be handled with the POSITION function, if you are careful.

$\delta(a = s)$	becomes `POSITION(a IN s)`
$\delta(a <> s)$	becomes `SIGN(1 - POSITION(a IN s))`

Rozenshtein's book gives more tricks, but many of them depend on Sybase's T-SQL functions and are not portable. Another problem is that the code can become very hard to read, and what is happening is not obvious to the next programmer to read the code.

CHAPTER 8

Other Schema Objects

Let's be picky about definitions. A *database* is the data that sits under the control of the database management system (DBMS). The DBMS has the schema, rules, and operators that apply to the database. The *schema* contains the definitions of the objects in the database. But we always just say "the database" as if it had no parts to it.

In the original SQL-89 language, the only data structure the user could access via SQL was the table, which could be permanent (*base tables*) or virtual (*views*). SQL-92 also allows the DBA to define other schema objects, but most of these new features are not yet available in SQL implementations or the available versions of them are proprietary. Let's take a quick look at these new features, but without spending much time on their details.

8.1 Schema Creation

Obviously, every product has a way to create a new database, but none of them have agreed on the syntax. Some products are very concerned with physical storage requirements in the creation process; others are less concerned. The SQL-92 syntax for creating a new schema is minimal and simple:

```
<schema definition> ::=
    CREATE SCHEMA <schema name clause>
```

```
        [<schema character set specification>]
        [<schema element>...]

<schema name clause> ::=
      <schema name>
    | AUTHORIZATION <schema authorization identifier>
    | <schema name> AUTHORIZATION <schema authorization identifier>

<schema authorization identifier> ::= <authorization identifier>

<schema character set specification> ::=
    DEFAULT CHARACTER SET <character set specification>

<schema element> ::=
      <domain definition>
    | <table definition>
    | <view definition>
    | <grant statement>
    | <assertion definition>
```

The schema can be created with an optional password or <schema authorization identifier>, set by the DBA. The DEFAULT CHARACTER SET clause is self-explanatory; it was added to satisfy ISO requirements for international use. I will discuss the other schema elements shortly.

The logical model for schema creation is that the whole schema comes into existence all at once. This is important because it means you can have circular references that would be impossible to add to the schema after creation. For example, you can let table T1 reference table T2 and vice versa. If T1 were created before T2, you would get an error message about a constraint referencing a nonexistent table. If T2 were created before T1, you would get the same problem in the other direction. The time of creation can be important—for example, consider this problem from Robert Stearns of the University of Georgia's computer science department. Suppose you have a table for issuing Internet domains that looks like this:

```
CREATE TABLE Internet
(owner CHAR(10) NOT NULL,
 domain INTEGER NOT NULL,
 subdlow INTEGER NOT NULL,
 subdupr INTEGER NOT NULL,
PRIMARY KEY (owner, domain),
CONSTRAINT super_sub_order CHECK (subdupr > subdlow),
```

```
UNIQUE (owner, domain, subdlow),
UNIQUE (owner, domain, subdupr));
```

If you are not familiar with Internet addresses, each one shows an owner who has unique numbered domains; within each of its domains, each subdomain r has an upper and a lower bound to its range. The problem is to add the constraint that subdomains within a domain do not overlap. For example, you might add these rows:

```
INSERT INTO Internet VALUES ('Jones ', 3, 2, 254);
INSERT INTO Internet VALUES ('Smith ', 4, 2, 51);
INSERT INTO Internet VALUES ('Adams ', 4, 52, 254);
```

but you could not add

```
INSERT INTO Internet VALUES ('Smith ', 3, 2, 51);
```

because within domain 3 it would overlap with the existing 'Jones' row in the table. Once you have some valid rows in place, however, you can then add this constraint to the table:

```
ALTER TABLE Internet
ADD CONSTRAINT non-overlap
CHECK (NOT EXISTS (SELECT *
                   FROM Internet AS I1
                   WHERE I1.owner <> Internet.owner
                     AND I1.domain = Internet.domain
                     AND (Internet.subdlow <= I1.subdupr
                          AND Internet.subdupr >= I1.subdupr)));
```

As an aside, if you have trouble with the final predicate in the constraint's subquery, draw a picture of the two possible nonoverlapping situations. Either the new interval is to the left or the right of an old interval; this would be expressed as (subdlow > I1.subdupr OR subdupr < I1.subdupr). Now, negate that expression to find the overlapping condition and you have the predicate we wanted.

The reason you have to add this constraint after you have some valid rows is that when the table is being initialized, the self-join will not work. The table does not exist yet, so the CHECK() clause cannot find rows with which to do the NOT EXISTS() predicate. Likewise, when you are inserting rows into an empty table, they are not there yet, so the predicate fails. The timing of the creation is very important.

8.1.1 Schema Tables

The usual way an SQL engine keeps the information it needs about the schema is to put it in SQL tables. No two vendors agree on how the schema tables should be named or structured. The SQL-92 standard defines a set of standard schema tables, which no one implements. Though I doubt that anyone will ever implement them, I do feel that vendors will generate schema information in those formats for data exchange.

Every SQL product will allow users to query the schema tables. User groups will have libraries of queries for getting useful information out of the schema tables; you should take the time to get copies of them.

The SQL-92 standard also includes tables for temporal functions, collations, character sets, and so forth, but they are not yet implemented in actual products.

8.2 Temporary Tables

Tables in SQL-92 can be defined as persistent base tables, local temporary tables, or global temporary tables. The syntax is

```
<table definition> ::=
    CREATE [ { GLOBAL | LOCAL } TEMPORARY ] TABLE <table name>
        <table element list>
        [ ON COMMIT { DELETE | PRESERVE } ROWS ]
```

A local temporary table belongs to a single user. A global temporary table is shared by more than one user. When a session using a temporary table COMMITs its work, the table can be either emptied or preserved for the next transaction in the user's session. This is a way of giving the users working storage without giving them CREATE TABLE (and therefore DROP TABLE and ALTER TABLE) privileges. This has been a serious problem in SQL products for some time.

8.3 CREATE ASSERTION

This schema object creates a constraint that is not attached to any table. The syntax is

```
<assertion definition> ::=
    CREATE ASSERTION <constraint name> <assertion check>
      [ <constraint attributes> ]
```

```
<assertion check> ::=
   CHECK <left paren> <search condition> <right paren>
```

As you would expect, there is a DROP ASSERTION statement, but no ALTER statement. An assertion can do things that a CHECK() clause attached to a table cannot do, because it is outside of the tables involved. For example, it is very hard to make a rule that the total number of employees in the company must be equal to the total number of employees in all the health program tables.

8.4 CREATE DOMAIN

The DOMAIN is a new schema element in SQL-92 that allows you to declare an in-line macro that will allow you to put a commonly used column definition in one place in the schema. You should expect to see this feature in SQL products shortly, since it is easy to implement. The syntax is

```
<domain definition> ::=
 CREATE DOMAIN <domain name> [AS] <data type>
      [<default clause>]
      [<domain constraint>...]
      [<collate clause>]

<domain constraint> ::=
   [<constraint name definition>]
   <check constraint definition> [<constraint attributes>]

<alter domain statement> ::=
   ALTER DOMAIN <domain name> <alter domain action>

<alter domain action> ::=
      <set domain default clause>
   | <drop domain default clause>
   | <add domain constraint definition>
   | <drop domain constraint definition>
```

It is important to note that a DOMAIN has to be defined with a basic datatype and not with other DOMAINs. Once declared, a DOMAIN can be used in place of a datatype declaration on a column.

The CHECK() clause is where you can put the code for validating data items with check digits, ranges, lists, and other conditions. Since the DOMAIN is in one place, you can make a good argument for writing

```
CREATE DOMAIN StateCode AS CHAR(2)
       DEFAULT '??'
       CONSTRAINT valid_state_code
       CHECK (VALUE IN ('AL', 'AK', 'AZ', ...  ));
```

instead of

```
CREATE DOMAIN StateCode AS CHAR(2)
       DEFAULT '??'
       CONSTRAINT valid_state_code
       CHECK (VALUE IN (SELECT state FROM StateCodeTable));
```

The second method would be better if you did not have a DOMAIN and had to replicate the CHECK() clause in multiple tables in the database. This would collect the values and their changes in one place instead of many.

8.5 TRIGGERs

There is a feature in many versions of SQL called a TRIGGER, which will execute a block of procedural code against the database when a table event occurs. This is not part of SQL-92, but has been proposed in the SQL3 working document. You can think of a TRIGGER as a generalization of the referential actions.

The procedural code is usually written in a proprietary language, but some products let you attach programs in standard procedural languages. A TRIGGER could be used to automatically handle discontinued merchandise, for example, by creating a credit slip in place of the original order item data.

There is a proposal for standardizing TRIGGERs in the current ANSI/ISO SQL3, using a procedural language based on ADA. The proposal is fairly complicated, and no product has implemented it completely. You should look at what your particular vendor has given you if you want to work with TRIGGERs.

The advantages of TRIGGERs over declarative referential integrity is that you can do everything that declarative referential integrity can and almost anything else, too. The disadvantages are that the optimizer cannot get any data from the procedural code, the TRIGGERs take longer to execute, and they are not portable from product to product.

My advice would be to avoid TRIGGERs when you can use declarative referential integrity instead. If you do use them, check the code very carefully and keep it simple so that you will not hurt performance.

8.6 CREATE PROCEDURE

The PROCEDURE is a proposed schema element in SQL3 that allows you to declare and name a body of procedural code using the same proprietary language as the TRIGGERs or to invoke a host-language library routine. The two major differences are that a PROCEDURE can accept and return parameters and it is invoked by a call from a user session.

Again, many SQL products have had their own versions of PROCEDURE, so you should look at what your particular vendor has given you, check the code very carefully, and keep it simple so that you will not hurt performance.

The SQL/PSM for procedural code is an ISO standards (Melton 1998). Still, even with the move to the ISO standard, existing implementations will retain their own proprietary syntax in many places.

Table Operations

THERE ARE ONLY three things you can do with a row in an SQL table: insert it into a table, delete it from a table, or update the values in it.

9.1 DELETE FROM Statement

The DELETE FROM statement in SQL removes zero or more rows of one table. Most, but not all, interactive SQL tools will tell the user how many rows were affected by an update operation, and the SQL-92 standard requires the database engine to raise a completion condition of "no data" if there were zero rows. There are two forms of DELETE FROM in SQL: *positioned* and *searched*. The positioned deletion is done with cursors; the searched deletion uses a WHERE clause like the search condition in a SELECT statement.

9.1.1 The DELETE FROM Clause

The syntax for a searched deletion statement is

```
<delete statement: searched> ::=
  DELETE FROM <table name>
  [WHERE <search condition>]
```

The DELETE FROM clause simply gives the name of the updatable table or view to be changed. Notice that no correlation name is allowed in the

DELETE FROM clause; this is to avoid some self-referencing problems that could occur. For this discussion, we will assume the user doing the deletion has applicable DELETE privileges for the table. The positioned deletion removes the row in the base table that is the source of the current cursor row. This means that the query from which the cursor is built must be a base table. The SQL-92 syntax is

```
<delete statement: positioned> ::=
  DELETE FROM <table name>
  WHERE CURRENT OF <cursor name>
```

Cursors in SQL-92 are more extensive but different from cursors in SQL-89 and in most current implementations, so this book will not spend too much time discussing them.

9.1.2 The WHERE Clause

The most important thing to remember about the WHERE clause is that it is optional. If there is no WHERE clause, all rows in the table are deleted. Most, but not all, interactive SQL tools give the user a warning when he is about to do this and ask for confirmation. Do an immediate ROLLBACK to restore the table; if you COMMIT or have set the tool to automatically commit the work, then the data is pretty much gone. The DBA will have to do something to save you. (But don't feel bad about doing it at least once while you are learning SQL.) The way most SQL implementations do a deletion is with two passes on the table. The first pass marks all of the candidate rows that meet the WHERE clause condition. The second pass removes them, either immediately or by marking them so that a housekeeping routine can later reclaim the storage space. The important point is that while the rows are being marked, the entire table is still available for the WHERE condition to use. In many, if not most, cases this two-pass method does not make any difference in the results. The WHERE clause is usually a fairly simple predicate that references constants or relationships among the columns of a row. For example, we could clear out some employees with this deletion

```
DELETE FROM Personnel
  WHERE iq <= 100;          -- constant in simple predicate
```

or with this one:

```
DELETE FROM Personnel
  WHERE hat_size = iq;      -- uses columns in the same row
```

A good optimizer could recognize that these predicates do not depend on the table as a whole and would use a single scan for them. The two passes make a difference when the table references itself. Let's fire employees whose IQs are below average for their departments.

```
DELETE FROM Personnel
 WHERE iq < (SELECT AVG(iq)
               FROM Personnel AS P1
               WHERE Personnel.dept = P1.dept);
```

We have the following data:

Personnel

emp	dept	iq
'Able'	'Acct'	101
'Baker'	'Acct'	105
'Charles'	'Acct'	106
'Henry'	'Mkt'	101
'Celko'	'Mkt'	170
'Popkin'	'HR'	120

. . .

If this were done one row at a time, we would first go to Accounting and find the average IQ, $(101 + 105 + 106)/3.0 = 104$, and fire Able. Then we would move sequentially down the table, and again find the average IQ, $(105 + 106)/2.0 = 105.5$ and fire Baker. Only Charles would escape the downsizing.

Now sort the table a little differently, so that the rows are visited in reverse alphabetic order. We first read Charles's IQ and compute the average for Accounting $(101 + 105 + 106)/3.0 = 104$, and retain Charles. Then we would move sequentially down the table with the average IQ unchanged, so we also retain Baker. Able, however, is downsized when that row comes up. It might be worth noting that DB2 would delete rows in the sequential order in which they appear in physical storage. WATCOM SQL has an optional ORDER BY clause that sorts the table, then does a sequential deletion on the table. This feature can be used to force a sequential deletion in cases where order does not matter, thus optimizing the statement by saving a second pass over the table. But it also can give the desired results in situations where you would otherwise have to use a cursor and a host language.

Anders Altberg, Johannes Becher, and I tested different versions of a
DELETE statement whose goal was to remove all but one row of a group (see
the ROWID trick in Section 9.1.4). The three statements tested were

D1:
```
DELETE FROM Test
 WHERE EXISTS (SELECT T1.id
                 FROM Test AS T1
                WHERE T1.id = Test.id
                  AND T1.dup_cnt < dup_cnt)
```

D2:
```
DELETE FROM Test
 WHERE dup_cnt > (SELECT MIN(T1.dup_cnt)
                    FROM Test AS T1
                   WHERE T1.id = Test.id);
```

D3:
```
BEGIN ATOMIC
INSERT INTO WorkingTable(id, min_dup_cnt)
SELECT id, MIN(dupcnt)
  FROM Test
 GROUP BY id;
DELETE FROM Test
 WHERE dupcnt > (SELECT min_dup_cnt
                   FROM WorkingTable
                  WHERE Working.id = Test.id);
END;
```

Their relative execution speeds in one SQL desktop product were

D1	3.20 seconds
D2	31.22 seconds
D3	0.17 seconds

Without seeing the execution plans, I would guess that D1 went to an
index for the EXISTS() test and returned TRUE on the first item it found. On
the other hand, D2 scanned each subset in the partitioning of Test by id to
find the MIN() over and over. Finally, the D3 version simply did a JOIN on
simple scalar columns.

With a full SQL-92 implementation, you could write D3 as

```
D3-2:
 DELETE FROM Test
  WHERE dupcnt >
        (SELECT min_dup_cnt
           FROM (SELECT id, MIN(dupcnt)
                   FROM Test
                 GROUP BY id) AS WorkingTable(id, min_dup_cnt)
          WHERE Working.id = Test.id);
```

9.1.3 Deleting Based on Data in a Second Table

The WHERE clause can be as complex as you wish. This means you can have subqueries that use other tables. For example, to remove customers who have paid their bills from the Deadbeats table, you can use a correlated EXISTS predicate:

```
DELETE FROM Deadbeats
 WHERE EXISTS (SELECT *
                 FROM Payments AS P1
                WHERE Deadbeats.custno = P1.custno
                  AND P1.amtpaid >= Deadbeats.amtdue);
```

The scope rules from SELECT statements also apply to the WHERE clause of a DELETE FROM statement, but it is a good idea to qualify all of the column names.

9.1.4 Deleting within the Same Table

SQL allows a DELETE FROM statement to use columns, constants, and aggregate functions drawn from the table itself. For example, you can remove everyone who is below average in a class with this statement:

```
DELETE FROM Students
 WHERE grade < (SELECT AVG(grade) FROM Students);
```

But the DELETE FROM clause does not allow for correlation names on the table in the DELETE FROM clause, so not all WHERE clauses that could be written as part of a SELECT statement will work in a DELETE FROM statement. For example, a self-join on the working table in a subquery is impossible:

```
DELETE FROM Employees AS B1 -- correlation name is INVALID SQL
  WHERE Employees.bossno = B1.empno
    AND Employees.salary > B1.salary);
```

There are ways to work around this. One trick is to build a VIEW of the
table and use the VIEW instead of a correlation name. Consider the problem
of finding all employees who are now earning more than their boss and
deleting them. The employee table being used has a column for the
employee's identification number, empno, and another column for the boss's
employee identification number, bossno.

```
CREATE VIEW Bosses
AS SELECT empno, salary FROM Employees;

 DELETE FROM Employees
   WHERE EXISTS (SELECT *
                    FROM Bosses AS B1
                  WHERE Employees.bossno = B1.empno
                    AND Employees.salary > B1.salary);
```

Simply using the Employees table in the subquery will not work. We need
an outer reference in the WHERE clause to the Employees table in the subquery, and we cannot get that if the Employees table is in the subquery. Such
views should be as small as possible so that the SQL engine can materialize
them in main storage.

Redundant Duplicates in a Table

Redundant duplicates are unneeded copies of a row in a table. You most
often get them because you did not put a UNIQUE constraint on the table and
then you inserted the same data twice. Removing the extra copies from a
table in SQL is much harder than you would think. If fact, if the rows are
exact duplicates, you cannot do it with a simple DELETE FROM statement.
Removing redundant duplicates involves saving one of them while deleting
the other(s). But if SQL has no way to tell them apart, it will delete all rows
that were qualified by the WHERE clause. Another problem is that the deletion
of a row from a base table can trigger referential actions, which can have
unwanted side effects. For example, if there is a referential integrity constraint that says a deletion in Table1 will cascade and delete matching rows
in Table2, removing redundant duplicates from T1 can leave me with no
matching rows in T2. Yet I still have a referential integrity rule that says there
must be at least one match in T2 for the single row I preserved in T1. SQL-92

allows constraints to be deferrable or nondeferrable, so you might be able to suspend the referential actions that the transaction below would cause:

```
BEGIN
INSERT INTO WorkingTable    -- use DISTINCT to kill duplicates
SELECT DISTINCT * FROM MessedUpTable;

DELETE FROM MessedUpTable;   -- clean out messed-up table
INSERT INTO MessedUpTable    -- put working table into it
SELECT * FROM WorkingTable;

DROP TABLE WorkingTable;     -- get rid of working table
END;
```

Redundant Duplicates Removal with ROWID

Leonard C. Medel came up with several interesting ways to delete redundant duplicate rows from a table in an Oracle database. Let's assume that we have this table:

```
CREATE TABLE Personnel
(id INTEGER NOT NULL,
 name CHAR(30) NOT NULL,
 . . . );
```

The classic Oracle "delete dups" solution is the statement

```
DELETE FROM Personnel
 WHERE ROWID < (SELECT MAX(P1.ROWID)
                  FROM Personnel AS P1
                 WHERE P1.id = Personnel.id
                   AND P1.name = Personnel.name);
                   AND . . . );
```

The column, or more properly pseudocolumn, ROWID is based on the physical location of a row in storage. It can change after a user session but not during the session. It is the fastest possible physical access method into an Oracle table because it goes directly to the physical address of the data.

Doing a quick test on a 100,000-row table, Medel achieved about a 10-fold improvement with these two alternatives. In English, the first alternative is to find the highest ROWID for each group of one or more duplicate rows, and then delete every row, except the one with highest ROWID.

```
DELETE FROM Personnel
 WHERE ROWID IN (SELECT P2.ROWID
                    FROM Personnel AS P2,
                        (SELECT P3.id, P3.name, ...
                                MAX(P3.ROWID) AS max_rowid
                            FROM Personnel AS P3
                            GROUP BY P3.id, P3.name, ...) AS P4
                        WHERE P2.ROWID <> P4.max_rowid
                          AND P2.id = P4.id
                          AND P2.name = P4.name);
```

Notice that the GROUP BY clause needs all the columns in the table.

The second approach is to notice that the set of all rows in the table minus the set of rows we want to keep defines the set of rows to delete. This gives us the following statement:

```
DELETE FROM Personnel
 WHERE ROWID IN (SELECT P2.ROWID
                    FROM Personnel AS P2
                 EXCEPT
                 SELECT MAX(P3.ROWID)
                    FROM Personnel AS P3
                 GROUP BY P3.id, P3.name, ... . );
```

The reason that both of these approaches are faster than the short classic version is that they avoid a correlated subquery expression in the WHERE clause.

9.1.5 Deleting in Multiple Tables without Referential Integrity

There is no way to directly delete rows from more than one table in a single DELETE FROM statement. There are two approaches to removing related rows from multiple tables. One is to use a temporary table of the deletion values; the other is to use referential integrity actions, as defined in SQL-92. For the purposes of this section, let us assume that we have a database with an Orders table and an Inventory table. Our business rule is that when something is out of stock, we delete it from all the orders.

Assume that no referential integrity constraints have been declared at all. First, create a temporary table of the products to be deleted based on your search criteria, then use that table in a correlated subquery to remove rows from each table involved.

```
CREATE MODULE Foobar
CREATE LOCAL TEMPORARY TABLE Discontinue
(partno INTEGER NOT NULL UNIQUE)
ON COMMIT DELETE ROWS;

  . . .

PROCEDURE CleanInventory(. .. )
BEGIN ATOMIC
INSERT INTO Discontinue
SELECT DISTINCT partno -- pick out the items to be removed
  FROM . . .
 WHERE . . . ;           -- using whatever criteria you require
DELETE FROM Orders
 WHERE partno IN (SELECT partno FROM Discontinue);
DELETE FROM Inventory
 WHERE partno IN (SELECT partno FROM Discontinue);
COMMIT WORK;
END;
END MODULE;
```

Not all products have the SQL-92 CREATE LOCAL TEMPORARY TABLE feature yet. The temporary table is persistent in the schema, but its content is not. TEMPORARY tables are always empty at the start of a session, and they always appear to belong to only the user of the session. The GLOBAL option means that each application gets one copy of the table for all the modules, while LOCAL would limit the scope to the module in which it is declared.

9.2 INSERT INTO Statement

The INSERT INTO statement is the only way to get new data into a base table. In practice, there are always other tools for loading large amounts of data into a table, but they are very vendor-dependent.

9.2.1 INSERT INTO Clause

The SQL-92 syntax for INSERT INTO is

```
<insert statement> ::=
  INSERT INTO <table name>
    <insert columns and source>

<insert columns and source> ::=
    [ (<insert column list>) ] <query expression>
```

```
    VALUES <table value constructor list>
    | DEFAULT VALUES

<table value constructor list> ::=
    <row value constructor> [ { <comma> <row value constructor> }
    . . . ]

<row value constructor> ::=
      <row value constructor element>
    | <left paren> <row value constructor list> <right paren>
    | <row subquery>

<row value constructor list> ::=
    <row value constructor element>
        [ { <comma> <row value constructor element> }. . . ]

<row value constructor element> ::=
      <value expression>
    | <null specification>
    | <default specification>

<null specification> ::=  NULL

<default specification> ::= DEFAULT
```

The two basic forms of an INSERT INTO are a table constant (usually a single row) insertion and a query insertion. The table constant insertion is done with a VALUES( ) clause. The list of insert values usually consists of constants or explicit NULLs, but in theory they could be almost any expression in the SQL-92 standard, including scalar SELECT subqueries. Though this is legal SQL, I have not yet found a use for it or a product that supports it.

The SQL-92 DEFAULT VALUES clause is a new shorthand for VALUES (DEFAULT, DEFAULT, . . . , DEFAULT), so it is just shorthand for a particular single row insertion.

The tabular constant insertion is a simple tool, mostly used in interactive sessions to put in small amounts of data. A query insertion executes the query and produces a working table, which is inserted into the target table all at once. In both cases, the optional list of columns in the target table has to be UNION-compatible with the columns in the query or with the values in the VALUES clause. Any column not in the list will be assigned NULL or its explicit DEFAULT value.

9.2.2 The Nature of Inserts

In theory, an insert using a query will place the rows from the query in the target table all at once. The set-oriented nature of an insertion means that a statement like

```
INSERT INTO SomeTable (somekey, transactiontime)
SELECT millions, CURRENT_TIMESTAMP
  FROM HugeTable;
```

will have one value for transactiontime in all the rows of the result, no matter how long it takes to load them into SomeTable. Keeping things straight requires a lot of checking behind the scenes. The insertion can fail if just one row violates a constraint on the target table. The usual physical implementation is to put the rows into the target table, but to mark the work as uncommitted until the whole transaction has been validated. Once the system knows that the insertion is to be committed, it must rebuild all the indexes. Rebuilding indexes will lock out other users and might require sorting the table if the table had a unique or clustered index. If you have had experience with a file system, your first thought might be to drop the indexes, insert the new data, sort the table, and reindex it. The utility programs for index creation can actually benefit from having a known ordering. Unfortunately, this trick does not always work in SQL. The indexes maintain the uniqueness and referential integrity constraints and cannot be easily dropped and restored. Files stand alone; tables are part of a whole database.

9.2.3 Bulk Load and Unload Utilities

All versions of SQL have a language extension or utility program that will let you read data from an external file directly into a table. There is no standard for this tool, so they are all different. Most of these utilities require the name of the file and the format it is written in. The simpler versions of the utility just read the file and put it into a single target table. At the other extreme, Oracle uses a miniature language that can do simple editing as each record is read. If you use a simpler tool, it is a good idea to build a working table in which you stage the data for cleanup before loading it into the actual target table. You can apply edit routines, look for duplicates, and put the bad data into another working table for inspection. The corresponding output utility, which converts a table into a file, usually offers a choice of format options; any computations and selection can be done in SQL. Some of these programs will accept a SELECT statement or a VIEW; some will only convert a base table.

Most tools now have an option to output INSERT INTO statements along with the appropriate CREATE TABLE and CREATE INDEX statements.

9.3 UPDATE Statement

The function of the UPDATE statement in SQL is to change the values in zero or more columns of zero or more rows of one table. SQL implementations will tell you how many rows were affected by an update operation or at a minimum return the SQLSTATE or SQLCODE value for zero rows affected. There are two forms of UPDATE in SQL: *positioned* and *searched.* The positioned UPDATE is done with cursors; the searched UPDATE uses a WHERE that resembles the search condition in a SELECT statement. I do not discuss positioned UPDATEs in this book, for two reasons. First, cursors are used in a host programming language, and we are concerned with pure SQL whenever possible. Second, cursors in SQL-92 are different from cursors in SQL-89 and in current implementations and are not completely available in any implementations at the time of this writing.

9.3.1 The UPDATE Clause

The syntax for a searched UPDATE statement is

```
<update statement> ::=
  UPDATE <table name>
    SET <set clause list>
  [WHERE <search condition>]

<set clause list> ::=
  <set clause> [{ , <set clause> }...]

<set clause> ::= <object column> = <update source>

<update source> ::= <value expression> | NULL | DEFAULT

<object column> ::= <column name>
```

The UPDATE clause simply gives the name of the UPDATEable table or view to be changed. Notice that no correlation name is allowed in the UPDATE clause; this is to avoid some self-referencing problems that could occur. The SET clause is a list of columns to be changed or made; the WHERE clause tells the statement which rows to use. For this discussion, we will assume the user doing the update has applicable UPDATE privileges for each <object column>.

9.3.2 The WHERE Clause

As mentioned, the most important thing to remember about the WHERE clause is that it is optional. If there is no WHERE clause, all rows in the table are changed. This is a common error; if you make it, immediately execute a ROLLBACK command.

9.3.3 The SET Clause

Each assignment in the <set clause list> is executed in parallel, and each SET clause changes all the qualified rows at once. Or at least that is the theoretical model. In practice, implementations will first mark all of the qualified rows in the table in one pass, using the WHERE clause. If there were no problems, such as finding zero rows that met the criteria, then the SQL engine makes a copy of each marked row in working storage. Each SET clause is executed based on the old row image, and the results are put in the new row image. Finally, the new rows replace the old rows. If an error occurs during all of this, then the table is left unchanged and the errors are reported.

This parallelism is not like what you find in a traditional third-generation programming language, so it may be hard to learn. This feature lets you write a statement that will swap the values in two columns:

```
UPDATE MyTable
SET a = b, b = a;
```

This is not the same thing as

```
BEGIN ATOMIC
UPDATE MyTable
SET a = b;
UPDATE MyTable
SET b = a;
END;
```

In the first UPDATE, columns a and b will swap values in each row. In the second pair of UPDATEs, column a will get all of the values of column b in each row. In the second UPDATE of the pair, a, which now has the same value as the original value of b, will be written back into column b—no change at all. There are some limits as to what the value expression can be. The same column cannot appear more than once in a <set clause list>—which makes sense, given the parallel nature of the statement. Since both go into effect at the same time, you would not know which SET clause to use.

9.3.4 Updating with a Second Table

Most updating is done with simple expressions of the form SET <column name> = <constant value> because UPDATEs are done via data entry programs. It is also possible to have the <column name> on both sides of the equal sign! This will not change any values in the table, but can be used as a way to trigger referential actions that have an ON UPDATE condition. However, the <set clause list> does not have to contain only simple expressions. It is possible to use one table to post summary data to another. The scope of the <table name> is the entire <update statement>, so it can be referenced in the WHERE clause. This is easier to explain with an example. Assume we have the following tables:

```
CREATE TABLE Customers
(custno INTEGER NOT NULL,
 acctbalance DECIMAL(8,2) NOT NULL);

CREATE TABLE Payments
(custno INTEGER NOT NULL,
 transno INTEGER NOT NULL,
 amt DECIMAL(8,2) NOT NULL);
```

The problem is to post all of the payment amounts to the balance in the Customers table, overwriting the old balance. Such a posting is usually a batch operation, so a searched UPDATE statement seems the logical approach. SQL-92 and some—but not all—current implementations allow you to use the updated table's names in a subquery:

```
UPDATE Customers
    SET acctbalance = acctbalance
                    - (SELECT SUM(amt)
                         FROM Payments AS P1
                        WHERE Customers.custno = P1.custno)
    WHERE EXISTS (SELECT *
                    FROM Payments AS P2
                   WHERE Customers.custno = P2.custno);
```

When there is no payment, the scalar query will return an empty set. The SUM() of an empty set is always NULL. One of the most common programming errors made when using this trick is to write a query that may return more than one row. If you did not think about it, you might have written the last example as

```
UPDATE Customers
   SET acctbalance = acctbalance
                     - (SELECT amt
                          FROM Payments AS P1
                         WHERE Customers.custno = P1.custno)
   WHERE EXISTS (SELECT *
                   FROM Payments AS P2
                  WHERE Customers.custno = P2.custno);
```

But consider the case where a customer has made more than one payment and we have both of them in the Payments table; the whole transaction will fail. The UPDATE statement should return an error message and ROLLBACK the entire UPDATE statement. In the first example, however, we know that we will get a scalar result because there is only one SUM(amt).

The second common programming error made with this kind of UPDATE is to use an aggregate function that does not return zero when it is applied to an empty table, such as the AVG(). Suppose we wanted to post the average payment amount in Customers; we could not just replace SUM() with AVG() and acctbalance with avgbalance in the above UPDATE. Instead, we would have to add a WHERE clause to the UPDATE that gives us only those customers who made a payment:

```
UPDATE Customers
   SET payment = (SELECT AVG(P1.amt)
                    FROM Payments AS P1
                   WHERE Customers.custno = P1.custno)
   WHERE EXISTS (SELECT *
                   FROM Payments AS P1
                  WHERE Customers.custno = P1.custno);
```

You can use the WHERE clause to avoid NULLs in cases where a NULL would propagate in a calculation.

9.3.5 Using the CASE Expression in UPDATEs

The CASE expression in SQL-92 is very handy for updating a table. The first trick is to realize that you can write "SET a = a" to do nothing to the table. The statement given above can be rewritten as

```
UPDATE Customers
   SET payment
       = CASE WHEN EXISTS (SELECT *
```

```
                    FROM Payments AS P1
                    WHERE Customers.custno = P1.custno)
        THEN (SELECT AVG(P1.amt)
              FROM Payments AS P1
              WHERE Customers.custno = P1.custno)
        ELSE payment;
```

This statement will scan the entire table since there is no WHERE clause. That might be a bad thing in this example—I would guess that only a small number of customers make a payment on any given day. But very often you were going to do a table scan anyway, and this version can be faster.

But the real advantage of the CASE expression is the ability to combine several UPDATE statements into one statement. The execution time will be greatly improved and will save you a lot of procedural code or really ugly SQL. Consider this example. We have an inventory of books and we want to (1) reduce the price of books priced $25.00 and over by 15% and (2) increase the price of the books under $25.00 by 10% to make up the difference. The immediate thought is to write

```
BEGIN ATOMIC -- wrong!
UPDATE Books
   SET price = price * 0.90
 WHERE price >= 25.00;
UPDATE Books
   SET price = price * 1.15
 WHERE price < 25.00;
END;
```

But this does not work. Consider a book priced at $25.00; it goes through the first UPDATE and is repriced at $22.50; it then goes through the second UPDATE and is repriced at $25.88, which is not what we wanted. Flipping the two statements will produce the desired results for this book, but given a book priced at $24.95, we will get $28.69 and then $25.82 as a final price.

```
UPDATE Books
   SET price = CASE WHEN price < 25.00
                    THEN price = price * 1.15
                    ELSE price = price * 0.90 END;
```

This is not only faster, but it is correct. However, you have to be careful and be sure that you did not really want a series of functions applied to the same columns in a particular order. If that is the case, then you need to try to make each assignment expression within the SET clause stand by itself as a complete function instead of one step in a process. Consider this example:

```
BEGIN ATOMIC
UPDATE Foobar
   SET a = x
 WHERE r = 1;
UPDATE Foobar
   SET b = y
 WHERE s = 2;
UPDATE Foobar
   SET c = z
 WHERE t = 3;
UPDATE Foobar
   SET c = z + 1
 WHERE t = 4;
END;
```

This can be replaced by

```
UPDATE Foobar
   SET a = CASE WHEN r = 1 THEN x ELSE a END,
       b = CASE WHEN s = 2 THEN y ELSE b END,
       c = CASE WHEN t = 3 THEN z
                WHEN t = 4 THEN z + 1
                ELSE c END
 WHERE r = 1
    OR s = 2
    OR t IN (3, 4);
```

The WHERE clause is optional, but might improve performance if the index is right and the candidate set is small. Notice that this approach is driven by the destination of the UPDATE—the columns appear only once in the SET clause. The traditional approach is driven by the source of the changes—you first make updates from one data source, then the next, and so forth. Think about how you would do this with a set of magnetic tapes applied against a master file.

9.3.6 Updating within the Same Table

An <update source> can have NULL or DEFAULT as a value, assuming that the <object column> allows them. Most of the time, however, an UPDATE will use a value expression, which will probably be a constant or a bit of simple arithmetic done on the column using the column itself or other columns in the same row. The one rule is that a value expression in a SET clause shall not directly contain a <set function specification>. That means I cannot write something like

```
UPDATE Customers SET age = AVG(age); -- Not valid SQL
```

However, it is sometimes handy to reference a table as a whole to make an update. The tricks for doing this involve creating VIEWs or a working table and can be shown easily with another example.

Rick Vicik had an article in *SQL Forum,* "Advanced Transact SQL" (Vicik 1993), in which he proposed the problem of finding all employees who are now earning as much as or more than their boss and reducing each such employee's salary to 90% of the boss's salary. The employee table being used has a column for the employee's identification number, empno, and another column for the boss's employee identification number, bossno. The reason that you cannot do this directly in most versions of SQL is that the UPDATE statement cannot use a correlation name in the SET clause. Sybase's old Transact SQL and Centura's SQLBase are two exceptions. The query could be done in SQLBase as

```
UPDATE Employees AS Boss     -- Not standard SQL!
   SET Employees.salary = (Boss.salary * 0.90)
 WHERE Employees.bossno = Boss.empno
   AND Employees.salary >= Boss.salary;
```

But another trick will work in standard SQL. First construct a working table or view of the employees who are being adjusted that looks like the original table:

```
CREATE VIEW Adjustment (empno, ..., newsalary)
AS SELECT worker.empno, ..., (boss.salary * 0.90)
    FROM Employees AS worker, Employees AS boss
   WHERE worker.bossno = boss.empno
     AND worker.salary >= boss.salary;
```

This view is also useful for generating a report on just what you did in case the auditor or an irate employee wants to know. Now use an UPDATE with this view to drive it, just as we used a second table to construct a scalar result before:

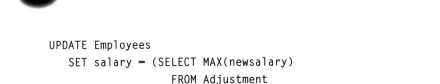

```
UPDATE Employees
   SET salary = (SELECT MAX(newsalary)
                    FROM Adjustment
                    WHERE Adjustment.empno = Employees.empno)
 WHERE empno IN (SELECT empno FROM Adjustment);
```

The expression MAX(newsalary) is a trick used to guarantee that only a single value is returned by the subquery. This will signal the SQL parser that this is always a scalar value, so the right-hand side of the SET clause assignment is correct. Some implementations of SQL do not check for multiple rows in a subquery until runtime, rather than at compile time. Use the MAX() trick to guarantee portability of your code.

If the WHERE clause in the UPDATE statement were not there, the salaries for the unadjusted employees would be set to NULL, the result of the subquery expression when it cannot find a matching empno in both tables.

9.3.7 Updating a Primary Key

Updating a primary key is different from updating a non-key column. You must still preserve the uniqueness of the key after the update. Early versions of DB2 and other SQLs did not implement UPDATE properly in the case of keys and other columns that were declared with a unique constraint. Consider a table defined as

```
CREATE TABLE MyList
(seqno INTEGER PRIMARY KEY,
stuff1 CHAR(1) NOT NULL,
stuffN CHAR(1) NOT NULL);
```

where seqno is a sequential identification number. The problem is to bump all of the existing item numbers by 1, so that we can add a new item number 1 to the table. This could be done with these two statements:

```
BEGIN ATOMIC
UPDATE MyList SET seqno = seqno + 1;
INSERT INTO MyList VALUES (1, 'a1', . . . . , 'aN');
END;
```

The reason this could fail in some early SQL implementations is that these versions of SQL attempted to do a row-at-a-time update inside the engine, as if they were using a cursor on the table, and to check the uniqueness after each row update. If the table is sorted in ascending order, the SQL engine reads the first row (seqno = 1) and changes it to (seqno = 2). However, the second row already has 2 for a key value, so the update fails immediately. This problem was present in DB2 at one time. If the table has been accessed in descending order, then it works just fine. If the table is not ordered, then the failure will occur at some random row and drive you crazy. The best way to handle this is to first convert all of the seqno values to negatives, update them, and then insert the new value:

```
BEGIN ATOMIC -- work around for nonstandard SQL
UPDATE MyList SET seqno = - (seqno + 1);
UPDATE MyList SET seqno = - (seqno);
INSERT INTO MyList VALUES (1, 'al', . . . ,'aN');
END;
```

Another method is to drop the UNIQUE or PRIMARY KEY constraints or indexes, do the update, insert the new row, and then use the ALTER statement to restore the constraints or a CREATE INDEX statement to rebuild unique indexes. However, the time required can be costly since you are going to lock everyone out of the database while you do it.

9.4 A Note on Flaws in a Common Vendor Extension

While I do not like to spend much time discussing nonstandard SQL-like languages, the T-SQL language from Sybase has a horrible flaw in it that users need to be warned about. This language treats an UPDATE or DELETE FROM as just another query. It builds a working table in a FROM clause that is added to the syntax, then uses that working table to go to the target base table mentioned in the DELETE or UPDATE clause.

If a base table row is represented more than once in the hidden query, then that row is operated on multiple times, in a total violation of relational principles. Here is a quick example:

```
CREATE TABLE T1 (x INTEGER NOT NULL);
INSERT INTO T1 VALUES (1), (2), (3), (4);

CREATE TABLE T2 (x INTEGER NOT NULL);
INSERT INTO T2 VALUES (1), (1), (1), (1);
```

Now try to update T1 by doubling all the rows that have a match in T2.

```
UPDATE T1
   SET T1.x = 2 * T1.x
```

```
FROM T2
WHERE T1.x = T2.x;
```

T1

x
16
2
3
4

The FROM clause gives you a CROSS JOIN, so you get a series of actions on the same row ($1 \Rightarrow 2 \Rightarrow 4 \Rightarrow 8 \Rightarrow 16$). Go one step further and include another table with no relation to anything:

```
CREATE TABLE T3 (x CHAR(1) NOT NULL);
INSERT INTO T3 VALUES ('a'), ('a'), ('a'), ('a');

UPDATE  T1
   SET T1.x = 2* T1.x
  FROM T2, T3
 WHERE T1.x = T2.x;
```

T1

x
65536
2
3
4

These are very simple examples, as you can see, but you get the idea. In the case of the DELETE FROM statement, removing the same row over and over does not change the results, but updating the same row over and over is a disaster. Some aspects of this problem have been fixed in the current version of Sybase, but the syntax is still not standard or portable.

CHAPTER 10

Comparison or Theta Operators

DR. E. F. CODD introduced the term *theta operators* in his early papers for what a programmer would have called a *comparison predicate operator*. The large number of datatypes in SQL makes doing comparisons a little harder than in other programming languages. Values of one datatype have to be promoted to values of the other datatype before the comparison can be done. The available datatypes are implementation- and hardware-dependent, so read the manuals for your product.

The comparison operators are overloaded and will work for <numeric>, <character>, and <datetime> datatypes. The symbols and meanings for comparison operators are shown in the table below.

operator	<numeric>	<character>	<datetime>
< :	less than	(collates before)	(earlier than)
= :	equal	(collates equal to)	(same time as)
> :	greater than	(collates after)	(later than)
<= :	at most	(collates before or equal to)	(occurs at or earlier than)
<> :	not equal	(not the same as)	(not the same time as)
>= :	at least	(collates after or equal to)	(occurs at or after)

You will also see != or ~= for "not equal to" in some older SQL implementations. These symbols are borrowed from the C and PL/I programming languages, respectively, and have never been part of standard SQL. It is a bad habit to use them since doing so destroys the portability of your code and makes it harder to read.

10.1 Converting Datatypes

NUMERIC datatypes are all mutually comparable and mutually assignable. If an assignment would result in a loss of the most significant digits, an exception condition is raised. If least significant digits are lost, the implementation defines what rounding or truncating occurs and does not report an exception condition. Most often, one value is converted to the same datatype as the other, and the comparison is then done in the usual way. The chosen datatype is the "higher" of the two, using the following ordering: SMALLINT, INTEGER, DECIMAL, NUMERIC, REAL, FLOAT, DOUBLEPRECISION.

Floating-point hardware will often affect comparisons for REAL, FLOAT, and DOUBLEPRECISION numbers. There is no good way to avoid this since it is not always reasonable to use DECIMAL or NUMERIC in their place. A host language will probably use the same floating-point hardware, so at least errors will be constant across the application.

CHARACTER and CHARACTER VARYING datatypes are comparable if and only if they are taken from the same character repertoire. That means that ASCII characters cannot be compared to graphics characters, English cannot be compared to Arabic, and so on. In most implementations this is not a problem because the database has only one repertoire.

The comparison takes the shorter of the two strings and pads it with spaces. The strings are compared position by position from left to right, using the collating sequence for the repertoire—ASCII or EBCDIC in most cases.

Temporal (or datetime, as they are called in the standard) datatypes are mutually assignable only if the source and target of the assignment have the same datetime fields. That is, you cannot compare a date and a time. The CAST() operator can do explicit type conversions before you do a comparison. Here is a table of the valid combinations of source and target datatypes in SQL-92. Y means that the combination is syntactically valid without restriction; M indicates that the combination is valid subject to other syntax rules; and N indicates that the combination is not valid. The codes mean yes, maybe, and no in English.

<value expr>	<cast target>										
	EN	AN	VC	FC	VB	FB	D	T	TS	YM	DT
EN	Y	Y	Y	Y	N	N	N	N	N	M	M
AN	Y	Y	Y	Y	N	N	N	N	N	N	N
C	Y	Y	M	M	Y	Y	Y	Y	Y	Y	Y
B	N	N	Y	Y	Y	Y	N	N	N	N	N
D	N	N	Y	Y	N	N	Y	N	Y	N	N
T	N	N	Y	Y	N	N	N	Y	Y	N	N
TS	N	N	Y	Y	N	N	Y	Y	Y	N	N
YM	M	N	Y	Y	N	N	N	N	N	Y	N
DT	M	N	Y	Y	N	N	N	N	N	N	Y

where

EN = exact numeric
AN = approximate numeric
C = character (fixed- or variable-length)
FC = fixed-length character
VC = variable-length character
B = bit string (fixed- or variable-length)
FB = fixed-length bit string
VB = variable-length bit string
D = date
T = time
TS = timestamp
YM = year-month interval
DT = day-time interval

10.2 Row Comparisons in SQL-92

SQL-92 generalized the theta operators so they would work on row expressions and not just on scalars. This is not a popular feature yet, but it is very handy for situations where a key is made from more than one column, and so forth. This makes SQL more orthogonal, and it has an intuitive feel to it. Take three row constants:

```
A = (10, 20, 30, 40);

B = (10, NULL, 30, 40);

C = (10, NULL, 30, 100);
```

It seems reasonable to define a tuple comparison as valid only when the datatypes of each corresponding column in the rows are UNION-compatible. If not, the operation is an error and should report a warning. It also seems reasonable to define the results of the comparison to the AND-ed results of each corresponding column using the same operator. That is, (A = B) becomes

```
((10, 20, 30, 40) = (10, NULL, 30, 40));
```

becomes

```
((10 = 10) AND (20 = NULL) AND (30 = 30) AND (40 = 40));
```

becomes

```
(TRUE AND UNKNOWN AND TRUE AND TRUE);
```

becomes

```
(UNKNOWN);
```

This seems to be reasonable and conforms to the idea that a NULL is a missing value that we expect to resolve at a future date, so we cannot draw a conclusion about this comparison just yet. Now consider the comparison (A = C), which becomes

```
((10, 20, 30, 40) = (10, NULL, 30, 100));
```

becomes

```
((10 = 10) AND (20 = NULL) AND (30 = 30) AND (40 = 100));
```

becomes

```
(TRUE AND UNKNOWN AND TRUE AND FALSE);
```

becomes

```
(FALSE);
```

There is no way to pick a value for column 2 of row C such that the UNKNOWN result will change to TRUE because the fourth column is always FALSE. This leaves you with a situation that is not very intuitive. The first case can resolve to TRUE or FALSE, but the second case can only go to FALSE.

The SQL-92 standard decided that the theta operators would work as shown in the table below. The expression RX <comp op> RY is shorthand for a row RX compared to a row RY; likewise, RXi means the *i*th column in the row RX. The results are still TRUE, FALSE, or UNKNOWN, if there is no error in type matching. The rules favor solid tests for TRUE or FALSE, using UNKNOWN as a last resort.

The idea of these rules is that as you read the rows from left to right, the values in one row are always greater than (or less than) those in the other row after some column. This is how it would work if you were alphabetizing words.

The rules are

1. RX = RY is TRUE if and only if RXi = RYi for all *i*.

2. RX <> RY is TRUE if and only if RXi <> RYi for some *i*.

3. RX < RY is TRUE if and only if RXi = RYi for all *i* < *n* and RXn < RYn for some *n*.

4. RX > RY is TRUE if and only if RXi = RYi for all *i* < *n* and RXn > RYn for some *n*.

5. RX <= RY is TRUE if and only if Rx = Ry or Rx < Ry.

6. RX >= RY is TRUE if and only if Rx = Ry or Rx > Ry.

7. RX = RY is FALSE if and only if RX <> RY is TRUE.

8. RX <> RY is FALSE if and only if RX = RY is TRUE.

9. RX < RY is FALSE if and only if RX >= RY is TRUE.

10. RX > RY is FALSE if and only if RX <= RY is TRUE.

11. RX <= RY is FALSE if and only if RX > RY is TRUE.

12. RX >= RY is FALSE if and only if RX < RY is TRUE.

13. RX <comp op> RY is UNKNOWN if and only if RX <comp op> RY is neither TRUE nor FALSE.

The negations are defined so that the NOT operator will still have its usual properties. Notice that a NULL in a row will give an UNKNOWN result in a comparison. These row comparisons can be done in SQL-89, but translating the predicates is messy.

Consider this SQL-92 expression:

```
(a, b, c) < (x, y, z)
```

which becomes

```
((a < x)
  OR ((a = x) AND (b < y))
  OR ((a = x) AND (b = y) AND (c < z)))
```

The SQL-89 standard allowed only scalar subqueries on the right-hand side and a single-value expression on the left-hand side of the <comp op> ALL <subquery> and <comp op> SOME <subquery> predicates. SQL-92 is more orthogonal; it allows a single-row expression of any sort, including a single-row subquery, on the left-hand side. Likewise, the BETWEEN predicate can use row expressions in any position in SQL-92.

CHAPTER 11

Valued Predicates

V*ALUED PREDICATES* IS my term for a set of related unary Boolean predicates that test for the logical value or NULL value of their operand. The IS NULL has always been part of SQL, but the logical IS predicate is new to SQL-92 and is not well implemented at this time.

11.1 IS NULL Predicate

The IS NULL predicate is a test for a NULL value in a column with the syntax

```
<null predicate> ::= <row value constructor> IS [NOT] NULL
```

It is the only way to test to see if an expression is NULL or not, and it has been in SQL-86 and all later versions of the standard. The SQL-92 standard extended it to accept <row value constructor> instead of a single column or scalar expression. This extended version will start showing up in implementations when other row expressions are allowed. If all the values in the row R are the NULL value, then R IS NULL is TRUE; otherwise, it is FALSE. If none of the values in R are NULL value, R IS NOT NULL is TRUE; otherwise, it is FALSE. The case where the row is a mix of NULL and non-NULL values is defined by the table below, where *Degree* means the number of columns in the row expression.

Expression	R IS NULL	R IS NOT NULL	NOT R IS NULL	NOT R IS NOT NULL
Degree = 1				
NULL	TRUE	FALSE	FALSE	TRUE
No NULL	FALSE	TRUE	TRUE	FALSE
Degree > 1				
All NULLs	TRUE	FALSE	FALSE	TRUE
Some NULLs	FALSE	FALSE	TRUE	TRUE
No NULLs	FALSE	TRUE	TRUE	FALSE

Note that R IS NOT NULL has the same result as NOT R IS NULL if and only if R is of degree 1. This is a break in the usual pattern of predicates with a NOT option in them. Here are some examples:

```
NOT (NULL, NULL, NULL) IS NULL = FALSE
NOT (NULL, NULL, NULL) IS NOT NULL = TRUE
(1, NULL, 3) IS NOT NULL = FALSE
(NULL, NULL, NULL) IS NULL = TRUE
(NULL, NULL, NULL) IS NOT NULL = FALSE
NOT (1, 2, 3) IS NULL = TRUE
NOT (1, NULL, 3) IS NULL = TRUE
NOT (1, NULL, 3) IS NOT NULL = TRUE
NOT (NULL, NULL, NULL) IS NULL = FALSE
NOT (NULL, NULL, NULL) IS NOT NULL = TRUE
```

11.1.1 Sources of NULLs

It is important to remember where NULLs can occur. They are not just a possible value in a column. Aggregate functions on empty sets, OUTER JOINs, arithmetic expressions with NULLs, and so forth all return NULLs. These constructs often show up as columns in VIEWs.

11.2 IS [NOT]{ TRUE | FALSE | UNKNOWN } Predicate

This predicate tests a condition that has the truth value TRUE, FALSE, or UNKNOWN, and returns TRUE or FALSE. The syntax is

```
<Boolean test> ::=
    <Boolean primary> [ IS [ NOT ] <truth value> ]

<truth value> ::= TRUE | FALSE | UNKNOWN
```

```
<Boolean primary> ::=
    <predicate> | <left paren> <search condition> <right paren>
```

As you would expect, the expression IS NOT <logical value> is the same as NOT (IS <logical value>), so the predicate can be defined by the table below:

IS condition	TRUE	FALSE	UNKNOWN
TRUE	TRUE	FALSE	FALSE
FALSE	FALSE	TRUE	FALSE
UNKNOWN	FALSE	FALSE	TRUE

If you are familiar with some of Chris Date's writings, you may remember that his MAYBE(x) predicate is not the same as the ANSI (x) IS NOT FALSE predicate, but is instead equivalent to the (x) IS UNKNOWN predicate. Date's predicate excludes the case where all conditions in the predicate are TRUE.

Date points out that it is difficult to ask a conditional question in English. To borrow one of Date's examples (Date 1990), consider the problem of finding employees who *might be* programmers born before 1941 January 18 and who have a salary less than $50,000. The statement of the problem is a bit unclear as to what the "might be" covers—just being a programmer, or all three conditions. Let's assume that we want some doubt on any of the three conditions. With this predicate, the answer is fairly easy to write:

```
SELECT *
  FROM Employees
 WHERE (job = 'Programmer'
        AND dob < CAST ('1941-01-18' TO DATE)
        AND salary < 50000) IS UNKNOWN;
```

It could be expanded out in SQL-89 to

```
SELECT *
  FROM Employees
 WHERE (job = 'Programmer'
   AND dob < CAST ('1941-01-18' TO DATE)
   AND salary < 50000)
     OR (job IS NULL
         AND dob < CAST ('1941-01-18' TO DATE)
         AND salary < 50000)
     OR (job = 'Programmer'
```

```
      AND dob IS NULL
      AND salary < 50000)
  OR (job = 'Programmer'
      AND dob < CAST ('1941-01-18' TO DATE)
      AND salary IS NULL)
  OR (job IS NULL
      AND dob IS NULL
      AND salary < 50000)
  OR (job IS NULL
      AND dob < CAST ('1941-01-18' TO DATE)
      AND salary IS NULL)
  OR (job = 'Programmer'
      AND dob IS NULL
      AND salary IS NULL)
  OR (job IS NULL
      AND dob IS NULL
      AND salary IS NULL);
```

The problem is that every possible combination of NULLs and non-NULLs has to be tested. Since there are three predicates involved, this gives us $(2^3) = 8$ combinations to check out. The IS NOT UNKNOWN predicate does not have to bother with the combinations, only the final logical value.

LIKE and SIMILAR Predicates

THE LIKE PREDICATE is a string pattern–matching test with the syntax

```
<like predicate> ::=
    <match value> [NOT] LIKE <pattern>
        [ESCAPE <escape character>]

<match value> ::= <character value expression>
<pattern> ::= <character value expression>
<escape character> ::= <character value expression>
```

The expression M NOT LIKE P is equivalent to NOT (M LIKE P), which follows the usual syntax pattern in SQL. There are two wildcards allowed in the <pattern> string. They are the '%' and '_' characters. The '_' character represents a single arbitrary character; the '%' character represents an arbitrary substring, possibly of length zero. Notice that there is no way to represent zero or one arbitrary character. This is not the case in many text-search languages and can lead to problems or very complex predicates.

Any other character in the <pattern> represents that character itself. This means that SQL patterns are case-sensitive, but many vendors allow you to set case sensitivity on or off at the database system level.

The <escape character> is part of the SQL-92 standard but is not yet widely implemented. The <escape character> is used in the <pattern> to specify that the character that follows it is to be interpreted as a literal rather than a wildcard. This means that the escape character is followed by the escape character itself, an '_', or a '%'. C programmers are used to this convention, where the language defines the escape character as '\', so this is also a good choice for SQL programmers.

12.1 Tricks with Patterns

The '_' character tests much faster than the '%' character. The reason is obvious: the parser that compares a string to the pattern needs only one operation to match an underscore before it can move to the next character, but has to do some look-ahead parsing to resolve a percentage sign. The wildcards can be inserted in the middle or beginning of a pattern. Thus, 'B%K' will match 'BOOK', 'BLOCK', and 'BK', but it will not match 'BLOCKS'.

The parser would scan each letter and classify it as a wildcard or an exact match. In the case of 'BLOCKS', the initial 'B' would be an exact match and the parser would continue; 'L', 'O', and 'C' have to be wildcard matches since they don't appear in the pattern string; 'K' cannot be classified until we read the last letter. The last letter is 'S', so the match fails.

For example, given a column declared to be seven characters long, and a LIKE predicate looking for names that start with "Mac," you would usually write

```
SELECT *
  FROM People
 WHERE (name LIKE 'Mac%');
```

but this might actually run faster:

```
SELECT *
  FROM People
 WHERE (name LIKE 'Mac_   ')
    OR (name LIKE 'Mac__  ')
    OR (name LIKE 'Mac___ ')
    OR (name LIKE 'Mac____');
```

The trailing blanks are also characters that can be matched exactly.

Putting a '%' at the front of a pattern is very time-consuming. For example, you might try to find all names that end in "son" with the query

```
SELECT *
  FROM People
 WHERE (name LIKE '%son');
```

The use of underscores instead will make a real difference in most SQL implementations for this query because most of them always parse from left to right.

```
SELECT *
  FROM People
 WHERE (name LIKE '_son  ')
    OR (name LIKE '__son ')
    OR (name LIKE '___son ')
    OR (name LIKE '____son');
```

Remember that the '_' character requires a matching character and the '%' character does not. Thus, the query

```
SELECT *
  FROM People
 WHERE (name LIKE 'John_%');
```

and the query

```
SELECT *
  FROM People
 WHERE (name LIKE 'John%');
```

are subtly different. Both will match to 'Johnson' and 'Johns', but the first will not accept 'John' as a match. This is how you get a "one-or-more-characters" pattern match in SQL.

Remember that the <pattern> as well as the <match value> can be constructed with concatenation operators, SUBSTRING( ), and other string functions. For example, let's find people whose first names are part of their last names with the query

```
SELECT *
  FROM People
 WHERE (lastname LIKE '%' || firstname || '%');
```

which will show us people like 'John Johnson', 'Anders Andersen', and 'Bob McBoblin'. This query will also run very slowly. However, this is case-sensitive and would not work for names such as 'Jon Anjon', so you might want to modify the statement to:

```
SELECT *
  FROM People
 WHERE (UPPER (lastname) LIKE '%' || UPPER(firstname) || '%');
```

12.2 Results with NULL Values and Empty Strings

As you would expect, a NULL in the predicate returns an UNKNOWN result. The NULL can be the escape character, pattern, or match value.

If M and P are both character strings of length zero, M LIKE P defaults to TRUE. If one or both are longer than zero characters, you use the regular rules to test the predicate.

12.3 LIKE Is Not Equality

A very important point that is often missed is that two strings can be equal but not LIKE in SQL. The test of equality first pads the shorter of the two strings with rightmost blanks, then matches the characters in each, one for one. Thus 'Smith' and 'Smith   ' (with three trailing blanks) are equal. However, the LIKE predicate does no padding, so 'Smith' LIKE 'Smith   ' tests FALSE because there is nothing to match to the blanks.

A good trick to get around these problems is to use the TRIM() function to remove unwanted blanks from the strings within either or both of the two arguments.

12.4 Avoiding the LIKE Predicate with a JOIN

Mark Saltzman, assistant director–info systems at the University of Wisconsin Extension, has another trick for doing a string search under certain conditions. For example, let's assume that we have a database of automobile license plates and we have a single character mismatch. To find all auto tags that might have been mistaken for the tag 'ABC-123', you use the LIKE query:

```
SELECT *
  FROM AutoTags
 WHERE plate = 'ABC-123'
    OR plate LIKE  '_BC-123'
    OR plate LIKE  'A_C-123'
    OR plate LIKE  'AB_-123'
    OR plate LIKE  'ABC-_23'
    OR plate LIKE  'ABC-1_3'
    OR plate LIKE  'ABC-12_';
```

Saltzman builds a table with pairs of actual and lookup values of strings. This puts the effort into creating a cross-reference table (Xref) that contains the actual and cross-referencing values. The table might look like this in part:

```
CREATE TABLE Xref
(actual CHAR(7) NOT NULL,
 lookup CHAR(7) NOT NULL);
```

Xref

actual	lookup
'ABC-123'	'_BC-123'
'ABC-123'	'A_C-123'
'ABC-123'	'AB_-123'
'ABC-123'	'ABC-_23'
'ABC-123'	'ABC-1_3'
'ABC-123'	'ABC-12_'
'ABC-124'	'_BC-124'
'ABC-124'	'A_C-124'
'ABC-124'	'AB_-124'
'ABC-124'	'ABC-_24'
'ABC-124'	'ABC-1_4'
'ABC-124'	'ABC-12_'
. . .	. . .

To find all auto tags that might have been mistaken for the tag `'ABC-123'`, you use the query

```
SELECT DISTINCT X1.actual
  FROM Xref AS X1, Xref AS X2
 WHERE X1.lookup = X2.lookup
   AND X1.actual <> X2.actual
   AND X2.actual = 'ABC-123';
```

The SELECT is actually quite efficient and can use any indexes you create on the columns, as opposed to using wildcard searches in a LIKE predicate. In a real situation, you would actually return thousands of possible matches from the database that differed by one character. You are trading speed for storage space, and you are saving yourself a table scan.

12.5 Other Pattern-Matching Predicates

Many SQL products have a version of grep(), a utility program from the UNIX operating system. The name is short for "general regular expression parser," and before you ask, a regular expression is a class of formal languages. If you are a computer science major, you have seen them; otherwise, don't worry about it. The bad news is that there are several verisons of grep() in the UNIX community, such as egrep(), fgrep(), xgrep(), and a dozen or so others.

There is a proposal in the SQL-99 standard for a predicate of the form "<string expression> SIMILAR TO <pattern>", which is based on the POSIX version of grep().

You should still read your product manual to get the details, but most grep() functions accept patterns based on regular expressions. A regular expression is a string with the following special pattern symbols:

Single character symbols:

    .   any character (same as the SQL underscore)
    ^   start of line (not used in an SQL string)
    $ end of line (not used in an SQL string)
    \\   next character is a literal

Repetition symbols:

    +   match one or more occurrences of the preceding character
    *   match zero or more occurrences of the preceding character

Sets of characters:

    []   match one of the characters inside the brackets
    [^]   match anything but the characters inside the brackets, after the caret
    -    match all the characters (in ASCII sort order) from the character on the left to the character on the right.

Examples:

    'x+' match a string of xs of any length
    '[aeiou0-9]' match one character to a, e, i, o, u, or 0 through 9
    '[^aeiou0-9]' match anything but a, e, i, o, u, and 0 through 9
    '\$ *[0-9]+\.[0-9] [0-9]' match a string for a dollar amount

CHAPTER 13

BETWEEN and OVERLAPS
Predicates

THE BETWEEN AND OVERLAPS predicates both offer a shorthand way of showing that one value lies within a range defined by two other values. BETWEEN works with scalar range limits; the OVERLAPS predicate looks at two time periods (defined either by start and end points or by a starting time and an INTERVAL) to see if they overlap in time.

13.1 BETWEEN Predicate

The predicate <value expression> [NOT] BETWEEN <low value expression> AND <high value expression> is a feature of SQL that is used enough to deserve special attention. It is also just tricky enough to fool beginning programmers. This predicate is actually just shorthand for the expression

```
((<low value expression> <= <value expression>)
    AND (<value expression> <= <high value expression>))
```

Please note that the end points are included in this definition. This predicate works with any datatypes that can be compared. Most programmers miss this fact and use it only for numeric values. It can be used for character strings and datetime data as well. The <high value expression> and <low value expression> can be expressions or constants, but again, programmers tend to use just constants.

13.1.1 Results with NULL Values

The results of this predicate with NULL values for <value expression>, <low value expression>, or <high value expression> follow directly from the definition. If both <low value expression> and <high value expression> are NULL, the result is UNKNOWN for any value of <value expression>. If <low value expression> or <high value expression> is NULL, but not both of them, the result is determined by the value of <value expression> and its comparison with the remaining non-NULL term. If <value expression> is NULL, the results are UNKNOWN for any values of <low value expression> and <high value expression>.

13.1.2 Results with Empty Sets

Notice that if <high value expression> is less than <low value expression>, the expression will always be FALSE unless the value is NULL; then it is UNKNOWN. That is a bit confusing since there is no value to which <value expression> could resolve itself that would produce a TRUE result. But this follows directly from expanding the definition.

13.1.3 Programming Tips

The BETWEEN range includes the end points, so you have to be careful. For example, changing a percent range on a test into a letter grade with

Grades

low	high	grade
90	100	'A'
80	90	'B'
70	80	'C'
60	70	'D'
00	60	'F'

will not work when a student gets a grade on the borderline (90, 80, 70, or 60). One way to solve the problem is to change the table by adding 1 to the low scores. Of course, the student who got 90.1 will argue that he should have gotten an A and not a B. If you add 0.01 to the low scores, the student who got 90.001 will argue that he should have gotten an A and not a B. This is a problem with a continuous variable.

A better solution might be to change the predicate to (score BETWEEN low AND high) AND (score > low) or simply to ((low < score) AND (score <=

high)). Neither approach will be much different in this example since few values will fall on the borders between grades and this table is very, very small.

However, some indexing schemes might make the BETWEEN predicate the better choice for larger tables of this sort. They will keep index values in trees whose nodes hold a range of values (look up a description of the B tree family in a computer science book). An optimizer can compare the range of values in the BETWEEN predicate to the range of values in the index nodes as a single action. If the BETWEEN predicate were presented as two comparisons, it might execute them as separate actions against the database, which would be slower.

13.2 OVERLAPS Predicate

The OVERLAPS predicate is a feature not yet available in most SQL implementations because it requires more of the SQL-92 temporal datatypes than most implementations have. Many programmers have been "faking" the functionality of the INTERVAL datatype with the existing date and time features of their products.

13.2.1 Time Periods and OVERLAPS Predicate

An INTERVAL in SQL-92 is a measure of temporal duration, expressed in units such as a day, an hour, and so forth. This is how you add or subtract days to or from a date, hours and minutes to or from a time, and so forth. The standard is more complete than any existing implementation. When INTERVALs are more generally available, you will also have an OVERLAPS predicate, which compares two time periods. These time periods are defined as row values with two columns. The first column (the starting time) of the pair is always a datetime datatype, and the second column (the termination time) is a datetime datatype that can be used to compute a datetime value. If the starting and termination times are the same, this is an instantaneous event.

The result of the <overlaps predicate> is formally defined as the result of the following expression:

```
(S1 > S2 AND NOT (S1 >= T2 AND T1 >= T2))
OR (S2 > S1 AND NOT (S2 >= T1 AND T2 >= T1))
OR (S1 = S2 AND (T1 <> T2 OR T1 = T2))
```

where S1 and S2 are the starting times of the two time periods and T1 and T2 are their termination times.

The rules for the OVERLAPS predicate should be intuitive, but they are not. The principles that we wanted in the standard were

1. A time period includes its starting point, but does not include its end point. The reason for this model is that it follows the ISO convention that there is no 24:00 Hrs today; it is 00:00 Hrs tomorrow. Open-ended durations have closure properties that are useful. The concatenation of two open-ended durations is an open-ended duration

2. If the time periods are not instantaneous, they overlap when they share a common time period.

3. If the first term of the predicate is an INTERVAL and the second term is an instantaneous event (a datetime datatype), they overlap when the second term is in the time period (but is not the end point of the time period).

4. If the first and second terms are both instantaneous events, they overlap only when they are equal.

5. If the starting time is NULL and the finishing time is a datetime value, the finishing time becomes the starting time and we have an event. If the starting time is NULL and the finishing time is an INTERVAL value, then both the finishing and starting times are NULL.

Please consider how your intuition reacts to these results, when the granularity is at the YEAR-MONTH-DAY level. Remember that a day begins at 00:00 Hrs.

```
(today, today) OVERLAPS (today, today) is TRUE
(today, tomorrow) OVERLAPS (today, today) is TRUE
(today, tomorrow) OVERLAPS (tomorrow, tomorrow) is FALSE
(yesterday, today) OVERLAPS (today, tomorrow) is FALSE
```

The OVERLAPS predicate is not common in SQL products, but let's see what we have to do to handle overlapping times. Consider a table of hotel guests with the days of their stays and a table of special events being held at the hotel. The tables might look like this:

```
CREATE TABLE Guests
(guestname CHARACTER(30) PRIMARY KEY
 arrival DATE NOT NULL,
 departure DATE NOT NULL,
 . . .);
```

Guests

guestname	arrival	departure
'Dorothy Gale'	'1999-02-01'	'1999-11-01'
'Indiana Jones'	'1999-02-01'	'1999-02-01'
'Don Quixote'	'1999-01-01'	'1999-10-01'
'James T. Kirk'	'1999-02-01'	'1999-02-28'
'Santa Claus'	'1999-12-01'	'1999-12-25'

```
CREATE TABLE Celebrations
(eventname CHARACTER(30) PRIMARY KEY,
 start_date DATE NOT NULL,
 finish_date DATE NOT NULL,
 . . .);
```

Celebrations

celebname	start_date	finish_date
'Apple Month'	'1999-02-01'	'1999-02-28'
'Christmas Season'	'1999-12-01'	'1999-12-25'
'Garlic Festival'	'1999-01-15'	'1999-02-15'
'National Pear Week'	'1999-01-01'	'1999-01-07'
'New Year's Day'	'1999-01-01'	'1999-01-01'
'St. Fred's Day'	'1999-02-24'	'1999-02-24'
'Year of the Prune'	'1999-01-01'	'1999-12-31'

The BETWEEN operator will work just fine with single dates that fall between the starting and finishing dates of these celebrations, but please remember that the BETWEEN predicate will include the end point of an interval and that the OVERLAPS predicate will not. To find out if a particular date occurs during an event, you can simply write queries like

```
SELECT guestname, ' arrived during ', celebname
  FROM Guests, Celebrations
 WHERE arrival BETWEEN start_date AND finish_date
   AND arrival <> finish_date;
```

which will find the guests who arrived at the hotel during each event. The final predicate can be kept, if you want to conform to the ANSI convention, or dropped if that makes more sense in your situation. From now on, we will keep both end points to make the queries easier to read.

```
SELECT guestname, ' arrived during ', celebname
  FROM Guests, Celebrations
 WHERE arrival BETWEEN start_date AND finish_date;
```

guestname	'arrived during'	celebname
'Dorothy Gale'	'arrived during'	'Apple Month'
'Dorothy Gale'	'arrived during'	'Garlic Festival'
'Dorothy Gale'	'arrived during'	'Year of the Prune'
'Indiana Jones'	'arrived during'	'Apple Month'
'Indiana Jones'	'arrived during'	'Garlic Festival'
'Indiana Jones'	'arrived during'	'Year of the Prune'
'Don Quixote'	'arrived during'	'National Pear Week'
'Don Quixote'	'arrived during'	'New Year's Day'
'Don Quixote'	'arrived during'	'Year of the Prune'
'James T. Kirk'	'arrived during'	'Apple Month'
'James T. Kirk'	'arrived during'	'Garlic Festival'
'James T. Kirk'	'arrived during'	'Year of the Prune'
'Santa Claus'	'arrived during'	'Christmas Season'
'Santa Claus'	'arrived during'	'Year of the Prune'

The obvious question is which guests were at the hotel during each event. A common programming error when trying to find out if two intervals overlap is to write the query with the BETWEEN predicate:

```
SELECT guestname, ' was here during ', celebname
  FROM Guests, Celebrations
 WHERE arrival BETWEEN start_date AND finish_date
    OR departure BETWEEN start_date AND finish_date;
```

This is wrong, because it does not cover the case where the event began and finished during the guest's visit. Seeing his error, the programmer will sit down and draw a timeline diagram of all four possible overlapping cases (Figure 13.1). So the programmer adds more predicates:

```
SELECT guestname, ' was here during ', celebname
  FROM Guests, Celebrations
 WHERE arrival BETWEEN start_date AND finish_date
    OR departure BETWEEN start_date AND finish_date
    OR start_date BETWEEN arrival AND departure
    OR finish_date BETWEEN arrival AND departure;
```

Fig. 13.1

Fig. 13.2

A thoughtful programmer will notice that the last predicate is not needed and might drop it, but either way, this is a correct query. But it is not the best answer. In the case of the overlapping intervals, there are two cases where a guest's stay at the hotel and an event do not both fall within the same time frame: Either the guest checked out before the event started or the event ended before the guest arrived. If you want to do the logic, that is what the first predicate will work out to be when you also add the conditions that `arrival <= departure` and `start_date <= finish_date`. But it is easier to see in a timeline diagram (Figure 13.2).

Both cases can be represented in one SQL statement as

```
SELECT guestname, celebname
  FROM Guests, Celebrations
 WHERE NOT ((departure < start_date) OR (arrival > finish_date));
```

VIEW GuestsEvents

guestname	celebname
'Dorothy Gale'	'Apple Month'
'Dorothy Gale'	'Garlic Festival'
'Dorothy Gale'	'St. Fred's Day'
'Dorothy Gale'	'Year of the Prune'
'Indiana Jones'	'Apple Month'

guestname	celebname
'Indiana Jones'	'Garlic Festival'
'Indiana Jones'	'Year of the Prune'
'Don Quixote'	'Apple Month'
'Don Quixote'	'Garlic Festival'
'Don Quixote'	'National Pear Week'
'Don Quixote'	'New Year's Day'
'Don Quixote'	'St. Fred's Day'
'Don Quixote'	'Year of the Prune'
'James T. Kirk'	'Apple Month'
'James T. Kirk'	'Garlic Festival'
'James T. Kirk'	'St. Fred's Day'
'James T. Kirk'	'Year of the Prune'
'Santa Claus'	'Christmas Season'
'Santa Claus'	'Year of the Prune'

(cont.) appears at top left.

This VIEW is handy for other queries. Using the NOT in the WHERE clause allows you to add or remove it to reverse the sense of the query. For example, to find out how many celebrations each guest could have seen, you would write

```
CREATE VIEW GuestCelebrations (guestname, celebname)
AS SELECT guestname, celebname
    FROM Guests, Celebrations
    WHERE NOT ((departure < start_date) OR (arrival > finish_date));

SELECT guestname, COUNT(*) AS celebcount
  FROM GuestCelebrations
 GROUP BY guestname;
```

Result

guestname	celebcount
'Dorothy Gale'	4
'Indiana Jones'	3
'Don Quixote'	6
'James T. Kirk'	4
'Santa Claus'	2

and then to find out how many guests were at the hotel during each celebration, you would write

Fig. 13.3

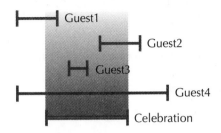

```
SELECT celebname, COUNT(*) AS guestcount
  FROM GuestCelebrations
 GROUP BY celebname;
```

Result

celebname	guestcount
'Apple Month'	4
'Christmas Season'	1
'Garlic Festival'	4
'National Pear Week'	1
'New Year's Day'	1
'St. Fred's Day'	3
'Year of the Prune'	5

This last query is only part of the story. What the hotel management really wants to know is how many room nights were sold for a celebration. A little algebra tells you that the length of an event is (Event.finish_date - Event.start_date + INTERVAL 1 DAY) and that the length of a guest's stay is (Guest.departure - Guest. arrival + INTERVAL 1 DAY). Let's do one of those timeline charts again (Figure 13.3). What we want is the part of the Guests interval that is inside the Celebrations interval.

Guests 1 and 2 spent only part of their time at the celebration; Guest 3 spent all of his time at the celebration and Guest 4 stayed even longer than the celebration. That interval is defined by the two points (GREATEST(arrival, start_date), LEAST(departure, finish_date)), to borrow a pair of functions from Oracle that are not standard SQL.

Instead, you can use the aggregate functions in SQL to build a VIEW on a VIEW, like this:

```
CREATE VIEW Working (guestname, celebname, entered, exited)
AS SELECT GE.guestname, GE.celebname, start_date, finish_date
```

```
    FROM GuestCelebrations AS GE, Celebrations AS E1
   WHERE E1.celebname = GE.celebname
UNION
    SELECT GE.guestname, GE.celebname, arrival, departure
     FROM GuestCelebrations AS GE, Guests AS G1
    WHERE G1.guestname = GE.guestname;
```

VIEW Working

guestname	celebname	entered	exited
'Dorothy Gale'	'Apple Month'	'1999-02-01'	'1999-02-28'
'Dorothy Gale'	'Apple Month'	'1999-02-01'	'1999-11-01'
'Dorothy Gale'	'Garlic Festival'	'1999-02-01'	'1999-11-01'
'Dorothy Gale'	'Garlic Festival'	'1999-01-15'	'1999-02-15'
'Dorothy Gale'	'St. Fred's Day'	'1999-02-01'	'1999-11-01'
'Dorothy Gale'	'St. Fred's Day'	'1999-02-24'	'1999-02-24'
'Dorothy Gale'	'Year of the Prune'	'1999-02-01'	'1999-11-01'
'Dorothy Gale'	'Year of the Prune'	'1999-01-01'	'1999-12-31'
'Indiana Jones'	'Apple Month'	'1999-02-01'	'1999-02-01'
'Indiana Jones'	'Apple Month'	'1999-02-01'	'1999-02-28'
'Indiana Jones'	'Garlic Festival'	'1999-02-01'	'1999-02-01'
'Indiana Jones'	'Garlic Festival'	'1999-01-15'	'1999-02-15'
'Indiana Jones'	'Year of the Prune'	'1999-02-01'	'1999-02-01'
'Indiana Jones'	'Year of the Prune'	'1999-01-01'	'1999-12-31'
'Don Quixote'	'Apple Month'	'1999-02-01'	'1999-02-28'
'Don Quixote'	'Apple Month'	'1999-01-01'	'1999-10-01'
'Don Quixote'	'Garlic Festival'	'1999-01-01'	'1999-10-01'
'Don Quixote'	'Garlic Festival'	'1999-01-15'	'1999-02-15'
'Don Quixote'	'National Pear Week'	'1999-01-01'	'1999-01-07'
'Don Quixote'	'National Pear Week'	'1999-01-01'	'1999-10-01'
'Don Quixote'	'New Year's Day'	'1999-01-01'	'1999-01-01'
'Don Quixote'	'New Year's Day'	'1999-01-01'	'1999-10-01'
'Don Quixote'	'St. Fred's Day'	'1999-02-24'	'1999-02-24'
'Don Quixote'	'St. Fred's Day'	'1999-01-01'	'1999-10-01'
'Don Quixote'	'Year of the Prune'	'1999-01-01'	'1999-12-31'
'Don Quixote'	'Year of the Prune'	'1999-01-01'	'1999-10-01'
'James T. Kirk'	'Apple Month'	'1999-02-01'	'1999-02-28'
'James T. Kirk'	'Garlic Festival'	'1999-02-01'	'1999-02-28'

'James T. Kirk'	'Garlic Festival'	'1999-01-15'	'1999-02-15'
'James T. Kirk'	'St. Fred's Day'	'1999-02-01'	'1999-02-28'
'James T. Kirk'	'St. Fred's Day'	'1999-02-24'	'1999-02-24'
'James T. Kirk'	'Year of the Prune'	'1999-02-01'	'1999-02-28'
'James T. Kirk'	'Year of the Prune'	'1999-01-01'	'1999-12-31'
'Santa Claus'	'Christmas Season'	'1999-12-01'	'1999-12-25'
'Santa Claus'	'Year of the Prune'	'1999-12-01'	'1999-12-25'
'Santa Claus'	'Year of the Prune'	'1999-01-01'	'1999-12-31'

This will put the earliest and latest points in both intervals into one column. Now we can construct a VIEW like this:

```
CREATE VIEW Attendees(guestname, celebname, entered, exited)
AS SELECT guestname, celebname, MAX(entered), MIN(exited)
     FROM Working
     GROUP BY guestname, celebname;
```

VIEW Attendees

guestname	celebname	entered	exited
'Dorothy Gale'	'Apple Month'	'1999-02-01'	'1999-02-28'
'Dorothy Gale'	'Garlic Festival'	'1999-02-01'	'1999-02-15'
'Dorothy Gale'	'St. Fred's Day'	'1999-02-24'	'1999-02-24'
'Dorothy Gale'	'Year of the Prune'	'1999-02-01'	'1999-11-01'
'Indiana Jones'	'Apple Month'	'1999-02-01'	'1999-02-01'
'Indiana Jones'	'Garlic Festival'	'1999-02-01'	'1999-02-01'
'Indiana Jones'	'Year of the Prune'	'1999-02-01'	'1999-02-01'
'Don Quixote'	'Apple Month'	'1999-02-01'	'1999-02-28'
'Don Quixote'	'Garlic Festival'	'1999-01-15'	'1999-02-15'
'Don Quixote'	'National Pear Week'	'1999-01-01'	'1999-01-07'
'Don Quixote'	'New Year's Day'	'1999-01-01'	'1999-01-01'
'Don Quixote'	'St. Fred's Day'	'1999-02-24'	'1999-02-24'
'Don Quixote'	'Year of the Prune'	'1999-01-01'	'1999-10-01'
'James T. Kirk'	'Apple Month'	'1999-02-01'	'1999-02-28'
'James T. Kirk'	'Garlic Festival'	'1999-02-01'	'1999-02-15'
'James T. Kirk'	'St. Fred's Day'	'1999-02-24'	'1999-02-24'
'James T. Kirk'	'Year of the Prune'	'1999-02-01'	'1999-02-28'
'Santa Claus'	'Christmas Season'	'1999-12-01'	'1999-12-25'
'Santa Claus'	'Year of the Prune'	'1999-12-01'	'1999-12-25'

The Attendees VIEW can be used to compute the total number of room days for each celebration. Assume that the difference of two dates will return an integer that is the number of days between them:

```
SELECT celebname,
       SUM(exited - entered + INTERVAL 1 DAY) AS roomdays
  FROM Attendees
 GROUP BY celebname;
```

Result

celebname	roomdays
'Apple Month'	85
'Christmas Season'	25
'Garlic Festival'	63
'National Pear Week'	7
'New Year's Day'	1
'St. Fred's Day'	3
'Year of the Prune'	602

If you would like to get a count of the room days sold in the month of January, you could use this query, which avoids a BETWEEN or OVERLAPS predicate completely:

```
SELECT SUM(CASE WHEN leave > DATE '1999-01-31'
                THEN DATE '1999-01-31'
                ELSE leave END
         - CASE WHEN arrival < DATE '1999-01-01'
                THEN DATE '1999-01-01'
                ELSE arrival END + INTERVAL 1 DAY) AS room_days
  FROM Guests
 WHERE leave > DATE '1999-01-01' AND arrival <= DATE '1999-01-31';
```

CHAPTER 14

The [NOT] IN Predicate

THE IN PREDICATE is very natural. It takes a value and checks if it is in a list of comparable values. SQL-89 allowed only simple scalar values, but SQL-92 also allows value expressions. The syntax is

```
<in predicate> ::=
<row value constructor> [NOT] IN <in predicate value>

<in predicate value> ::=
    <table subquery> | (<in value list>)

<in value list> ::=
    <row value expression> { <comma> <row value expression> } . . .
```

The expression `<row value constructor>` NOT IN `<in predicate value>` has the same effect as NOT (`<row value constructor>` IN `<in predicate value>`). This pattern for the use of the keyword NOT is found in most of the other predicates in SQL-92.

The expression `<row value constructor>` IN `<in predicate value>` has the same effect as `<row value constructor>` = ANY `<in predicate value>` by definition. Most optimizers will recognize this and execute the same code for both expressions. This means that if the `<in predicate value>` is empty, such as one you would get from a subquery that returns no rows, the results will be equivalent to (`<row value constructor>` = (NULL, . . . , NULL)), which is always evaluated to UNKNOWN. Likewise, if the `<in predicate value>` is an explicit list of NULLs, the results will be UNKNOWN. However, please remember that there is a difference between an empty table and a table with rows of all NULLs.

IN predicates with a subquery can sometimes be converted into EXISTS predicates, but there are some problems and differences in the predicates. Conversion to an EXISTS predicate is often a good way to improve performance, but it will not be as easy to read as the original IN predicate. An EXISTS predicate can use indexes to find (or fail to find) a single value that confirms (or denies) the predicate, whereas the IN predicate often has to build the results of the subquery in a working table.

14.1 Optimizing the IN Predicate

Most database engines have no statistics about the relative frequency of the values in a list of constants, so they will scan that list in the order in which they appear. People like to order lists alphabetically or by magnitude, but it would be better to order the list from most frequently occurring values to least frequent. It is also pointless to have duplicate values in the constant list since the predicate will return TRUE if it matches the first duplicate it finds and never get to the second occurrence. Likewise, if the predicate is FALSE for that value, traversing a needlessly long list wastes computer time.

Many SQL engines perform an IN predicate with a subquery by building the result set of the subquery first as a temporary working table, then scanning that result table from left to right. This can be expensive in many cases; for example, in a query to find who works for us in a city with a major sports team (we want to get tickets), we could write

```
SELECT *
  FROM Personnel
 WHERE city_state IN (SELECT city_state
                        FROM SportTeams);
```

assuming that the combination of (city, state) is unique. But let us further assume that our personnel are located in n cities and the sports teams are in m cities, where m is much greater than n. If the matching cities appear near the front of the list generated by the subquery expression, it will perform much faster than if they appear at the end of the list. In the case of a subquery expression you have no control over how the subquery is presented back in the containing query.

However, you can order the expressions in a list in the most-likely-to-occur order, such as

```
SELECT *
  FROM Personnel
 WHERE city_state IN ('New York', 'Chicago', 'Atlanta',
 . . . );
```

Incidentally, SQL-92 allows row expression comparisons, so if you have a SQL-92 implementation with separate columns for the city and state, you could write

```
SELECT *
  FROM Personnel
 WHERE (city, state) IN (SELECT city, state
                           FROM SportTeams);
```

Teradata did not get correlated subqueries until 1996, so they often used this SQL-92 feature as a workaround. I am not sure if you should count them as being ahead or behind the technology for that.

Unfortunately, some older versions of SQL do not remove duplicates in the result table of the subquery. This can handled by using a SELECT DISTINCT in the subquery, but that will usually force a sort on the result set. You have to figure out if the amount of duplication justifies the sort.

A trick that can work for large lists on some products is to force the engine to construct a list ordered by frequency. This involves first constructing a VIEW that has an ORDER BY clause; this is not part of the SQL standard, which does not allow a VIEW to have an ORDER BY clause. For example, a paint company wants to find all the products offered by competitors that use the same color as one of its products. First construct a VIEW that orders the colors by frequency of appearance:

```
CREATE VIEW PopColor (color, tally)
AS SELECT color, COUNT(*) AS tally
     FROM Paints
    GROUP BY color
    ORDER BY tally DESC;
```

Then go to the Competitor data and do a simple column SELECT on the VIEW:

```
SELECT *
  FROM Competitor
 WHERE color IN (SELECT color FROM PopColor);
```

The VIEW is grouped, so it will be materialized in sort order. The subquery will then be executed and (we hope) the sort order will be maintained and passed along to the IN predicate.

Another trick is to replace the IN predicate with a JOIN operation. For example, you have a table of restaurant telephone numbers and a guidebook and you want to pick out the four-star places, so you write this query:

```
SELECT restname, phone
  FROM Restaurants
 WHERE restname IN (SELECT restname
                      FROM QualityGuide
                     WHERE stars = 4);
```

If there is an index on QualityGuide.stars, the SQL engine will probably build a temporary table of the four-star places and pass it on to the outer query. The outer query will then handle it as if it were a list of constants.

However, this is not the sort of column that you would normally index. Without an index on stars, the engine will simply do a sequential search of the QualityGuide table. This query can be replaced with a JOIN query:

```
SELECT restname, phone
  FROM Restaurants, QualityGuide
 WHERE stars = 4
   AND Restaurants.restname = QualityGuide.restname;
```

This query should run faster, since restname is a key for both tables and will be indexed to ensure uniqueness. However, this can return duplicate rows in the result table that you can handle with a SELECT DISTINCT. Consider a more budget-minded query, where we want places with a meal priced at under $10 and the menu guidebook lists all the meals. The query looks about the same:

```
SELECT restname, phone
  FROM Restaurants
 WHERE restname IN (SELECT restname
                      FROM MenuGuide
                     WHERE price <= 10.00);
```

And you would expect to be able to replace it with

```
SELECT restname, phone
  FROM Restaurants, MenuGuide
```

```
WHERE price <= 10.00
  AND Restaurants.restname = MenuGuide.restname;
```

Every item in Murphy's Two-Dollar Hash House will get a line in the results of the JOINed version, however. This can be fixed by changing SELECT restname, phone to SELECT DISTINCT restname, phone, but it will cost more time to do a sort to remove the duplicates. There is no good general advice, except to experiment with your particular product.

The NOT IN predicate is probably better replaced with a NOT EXISTS predicate. Using the restaurant example again, we find out that our friend John has a list of eateries and we want to see those that are not in the guidebook. The natural formation of the query is

```
SELECT *
  FROM JohnsBook
WHERE restname NOT IN (SELECT restname FROM QualityGuide);
```

But you can write the same query with a NOT EXISTS predicate and it will probably run faster:

```
SELECT *
  FROM JohnsBook AS J1
WHERE NOT EXISTS (SELECT *
                    FROM QualityGuide AS Q1
                   WHERE Q1.restname = J1.restname);
```

The reason the second version will probably run faster is that it can test for existence using the indexes on both tables. The NOT IN version has to test all the values in the subquery table for inequality. Many SQL implementations will construct a temporary table from the IN predicate subquery if it has a WHERE clause, but the temporary table will not have any indexes. The temporary table can also have duplicates and a random ordering of its rows, so that the SQL engine has to do a full-table scan.

14.2 Replacing ORs with the IN Predicate

A simple trick that beginning SQL programmers often miss is using an IN predicate to replace a set of OR-ed predicates. For example,

```
SELECT *
  FROM QualityControlReport
WHERE test_1 = 'passed'
```

```
    OR test_2 = 'passed'
    OR test_3 = 'passed'
    OR test_4 = 'passed';
```

can be rewritten as

```
SELECT *
  FROM QualityControlReport
 WHERE 'passed' IN (test_1, test_2, test_3, test_4);
```

The reason this is hard to see is that programmers get used to thinking of either a subquery or a simple list of constants. They miss the fact that the IN predicate list can be a list of expressions. The optimizer would have handled each of the original predicates separately in the WHERE clause, but it has to handle the IN predicate as a single item, which can change the order of evaluation. This might or might not be faster than the list of OR-ed predicates for a particular query.

14.3 NULLs and the IN Predicate

NULLs create some special problems in a NOT IN predicate with a subquery. Consider these two tables:

```
CREATE TABLE Table1 (x INTEGER);
INSERT INTO Table1 VALUES (1), (2), (3), (4);

CREATE TABLE Table2 (x INTEGER);
INSERT INTO Table2 VALUES (1), (NULL), (2);
```

Now execute this query:

```
SELECT *
  FROM Table1
 WHERE x NOT IN (SELECT x FROM Table2)
```

Let's work it out step by painful step:

1. Do the subquery:

    ```
    SELECT *
      FROM Table1
     WHERE x NOT IN (1, NULL, 2);
    ```

2.   Convert the NOT IN to its definitional form:

```
SELECT *
  FROM Table1
 WHERE NOT (x IN (1, NULL, 2));
```

3.   Expand the IN predicate:

```
SELECT *
  FROM Table1
 WHERE NOT ((x = 1) OR (x = NULL) OR (x = 2));
```

4.   Apply DeMorgan's law:

```
SELECT *
  FROM Table1
 WHERE ((x <> 1) AND (x <> NULL) AND (x <> 2));
```

5.   Use the constant logical expression:

```
SELECT *
  FROM Table1
 WHERE ((x <> 1) AND UNKNOWN AND (x <> 2));
```

6.   Reduce OR to a constant:

```
SELECT *
 FROM Table1
 WHERE UNKNOWN;
```

7.   The results are always empty.

Now try this with another set of tables:

```
CREATE TABLE Table3 (x INTEGER);
INSERT INTO Table3 VALUES (1), (2), (NULL), (4);

CREATE TABLE Table4 (x INTEGER);
INSERT INTO Table3 VALUES (1), (3), (2);
```

Let's work out the same query again, step by painful step:

1. Do the subquery:

    ```
    SELECT *
      FROM Table3
     WHERE x NOT IN (1, 3, 2);
    ```

2. Convert the NOT IN to a Boolean expression:

    ```
    SELECT *
      FROM Table3
     WHERE NOT (x IN (1, 3, 2));
    ```

3. Expand the IN predicate:

    ```
    SELECT *
      FROM Table3
     WHERE NOT ((x = 1) OR (x = 3) OR (x = 2));
    ```

4. Apply DeMorgan's law:

    ```
    SELECT *
      FROM Table3
     WHERE ((x <> 1) AND (x <> 3) AND (x <> 2));
    ```

5. Compute the result set. I will show it as a UNION with substitutions:

    ```
    SELECT *
      FROM Table3
     WHERE ((1 <> 1) AND (1 <> 3) AND (1 <> 2)) -- FALSE
    UNION ALL
    SELECT *
      FROM Table3
     WHERE ((2 <> 1) AND (2 <> 3) AND (2 <> 2)) -- FALSE
    UNION ALL
    SELECT *
      FROM Table3
     WHERE ((NULL <> 1) AND (NULL <> 3) AND (NULL <> 2)) -- UNKNOWN
    UNION ALL
    SELECT *
      FROM Table3
     WHERE ((4 <> 1) AND (4 <> 3) AND (4 <> 2)); -- TRUE
    ```

6.   The result is one row = (4).

14.4 IN Predicate and Referential Constraints

One of the most popular uses for the IN predicate is in a CHECK( ) clause on a table. The usual form is a list of values that are legal for a column, such as

```
CREATE TABLE Addresses
(name CHAR(25) NOT NULL PRIMARY KEY,
 street CHAR(25) NOT NULL,
 city CHAR(20) NOT NULL,
 state_code CHAR(2) NOT NULL
       CONSTRAINT valid_state_code
       CHECK (state_code IN ('AL', 'AK', ...)),
 . . . );
```

This method works fine with a small list of values, but it has problems when applied to a longer list. To speed up the search, it is very important to arrange the values in the order they are most likely to match the two-letter state_code.

In full SQL-92, it became possible to reference other tables, so you could write the same constraint as

```
CREATE TABLE Addresses
(name CHAR(25) NOT NULL PRIMARY KEY,
 street CHAR(25) NOT NULL,
 city CHAR(20) NOT NULL,
 state_code CHAR(2) NOT NULL,
 CONSTRAINT valid_state_code
 CHECK (state_code
        IN (SELECT state_code
              FROM ZipCodeData AS Z1
             WHERE Z1.state_code = Addresses.state_code)),
 . . . );
```

The advantage of this is that you can change the ZipCodeData and thereby change the effect of the constraint on the Addresses table. This is fine for adding more data in the outer reference (e.g., Quebec joins the Union and gets the state code 'QB'), but it has a bad effect when you try to delete data in the outer reference (e.g., California secedes from the Union and every row with 'CA' for a state code is now invalid).

I am not sure at the time of this writing how many products will allow this method and what the results will be. Notice that you also get some weird results with a NULL in the IN predicate list.

EXISTS() Predicate

T HE EXISTS PREDICATE is very natural: It is a test for a nonempty set. If there are any rows in its subquery, it is TRUE; otherwise, it is FALSE. You cannot get an UNKNOWN result. The syntax is

```
<exists predicate> ::= EXISTS <table subquery>
```

It is worth mentioning that a <table subquery> is always inside parentheses to avoid problems in the grammar during parsing.

In SQL-89, the rules stated that the subquery had to have a SELECT clause with one column or a *. If the SELECT * option was used, the database engine would (in theory) pick one column and use it. This fiction was needed because SQL-89 defined subqueries as having only one column. SQL-92 can handle row-valued comparisons and does not need that restriction.

There are three popular options for the programmer to use.

1. EXISTS (SELECT * FROM . . .)

In general, the SELECT * option should perform better than an actual column. It lets the query optimizer decide which column to use. If a column has an index on it, then simply seeing a pointer in the index is enough to determine that something exists. We do not need to know what the actual value was.

2.   EXISTS (SELECT <column> FROM . . .)

   Although I just said that the * should be better, you will find situations where directing the SQL compiler to a particular column is a better choice. Unfortunately, old SQL products would actually execute all of the subquery expression instead of stopping early.

3.   EXISTS (SELECT <constant> FROM . . .)

   Oracle and some other products prefer a constant in the SELECT clause list because this tells them that they do not have to read a row to get a value once they have a pointer to a row. Yes, the optimizer ought to be smart enough to figure that out, but it isn't.

If some columns have indexes that can be used to answer the query, the optimizer can access just the indexes and never has to look at the table itself. For example, we want to find all the personnel who were born on the same day as any famous person. The query could be

```
SELECT P1.name, ' has the same birthday as a famous person!'
  FROM Personnel AS P1
 WHERE EXISTS (SELECT *
                 FROM Celebrities AS C1
                WHERE P1.birthday = C1.birthday);
```

If the table Celebrities has an index on its birthday column, the optimizer will get the current employee's birthday P1.birthday and look up that value in the index. If the value is in the index, the predicate is TRUE and we don't need to look at the Celebrities table at all.

If it is not in the index, the predicate is FALSE and there is still no need to look at the Celebrities table. This should be fast, since indexes are smaller than their tables and are structured for very fast searching.

However, if Celebrities has no index on its birthday column, the query may have to look at every row to see if there is a birthday that matches the current employee's birthday. There are some tricks that a good optimizer can use to speed things up in this situation.

If the number of values is small and there is a lot of duplication, the SQL engine can build a temporary table of Celebrity birthdates, sort it, and remove duplicates during the sort. This will work if the schema tables track how many unique values can appear in a column. You can find this from constraints and from data declarations as well as from statistics. In this example, we know that we would have at most 366 possible birthdays and a lot of duplication. A binary search on this temporary table could be fast enough to make up for the time lost in building it.

15.1 EXISTS and NULLs

A NULL might not be a value, but it does exist in SQL. This is often a problem for a new SQL programmer who is having trouble with NULLs and how they behave. Think of them as being like a brown paper bag—you know that something is inside, but you do not know exactly what it is. For example, we want to find all the personnel who were not born on the same day as a famous person. This can be answered with the negation of the original query:

```
SELECT P1.name, ' was born on a day without a famous person!'
  FROM Personnel AS P1
 WHERE NOT EXISTS (SELECT *
                     FROM Celebrities AS C1
                    WHERE P1.birthday = C1.birthday);
```

But assume that among the Celebrities, we have a movie star who will not admit her age, shown in the row ('Gloria Glamour', NULL). A new SQL programmer might expect that Gloria Glamour will not match to anyone since we don't know her birthday yet. Actually, she will match to everyone since there is a chance that they may match when some tabloid newspaper finally gets a copy of her birth certificate. But work out the subquery in the usual way to convince yourself:

```
  . . .
 WHERE NOT EXISTS (SELECT *
                     FROM Celebrities AS C1
                    WHERE P1.birthday = NULL);
```

becomes

```
  . . .
 WHERE NOT EXISTS (SELECT *
                     FROM Celebrities AS C1
                    WHERE UNKNOWN);
```

becomes

```
  . . .
 WHERE TRUE;
```

You will see that the predicate tests to UNKNOWN because of the NULL comparison and therefore fails whenever we look at Gloria Glamour.

Another problem with NULLs becomes apparent when you attempt to convert IN predicates to EXISTS predicates. In our example of matching our personnel to famous people, the query can be rewritten as

```
SELECT P1.name, ' was born on a day without a famous person!'
  FROM Personnel AS P1
 WHERE P1.birthday NOT IN (SELECT C1.birthday
                             FROM Celebrities AS C1);
```

However, consider a more complex version of the same query, where the celebrity has to have been born in New York City. The IN predicate would be

```
SELECT P1.name, ' was born on a day without a famous New Yorker!'
  FROM Personnel AS P1
 WHERE P1.birthday NOT IN (SELECT C1.birthday
                             FROM Celebrities AS C1
                            WHERE C1.birthcity = 'New York');
```

You would think that the EXISTS version would be

```
SELECT P1.name, ' was born on a day without a famous New Yorker!'
  FROM Personnel AS P1
 WHERE NOT EXISTS (SELECT *
                     FROM Celebrities AS C1, Personnel AS E1
                    WHERE C1.birthcity = 'New York'
                      AND C1.birthday = E1.birthday);
```

But assume that Gloria Glamour is our only New Yorker and that we still don't know her birthday. The subquery will be empty for every employee in the EXISTS predicate version because her NULL birthday will not test equal to the known employee birthdays. That means that the NOT EXISTS predicate will return TRUE and we will get every employee to match to Gloria Glamour. But now look at the IN predicate version, which will have a single NULL in the subquery result. This predicate will be equivalent to (Personnel.birthday = NULL), which is always UNKNOWN, and we will get no Personnel back.

Likewise, you cannot, in general, transform the quantified comparison predicates into EXISTS predicates because of the possibility of NULL values. Remember that "x <> ALL <subquery>" is shorthand for "x NOT IN <subquery>" and "x = ANY <subquery>" is shorthand for "x IN <subquery>", and it will not surprise you.

Different versions of SQL may handle these situations differently, in violation of the standard. (For an example of such differences involving DB2 and Oracle, see van der Lans 1991.) In general, the EXISTS predicates will run faster than the IN predicates. The problem is in deciding whether to build the query or the subquery first; the optimal approach depends on the size and distribution of the values in each, and that cannot usually be known until runtime.

15.2 EXISTS and JOINs

The EXISTS predicate is almost always used with a correlated subquery. Very often the subquery can be "flattened" into a JOIN, which will often run faster than the original query. Our sample query can be converted into

```
SELECT P1.name, ' has the same birthday as a famous person!'
  FROM Personnel AS P1, Celebrities AS C1
 WHERE (P1.birthday = C1.birthday);
```

The advantage of the JOIN version is that it allows us to show columns from both tables. We should make the query more informative by rewriting it:

```
SELECT P1.name, ' has the same birthday as ', C1.name
  FROM Personnel AS P1, Celebrities AS C1
 WHERE P1.birthday = C1.birthday;
```

This new query could be written with an EXISTS predicate, but that would be a waste of resources.

```
SELECT P1.name, ' has the same birthday as ', C1.name
  FROM Personnel AS P1, Celebrities AS C1
 WHERE EXISTS (SELECT *
                 FROM Celebrities AS C2
                WHERE P1.birthday = C2.birthday
                  AND C1.name = C2.name);
```

15.3 EXISTS and Quantifiers

Formal logic makes use of quantifiers that can be applied to propositions. The two forms are "For all x, $P(x)$" and "For some x, $P(x)$". The first is written as $\forall$ and the second is written as $\exists$, if you want to look up the formulas in a textbook. The quantifiers put into symbols such statements as "All men are mortal" or "Some Cretans are liars" so they can be manipulated.

The big question over 100 years ago was that of *existential import* in formal logic. Everyone agreed that saying "All men are mortal" implies that "No men are not mortal," but does it also imply that "some men are mortal"— that we have to have at least one man who is mortal?

Existential import lost the battle, and the modern convention is that "All men are mortal" has the same meaning as "There are no men who are immortal" but does not imply that any men exist at all. This is the convention followed in the design of SQL, with the exception of Sybase (before Sybase System 10) and Microsoft SQL Server products. Consider the statement "Some salesmen are liars" and the way we would write it with the EXISTS predicate in SQL:

```
EXISTS (SELECT *
          FROM Personnel AS P1
         WHERE P1.job = 'Salesman'
           AND P1.name IN (SELECT L1.name FROM Liars AS L1));
```

This query could also be written with (P1.name = L1.name) instead of the IN predicate by putting the references to the Liars table in the FROM clause. The reason for doing it this way is to show the relationship between this query and the next step.

If we are more cynical about salesmen, we might want to formulate the predicate "All salesmen are liars" with the EXISTS predicate in SQL, using the transform rule just discussed:

```
NOT EXISTS (SELECT *
              FROM Personnel AS P1
             WHERE P1.job = 'Salesman'
               AND P1.name NOT IN
                     (SELECT L1.name
                        FROM Liars AS L1));
```

which, informally, says, "There are no salesmen who are not liars" in English. In both these cases, the IN predicate can be changed into an EXISTS predicate, which should improve performance, but it would not be as easy to read.

15.4 EXISTS() and Referential Constraints

The SQL-92 standard was designed so that the declarative referential constraints could be expressed as EXISTS() predicates in a CHECK() clause. For example,

```
CREATE TABLE Addresses
(name CHAR(25) NOT NULL PRIMARY KEY,
 street CHAR(25) NOT NULL,
 city CHAR(20) NOT NULL,
 state_code CHAR(2) NOT NULL
            REFERENCES ZipCodeData(state_code),
 . . . );
```

could be written as

```
CREATE TABLE Addresses
(name CHAR(25) NOT NULL PRIMARY KEY,
 street CHAR(25) NOT NULL,
 city CHAR(20) NOT NULL,
 state_code CHAR(2) NOT NULL,
 CONSTRAINT valid_state_code
 CHECK (EXISTS (SELECT *
                FROM ZipCodeData AS Z1
                WHERE Z1.state_code = Addresses.state_code)),
 . . . );
```

There is no advantage to this expression for the DBA since you cannot attach referential actions with the CHECK( ) constraint. However, a SQL database can use the same mechanisms in the SQL compiler for both constructions.

Quantified Subquery Predicates

A QUANTIFIER IS A logical operator that states the quantity of objects for which a statement is TRUE. This is a logical quantity, not a numeric quantity; it relates a statement to the whole set of possible objects. In everyday life, you see quantified statements like "There is only one mouthwash that stops dinosaur breath," "All doctors drive Mercedes," or "Some people got rich investing in cattle futures."

The first statement, about the mouthwash, is a *uniqueness quantifier.* If there were two or more products that could save us from dinosaur breath, it would be FALSE. The second statement has what is called a *universal quantifier* since it deals with all doctors—find one exception and the statement is FALSE. The last statement has an *existential quantifier,* since it asserts that one or more people exist who got rich by investing in cattle futures—find one example and the statement is TRUE.

SQL has forms of these quantifiers that are not quite like those in formal logic. They are based on extending the use of comparison predicates to allow result sets to be quantified, and they use SQLs three-valued logic, so they do not return just TRUE or FALSE.

16.1 Scalar Subquery Comparisons

A comparison in SQL-89 was always done between scalar values; SQL-92 now allows row comparisons (see Section 10.2). If a subquery returns a single-row, single-column result table, it is treated as a scalar value in

SQL-92 in virtually any place a scalar could appear. SQL-89 allowed a limited form of comparison between a scalar expression and a quantified scalar subquery. The SQL-89 syntax required that the scalar expression appear on the left-hand side of the quantified comparison operator and the subquery on the right.

Though it is not part of the SQL-89 standard, many old SQL implementations also allowed a predicate of the form `<expression> <comp op> <scalar subquery>`, which is the same as the `<comp op> ANY` predicate restricted to a `<scalar subquery>`. The scalar subquery can be correlated or uncorrelated. For example, to find out if we have any teachers who are more than one year older than the students, I could write

```
SELECT name
  FROM Teachers AS T1
 WHERE T1.age > (SELECT MAX(S1.age) + INTERVAL 365 DAYS)
                  FROM Students AS S1);
```

In this case, the scalar subquery will be run only once and reduced to a constant value by the optimizer before scanning the Teachers table. I am finding the unique maximum student age to do the query.

A correlated subquery is more complex because it will have to be executed for each value from the containing query. For example, to find which suppliers have sent us fewer than 100 parts, we would use this query. Notice how the SUM(`quantity`) has to be computed for each supplier number, sno.

```
SELECT sno, sname
  FROM Suppliers
 WHERE 100 > (SELECT SUM(quantity)
                FROM Shipments
               WHERE Shipments.sno = Suppliers.sno);
```

If a scalar subquery returns a NULL, we can use the rules for handling comparison with NULLs. But what if it returns an empty result—a supplier that has not shipped us anything? In SQL-92, the empty result table is also a NULL; however, it is wise to check your implementation since this is a new feature in the language.

In SQL-92, you can place scalar or row subqueries on either side of a comparison predicate as long as they return comparable results. But you must be aware of the rules for row comparisons. For example, the following query will find the product manager who has more of his product at stores than in the warehouse:

```
SELECT manager, product
  FROM Personnel AS P1
 WHERE (SELECT SUM(qty)
           FROM Warehouses AS W1
          WHERE P1.product = W1.product)
         < (SELECT SUM(qty)
               FROM Stores AS S1
              WHERE P1.product = S1.product);
```

Here is a programming tip: The main problem with writing these queries is getting a result with more than one row in it. You can guarantee uniqueness in several ways. An aggregate function on an ungrouped table will always be a single value. A JOIN with the containing query based on a key will always be a single value.

16.2 Quantifiers and Missing Data

The quantified predicates are used with subquery expressions to compare a single value to those of the subquery, and take the general form <value expression> <comp op> <quantifier> <subquery>. These predicates are based on the formal logical quantifiers "For all," written as ∀ in formal logic, and "There exists," written as ∃ in formal logic; SQL tries to preserve similar properties.

The predicate <value expression> <comp op> ANY table S is equivalent to taking each row s (assume that they are numbered from 1 to n) of table S and testing <value expression> <comp op> s with ORs between the expanded expressions:

```
((<value expression> <comp op> s1)
OR (<value expression> <comp op> s2)
    . . .
OR (<value expression> <comp op> sn))
```

When you get a single TRUE result, the whole predicate is TRUE.

As long as table S has cardinality greater than zero and one non-NULL value, you will get a result of TRUE or FALSE. The keyword SOME is the same as ANY—just a matter of style and readability. Likewise, <value expression> <comp op> ALL table S takes each row s of table S and tests <value expression> <comp op> s with ANDs between the expanded expressions:

```
((<value expression> <comp op> s1)
AND (<value expression> <comp op> s2)
```

```
. . .
AND (<value expression> <comp op> sn))
```

When you get a single FALSE result, the whole predicate is FALSE. As long as table S has cardinality greater than zero and all non-NULL values, you will get a result of TRUE or FALSE.

That sounds reasonable so far. Now let EmptyTable be an empty table (no rows, cardinality zero) and NullTable be a table with only NULLs in its rows (cardinality greater than zero). The rules for SQL say that <value expression> <comp op> ALL NullTable always returns UNKNOWN, and likewise <value expression> <comp op> ANY NullTable always returns UNKNOWN. This makes sense because every row comparison test in the expansion would return UNKNOWN, so the series of OR and AND operators would behave in the usual way.

However, <value expression> <comp op> ALL EmptyTable always returns TRUE, and <value expression> <comp op> ANY EmptyTable always returns FALSE. Most people have no trouble seeing why the ANY predicate works that way; you cannot find a match, so the result is FALSE. But most people have lots of trouble seeing why the ALL predicate is TRUE. This convention is called *existential import,* which I have just discussed in Chapter 15 on the EXISTS predicate. If I were to walk into a bar and announce that I can beat any pink elephant in the bar, that would be a true statement. The fact that there are no pink elephants in the bar merely shows that the problem is reduced to the minimum case.

If this seems unnatural, then convert the ALL and ANY predicates into EXISTS predicates and look at the way that this rule preserves the properties that

1. $\forall x\, P(x) = \neg\, \exists x \neg\, P(x)$

2. $\exists x\, P(x) = \neg\, \forall x \neg\, P(x)$

The "Table1 x <comp op> ALL (SELECT y FROM Table2 WHERE <search condition>)" predicate converts to

```
. . . NOT EXISTS (SELECT *
                  FROM Table1, Table2
                  WHERE Table1.x <comp op> Table2.y
                  AND NOT <search condition>). . .
```

The "Table1 x <comp op> ANY (SELECT y FROM Table2 WHERE <search condition>)" predicate converts to

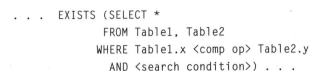

```
. . .  EXISTS (SELECT *
               FROM Table1, Table2
               WHERE Table1.x <comp op> Table2.y
               AND <search condition>) . . .
```

Of the two quantified predicates, the `<comp op>` ALL predicate is used more. The ANY predicate is more easily replaced and more naturally written with an EXISTS() predicate or an IN predicate. In fact, the SQL standard defines the IN predicate as shorthand for = ANY and the NOT IN predicate as shorthand for <> ANY, which is how most people would construct them in English.

The `<comp op>` ALL predicate is probably the more useful of the two since it cannot be written in terms of an IN predicate. The trick with it is to make sure that its subquery defines the set of values in which you are interested. For example, to find the authors whose books all sell for $19.95 or more, you could write

```
SELECT *
  FROM Authors AS A1
 WHERE  19.95 < ALL (SELECT price
                       FROM Books AS B1
                       WHERE A1.authorname = B1.authorname);
```

The best way to think of this is to reverse the usual English sentence "Show me all *x* that are *y*" in your mind so that it says "*y* is the value of all *x*" instead. We will see another use for this predicate in Chapter 24, "Regions, Runs, and Sequences."

16.3 The ALL Predicate and Extrema Functions

It is counterintuitive at first that these two predicates are not the same in SQL:

```
x >= (SELECT MAX(y) FROM Table1)
x >= ALL (SELECT y FROM Table1)
```

but you have to remember the rules for the extrema functions—they drop out all the NULLs before returning the greater or least values. The ALL predicate does not drop NULLs, so you can get them in the results.

However, if you know that there are no NULLs in a column or are willing to drop the NULLs yourself, you can use the ALL predicate to construct single queries to do work that would otherwise be done by two queries. For example, given the product manager table we used earlier in this chapter, to find which manager handles the largest number of products, you would first construct a grouped VIEW and group it again:

```
CREATE VIEW TotalProducts (manager, product_tally)
AS SELECT manager, COUNT(*)
     FROM Personnel
   GROUP BY manager;
```

```
SELECT manager
  FROM TotalProducts
 WHERE product_tally =
        (SELECT MAX(product_tally)
           FROM TotalProducts);
```

But Alex Dorfman found a single-query solution instead:

```
SELECT manager, COUNT(*)
  FROM Personnel
 GROUP BY manager
HAVING COUNT(*) + 1
      > ALL (SELECT DISTINCT COUNT(*)
               FROM Personnel
               GROUP BY manager);
```

The use of the SELECT DISTINCT in the subquery is to guarantee that we do not get duplicate rows when two managers handle the same number of products. You can also add a ". . . WHERE dept IS NOT NULL" clause to the subquery to get the effect of a true MAX() aggregate function.

16.4 UNIQUE Predicate

This subquery predicate is defined for Intermediate Level SQL-92 and is not widely implemented yet. It is a test for the absence of duplicate rows in a subquery. The UNIQUE keyword is also used as a table or column constraint, but don't confuse those two with this predicate. This predicate is used to define them. The UNIQUE column constraint is implemented in many SQL implementations with a CREATE UNIQUE INDEX <indexname> ON <table>(<column list>) statement. These are not the same thing.

The syntax for this predicate is

```
<unique predicate> ::= UNIQUE <table subquery>
```

If any two rows in the subquery are equal to each other, the predicate is FALSE. However, the definition in the standard is worded in the negative, so that NULLs get the benefit of the doubt. The query can be written as an EXISTS predicate that counts rows:

```
EXISTS (SELECT <column list>
          FROM <subquery>
          GROUP BY <column list>
          HAVING COUNT(*) > 1);
```

An empty subquery is always TRUE since you cannot find two rows, and therefore duplicates do not exist. This makes sense on the face of it.

NULLs are easier to explain with an example, say, a table with only two rows, ('a', 'b') and ('a', NULL). The first columns of each row are non-NULL and are equal to each other, so we have a match so far. The second column in the second row is NULL and cannot compare to anything, so we skip the second column pair and go with what we have, and the test is TRUE. This is giving the NULLs the benefit of the doubt, since the NULL in the second row could become 'b' some day and give us a duplicate row.

Now consider the case where the subquery has two rows, ('a', NULL) and ('a', NULL). The predicate is still TRUE because the NULLs do not test equal or unequal to each other—not because we are making NULLs equal to each other.

CHAPTER 17

The SELECT Statement

T HE GOOD NEWS about SQL is that the programmer only needs to learn the SELECT statement to do almost all his work! The bad news is that the statement can have so many nested clauses that it looks like a Victorian novel! The SELECT statement is used to query the database. It combines one or more tables, can do some calculations, and finally puts the results into a result table that can be passed on to the host language.

The SQL-89 SELECT statement is a subset of the SQL-92 SELECT statement, and in the first edition of this book, I favored SQL-89 syntax instead of SQL-92 syntax in the examples. When there was no SQL-89 syntax, I used the minimal SQL-92 syntax to do the job. But SQL implementations have more SQL-92 features today, so I have also used more of the newer syntax.

The one thing I have not done in this book is give a series of simple one-table SELECT statements. I am assuming that readers are experienced SQL programmers and got enough of those queries when they were learning SQL.

17.1 SELECT and JOINs

There is an order to the execution of the clauses of an SQL SELECT statement that does not seem to be covered in most beginning SQL books. It explains why some things work in SQL and others do not.

17.1.1 One-Level SELECT Statement

The simplest possible SELECT statement is just "SELECT * FROM Sometable;" which returns the entire table as it stands. You can actually write this as TABLE Sometable in SQL-92, but no product has that feature yet. Though the syntax rules say that all you need are the SELECT and FROM clauses, in practice there is almost always a WHERE clause.

Let's look at the SELECT statement in detail. The syntax for the statement is

```
SELECT [ALL | DISTINCT] <scalar expression list>
   FROM <table expression>
[WHERE <search condition>]
[GROUP BY <grouping column list>]
[HAVING <group condition>];
```

The order of execution is as follows:

1.   Execute the FROM <table expression> clause and construct the working result table defined in that clause. In SQL-89, the <table expression> is a list of tables or views that might be given correlation names, but it can get pretty fancy in SQL-92. The result is the CROSS JOIN (or the Cartesian product, to use an older term) of all the rows in the tables listed. What this does is take each row from the first table and concatenate each row from the second table to it to build a new row in the result table. You get all possible combinations.

     The result table preserves the order of the tables and the order of the rows within each in the result. The result table is different from other tables in that each column retains the table name from which it was derived. Thus, if table A and table B both have a column named x, there will be a column A.x and a column B.x in the results of the FROM clause. No product actually uses a CROSS JOIN to construct the intermediate table—the working table would get too large, too fast. For example, a 1,000-row table and a 1,000-row table would CROSS JOIN to get a 1,000,000-row working table. This is just the conceptual model we use to describe behavior.

     In SQL-92, the FROM can have all sorts of other table expressions, but the point is that they return a working table as a result. We will get into the details of those expressions later, with particular attention to the JOIN operators.

2. If there is a WHERE clause, the predicate in it is applied to each row of
    the FROM clause result table. The rows that test TRUE are retained; the
    rows that test FALSE or UNKNOWN are deleted from the working set.

    The WHERE clause is where the action is. The predicate can be
    quite complex and have nested subqueries. The syntax of a subquery
    is a SELECT statement, which is inside parentheses—failure to use
    parentheses is a common error for new SQL programmers. Sub-
    queries are where the original SQL got the name "Structured English
    Query Language"—the ability to nest SELECT statements was the
    "structured" part. We will deal with those in another section.

3. If there is a GROUP BY <grouping column list> clause, it is executed
    next. It uses the FROM and WHERE clause results and breaks these
    rows into groups where the columns in the <grouping column
    list> all have the same value. NULLs are treated as if they were all
    equal to each other and form their own group. Each group is then
    reduced to a single row in a new result table that replaces the old
    one. (See Chapter 20 on groups for more details.)

    Each row represents information about its group. SQL-92 does
    not allow you to use the name of a calculated column, such as
    (salary + commission) AS totalpay, in the GROUP BY clause
    because that column is named only in the SELECT clause of this
    query. However, you will find products that allow it because they
    create a result table first, using names in the SELECT cause, then fill
    it with rows created by the query. There are ways to get the same
    result by using VIEWs and tabular subquery expressions, which we
    will discuss later.

    Only four things make sense as group characteristics: the group-
    ing columns that define it, the aggregate functions that summarize
    group characteristics, function calls and constants, and expressions
    built from them.

4. If there is a HAVING clause, it is applied to each of the groups. The
    groups that test TRUE are retained; the groups that test FALSE or
    UNKNOWN are deleted. If there is no GROUP BY clause, the HAVING
    clause treats the whole table as a single group. SQL-92 prohibits cor-
    related queries in a HAVING clause.

    The <group condition> must apply to columns in the grouped
    working table or to group properties, not to the individual rows that
    originally built the group. Many implementations require that aggre-
    gate functions used in the HAVING clause also appear in the SELECT

clause, but that is not part of the standard. However, the SELECT clause of a grouped query must include all the grouping columns.

5.   Finally, the SELECT clause is applied to the result table. If a column does not appear in the <expression list>, it is dropped from the final results. Expressions can be constants or column names, or they can be calculations made from constants, columns, and functions.

   If the SELECT clause has the DISTINCT option, all the duplicate rows are deleted from the final results table. If the SELECT clause has the explicit ALL option or is missing the [ALL | DISTINCT], then all duplicate rows are preserved in the final results table. (Frankly, although it is legal syntax, nobody really uses the SELECT ALL option.) Finally, the results are returned.

Let's carry an example out in detail.

```
SELECT sex, COUNT(*), AVG(age), (MAX(age) - MIN(age)) AS age_range
  FROM Students, Gradebook
 WHERE grade = 'A'
   AND Students.stud_nbr = Gradebook.stud_nbr
 GROUP BY sex
HAVING COUNT(*) > 3;
```

The two starting tables look like this:

```
CREATE TABLE Students
(stud_nbr INTEGER PRIMARY KEY,
 sname CHAR(10) NOT NULL,
 sex CHAR(1) NOT NULL,
 age INTEGER NOT NULL);
```

Students

stud_nbr	sname	sex	age
1	'Smith'	'M'	16
2	'Smyth'	'F'	17
3	'Smoot'	'F'	16
4	'Adams'	'F'	17
5	'Jones'	'M'	16
6	'Celko'	'M'	17
7	'Vennor'	'F'	16
8	'Murray'	'M'	18

```
CREATE TABLE Gradebook
(stud_nbr INTEGER PRIMARY KEY,
grade CHAR(1) NOT NULL);
```

Gradebook

stud_nbr	grade
1	'A'
2	'B'
3	'C'
4	'D'
5	'A'
6	'A'
7	'A'
8	'A'

The CROSS JOIN in the FROM clause looks like this:

CROSS JOIN working table

Students				Gradebook	
stud_nbr	sname	sex	age	stud_nbr	grade
1	'Smith'	'M'	16	1	'A'
1	'Smith'	'M'	16	2	'B'
1	'Smith'	'M'	16	3	'C'
1	'Smith'	'M'	16	4	'D'
1	'Smith'	'M'	16	5	'A'
1	'Smith'	'M'	16	6	'A'
1	'Smith'	'M'	16	7	'A'
1	'Smith'	'M'	16	8	'A'
2	'Smyth'	'F'	17	1	'A'
2	'Smyth'	'F'	17	2	'B'
2	'Smyth'	'F'	17	3	'C'
2	'Smyth'	'F'	17	4	'D'
2	'Smyth'	'F'	17	5	'A'
2	'Smyth'	'F'	17	6	'A'
2	'Smyth'	'F'	17	7	'A'
2	'Smyth'	'F'	17	8	'A'
3	'Smoot'	'F'	16	1	'A'
3	'Smoot'	'F'	16	2	'B'

| Students | | | | | Gradebook | |
(cont.) stud_nbr	sname	sex	age		stud_nbr	grade
3	'Smoot'	'F'	16		3	'C'
3	'Smoot'	'F'	16		4	'D'
3	'Smoot'	'F'	16		5	'A'
3	'Smoot'	'F'	16		6	'A'
3	'Smoot'	'F'	16		7	'A'
3	'Smoot'	'F'	16		8	'A'
4	'Adams'	'F'	17		1	'A'
4	'Adams'	'F'	17		2	'B'
4	'Adams'	'F'	17		3	'C'
4	'Adams'	'F'	17		4	'D'
4	'Adams'	'F'	17		5	'A'
4	'Adams'	'F'	17		6	'A'
4	'Adams'	'F'	17		7	'A'
4	'Adams'	'F'	17		8	'A'
5	'Jones'	'M'	16		1	'A'
5	'Jones'	'M'	16		2	'B'
5	'Jones'	'M'	16		3	'C'
5	'Jones'	'M'	16		4	'D'
5	'Jones'	'M'	16		5	'A'
5	'Jones'	'M'	16		6	'A'
5	'Jones'	'M'	16		7	'A'
5	'Jones'	'M'	16		8	'A'
6	'Celko'	'M'	17		1	'A'
6	'Celko'	'M'	17		2	'B'
6	'Celko'	'M'	17		3	'C'
6	'Celko'	'M'	17		4	'D'
6	'Celko'	'M'	17		5	'A'
6	'Celko'	'M'	17		6	'A'
6	'Celko'	'M'	17		7	'A'
6	'Celko'	'M'	17		8	'A'
7	'Vennor'	'F'	16		1	'A'
7	'Vennor'	'F'	16		2	'B'
7	'Vennor'	'F'	16		3	'C'
7	'Vennor'	'F'	16		4	'D'
7	'Vennor'	'F'	16		5	'A'

7	'Vennor'	'F'	16	6	'A'
7	'Vennor'	'F'	16	7	'A'
7	'Vennor'	'F'	16	8	'A'
8	'Murray'	'M'	18	1	'A'
8	'Murray'	'M'	18	2	'B'
8	'Murray'	'M'	18	3	'C'
8	'Murray'	'M'	18	4	'D'
8	'Murray'	'M'	18	5	'A'
8	'Murray'	'M'	18	6	'A'
8	'Murray'	'M'	18	7	'A'
8	'Murray'	'M'	18	8	'A'

There are two predicates in the WHERE. The first predicate, grade = 'A', needs only the Students table. In fact, an optimizer in a real SQL engine would have removed those rows in the Students table that failed the test before doing the CROSS JOIN. The second predicate is Student.student = Gradebook.student, which requires both tables and the whole constructed row. Predicates that use two tables are called JOIN conditions for obvious reasons. Now remove the rows that don't meet the conditions. After the WHERE clause, the result table looks like this:

CROSS JOIN after WHERE clause

| Students | | | | Gradebook | |
stud_nbr	sname	sex	age	stud_nbr	grade
1	'Smith'	'M'	16	1	'A'
5	'Jones'	'M'	16	5	'A'
6	'Celko'	'M'	17	6	'A'
7	'Vennor'	'F'	16	7	'A'
8	'Murray'	'M'	18	8	'A'

We have a GROUP BY clause that will group the working table by sex:

by sex

| Students | | | | Gradebook | |
stud_nbr	sname	sex	age	stud_nbr	grade
1	'Smith'	'M'	16	1	A sex = 'M' group
5	'Jones'	'M'	16	5	A
6	'Celko'	'M'	17	6	A
8	'Murray'	'M'	18	8	A
7	'Vennor'	'F'	16	7	A sex = 'F' group

and the aggregate functions in the SELECT clause are computed for each group:

Aggregate functions

sex	COUNT(*)	AVG(age)	(MAX(age) – MIN(age)) AS age_range
'F'	1	16.00	(16 – 16) = 0
'M'	4	16.75	(18 – 16) = 2

The HAVING clause is applied to each group, the SELECT statement is applied last, and we get the final results:

Full query with HAVING clause

sex	COUNT(*)	AVG(age)	Age_range
'M'	4	16.75	2

Obviously, no real implementation actually produces these intermediate tables; that would be insanely expensive. They are just a model of how a statement works. In the case of SQL-92, the FROM clause can have JOINs and other operators that create working tables, but the same steps are followed in this order. A real query could have subqueries in the WHERE clause that would have to be parsed and expanded the same way.

17.1.2 Correlated Subqueries in a SELECT Statement

A *correlated subquery* is a subquery that references columns in the tables of its containing query. This is a way to "hide a loop" in SQL. Consider a query to find all the students who are younger than the oldest student of their gender:

```
SELECT *
  FROM Students AS S1
 WHERE age < (SELECT MAX(age)
               FROM Students AS S2
              WHERE S1.sex = S2.sex);
```

1. A copy of the table is made for each correlation name, S1 and S2. Students AS S1

stud_nbr	sname	sex	age
1	'Smith'	'M'	16
2	'Smyth'	'F'	17

3	'Smoot'	'F'	16
4	'Adams'	'F'	17
5	'Jones'	'M'	16
6	'Celko'	'M'	17
7	'Vennor'	'F'	16
8	'Murray'	'M'	18

2. When you get to the WHERE clause and find the innermost query, you will see that you need to get data from the containing query. The model of execution says that each outer row has the subquery executed on it in parallel with the other rows. Assume we are working on student (1,'Smith'), who is male. The query in effect becomes

```
SELECT 1, 'Smith', 'M', 16
  FROM Students AS S1
 WHERE 16 < (SELECT MAX(age)
               FROM Students AS S2
              WHERE 'M' = S2.sex);
```

3. The subquery can now be calculated for male students; the maximum age is 18. When we expand this out for all the other rows, this will give us

```
SELECT 1, 'Smith', 'M', 16 FROM Students AS S1 WHERE 16 < 18;
SELECT 2, 'Smyth', 'F', 17 FROM Students AS S1 WHERE 17 < 17;
SELECT 3, 'Smoot', 'F', 16 FROM Students AS S1 WHERE 16 < 17;
SELECT 4, 'Adams', 'F', 17 FROM Students AS S1 WHERE 17 < 17;
SELECT 5, 'Jones', 'M', 16 FROM Students AS S1 WHERE 16 < 18;
SELECT 6, 'Celko', 'M', 17 FROM Students AS S1 WHERE 17 < 18;
SELECT 7, 'Vennor', 'F', 16 FROM Students AS S1 WHERE 16 < 17;
SELECT 8, 'Murray', 'M', 18 FROM Students AS S1 WHERE 18 < 18;
```

4. These same steps have been done for each row in the containing query. The model is that all of the subqueries are resolved at once, but again, no implementation really does it that way. The usual approach is to build procedural loops in the database engine that scan through both tables. Which table is in which loop is decided by the optimizer. The final results are

stud_nbr	sname	sex	age
1	'Smith'	'M'	16
3	'Smoot'	'F'	16
5	'Jones'	'M'	16
6	'Celko'	'M'	17
7	'Vennor'	'F'	16

17.1.3 SQL-92 SELECT Statement

To ensure upward compatibility, an SQL-89 statement will produce the same results in SQL-92. However, the SQL-92 syntax for JOINs is an infixed operator in the FROM clause. The JOIN operators are quite general and flexible, allowing you to do things in a single statement that you could not do in the older notation. The basic syntax is

```
<joined table> ::=
    <cross join> | <qualified join> | (<joined table>)

<cross join> ::= <table reference> CROSS JOIN <table reference>

<qualified join> ::=
    <table reference> [NATURAL] [<join type>] JOIN
        <table reference> [<join specification>]

<join specification> ::= <join condition> | <named columns join>

<join condition> ::= ON <search condition>

<named columns join> ::= USING (<join column list>)

<join type> ::= INNER | <outer join type> [OUTER] | UNION

<outer join type> ::= LEFT | RIGHT | FULL

<join column list> ::= <column name list>

<table reference> ::=
    <table name> [[AS] <correlation name>[(<derived column list>)]]
        | <derived table>
            [AS] <correlation name> [(<derived column list>)]
        | <joined table>

<derived table> ::= <table subquery>
```

```
<column name list> ::=
    <column name> [{ <comma> <column name> } . . . ]
```

The INNER JOIN and CROSS JOIN were all you had in the SQL-89 standard. An INNER JOIN is done by forming the CROSS JOIN and then removing the rows that do not meet the JOIN specification given in the ON clause, as we just showed in the last section. The ON clause can be as elaborate as you want to make it, as long as it refers to tables and columns within its scope. If a <qualified join> is used without a <join type>, INNER is implicit.

However, in the real world, most INNER JOINs are done using equality tests on columns with the same names in different tables, rather than on elaborate predicates. Equi-joins are so common that SQL-92 has two short-hand ways of specifying them. The USING (c1, c2, . . . , cn) clause takes the column names in the list and replaces them with the clause ON ((T1.c1, T1.c2, . . . , T1.cn) = (T2.c1, T2.c2, . . . , T2.cn)). Likewise, the NATURAL option is shorthand for a USING() clause that is a list of all the column names that are common to both tables. If NATURAL is specified, a JOIN specification cannot be given; it is already there.

The UNION JOIN and OUTER JOIN are topics in themselves and will be covered in separate sections.

17.1.4 The ORDER BY Clause

Contrary to popular belief, the ORDER BY clause is not part of the SELECT statement; it is part of a CURSOR declaration. People think it is part of the SELECT statement because the only way you can get to the result set of a query in a host language is via a cursor, so when a vendor tool builds a cursor under the covers for you, it usually allows you to include an ORDER BY clause on the query.

Most optimizers will look at the result set and see from the query if it is already in sorted order as a result of fetches done with an index, thus avoiding a redundant sorting operation. The bad news is that many programmers have written code that depends on the way that their particular release of a particular brand of SQL product presented the result. This automatic ordering can disappear when an index is dropped or changed, or when the database is upgraded to a new release or ported to another product.

As part of a cursor, the ORDER BY clause has some properties that you probably did not know existed. But first let's get the syntax correct.

```
<order by clause> ::=
    ORDER BY <sort specification list>
```

```
<sort specification list> ::=
    <sort specification> [{ <comma> <sort specification> } . . . ]

<sort specification> ::=
    <sort key> [<collate clause >] [<ordering specification>]

<sort key> ::= <column name> | <unsigned integer>

<ordering specification> ::= ASC | DESC
```

The first thing to note is that the sort keys are either column names or the positional number of the column within the result table in the cursor. The use of the positional number of a column is a deprecated feature in SQL-92. *Deprecation* is a term in the standards world meaning this feature will be removed from the next release of the standard (in this case, SQL-99) and should therefore not be used, and that old code should be updated.

The column names used are the names that appear in the result query and not the names used in the original tables. These are illegal sorts:

```
SELECT a, (b+c) AS d  -- illegal!!
  FROM Foobar
 ORDER BY a, b, c;
```

The columns b and c simply do not exist in the result set of the cursor, so there is no way to sort on them.

```
SELECT a, b, c -- illegal!!
  FROM Foobar
 ORDER BY SIN(a), COS(b);
```

You cannot sort on a function result, only a column, but this is a common vendor extension.

The sort order is based on the collation sequence of the column to which it is attached. In full SQL-92, the collation can be defined in the schema on character columns, but in most SQL products today collation is either ASCII or EBCDIC.

Whether a sort key value that is NULL is considered greater or less than a non-NULL value is implementation-defined, but all sort key values that are NULL will either be considered greater than all non-NULL values or be considered less than all non-NULL values. There are SQL products that do it either way. And there are those that have it all wrong; the Sybase family simply treats the NULLs as if they were really values—that is, they sort low for ascending and high for descending.

In 1999 March, Chris Farrar received a question from one of Compaq's developers that caused him to examine a part of the SQL standard that I thought I understood. Farrar then found some differences between the general understanding and the actual wording of the specification. The situation can be described as follows: a table, Sortable, with two integer columns, a and b, containing two rows that happen to be in this physical order:

Sortable

a	b
NULL	8
NULL	4

Given the pseudoquery

```
SELECT a, b
  FROM Sortable
 ORDER BY a, b;
```

the first question is whether it is legal SQL-92 for the cursor to produce the result sequence

Cursor Result Sequence

a	b
NULL	8
NULL	4

The problem is that while the standard set a rule to make the NULLs group together either before or after the known values, it did not specify whether they have to act as if they were equal to each other. What is missing is a statement that when comparing NULL to NULL, the result in the context of ORDER BY is that NULL is equal to NULL, just as it is in a GROUP BY. This was the intent of the committee, so the expected result should have been

Cursor Result Sequence

a	b
NULL	4
NULL	8

Phil Shaw, former IBM representative and a long-standing member of the committee, dug up the section of the SQL-89 standard that addressed this question. In SQL-89, this was specified by the last General Rule of `<compar-ison predicate>`:

> Although "$x = y$" is unknown if both x and y are NULL values, in the context of GROUP BY, ORDER BY, and DISTINCT, a NULL value is identical to or is a duplicate of another NULL value.

That's the rule that causes all NULLs to go into the same group in GROUP BY, rather than each into its own group. Applying that rule, and then applying the rules for ORDER BY, the NULL values of column a of the two rows are equal, so you have to order the rows by the columns to the right in the ORDER BY. Which is what every SQL product does. Hopefully, by the time that this book is in print, this matter will have been settled.

The sort keys are applied from left to right, and a column name can appear only once in the list. But there is no obligation on the part of SQL to use a stable (sequence-preserving) sort. A stable sort on cities, followed by a stable order on states, would result in a list with cities sorted within each state, and the states sorted. While stability is a nice property, nonstable sorts are generally much faster.

Cursors include an `<updatability clause>`, which tells you if the cursor is FOR READ ONLY or for UPDATE [OF `<column name list>`], but this clause is optional. If ORDER BY is specified or if the result table is a read-only table, then the `<updatability clause>` defaults to FOR READ ONLY.

17.2 OUTER JOINs

OUTER JOINs exist in most current SQL implementations, but they use a vendor syntax rather than the ANSI SQL-92 syntax. The recent ODBC specification from Microsoft, SQL Anywhere (nee WATCOM SQL), and other products are now using all or part of the SQL-92 syntax, and we can expect other vendors to follow.

An OUTER JOIN is a JOIN that preserves all the rows in one or both tables, even when they do not have matching rows in the second table. Let's take a real-world situation. I have a table of orders and a table of suppliers that I wish to join for a report to tell us how much business we did with each supplier. With a NATURAL JOIN, the query would be this:

```
SELECT Suppliers.supno, supname, orderno, amt
  FROM Suppliers, Orders
 WHERE Suppliers.supno = Orders.supno;
```

Some suppliers' totals include credits for returned merchandise, and our total business with them works out to zero dollars. Other suppliers never got an order from us at all, so we did zero dollars' worth of business with them, too. But the first case will show up in the query result and be passed on to the report, whereas the second case will disappear in the INNER JOIN.

If we had used an OUTER JOIN, preserving the Suppliers table, we would have all the suppliers in the results. When a supplier with no orders was found in the Orders table, the orderno and amt columns would be given a NULL value in the result row.

17.2.1 Vendor Syntax for OUTER JOINs

In the old SQL-89 standard, there was no OUTER JOIN, so in products like earlier versions of DB2 from IBM you had to construct it by hand with a messy UNION:

```
SELECT supno, supname, amt      -- regular INNER JOIN
  FROM Suppliers, Orders
 WHERE Suppliers.supno = Orders.supno
UNION ALL
SELECT supno, supname, NULL    -- preserved rows of LEFT JOIN
  FROM Suppliers
 WHERE NOT EXISTS (SELECT *
                     FROM Orders
                    WHERE Suppliers.supno = Orders.supno);
```

The SQL-89 standard actually does not allow NULL to appear as a value expression in a SELECT clause list, but it is a very common vendor extension. DB2 and a few other versions of SQL followed the SQL-89 standard, so they would have to replace NULL with a constant of the correct datatype to make the UNION work. This is easy in the case of a CHARACTER column, where a message like '<<NONE>>' can be quickly understood. It is much harder to do in the case of a numeric column, where we could have a balance with a supplier that is positive, zero, or negative because of returns and credits. There really is a difference between a supplier that we did not use and a supplier whose returns canceled out its orders.

The most common vendor extensions are just for the LEFT OUTER JOIN. They use a plus sign or an asterisk to mark the preserved table. The special token either is put on the table name (XDB, DB2, Oracle, and SQLBase use (+) after the table name) or is part of an extended equality sign (Sybase uses *=, Universe uses =?, and so forth). The important property of either syntax is that an extended equality sign appears in the WHERE clause, and this has some side effects. The LEFT OUTER JOIN for our example might be written as

```
SELECT supno, supname, orderno, amt
  FROM Suppliers, Orders
 WHERE Suppliers.supno *= Orders.supno;
```

The name LEFT OUTER JOIN comes from the fact that the preserved table is on the left side of the equality sign. Likewise, a RIGHT OUTER JOIN would have the preserved table on the right-hand side, and the FULL OUTER JOIN would preserve both tables. These extended equality notations have a lot of problems, which is why they were not used in SQL-92. A table cannot be both preserved and unpreserved in the same WHERE clause in implementations that use this notation, so self OUTER JOINs are impossible without using VIEWs. The only JOIN condition allowed is equality, so you cannot write other outer theta JOINs. In fact, you cannot safely write something like NOT (Suppliers.supno *= Orders.supno) and predict the results. And, worst of all, the simple syntax is ambiguous.

Even WATCOM SQL Version 4.0, which was the best implementation of the SQL-92 OUTER JOIN syntax at that time, had many problems with resolving nested INNER JOIN and OUTER JOIN operations. For example, the WATCOM NATURAL operator set up an equi-join on columns that had the same names in both tables, but did not collapse the pair into a single column with the common name in the results. Thus, both column names were available to the next JOIN, which could lead to serious conflicts.

Here is how OUTER JOINs work in SQL-92. Assume you are given

Table1

a	b
1	w
2	x
3	y
4	z

Table2

a	c
1	r
2	s
3	t

and the OUTER JOIN expression

```
Table1
LEFT OUTER JOIN
Table2
```

```
ON Table1.a = Table2.a       <== join condition
   AND Table2.c = 't';        <== single table condition
```

We call Table1 the "preserved table" and Table2 the "unpreserved table" in the query. What I am going to give you is a little different, but equivalent to the ANSI/ISO standards.

1. We build the CROSS JOIN of the two tables. Scan each row in the result set.

2. If the predicate tests TRUE for that row, you keep it. You also remove all rows derived from it from the CROSS JOIN.

3. If the predicate tests FALSE or UNKNOWN for that row, keep the columns from the preserved table, convert all the columns from the unpreserved table to NULLs, and remove the duplicates.

So let us execute this by hand:

Let @ = passed the first predicate

Let * = passed the second predicate

Table1 CROSS JOIN Table2

a	b	a	c
1	w	1	r @
1	w	2	s
1	w	3	t *
2	x	1	r
2	x	2	s @
2	x	3	t *
3	y	1	r
3	y	2	s
3	y	3	t @* <== the TRUE set
4	z	1	r
4	z	2	s
4	z	3	t *

Table1 LEFT OUTER JOIN Table2

a	b	a	c	
3	y	3	t	<= only TRUE row
1	w	NULL	NULL	Sets of duplicates
1	w	NULL	NULL	
1	w	NULL	NULL	
2	x	NULL	NULL	
2	x	NULL	NULL	
2	x	NULL	NULL	
3	y	NULL	NULL	<== derived from the TRUE set - Remove
3	y	NULL	NULL	
4	z	NULL	NULL	
4	z	NULL	NULL	
4	z	NULL	NULL	

This yields the final results:

Table1 LEFT OUTER JOIN Table2

a	b	a	c
1	w	NULL	NULL
2	x	NULL	NULL
3	y	3	t
4	z	NULL	NULL

The basic rule is that every row in the preserved table is represented in the results in at least one result row.

There are limitations and very serious problems with the extended equality version of an OUTER JOIN used in some diseased, mutant products. Consider the two Chris Date tables:

Supplier   SupParts

supno	supno	partno	qty
S1	S1	P1	100
S2	S1	P2	250
S3	S2	P1	100
	S2	P2	250

Let's do an extended equality OUTER JOIN like this:

```
SELECT *
 FROM Supplier, SupParts
WHERE Supplier.supno *= SupParts.supno
  AND qty < 200;
```

If I do the OUTER JOIN first, I get

Suppliers LOJ SupParts

supno	supno	partno	qty
S1	S1	P1	100
S1	S1	P2	250
S2	S2	P1	100
S2	S2	P2	250
S3	NULL	NULL	NULL

Then I apply the (qty < 200) predicate and get

Suppliers LOJ SupParts

supno	supno	partno	qty
S1	S1	P1	100
S2	S2	P1	100

Doing it in the opposite order yields

Suppliers LOJ SupParts

supno	supno	partno	qty
S1	S1	P1	100
S2	S2	P1	100
S3	NULL	NULL	NULL

Sybase does it one way, Oracle does it the other, and Centura (nee Gupta) lets you pick which one—the worst of both nonstandard worlds! In SQL-92, you have a choice and can force the order of execution. Either do the predicates after the JOIN . . .

```
SELECT *
  FROM Supplier
       LEFT OUTER JOIN
       SupParts
```

```
        ON Supplier.supno = SupParts.supno
WHERE qty < 200;
```

. . . or do it in the joining:

```
SELECT *
 FROM Supplier
      LEFT OUTER JOIN
      SupParts
      ON Supplier.supno = SupParts.supno
        AND qty < 200;
```

Another problem is that you cannot show the same table as preserved and unpreserved in the extended equality version, but doing so is easy in SQL-92. For example, to find the students who have taken Math 101 and might have taken Math 102:

```
SELECT C1.student, C1.math, C2.math
  FROM (SELECT * FROM Courses WHERE math = 'Math 101') AS C1
       LEFT OUTER JOIN
       (SELECT * FROM Courses WHERE math = 'Math 102') AS C2
       ON C1.student = C2.student;
```

As an actual example you can try yourself, consider this problem from Jarle Javenes to compare OUTER JOINs run on Centura SQLBase and Sybase SQLServer 11.

```
CREATE TABLE A (type INTEGER NOT NULL, nbr INTEGER NOT NULL);
CREATE TABLE B (nbr INTEGER NOT NULL, name CHAR(10) NOT NULL);

INSERT INTO A VALUES (1, 1), (2, 2), (3, 3), (4, 4);
INSERT INTO B VALUES (1, 'Joe'), (2, 'Debbie');
```

This query gives the same result for both databases.

```
SELECT *
  FROM A, B
 WHERE A.nbr *= B.nbr;
```

A.type	A.nbr	B.nbr	B.name
1	1	1	'Joe'
2	2	2	'Debbie'

| 3 | 3 | NULL | NULL |
| 4 | 4 | NULL | NULL |

However, this second query produces different results.

```
SELECT *
  FROM B, A
 WHERE B.nbr *= A.nbr
   AND name = 'Joe';
```

Result for Sybase 11.0

A.type	A.nbr	B.nbr	B.name
1	1	1	'Joe'
2	2	NULL	NULL
3	3	NULL	NULL
4	4	NULL	NULL

Result for Centura SQLBase

A.type	A.nbr	B.nbr	B.name
1	1	1	'Joe'

17.2.2 SQL-92 Syntax for JOINs

The SQL-92 syntax for OUTER JOINs is an infixed operator in the FROM clause. The SQL-92 syntax also defines other types of JOINs, some of which are discussed in other parts of this book. Since the OUTER JOIN is being implemented, it is more important than some of the really exotic JOINs. Right now, the OUTER JOIN operators that are actually implemented use only a subset of the possible options. This flexibility allows you to do things that you could not do in any reasonable fashion in the older notation. Below is a realistic version of what an OUTER JOIN syntax will be in your actual SQL product.

Remember to read the manual and find out what is there. Assuming that supno is the only column that appears with the same name in both the Suppliers and the Orders tables, our example of orders and suppliers could be written as

```
SELECT supno, supname, orderno, amt
  FROM Suppliers LEFT OUTER JOIN Orders
       ON (Suppliers.supno = Orders.supno);
```

or

```
SELECT supno, supname, orderno, amt
  FROM Suppliers LEFT OUTER JOIN Orders
       USING (supno);
```

or

```
SELECT supno, supname, orderno, amt
 FROM Suppliers NATURAL LEFT OUTER JOIN Orders;
```

An interesting feature of the SQL-92 standard is that a SELECT expression that returns a single row with a single value can be used where a scalar expression can be used. If the result of the scalar query is empty, it is converted to a NULL. This will sometimes—not always!—let you write an OUTER JOIN as a query within the SELECT clause. Thus, this query will work only if each supplier has one or zero orders:

```
SELECT supno, supname, orderno,
       (SELECT amt FROM Orders WHERE Suppliers.supno =
       Orders.supno) AS amt
  FROM Suppliers;
```

However, I could write

```
SELECT supno, supname,
       (SELECT COUNT(*)
          FROM Orders
         WHERE Suppliers.supno = Orders.supno)
 FROM Suppliers;
```

instead of writing

```
SELECT supno, supname, COUNT(*)
  FROM Suppliers LEFT OUTER JOIN Orders
       ON (Suppliers.supno = Orders.supno)
 GROUP BY supno, supname;
```

Though the standard OUTER JOIN syntax is still new to most implementations, it would seem reasonable that it will be more efficient than a correlated subquery in the SELECT list. However, you should experiment with your particular product to find out which is better.

17.2.3 NULLs and OUTER JOINs

The NULLs generated by the OUTER JOIN can occur in columns derived from source table columns that have been declared to be NOT NULL. Even if you tried to avoid all the problems with NULLs by making every column in every table of your database schema NOT NULL, they could still occur in OUTER JOIN results. However, a table can have NULLs and still be used in an OUTER JOIN. Consider different JOINs on the following two tables, which have NULLs in the common column:

T1		T2	
a	**x**	**b**	**x**
1	'r'	7	'r'
2	'v'	8	's'
3	NULL	9	NULL

A natural INNER JOIN on column x can only match those values that are equal to each other. But NULLs do not match to anything, not even to other NULLs. Thus, there is one row in the result, on the value 'r' in column x in both tables.

T1 INNER JOIN T2 ON (T1.x = T2.x)

a	**T1.x**	**b**	**T2.x**
1	'r'	7	'r'

Now do a LEFT OUTER JOIN on the tables, which will preserve table T1, and you get

T1 LEFT OUTER JOIN T2 ON (T1.x = T2.x)

a	**T1.x**	**b**	**T2.x**
1	'r'	7	'r'
2	'v'	NULL	NULL
3	NULL	NULL	NULL

Again, there are no surprises. The original INNER JOIN row is still in the results. The other two rows of T1 that were not in the equi-JOIN do show up in the results, and the columns derived from table T2 are filled with NULLs. The RIGHT OUTER JOIN would also behave the same way. The problems start with the FULL OUTER JOIN, which looks like this:

```
T1 FULL OUTER JOIN T2 ON (T1.x = T2.x)
```

a	T1.x	b	T2.x
1	'r'	7	'r'
2	'v'	NULL	NULL
3	NULL	NULL	NULL
NULL	NULL	8	's'
NULL	NULL	9	NULL

The way this result is constructed is worth explaining in detail. First, do an INNER JOIN on T1 and T2, using the ON clause condition, and put those rows (if any) in the results. Then all rows in T1 that could not be joined are padded out with NULLs in the columns derived from T2 and inserted into the results. Finally, take the rows in T2 that could not be joined, pad them out with NULLs, and insert them into the results. The bad news is that the original tables cannot be reconstructed from an OUTER JOIN. Look at the results of the FULL OUTER JOIN, which we will call R1, and SELECT the first columns from it:

```
SELECT T1.a, T1.x FROM R1
```

a	x
1	'r'
2	'v'
3	NULL
NULL	NULL
NULL	NULL

The created NULLs remain and cannot be differentiated from the original NULLs. But you cannot throw out those duplicate rows because they may be in the original table T1. Since many products have only a LEFT OUTER JOIN, beginning programmers might try to construct a FULL OUTER JOIN with

```
SELECT * FROM T1 LEFT OUTER JOIN T2 ON (T1.x = T2.x)
  UNION ALL
SELECT * FROM T2 LEFT OUTER JOIN T1 ON (T1.x = T2.x);
```

But the UNION ALL will give you false duplicate rows from the rows that were part of the INNER JOIN, namely, (1, 'r', 7, 'r') in this example. However, a simple UNION could remove true duplicate rows from the original tables.

17.2.4 NATURAL versus Conditional OUTER JOINs

It is worth mentioning in passing that the SQL-92 standard has a NATURAL LEFT OUTER JOIN, but it is not implemented in most current versions of SQL. Even those that have the syntax are actually creating an ON clause with equality tests, like the examples we have been using in this section.

A NATURAL JOIN has only one copy of the common column pairs in its result. The conditional OUTER JOIN has both of the original columns, with their table-qualified names. The NATURAL JOIN has to have a correlation name for the result table to identify the shared columns. We can build a NAT- URAL LEFT OUTER JOIN by using the COALESCE() function to combine the common column pairs into a single column and put the results into a VIEW where the columns can be properly named, thus:

```
CREATE VIEW NLOJ12 (x, a, b)
AS SELECT COALESCE(T1.x, T2.x), T1.a, T2.b
     FROM T1 LEFT OUTER JOIN T2 ON T1.x = T2.x;
```

NLOJ12

x	a	b
'r'	1	7
'v'	2	NULL
NULL	3	NULL

Unlike the NATURAL JOINs, the conditional OUTER JOIN does not have to use a simple one-column equality as the join condition. The condition can have several predicates, use other comparisons, and so forth—for example,

```
T1 LEFT OUTER JOIN T2 ON (T1.x < T2.x)
```

a	T1.x	b	T2.x
1	'r'	8	's'
2	'v'	NULL	NULL
3	NULL	NULL	NULL

as compared to

```
T1 LEFT OUTER JOIN T2 ON (T1.x > T2.x)
```

a	T1.x	b	T2.x
1	'r'	NULL	NULL
2	'v'	7	'r'
2	'v'	8	's'
3	NULL	NULL	NULL

Again, so much of current OUTER JOIN behavior is vendor-specific that you should experiment with the particular product you are using to see what actually happens.

17.2.5 Self-OUTER JOINs

There is no rule that forbids an OUTER JOIN on the same table. In fact, the self-OUTER JOIN is a good trick for "flattening" a normalized table into a horizontal report. To illustrate the method, start with a table defined as

```
CREATE TABLE Credits
(student INTEGER NOT NULL,
 course CHAR(8) NOT NULL);
```

This table represents student numbers and a course code for each class they have taken. However, our rules say that students cannot get credit for CS-102 until they have taken the prerequisite CS-101 course, they cannot get credit for CS-103 until they have taken the prerequisite CS-102 course, and so forth. Let's first load the table with some sample values. Notice that student 1 has taken both courses, student 2 has only the first of the series, and student 3 jumped ahead of sequence and therefore cannot get credit for his CS-102 course until he goes back and takes CS-101.

Credits

student	course
1	'CS-101'
1	'CS-102'
2	'CS-101'
3	'CS-102'

What we want is basically a histogram (bar chart) for each student, showing how far they have gone in their degree programs. Assume that we are looking only at two courses; the result of the desired query might look like this (NULL is used to represent a missing value):

```
(1, 'CS-101', 'CS-102')
(2, 'CS-101', NULL)
```

Clearly, this will need a self-JOIN, since the last two columns come from the same table, Credits. You have to give correlation names to both uses of the Credits table in the OUTER JOIN operator when you construct a self-OUTER JOIN, just as you would with any other self-JOIN, thus:

```
SELECT student, C1.course, C2.course
  FROM Credits AS C1 LEFT OUTER JOIN Credits AS C2
       ON C1.student = C2.student
          AND C1.course = 'CS-101'
          AND C2.course = 'CS-102';
```

17.2.6 Two or More OUTER JOINs

Some relational purists feel that every operator should have an inverse, and therefore they do not like the OUTER JOIN. Others feel that the created NULLs are fundamentally different from the explicit NULLs in a base table and should have a special token. SQL uses its general-purpose NULLs and leaves things at that. Regardless of what theory may say, you also will find that vendors have often done strange things with the ways their products work.

A major problem is that OUTER JOIN operators do not have the same properties as INNER JOIN operators. The order in which FULL OUTER JOINs are executed will change the results (a mathematician would say that they are not associative). To show some of the problems that can come up when you have more than two tables, let us use three very simple two-column tables. Notice that some of the column values match and some do not match, but the three tables contain all possible pairs of column names.

```
CREATE TABLE T1 (a INTEGER NOT NULL, b INTEGER NOT NULL);
INSERT INTO T1 VALUES (1, 2);

CREATE TABLE T2 (a INTEGER NOT NULL, c INTEGER NOT NULL);
INSERT INTO T2 VALUES (1, 3);

CREATE TABLE T3 (b INTEGER NOT NULL, c INTEGER NOT NULL);
INSERT INTO T3 VALUES (2, 100);
```

Now let's try some of the possible orderings of the three tables in a chain of LEFT OUTER JOINs. The problem is that a table can be preserved or unpreserved in the immediate JOIN and in the opposite state in the containing JOIN.

```
SELECT T1.a, T1.b, T3.c
   FROM ((T1 NATURAL LEFT OUTER JOIN T2)
      NATURAL LEFT OUTER JOIN T3);
```

Result

a	b	c
1	2	NULL

```
SELECT T1.a, T1.b, T3.c
   FROM ((T1 NATURAL LEFT OUTER JOIN T3)
      NATURAL LEFT OUTER JOIN T2);
```

Result

a	b	c
1	2	100

```
SELECT T1.a, T1.b, T3.c
   FROM ((T2 NATURAL LEFT OUTER JOIN T3)
      NATURAL LEFT OUTER JOIN T2);
```

Result

a	b	c
NULL	NULL	NULL

Even worse, the choice of column in the SELECT list can change the output. Instead of displaying T3.c, use T2.c and you will get

```
SELECT T1.a, T1.b, T2.c
   FROM ((T2 NATURAL LEFT OUTER JOIN T3)
      NATURAL LEFT OUTER JOIN T1);
```

Result

a	b	c
NULL	NULL	3

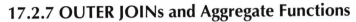

17.2.7 OUTER JOINs and Aggregate Functions

At the start of this chapter, we had a table of orders and a table of suppliers, which were to be used to build a report to tell us how much business we did with each supplier. The query that will do this is

```
SELECT Suppliers.supno, supname, SUM(amt)
  FROM Suppliers LEFT OUTER JOIN Orders
       ON Suppliers.supno = Orders.supno
 GROUP BY supno, supname;
```

Some suppliers' totals include credits for returned merchandise, such that our total business with them worked out to zero dollars. Each supplier with which we did no business will have a NULL in its amt column in the OUTER JOIN. The usual rules for aggregate functions with NULL values apply, so these suppliers will also show a zero total amount. It is possible to use a function inside an aggregate function, so you could write SUM(COALESCE (T1.x, T2.x)) for the common column pairs.

If you need to tell the difference between a true sum of zero and the result of a NULL in an OUTER JOIN, use the MIN() or MAX() function on the questionable column. These functions both return a NULL result for a NULL input, so an expression inside the MAX() function could be used to print the message MAX(COALESCE(amt, 'No Orders')), for example.

Likewise, these functions could be used in a HAVING clause, but that would defeat the purpose of using an OUTER JOIN.

17.2.8 FULL OUTER JOIN

The FULL OUTER JOIN was introduced in SQL-92, but has not been implemented in most SQLs yet. This operator is a mix of the LEFT and RIGHT OUTER JOINs, with preserved rows constructed from both tables. The statement takes two tables and puts them in one result table. Again, this is easier to explain with an example than with a formal definition. It is also a way to show how to form a query that will perform the same function. Using Suppliers and Orders again, we find that we have suppliers with which we have done no business, but we also have orders for which we have not decided on suppliers. To get all orders and all suppliers in one result table, we could use the SQL-89 query:

```
SELECT supno, supname, amt      -- regular INNER JOIN
  FROM Suppliers, Orders
 WHERE Suppliers.supno = Orders.supno
```

```
UNION ALL
SELECT supno, supname, NULL   -- preserved rows of LEFT JOIN
   FROM Suppliers
  WHERE NOT EXISTS (SELECT *
                        FROM Orders
                       WHERE Suppliers.supno = Orders.supno)
UNION ALL
SELECT NULL, NULL, amt     -- preserved rows of RIGHT JOIN
   FROM Orders
  WHERE NOT EXISTS (SELECT *
                        FROM Suppliers
                       WHERE Suppliers.supno = Orders.supno);
```

The same thing in SQL-92 would be

```
SELECT supno, supname, amt
   FROM Orders FULL OUTER JOIN Suppliers
        ON (Suppliers.supno = Orders.supno);
```

The FULL OUTER JOIN is not used as much as a LEFT or RIGHT OUTER JOIN. Reports are usually done from a viewpoint that leads to preserving only one side of the JOIN. That is, you might ask, "What suppliers got no business from us?" or ask, "What orders have not been assigned a supplier?" but a combination of the two questions is not likely to be in the same report.

17.2.9 WHERE Clause OUTER JOIN Operators

As we have seen, SQL engines that use special operators in the WHERE clause for OUTER JOIN syntax get strange results. But with the SQL-92 syntax for OUTER JOINs, the programmer has to be careful in the WHERE to qualify the JOIN columns of the same name to be sure that he picks up the preserved column. Both of these are legal queries:

```
SELECT *
  FROM T1 LEFT OUTER JOIN T2
       ON T1.a = T2.a
 WHERE T1.a = 15;
```

and

```
SELECT *
  FROM T1 LEFT OUTER JOIN T2
```

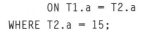

```
        ON T1.a = T2.a
 WHERE T2.a = 15;
```

However, the second one will reject the rows with generated NULLs in them. If that is what you wanted, then why bother with an OUTER JOIN in the first place?

17.3 Old versus New JOIN Syntax

ODBC and other call-level interfaces support at least the SQL-92 LEFT OUTER JOIN syntax, often by translating the SQL statement passed from the application into the proprietary syntax of the backend database. With the SQL/CLI standard in place now, you can expect to see more and more products with the full SQL-92 JOIN syntax.

However, you may find that using the INNER JOIN instead of putting the JOIN conditions in the WHERE clause does not work as well. Most optimizers will do elaborate inspections in the WHERE clause, but have not yet gotten the same degree of sophistication with the explicit operators in the new syntax. Instead, the JOINs are executed in the order in which they appear, in effect letting you write out an execution plan yourself. If you wanted to do that, this is great, but it can also harm you.

When the JOIN conditions were in the WHERE clause, the optimizer picked the best order of execution it could find. Recompiling in the old syntax would force the optimizer to look at current indexes, statistics, and whatever else it used for its decisions and produce a completely new plan based on the current state of the database.

However, a FROM clause with heavily parenthesized JOIN operators can be forced into one and only one JOIN sequence for the tables; this means the only optimization open to it would be to look for new indexes. This will not be true in a few years, after the new syntax is integrated into the SQL products, but it means that you should test different versions of the same query for speed.

17.4 Exotic JOINs

Most JOINs are done using an equality test between the columns in the JOINed tables. In fact, of these equi-JOINs, the columns usually have the same names, so we give them the special name NATURAL JOINs. Among NATURAL JOINs, the most common case is a foreign key to the primary key of the table it references. Since these simple JOINs constitute 80% to 85% of the SQL queries in real applications, it is easy to forget that you can also have other kinds of JOINs. This section will discuss other types of JOINs that are not used often, but are very helpful when they are needed. For lack of a better term, I am calling them exotic JOINs.

17.4.1 Self Non-Equi-JOINs

A non-equi-JOIN is simply that—a JOIN based on a comparison other than an equality in columns of the two tables. Here are some common uses for them. A self-JOIN is a JOIN of one copy of a table to itself or to a subset of itself. A common use for a self non-equi-JOIN is to JOIN a table to itself in such a way as to avoid making redundant pairs. For example, you are given a table of products and you want to make a list of pairs of them, which you will use for market analysis. The first-attempt query is usually

```
SELECT P1.prodname, P2.prodname
  FROM Products AS P1, Products AS P2;
```

but this is quickly rejected because it produces too much data and most of it is redundant.

You would get the four rows ('peanut butter', 'jelly'), ('jelly', 'peanut butter'), ('peanut butter', 'peanut butter'), and ('jelly', 'jelly') when you really wanted just ('jelly', 'peanut butter'). The trick is to use a nonequality to remove the unwanted combinations:

```
SELECT P1.prodname, P2.prodname
  FROM Products AS P1, Products AS P2
 WHERE P1.prodname < P2.prodname;
```

To keep the pairs where both members are identical, change the "less than" to a "less than or equal" operator. This pattern can be extended to produce triples, quadruples, and so forth. It is a good idea to use a "less than" sign instead of a "greater than" sign, so that the first column in the result table will have the lowest value of the group. This horizontal sorting will be easier to read.

17.4.2 Range JOINs

Most JOINs are based on simple predicates that involve scalar comparisons. But it is also possible to do JOINs based on relationships between sets of columns in two or more tables. The most common form of this is an interval JOIN, where a time period or a range of values is related to another value in the second table.

A common example of translating an interval or range into a scalar value is grading such that 100% to 90% on a test is an A, 80% to 89% is a B, 70% to 79% is a C, 60% to 69% is a D, and 59% or less is a failure. The use of this type of query for code translation or as a way of partitioning a database is discussed in Section 19.1.

17.4.3 JOINs by Function Calls

JOINs can also be done inside functions that relate columns from one or more tables in their parameters. This is easier to explain with an actual example from John Botibol of Deverill plc in Dorset, England. His problem was how to "flatten" legacy data that was stored in a flat file database into a relational format for a data warehouse. There was a vast amount of demographic information on people that related to their subjects of interest. The subjects of interest were selected from a list; some subjects required just one answer and others allowed multiple selections.

The problem was that the data for multiple selections was stored as a string with 1 or 0 in positional places to indicate "Interested" or "Not interested" in that item. The actual list of products was stored in another file as a list. Thus, for a person we might have something like '101110' together with a list like 1 = Bananas, 2 = Apples, 3 = Bread, 4 = Fish, 5 = Meat, 6 = Butter, if the subject area was foods.

The data was first moved into working tables like this:

```
CREATE TABLE RawSurvey
(rawkey INTEGER NOT NULL PRIMARY KEY,
 rawstring CHAR(20) NOT NULL);

CREATE TABLE SurveyList
(survey_id INTEGER NOT NULL PRIMARY KEY,
 surveytext CHAR(30) NOT NULL);
```

There were always the correct number of 1s and 0s for the number of question options in any group (thus, in this case the answer strings always have six characters), and the list was in the correct order to match the positions in the string. The data had to be ported into SQL, which meant that each survey had to be broken down into a row for each response.

```
CREATE TABLE Survey
(survey_id INTEGER NOT NULL,
 surveytext CHAR(30) NOT NULL,
```

```
ticked INTEGER NOT NULL
     CONSTRAINT tick_mark
     CHECK (ticked IN (0,1)) DEFAULT 0,
PRIMARY KEY (survey_id, surveytext));
```

This table can be loaded with the query

```
INSERT INTO Survey(survey_id, surveytext, ticked)
SELECT rawkey, surveytext,
       SUBSTRING(rawstring FROM survey_id FOR 1)
  FROM RawSurvey, SurveyList
```

The tables are joined in the SUBSTRING() function instead of with a theta operator. The SUBSTRING() function returns an empty string if survey_id goes beyond the end of the string. The query will always return a number of rows that is equal to or less than the number of characters in rawstring. The technique will adjust itself correctly for any number of possible survey answers.

Given that in the real problem, the table SurveyList always contained exactly the right number of entries for the length of the string to be exploded and that the string to be exploded always had exactly the right number of characters, you did not need a WHERE clause to check for bad data.

17.4.4 The UNION JOIN

The UNION JOIN was defined in SQL-92, but I know of no SQL product that has implemented it. As the name implies, it is a cross between a UNION and a FULL OUTER JOIN. The definition followed easily from the other infixed JOIN operators. The syntax has no conditional clause:

```
<table expression 1> UNION JOIN <table expression 2>
```

The statement takes two dissimilar tables and puts them into one result table. It preserves all the rows from both tables and does not try to consolidate them. Columns that do not exist in one table are simply padded out with NULLs in the result rows. Columns with the same names in the tables have to be renamed differently in the result. This is equivalent to

```
<table expression 1>
 FULL OUTER JOIN
 <table expression 2>
 ON 1 = 2;
```

Any conditional expression that is always FALSE will work. As an example of this, you might want to combine the medical records of male and female patients into one table with this query:

```
SELECT *
  FROM (SELECT 'male', prostate FROM Males)
       OUTER JOIN
       (SELECT 'female', pregnancy FROM Females);
```

You'll get a result table like this:

Result

male	prostate	female	pregnancy
'male'	no	NULL	NULL
'male'	no	NULL	NULL
'male'	yes	NULL	NULL
'male'	yes	NULL	NULL
NULL	NULL	'female'	no
NULL	NULL	'female'	no
NULL	NULL	'female'	yes
NULL	NULL	'female'	yes

To be honest, I have never seen a use for this, but such a query was requested on an Internet chat group for use with a display screen that used "combo boxes" to create computer configuration options.

17.5 Dr. Codd's T-JOIN

Dr. E. F. Codd introduced a set of new theta operators, called *T-operators,* which were based on the idea of a best fit or approximate equality (Codd 1990). The algorithm for the operators is easier to understand with an example borrowed from Dr. Codd (Codd 1990) and modified.

The problem is to assign the classes to the available classrooms. We want (class_size < room_size) to be true after the assignments are made. This will allow us a few empty seats in each room for late students. We can do this in one of two ways. The first way is to sort the tables in ascending order by classroom size and the number of students in a class. We start with the following tables:

```
CREATE TABLE Rooms
(room_nbr CHAR(2) PRIMARY KEY,
 room_size INTEGER NOT NULL);

CREATE TABLE Classes
(class_nbr CHAR(2) PRIMARY KEY,
 class_size INTEGER NOT NULL);
```

These tables have the following rows:

Classes

class_nbr	class_size
'c1'	80
'c2'	70
'c3'	65
'c4'	55
'c5'	50
'c6'	40

Rooms

room_nbr	room_size
'r1'	'70'
'r2'	'40'
'r3'	'50'
'r4'	'85'
'r5'	'30'
'r6'	'65'
'r7'	'55'

The goal of the T-Join problem is to assign a class that is smaller than the classroom given it (class_size < room_size). Dr. Codd gives two approaches to the problem:

1. Ascending-order algorithm
   Sort both tables into ascending order. Reading from the top of the Rooms table, match each class with the first room that will fit.

Classes		Rooms	
class_nbr	class_size	room_nbr	room_size
c6'	40	'r5'	30
'c5'	50	'r2'	40

'c4'	55	'r3'	50
'c3'	65	'r7'	55
'c2'	70	'r6'	65
'c1'	80	'r1'	70
		'r4'	85

This gives us

Results

class_nbr	class_size	room_nbr	room_size
'c2'	70	'r4'	85
'c3'	65	'r1'	70
'c4'	55	'r6'	65
'c5'	50	'r7'	55
'c6'	40	'r3'	50

2. Descending-order algorithm

Sort both tables into descending order. Reading from the top of the Classes table, match each class with the first room that will fit.

Classes   Rooms

class_nbr	class_size	room_nbr	room_size
'c1'	80	'r4'	85
'c2'	70	'r1'	70
'c3'	65	'r6'	65
'c4'	55	'r7'	55
'c5'	50	'r3'	50
'c6'	40	'r2'	40
		'r5'	30

Results

class_nbr	class_size	room_nbr	room_size
'c1'	80	'r4'	85
'c3'	65	'r1'	70
'c4'	55	'r6'	65
'c5'	50	'r7'	55
'c6'	40	'r3'	50

Notice that the answers are different! Dr. Codd has never given a definition in relational algebra of the T-Join, so I propose that we need one. Informally, for each class, we want the smallest room that will hold it, while maintaining the T-Join condition. Or for each room, we want the largest class that will fill it, while maintaining the T-Join condition. These can be two different things, so you must decide which table is the driver. But either way, I am advocating a "best fit" over Codd's "first fit" approach.

In effect, the Swedish and Croatian solutions given later in this section use my definition instead of Dr. Codd's; the Colombian solution is true to the algorithmic approach.

Other theta conditions can be used in place of the "less than" shown here. If "less than or equal" is used, all the classes are assigned to a room in this case, but not in all cases. This is left to the reader as an exercise.

The first attempts in standard SQL are versions grouped by queries. They can, however, produce some rows that would be left out of the answers Dr. Codd was expecting. The first JOIN can be written as

```
SELECT class_nbr, class_size, MIN(room_size)
  FROM Rooms, Classes
 WHERE Classes.class_size < Rooms.room_size
 GROUP BY class_nbr, class_size;
```

This will give a result table with the desired room sizes, but not the room numbers. You cannot put the other columns in the SELECT list since it would conflict with the GROUP BY clause. But also note that the classroom with 85 seats (r4) is used twice, once by class 'c5' and then by class 'c6':

Result

class_nbr	class_size	MIN(room_size)
'c1'	80	85 ← room r4
'c2'	70	85 ← room r4
'c3'	65	70
'c4'	55	65
'c5'	50	55
'c6'	40	50

Your best bet after this is to use the query in an EXISTS clause.

```
SELECT *
  FROM Rooms, Classes
```

```
WHERE EXISTS (SELECT class_nbr, class_size, MIN(room_size)
              FROM Rooms, Classes
              WHERE Classes.class_size < Rooms.room_size
              GROUP BY class_nbr, class_size);
```

However, some versions of SQL will not allow a grouped subquery, and others will balk at an aggregate function in an EXISTS predicate. The only way I have found to rectify this is to save the results to a temporary table, then JOIN it back to the Cartesian product of Rooms and Classes. The second T-JOIN can be done by putting the columns for Rooms into the SELECT list of the same query schema:

```
SELECT room_nbr, room_size, MAX(class_size)
  FROM Rooms, Classes
 WHERE Classes.class_size < Rooms.room_size
 GROUP BY room_nbr, room_size;
```

This time, the results are the same as those Dr. Codd got with his procedural algorithm:

Result

room_nbr	room_size	MAX(class_size)
'r4'	85	80
'r1'	70	65
'r6'	65	55
'r7'	55	50
'r3'	50	40

If you do a little arithmetic on the data, you find that we have 360 students and 395 seats, 6 classes and 7 rooms. This solution uses the fewest rooms, but note that the 70 students in class 'c2' are left out completely. Room 'r2' is left over, but it has only 40 seats.

As it works out, the best fit of rooms to classes is given by changing the matching rule to "less than or equal." This will leave the smallest room empty and pack the other rooms to capacity:

```
SELECT class_nbr, class_size, MIN(room_size)
  FROM Rooms, Classes
 WHERE Classes.class_size <= Rooms.room_size
 GROUP BY class_nbr, class_size;
```

17.5.1 The Croatian Solution

I published this same problem in an article in *DBMS* magazine (Celko 1992a) and got an answer in QUEL from Miljenko Martinis of Croatia in our Letters column (Miljenko 1992). He then translated it from QUEL into SQL with two views:

```
CREATE VIEW Classrooms -- all possible legal pairs
AS SELECT *
    FROM Classes, Rooms
   WHERE class_size < room_size;

CREATE VIEW Classrooms1 -- smallest room for the class
AS SELECT *
    FROM Classrooms AS CR1
   WHERE room_size = (SELECT MIN(room_size)
                        FROM Classrooms
                       WHERE class_nbr = CR1.class_nbr);
```

We find the answer with the simple query

```
SELECT class_nbr, class_size, room_size, room_nbr
  FROM Classrooms1 AS CR1
 WHERE class_size = (SELECT MAX(class_size)
                       FROM Classrooms1
                      WHERE room_nbr = CR1.room_nbr);
```

This is a pure SQL-89 solution. I tried this in XDB on my PC; it runs very, very slowly, but it works and gives true "best-fit" results.

class_nbr	class_size	room_size	room_nbr
'c6'	40	50	'r3'
'c5'	50	55	'r7'
'c4'	55	65	'r6'
'c3'	65	70	'r1'
'c1'	80	85	'r4'

17.5.2 The Swedish Solution

I got another solution from Anders Karlsson of Mr. K Software AB in Stockholm, Sweden. Here is a version of that query:

```
SELECT C1.class_nbr, C1.class_size, R1.room_size, R1.room_nbr
  FROM Classes AS C1, Rooms AS R1
 WHERE C1.class_size = (SELECT MAX(C2.class_size)
                          FROM Classes AS C2
                         WHERE R1.room_size > C2.class_size)
   AND NOT EXISTS (SELECT *
                     FROM Rooms AS R2
                    WHERE R2.room_size > C1.class_size
                      AND R2.room_size < R1.room_size);
```

The first predicate says that we have the largest class that will go into this room. The second predicate says that there is no other room which would fit this class better (i.e., that is smaller than the candidate room and still larger than the class at which we are looking).

17.5.3 The Colombian Solution

Francisco Moreno of the Department of Systems Engineering at the University of Antioquia in Colombia came up with another approach and data to demonstrate the problems in the T-Join.

Clean out the existing tables and insert this data:

```
DELETE FROM Classes;
INSERT INTO Classes
VALUES ('c1', 106),
       ('c2', 105),
       ('c3', 104),
       ('c4', 100),
       ('c5', 99),
       ('c6', 90),
       ('c7', 89),
       ('c8', 88),
       ('c9', 83),
       ('c10', 82),
       ('c11', 81),
       ('c12', 65),
       ('c13', 50),
       ('c14', 49),
       ('c15', 30),
       ('c16', 29),
       ('c17', 28),
```

```
          ('c18', 20),
          ('c19', 19);

DELETE FROM Rooms;
INSERT INTO Rooms
VALUES ('r1', 102),
          ('r2', 101),
          ('r3', 95),
          ('r4', 94),
          ('r5', 85),
          ('r6', 70),
          ('r7', 55),
          ('r8', 54),
          ('r9', 35),
          ('r10', 34),
          ('r11', 25),
          ('r12', 18);
```

Using Codd's T-Join algorithm for descending lists, you would have this mapping:

```
'c1'      106
'c2'      105
'c3'      104
'c4'      100      <--->      'r1'    102
'c5'       99      <--->      'r2'    101
'c6'       90      <--->      'r3'     95
'c7'       89      <--->      'r4'     94
'c8'       88
'c9'       83      <--->      'r5'     85
'c10'      82
'c11'      81
'c12'      65      <--->      'r6'     70
'c13'      50      <--->      'r7'     55
'c14'      49      <--->      'r8'     54
'c15'      30      <--->      'r9'     35
'c16'      29      <--->      'r10'    34
'c17'      28
'c18'      20      <--->      'r11'    25
'c19'      19

                             'r12'    18
```

There are 1,317 students in classes and 768 seats for them. You can see by inspection that some classes are too large for any room we have. If you start in ascending order, class 'c19' pairs with room 'r11', and you get another result set.

This algorithm is not a best fit answer but a first fit answer. This is an important difference. To explain further, the first fit to class 'c4' is room 'r1', which has 102 seats; the best fit is room 'r2', which has 101 seats. The algorithm would give us this result table:

Results

class_nbr	class_size	room_size	room_nbr
'c4'	100	102	'r1'
'c5'	99	101	'r2'
'c6'	90	95	'r3'
'c7'	89	94	'r4'
'c9'	83	85	'r5'
'c12'	65	70	'r6'
'c13'	50	55	'r7'
'c14'	49	54	'r8'
'c15'	30	35	'r9'
'c16'	29	34	'r10'
'c18'	20	25	'r11'

704 students served.

If you use the Swedish or Croatian solution on this data, the answer is

Swedish Result

class_nbr	class_size	room_size	room_nbr
c4'	100	101	'r2'
'c6'	90	94	'r4'
'c9'	83	85	'r5'
'c12'	65	70	'r6'
'c13'	50	54	'r8'
'c15'	30	34	'r10'
'c18'	20	25	'r11'

438 students served.

At this point you have a result that is not complete but has the tightest mapping of each class into a room. There is another problem that was not mentioned. We have not had two classes or two rooms of the same size in the data, and this will cause other problems.

Instead of trying to use a single static SQL query, we can use SQL to generate SQL code, then execute it dynamically. This solution is right but is horrible from a performance viewpoint.

```
-- build a table of possible T-Join pairings
DROP TABLE T-Join;
CREATE TABLE T-Join AS
SELECT *
  FROM Classes, Rooms
 WHERE room_size > class_size;

-- create a temporary working table
DROP TABLE Ins;
CREATE TABLE Ins
(class_nbr CHAR(3) NOT NULL,
 class_size INTEGER NOT NULL,
 room_nbr CHAR(3) NOT NULL,
 room_size INTEGER NOT NULL);

-- create a table with the insertion code for each row
SELECT
'INSERT INTO Ins
SELECT class_nbr, class_size, room_nbr, room_size
  FROM T-Join AS T1
 WHERE room_size
       = (SELECT MAX(room_size)
            FROM T-Join
           WHERE room_size NOT IN (SELECT room_size FROM Ins))
   AND class_size
       = (SELECT MAX(class_size)
            FROM T-Join AS T2
           WHERE class_size NOT IN (SELECT class_size FROM Ins)
             AND T2.class_size < T1.room_size);'
  FROM Rooms
 WHERE room_size > (SELECT MIN(class_size) FROM Classes);
COMMIT;
```

Now use "SELECT * FROM Ins;" query in a host program with dynamic SQL and execute each statement in the temporary table in order. This will give us the first answer at the beginning of Section 17.5.3, and it also works for the original data.

Moreno's second solution, which handles duplicates, is more complex, and I will not give it here. It uses the keys of the tables to make rows with duplicate values unique.

VIEWs and TEMPORARY TABLEs

A VIEW IS ALSO called a virtual table, to distinguish it from temporary and base tables. Before the SQL-92 standard was adopted, we thought of a VIEW as a new table that was constructed from base tables or other VIEW s upon its first use in a query. It simply ceases to exist upon the end of the query in which it appeared. Whether or not the database system actually materializes a VIEW as a physical table or uses other mechanisms is implementation-defined according to the ISO standard, but the VIEW must always act as if it were materialized.

With SQL-92, a much better way to explain a VIEW is to say that it is a table subquery expression that is kept in the schema tables to be invoked by name wherever a table could be used. If the VIEW is updatable, then additional rules apply.

This is a better definition because the standard separates administrative (DBA) privileges from user privileges. Table creation is administrative and query execution is a user privilege, and this model maintains that separation.

18.1 VIEWs in Queries

The SQL-92 syntax for the VIEW definition is

```
CREATE VIEW <table name> [(<view column list>)]
AS <query expression>
[WITH [<levels clause>] CHECK OPTION]
```

```
<levels clause> ::= CASCADED | LOCAL
```

The `<levels clause>` option in the `WITH CHECK OPTION` did not exist in SQL-89, and it is still not widely implemented yet. Section 18.5 of this chapter will discuss this clause in detail. It has no effect on queries, but only on `UPDATE`, `INSERT INTO`, and `DELETE FROM` statements.

A `VIEW` is different from both a `TEMPORARY TABLE` and from a base table. You cannot put indexes or constraints on a `VIEW`, as you can with base and `TEMPORARY TABLE`s. A `VIEW` has no existence in the database until it is invoked, while a `TEMPORARY TABLE` is persistent.

In SQL-92, the `AS` operator allows us to give names to the results of sub-query expressions and to use them. Thus a `VIEW` can be thought of as a persistent table subquery expression, stored in the schema tables and invoked by its name. In effect every occurrence of a `VIEW` name is replaced by the expression

```
<query expression>
AS <table name> [(<column list>)]
```

Here is a list of database schema objects and their properties in a query (i.e., how they are seen by a user as opposed to the DBA):

	physical existence	accessed by user
Domain	no	no
View	no	yes
Index	yes	no
Table	yes	yes

Those of you who are more cynical might also add a line to this chart that defines a "backup copy" as having neither existence nor accessibility.

The name of the `VIEW` must be unique within the database schema, like a table name. The `VIEW` definition cannot reference itself since it does not exist yet. Nor can the definition reference only other `VIEW`s; the nesting of `VIEW`s must eventually resolve to underlying base tables. This makes sense; if no base tables were involved, what would you be viewing?

18.2 Updatable and Read-Only VIEWs

Unlike base tables, `VIEW`s are either updatable or read-only, but not both. `INSERT`, `UPDATE`, and `DELETE` operations are allowed on updatable `VIEW`s and base tables, subject to any other constraints. `INSERT`, `UPDATE`, and `DELETE` are not allowed on read-only VIEWs, but you can change their base tables, as you would expect.

An updatable VIEW is one that can have each of its rows associated with exactly one row in an underlying base table. When the VIEW is changed, the changes pass through the VIEW to that underlying base table unambiguously. Updatable VIEWs in SQL-92 are defined only for queries on only one table, with no GROUP BY clause; no HAVING clause; no aggregate functions; no calculated columns; no UNION-ed, INTERSECT-ed, or EXCEPT-ed queries; and no SELECT DISTINCT clause. Any columns excluded from the VIEW must be NULL-able in the base table, so that a whole row can be constructed for insertion. By implication, the VIEW must also contain a key of the table. In short, we are absolutely sure that each row in the VIEW maps back to one and only one row in the base table.

Some updating is handled by the CASCADE option in the referential integrity constraints on the base tables, not by the VIEW declaration.

The definition of updatability in SQL-92 is actually pretty limited, but very safe. The database system could look at information it has in the referential integrity constraints to widen the set of allowed updatable VIEWs. You will find that some implementations are now doing just that, but it is not common yet. The SQL standard definition of an updatable VIEW is actually a subset of the possible updatable VIEWs, and a very small subset at that. The major advantage of this definition is that it is based on syntax and not semantics. For example, these VIEWs are logically identical:

```
CREATE VIEW Foo1
AS SELECT *
     FROM Foobar
    WHERE x IN (1,2);

CREATE VIEW Foo2    -- Illegal!
AS SELECT *
     FROM Foobar
    WHERE x = 1
   UNION ALL
   SELECT *
     FROM Foobar
    WHERE x = 2;
```

But Foo1 is legal and Foo2 is not. While I know of no formal proof, I suspect that determining if a complex query resolves to an updatable query for allowed sets of data values possible in the table is an NP-complete problem.

Without going into details, here is a list of types of queries that can yield updatable VIEWs, as taken from "VIEW Update Is Practical" (Goodman 1990):

1. Projection from a single table (ANSI SQL)
2. Restriction/projection from a single table (ANSI SQL)
3. UNION VIEWs
4. Set difference VIEWs
5. One-to-one JOINs
6. One-to-one OUTER JOINs
7. One-to-many JOINs
8. One-to-many OUTER JOINs
9. Many-to-many JOINs
10. Translated and coded fields

The SQL3 document has a CREATE TRIGGER mechanism for tables that allows a triggered action to be performed BEFORE, AFTER, or INSTEAD OF a regular INSERT, UPDATE, or DELETE to that table. It might be possible for a user to write INSTEAD OF triggers on VIEWs, which would catch the changes and route them to the base tables that make up the VIEW. The database designer would then have complete control over the way VIEWs are handled.

18.3 Types of VIEWs

VIEWs can be classified by the type of SELECT statement they use and the purpose they are meant to serve.

18.3.1 Single-Table Projection and Restriction

In practice, many VIEWs are projections or restrictions on a single base table. This is a common method for obtaining security control by removing rows or columns that a particular group of users is not allowed to see. These VIEWs are best done as in-line text expansion since the optimizer can easily fold their code into the final query plan.

18.3.2 Calculated Columns

One common use for a VIEW is to provide summary data across a row. For example, given a table with measurements in metric units, we can construct a VIEW that hides the calculations that convert them into English units.

It is important to be sure that you have no problems with NULL values when constructing a calculated column. For example, given a table of employees with columns for both salary and commission, you might construct this VIEW:

```
CREATE VIEW EmpPay (empno, totpay)
AS SELECT empno, (salary + commission)
    FROM Employees;
```

However, office workers do not get commissions, so the value of their commission column will be NULL (it cannot be zero, since that could represent a bad month for a commissioned salesman). The value of the totpay column in the VIEW will therefore be NULL. You should use the COALESCE() function to change the NULLs to zeros.

18.3.3 Translated Columns

Another common use of a VIEW is to translate codes into text or other codes by doing table lookups. This is a special case of a JOINed VIEW based on a FOREIGN KEY relationship between two tables. For example, an order table might use a part number that we wish to display with a part name on an order entry screen. This is done with a JOIN between the order table and the inventory table:

```
CREATE VIEW Screen (partid, pname, . . .
AS SELECT Orders.partid, Inventory.pname, . . . )
    FROM Inventory, Orders
  WHERE Inventory.partid = Orders.partid;
```

Sometimes the original code is kept, and sometimes it is dropped from the VIEW. As a general rule, it is a better idea to keep both values even though they are redundant. The redundancy can be used as a check for users as well as a hook for nested JOINs in either of the codes.

The idea of JOIN VIEWs to translate codes can be expanded to show more than just one translated column. The result is often a "star" query with one table in the center, joined by FOREIGN KEY relations to many other tables to produce a result that is more readable than the original central table.

Missing values are a problem, however. If there is no translation for a given code, no row appears in the VIEW, or if an outer JOIN was used, a NULL will appear. The programmer should establish a referential integrity constraint to CASCADE changes between the tables to prevent loss of data.

18.3.4 Grouped VIEWs

A grouped VIEW is based on a query with a GROUP BY clause. Since each of the groups may have more than one row in the base from which it was built, these are necessarily read-only VIEWs. Such VIEWs usually have one or more aggregate functions, and they are used for reporting purposes. They are also handy for working around weaknesses in SQL. Consider a VIEW that shows the largest sale in each state. The query is straightforward:

```
CREATE VIEW BigSales (state, bigamt)
AS SELECT STATE, MAX(amt)
     FROM Sales
   GROUP BY state;
```

However, SQL requires that the grouping column(s) appear in the select clause. If I simply want a list of the largest sales without their states, I cannot get it with this VIEW. I have to construct another VIEW from this grouped VIEW:

```
CREATE VIEW BigAmts (amt)
AS SELECT bigamt FROM BigSales;
```

Since this is a single-column table, it can be used with predicates that require a subquery in SQL-89. See Section 17.5 on T-JOINs for more details on how useful this can be for certain queries.

These VIEWs are also useful for "flattening out" one-to-many relationships. For example, consider a table of employees, keyed on the employee code number (empno), and a table of dependents, keyed on a combination of the code number for each dependent's parent (empno) and the dependent's own serial number (depid). The goal is to produce a report of the employees by name with the number of dependents each has.

```
CREATE VIEW DepTally1 (empno, totdeps)
AS SELECT empno, COUNT(*)
     FROM Dependents
   GROUP BY empno;
```

The report is then simply an OUTER JOIN between this VIEW and the Employees table.

The OUTER JOIN is needed to account for employees without dependents with a NULL value. Using SQL-92 syntax, the report query looks like this:

```
SELECT empname, totdeps
 FROM Employees LEFT OUTER JOIN DepTally1 ON empno;
```

18.3.5 UNION VIEWs

A VIEW based on a UNION or UNION ALL operation is read-only because there is no way to map a change onto just one row in one of the base tables. The UNION operator will remove duplicate rows from the results. Both the UNION and UNION ALL operators hide which table the rows came from. Such VIEWs must use a <view column list> because the columns in a UNION [ALL] have no names of their own. In theory, a UNION of two disjoint tables, neither of which has duplicate rows in itself, should be updatable. Most systems cannot detect this and make all such VIEWs read-only.

The problem given in Section 18.3.4 on grouped VIEWs could also be done with a UNION query that would assign a count of zero to employees without dependents, thus:

```
CREATE VIEW DepTally2 (empno, cntdeps)
AS (SELECT empno, COUNT(*)
      FROM Dependents
    GROUP BY empno)
   UNION
   (SELECT empno, 0
     FROM Employees AS E2
    WHERE NOT EXISTS (SELECT *
                       FROM Dependents AS D2
                      WHERE D2.empno = E2.empno));
```

The report is now a simple INNER JOIN between this VIEW and the Employees table. The zero value, instead of a NULL value, will account for employees without dependents. The report query looks like this:

```
SELECT empname, cntdeps
  FROM Employees, DepTally2
 WHERE (DepTally2.empno = Employees.empno);
```

18.3.6 JOINs in VIEWs

A VIEW whose query expression is a JOINed table is not usually updatable even in theory. One of the major purposes of a JOINed view is to "flatten out" a one-to-many or many-to-many relationship. Such relationships cannot map one row in the VIEW back to one row in the underlying tables on the "many" side of the JOIN. Anything said about a JOIN query could be said about a JOINed VIEW, so they will not be dealt with here (see Chapter 17 for a full discussion of JOINs).

18.3.7 Nested VIEWs

A point that is often missed, even by experienced SQL programmers, is that a VIEW can be built on other VIEWs. The only restrictions are that circular references within the query expressions of the VIEWs are illegal and that a VIEW must ultimately be built on base tables. One problem with nested VIEWs is that different updatable VIEWs can reference the same base table at the same time. If these VIEWs then appear in another VIEW, it becomes hard to determine what has happened when the highest-level VIEW is changed. As an example, consider a table with two keys:

```
CREATE TABLE Canada
(english INTEGER,
 french INTEGER,
 engword CHAR(30),
 frenword CHAR(30));

INSERT INTO Canada
VALUES (1, 2, 'muffins', 'croissants'),
       (2, 1, 'bait', 'escargots');

CREATE VIEW EnglishWords
AS SELECT english, engword
     FROM Canada
    WHERE engword IS NOT NULL;

CREATE VIEW FrenchWords
AS SELECT french, frenword
     FROM Canada
    WHERE frenword IS NOT NULL);
```

We have now tried the escargots and decided that we wish to change our opinion of them:

```
UPDATE EnglishWords
   SET engword = 'appetizer'
 WHERE english = 2;
```

Our French user has just tried haggis and decided to insert a new record of his experience:

```
INSERT INTO FrenchWords
   (3, 'Le swill')
```

The row that is created is (NULL, 3, NULL, 'Le swill') since there is no way for VIEW FrenchWords to get to the VIEW EnglishWords columns. Likewise, the English VIEW user can construct a row to record his translation, (3, NULL, 'Haggis', NULL). But neither of them can consolidate the two rows into a meaningful piece of data.

To delete a row is also to destroy data; the French speaker who drops 'croissants' from the table also drops 'muffins' from VIEW EnglishWords.

18.4 How VIEWs Are Handled in the Database System

The SQL-92 standard requires a system schema table with the text of the VIEW declarations in it. What would be handy, but is not easily done in all SQL implementations, is to trace the VIEWs down to their base tables by printing out a tree diagram of the nested structure. You should check your user library and see if such a utility program exists (such as, for example, FINDVIEW in the SPARC library for SQL/DS). There are several ways to handle VIEWs, and systems will often use a mixture of them. The major categories of algorithms are materialization and in-line text expansion.

18.4.1 View Column List

The <view column list> is optional; when it is not given, the VIEW will inherit the column names from the query. The number of column names in the <view column list> has to be the same as the degree of the query expression. If any two columns in the query have the same column name, you must have a <view column list> to resolve the ambiguity. The same column name cannot be specified more than once in the <view column list>.

18.4.2 VIEW Materialization

Materialization means that whenever you use the name of the VIEW, the database engine finds its definition in the schema tables and creates a working table with that name that has the appropriate column names with the appropriate datatypes. Finally, this new table is filled with the results of the SELECT statement in the body of the VIEW definition.

The decision to materialize a VIEW as an actual physical table is implementation-defined in the ANSI SQL standard, but the VIEW must act as if it were a table when accessed for a query. If the VIEW is not updatable, this approach automatically protects the base tables from any improper changes and is guaranteed to be correct. It uses existing internal procedures in the database engine (create table, insert from query), so this is easy for the database to do.

The downside of this approach is that it is not very fast for large VIEWs, uses extra storage space, cannot take advantage of indexes already existing on the base tables, usually cannot create indexes on the new table, and cannot be optimized as easily as other approaches. However, certain VIEWs are best done by materialization. A VIEW whose construction has a hidden sort is usually materialized. Queries with SELECT DISTINCT, UNION, GROUP BY, and HAVING clauses are usually implemented by sorting to remove duplicate rows or to build groups. As each row of the VIEW is built, it has to be saved to compare it to the other rows, so it makes sense to materialize it.

18.4.3 In-Line Text Expansion

Another approach is to store the text of the CREATE VIEW statement and work it into the parse tree of the SELECT, INSERT, UPDATE, or DELETE statements that use it. This allows the optimizer to blend the VIEW definition into the final query plan. For example, you can create a VIEW based on a particular department:

```
CREATE VIEW SalesDept (deptname, city, . . .)
AS SELECT *
    FROM Departments
   WHERE deptname = 'Sales';
```

and then use it as a query:

```
SELECT *
  FROM SalesDept
 WHERE city = 'New York';
```

The parser expands the VIEW into text (or an intermediate tokenized form) within the FROM clause. The syntax shown below is not legal SQL-89, but is part of SQL-92. Since many implementations already have the mechanisms for doing this, expect it to be an early SQL-92 feature. The query would become, in effect,

```
SELECT *
  FROM (SELECT *
          FROM Departments
          WHERE deptname = 'Sales')
        AS SalesDept (deptname, city, . . . )
  WHERE city = 'New York';
```

and the query optimizer would then "flatten it out" into

```
SELECT *
  FROM Departments
  WHERE deptname = 'Sales'
    AND city = 'New York';
```

Though this sounds like a nice approach, it has problems in many systems where the in-line expansion does not result in proper SQL. An earlier version of DB2 was one such system. To illustrate the problem, imagine that you are given a DB2 table that has a long identification number and some figures in each row. The long identification number is like those 40-digit monsters they give you on a utility bill—they are unique only in the first few characters, but the utility company prints the whole thing out anyway. Your task is to create a report that is grouped according to the first six characters of the long identification number. The immediate naive query uses the substring operator:

```
SELECT SUBSTRING(id FROM 1 TO 6), SUM(amt1), SUM(amt2), . . .
  FROM TableA
  GROUP BY id;
```

This does not work; it is incorrect SQL since the SELECT and GROUP BY lists do not agree. Other common attempts include GROUP BY SUBSTRING(id FROM 1 TO 6), which will fail because you cannot use a function; and GROUP BY 1, which will fail because you can use a column position only in a UNION statement (this feature is now deprecated in SQL-92) and in the ORDER BY in some products. The GROUP BY has to have a list of simple column names drawn from the tables of the FROM clause. The next attempt is to build a VIEW:

```
CREATE VIEW BadTry (Shortid, amt1, amt2, . . . )
AS SELECT SUBSTRING(id FROM 1 TO 6), amt1, amt2, . . .
    FROM TableA;
```

and then do a grouped select on it. This is correct SQL, but it does not work in DB2. DB2 apparently tries to insert the VIEW into the FROM clause, as we have seen, but when it expands the clause out, the results are the same as those of the incorrect first query attempt with a function call in the GROUP BY clause. The trick is to force DB2 to materialize the VIEW so that you can name the column constructed with the SUBSTRING() function. Anything that causes a sort will do this—the SELECT DISTINCT, UNION, GROUP BY, and HAVING clauses, for example.

Since we know that the short identification number is a key, we can use this VIEW:

```
CREATE VIEW Shorty (Shortid, amt1, amt2, . . . )
AS SELECT DISTINCT SUBSTRING(id FROM 1 TO 6), amt1, amt2, . . .
    FROM TableA;
```

Then the report query is

```
SELECT Shortid, SUM(amt1), SUM(amt2), . . .
  FROM Shorty
 GROUP BY Shortid;
```

This works fine in DB2. I am indebted to Susan Vombrack of Loral Aerospace for this example. Incidentally, this can be written in SQL-92 as

```
SELECT *
  FROM (SELECT SUBSTRING(id FROM 1 TO 6) AS shortid,
               SUM(amt1), SUM(amt2), . . .
          FROM TableA
         GROUP BY id);
```

The name on the substring result column in the subquery expression makes it recognizable to the parser.

18.4.4 Pointer Structures

Finally, the system can handle VIEWs with special data structures for the VIEW. This is usually an array of pointers into a base table constructed from the VIEW definition. This is a good way to handle updatable VIEWs in standard SQL since the target row in the base table is at the end of a pointer chain in the VIEW structure. Access will be as fast as possible.

The pointer structure approach cannot easily use existing indexes on the base tables. But the pointer structure can be implemented as an index with restrictions. Furthermore, multiple table VIEWs can be constructed as pointer structures that allow direct access to the related rows in the table involved in the JOIN. This approach is very product-dependent, so you cannot make any general assumptions.

18.4.5 Indexing and VIEWs

Note that VIEWs cannot have their own indexes. However, VIEWs can inherit the indexing on their base tables in some implementations. Like tables, VIEWs have no inherent ordering, but a programmer who knows his particular SQL implementation will often write code that takes advantage of the quirks of that product. In particular, some implementations allow you to use an ORDER BY clause in a VIEW (they are allowed only on cursors in standard SQL). This will force a sort and could materialize the VIEW as a working table. When the SQL engine has to do a table scan (a sequential read of the table), the sort might help or hinder a particular query: There is no way to predict the results.

18.5 WITH CHECK OPTION Clause

If WITH CHECK OPTION is specified, the viewed table has to be updatable. This is actually a fast way to check how your particular SQL implementation handles updatable VIEWs. Try to create a version of the VIEW in question using the WITH CHECK OPTION and see if your product will allow you to create it. The WITH CHECK OPTION is part of the SQL-89 standard, which was extended in SQL-92 by adding an optional <levels clause>. CASCADED is implicit if an explicit <levels clause> is not given. Consider a VIEW defined as

```
CREATE VIEW V1
AS SELECT *
     FROM Table1
    WHERE col1 = 'A';
```

and now UPDATE it with

```
UPDATE V1 SET col1 = 'B';
```

The UPDATE will take place without any trouble, but the rows that were previously seen now disappear when we use V1 again. They no longer meet the WHERE clause condition! Likewise, an INSERT INTO statement with VALUES (col1 = 'B') would insert just fine, but its rows would never be seen again in this VIEW. VIEWs created this way will always have all the rows that meet the criteria, and that can be handy. For example, you can set up a VIEW of records with a status code of 'to be done', work on them, and change a status code to 'finished', and they will disappear from your view. The important point is that the WHERE clause condition was checked only at the time when the VIEW was invoked.

The WITH CHECK OPTION makes the system check the WHERE clause condition upon insertion or UPDATE. If the new or changed row fails the test, the change is rejected and the VIEW remains the same. Thus, the previous UPDATE statement would get an error message, and you could not change certain columns in certain ways. For example, consider a VIEW of salaries under $30,000 defined with a WITH CHECK OPTION to prevent anyone from giving a raise above that ceiling.

SQL-92 has introduced an optional levels clause, which can be either CASCADED or LOCAL. If no levels clause is given, a levels clause of CASCADED is implicit. The idea of a CASCADED check is that the system checks all the underlying levels that built the VIEW, as well as the WHERE clause condition in the VIEW itself. If anything causes a row to disappear from the VIEW, the UPDATE is rejected. The idea of a WITH LOCAL CHECK OPTION is that only the local WHERE clause is checked. The underlying VIEWs or tables from which this VIEW is built might also be affected, but we do not test for those effects. Consider two VIEWs built on each other from the salary table:

```
CREATE VIEW Lowpay
AS SELECT *
    FROM Employees
    WHERE salary <= 250;

CREATE VIEW Mediumpay
AS SELECT *
    FROM Lowpay
    WHERE salary >= 100;
```

If neither VIEW has a WITH CHECK OPTION, the effect of updating Mediumpay by increasing every salary by $1,000 will be passed without any check to Lowpay. Lowpay will pass the changes to the underlying Employees table. The next time Mediumpay is used, Lowpay will be rebuilt in its own right and Mediumpay rebuilt from it, and all the employees will disappear from Mediumpay.

If only Mediumpay has a WITH CASCADED CHECK OPTION on it, the UPDATE will fail. Mediumpay has no problem with such a large salary, but it would cause a row in Lowpay to disappear, so Mediumpay must reject it. However, if only Mediumpay has a WITH LOCAL CHECK OPTION on it, the UPDATE will succeed. Mediumpay has no problem with such a large salary, so it passes the change along to Lowpay. Lowpay, in turn, passes the change to the Employees table and the UPDATE occurs. If both VIEWs have a WITH CASCADED CHECK OPTION, the effect is a set of conditions, all of which have to be met. The Employees table can accept UPDATEs or INSERTs only where the salary is between $100 and $250.

This can become very complex. Consider an example from an ANSI X3H2 paper by Nelson Mattos of IBM (Celko 1993). Let us build a five-layer set of VIEWs, using xx and yy as place holders for CASCADED or LOCAL, on a base table T1 with columns c1, c2, c3, c4, and c5, all set to a value of 10:

```
CREATE VIEW V1 AS SELECT * FROM T1 WHERE (c1 > 5);

CREATE VIEW V2 AS SELECT * FROM V1 WHERE (c2 > 5)
       WITH xx CHECK OPTION;

CREATE VIEW V3 AS SELECT * FROM V2 WHERE (c3 > 5);

CREATE VIEW V4 AS SELECT * FROM V3 WHERE (c4 > 5)
       WITH yy CHECK OPTION;

CREATE VIEW V5 AS SELECT * FROM V4 WHERE (c5 > 5);
```

When we set each one of the columns to zero, we get different results, which can be shown in this chart, where S means success and F means failure:

xx/yy	c1	c2	c3	c4	c5
cascade/cascade	F	F	F	F	S
local/cascade	F	F	F	F	S
local/local	S	F	S	F	S
cascade/local	F	F	S	F	S

To understand the chart, look at the last line. If xx = CASCADED and yy = LOCAL, updating column c1 to zero via V5 will fail, whereas updating c5 will succeed. Remember that a successful UPDATE means that the row(s) disappear from V5.

Follow the action for UPDATE V5 SET c1 = 0; VIEW V5 has no WITH CHECK OPTIONs, so the changed rows are immediately sent to V4 without any testing. VIEW V4 does have a WITH LOCAL CHECK OPTION, but column c1 is not involved, so V4 passes the rows to V3. VIEW V3 has no with check options, so the changed rows are immediately sent to V2. VIEW V2 does have a WITH CASCADED CHECK OPTION, so V2 passes the rows to V1 and awaits results. VIEW V1 is built on the original base table and has the condition c1 > 5, which is violated by this UPDATE. VIEW V1 then rejects the UPDATE to the base table, so the rows remain in V5 when it is rebuilt. Now the action for

```
UPDATE V5 SET c3 = 0;
```

VIEW V5 has no WITH CHECK OPTIONs, so the changed rows are immediately sent to V4, as before. VIEW V4 does have a WITH LOCAL CHECK OPTION, but column c3 is not involved, so V4 passes the rows to V3 without awaiting the results. VIEW V3 is involved with column c3 and has no WITH CHECK OPTIONs, so the rows can be changed and passed down to V2 and V1, where they UPDATE the base table. The rows are not seen again when V5 is invoked because they fail to get past VIEW V3. The real problem comes with UPDATE statements that change more than one column at a time. For example,

```
UPDATE V5 SET c1 = 0, c2 = 0, c3 = 0, c4 = 0, c5 = 0;
```

will fail for all possible combinations of <levels clause>s in the example schema.

A change in the SQL-92 standard in March 1993 defined the idea of a set of conditions that are inherited by the levels of nesting. In our sample schema, these implied tests would be added to each VIEW definition:

```
local/local
V1 = none
V2 = (c2 > 5)
V3 = (c2 > 5)
V4 = (c2 > 5) AND (c4 > 5)
V5 = (c2 > 5) AND (c4 > 5)

cascade/cascade
V1 = none
V2 = (c1 > 5) AND (c2 > 5)
V3 = (c1 > 5) AND (c2 > 5)
```

```
V4 = (c1 > 5) AND (c2 > 5) AND (c3 > 5) AND (c4 > 5)
V5 = (c1 > 5) AND (c2 > 5) AND (c3 > 5) AND (c4 > 5)

local/cascade
V1 = none
V2 = (c2 > 5)
V3 = (c2 > 5)
V4 = (c1 > 5) AND (c2 > 5) AND (c4 > 5)
V5 = (c1 > 5) AND (c2 > 5) AND (c4 > 5)

cascade/local
V1 = none
V2 = (c1 > 5) AND (c2 > 5)
V3 = (c1 > 5) AND (c2 > 5)
V4 = (c1 > 5) AND (c2 > 5) AND (c4 > 5)
V5 = (c1 > 5) AND (c2 > 5) AND (c4 > 5)
```

18.6 Dropping VIEWs

VIEWs, like tables, can be dropped from the schema. The SQL-92 syntax for the statement is

```
DROP VIEW <table name> <drop behavior>

<drop behavior> ::= [CASCADE | RESTRICT]
```

The <drop behavior> clause did not exist in SQL-86, so vendors had different behaviors in their implementations. The usual way of storing VIEWs was in a schema-level table with the VIEW name, the text of the VIEW, and perhaps other information. When you dropped a VIEW, the engine usually removed the appropriate row from the schema tables. You found out about dependencies when you tried to use VIEWs built on other VIEWs that no longer existed. Likewise, dropping a base table could cause the same problem when the VIEW was accessed.

The new CASCADE option will find all other VIEWs that use the dropped VIEW and remove them also. If RESTRICT is specified, the VIEW cannot be dropped if anything is dependent on it. This implies that the schema tables have a structure that is different from just a simple single table.

18.7 TEMPORARY TABLEs

A TEMPORARY TABLE can be used with SQL/PSM code to hold intermediate results rather than requerying or recalculating them over and over. The syntax for creating a TEMPORARY TABLE is

```
CREATE [GLOBAL | LOCAL] TEMP[ORARY] TABLE <table name>
 (<table element list>)
ON COMMIT [PRESERVE | DELETE] ROWS;
```

This is just like the usual CREATE TABLE statement with the addition of two pieces of syntax. The <table element>s can be column declarations, constraints, or declarative referential integrity clauses, just as if this were a base table. The differences come from the additional clauses.

The GLOBAL option in the TEMPORARY TABLE means that one copy of the table is available to *all* the modules of the application program in which it appears. The GLOBAL TEMPORARY TABLE is generally used to pass shared data between sessions.

The LOCAL option means that one copy of the table is available to *each* module of the application program in which the TEMPORARY TABLE appears. The LOCAL TEMPORARY TABLE is generally used as a "scratch table" by the user within a single module. If more than one user accesses the same LOCAL TEMPORARY TABLE, they each get a copy of the table, initially empty, for their session or within the scope of the module that uses it.

If you have trouble imagining multiple tables in the schema with the same name (a violation of a basic rule of SQL about uniqueness of schema objects), then imagine a single table created as declared, but with an extra phantom column that contains a user identifier. What the users are then seeing is an updatable VIEW on the LOCAL TEMPORARY TABLE, which shows them only the rows where this phantom column is equal to their user identifier, but not the phantom column itself. New rows are added to the LOCAL TEMPORARY TABLE with a DEFAULT of CURRENT USER.

The concept of modules in SQL is discussed in detail in Jim Melton's *Understanding SQL's Stored Procedures* (Melton 1998), but you can think of them as programs, procedures, functions, subroutines, or blocks of code, depending on the procedural language you use.

Since this is a table in the schema, you can get rid of it with a DROP TABLE <table name> statement, and you can change it with the usual INSERT INTO, DELETE FROM, and UPDATE statements. The differences are at the start and end of a session or module.

The ON COMMIT [PRESERVE | DELETE] ROWS clause describes the action taken when a COMMIT statement is executed successfully. The PRESERVE option means that the next time this table is used, the rows will still be there and will be deleted only at the end of the session. The DELETE option means that the rows will be deleted whenever a COMMIT statement is executed during the session. In both cases, the table will be cleared out at the end of the session or module.

18.8 Hints on Using VIEWs and TEMPORARY TABLEs

Sometimes it's easy for a programmer to decide whether to use VIEWs and TEMPORARY TABLEs. In the SQL-92 model, the user cannot create either a VIEW or a TEMPORARY TABLE. The creation of any schema object belongs to the database administrator, so the user has to use what he is given. However, you should know how to use each structure and which one is best for which situation.

18.8.1 Using VIEWs

Do not nest VIEWs too deeply; the overhead of building several levels eats up execution time, and the extra storage for materialized VIEWs can be expensive. Complex nestings are also hard to maintain. One way to figure out what VIEWs you should have is to inspect the existing queries and see if certain subqueries or expressions are repeated. These are good candidates for VIEWs.

One of the major uses of VIEWs is security. The DBA can choose to hide certain columns from certain classes of users through a combination of security authorizations and VIEWs. SQL-92 has provisions for restricting access to tables at the column level, but most implementations do not have that feature yet.

Another security trick is to add a column to a table that has a special user or security-level identifier in it. The VIEW hides this column and gives the user only what he is supposed to see. One possible problem is that a user could try to change something in the VIEW that violates other table constraints; when his attempt returns an error message, he has gotten some information about the security system that we might like to have hidden from him.

The best way to approach VIEWs is to think of how a user wants to see the database and then give him a set of VIEWs that make it look as if the database had been designed just for his applications.

18.8.2 Using TEMPORARY TABLEs

The GLOBAL TEMPORARY TABLE can be used to pass data among users, which is something that a VIEW cannot do. The LOCAL TEMPORARY TABLE has two major advantages. The user can load it with the results of a complex, time-consuming query once and use that result set over and over in his session, greatly improving performance. This also prevents the system from locking out other users from the base tables from which the complex query was built.

Codd discussed the idea of a snapshot, which is an image of a table at a particular moment in time. But it is important to know just what that moment was. You can use a TEMPORARY TABLE to hold such a snapshot by adding a column with a DEFAULT of the CURRENT TIMESTAMP.

The SQL-92 model of TEMPORARY TABLEs I have just described is not yet common in most implementations. In fact, many SQL products do not include the concept of a TEMPORARY TABLE at all. The exception is the Sybase family, Microsoft SQL Server and Sybase 11. But in their model, the users can dynamically create LOCAL TEMPORARY TABLEs that last only for their session and are visible only to their creator. These TABLEs cannot have indexes, constraints, VIEWs, referential integrity, or much of anything else declared on them; they serve only as "scratch tables" for the user.

A GLOBAL TEMPORARY TABLE can be created in a special database called tempdb within the schema (Sybase allows multiple databases within a single schema—again, not the ISO model).

18.8.3 Flattening a Table with a VIEW

Given a table with the monthly sales data shown as an attribute (the monthly amounts have to be NULL-able to hold missing values for the future) like this

```
CREATE TABLE AnnualSales1
(salesman CHAR(15) NOT NULL PRIMARY KEY,
 jan DECIMAL(5,2),
 feb DECIMAL(5,2),
 mar DECIMAL(5,2),
 apr DECIMAL(5,2),
 may DECIMAL(5,2),
 jun DECIMAL(5,2),
 jul DECIMAL(5,2),
 aug DECIMAL(5,2),
 sep DECIMAL(5,2),
 oct DECIMAL(5,2),
```

```
nov DECIMAL(5,2),
"dec" DECIMAL(5,2) -- reserved word!
);
```

the goal is to "flatten" it out so that it looks like this:

```
CREATE TABLE AnnualSales2
(salesman CHAR(15) NOT NULL PRIMARY KEY,
 month CHAR(3) NOT NULL
        CONSTRAINT valid_month_abbrev
        CHECK (month IN ('Jan', 'Feb', 'Mar', 'Apr',
                         'May', 'Jun', 'Jul', 'Aug',
                         'Sep', 'Oct', 'Nov', 'Dec'),
 amount DECIMAL(5,2) NOT NULL,
 PRIMARY KEY(salesman, month));
```

The trick is to build a VIEW of the original table with a number beside each month:

```
CREATE VIEW NumberedSales
AS SELECT salesman,
          1 AS M01, jan,
          2 AS M02, feb,
          3 AS M03, mar,
          4 AS M04, apr,
          5 AS M05, may,
          6 AS M06, jun,
          7 AS M07, jul,
          8 AS M08, aug,
          9 AS M09, sep,
         10 AS M10, oct,
         11 AS M11, nov,
         12 AS M12, "dec" --has to be in double quotes; DEC[IMAL] is a
                          keyword
   FROM AnnualSales1;
```

You can now use the auxiliary table of sequential numbers, or you can use a VALUES table constructor to build one. The flattened VIEW is

```
CREATE VIEW AnnualSales2 (salesman, month, amount)
AS SELECT S1.salesman,
     (CASE WHEN A.nbr = M01 THEN 'Jan'
```

```
            WHEN A.nbr = M02 THEN 'Feb'
            WHEN A.nbr = M03 THEN 'Mar'
            WHEN A.nbr = M04 THEN 'Apr'
            WHEN A.nbr = M05 THEN 'May'
            WHEN A.nbr = M06 THEN 'Jun'
            WHEN A.nbr = M07 THEN 'Jul'
            WHEN A.nbr = M08 THEN 'Aug'
            WHEN A.nbr = M09 THEN 'Sep'
            WHEN A.nbr = M10 THEN 'Oct'
            WHEN A.nbr = M11 THEN 'Nov'
            WHEN A.nbr = M12 THEN 'Dec'
            ELSE NULL END),
     (CASE WHEN A.nbr = M01 THEN jan
            WHEN A.nbr = M02 THEN feb
            WHEN A.nbr = M03 THEN mar
            WHEN A.nbr = M04 THEN apr
            WHEN A.nbr = M05 THEN may
            WHEN A.nbr = M06 THEN jun
            WHEN A.nbr = M07 THEN jul
            WHEN A.nbr = M08 THEN aug
            WHEN A.nbr = M09 THEN sep
            WHEN A.nbr = M10 THEN oct
            WHEN A.nbr = M11 THEN nov
            WHEN A.nbr = M12 THEN "dec"
            ELSE NULL END)
FROM AnnualSales AS S1
   CROSS JOIN
   (VALUES (1), (2), (3), (4), (5), (6),
           (7), (8), (9), (10), (11), (12)) AS A(nbr);
```

If your SQL product has derived tables, this can be written as a single VIEW query.

This technique lets you convert an attribute into a value, which is highly nonrelational but very handy for a report. The advantage of using a VIEW over using a TEMPORARY TABLE to hold the crosstabs query (given in Section 23.6) is that the VIEW will change automatically when the underlying base table is changed.

CHAPTER 19

Partitioning Data

DATA IS NOT information until you reduce it from a pile of detailed facts into some sort of summary. Statistics are one method of summarizing data that takes a set of data and reduces the set to a single number, for example, the average age of a firm's employees. But before you can produce statistics, you must have that dataset. This chapter is concerned with how to break the data in SQL into meaningful subsets that can then be presented to the user or passed along for further reduction.

19.1 Coverings and Partitions

We need to define some basic set operations. A *covering* is a collection of subsets, drawn from a set, whose union is the original set. A *partition* is a covering whose subsets do not intersect each other. Cutting up a pizza is a partitioning; smothering it in two layers of pepperoni slices is a covering. Partitions are the basis for most reports. The property that makes partitions useful for reports is *aggregation:* The whole is the sum of its parts. For example, a company budget is broken into divisions, divisions are broken into departments, and so forth. Each division budget is the sum of its department's budgets, and the sum of the division budgets is the total for the whole company. We would not be sure what to do if a department belonged to two different divisions because that would be a covering and not a partition.

19.1.1 Partitioning by Ranges

A common problem in data processing is classifying things by the way they fall into a range on a numeric or alphabetic scale. For example, for test paper grades, the range 100% to 90% is an A, 80% to 89% is a B, 70% to 79% is a C, 60% to 69% is a D, and 59% or less is an F. Mail-order companies compute shipping and handling charges based on ranges for the amounts of the purchases. ZIP codes in a certain range will belong to a particular city, state, and parcel mailing zone.

Range Tables

The best approach to translating a code into a value when ranges are involved is to set up a table with the high and low values for each translated value in it. Any missing values will easily be detected, and the table can be validated for completeness. For example, we could create a table of ZIP code ranges and two-character state abbreviation codes like this:

```
CREATE TABLE StateZip
(state CHAR(2) NOT NULL,
 city CHAR(20) NOT NULL,
 lowzip CHAR(5) NOT NULL UNIQUE,
 highzip CHAR(5) NOT NULL UNIQUE,
 CONSTRAINT zip_order_okay CHECK(lowzip < highzip),
 PRIMARY KEY (city, state)
 );
```

Here is a query that looks up the city name and state code from the ZIP code in the AddressBook table to complete a mailing label with a simple JOIN that looks like this:

```
SELECT A1.name, A1.street, SZ.city, SZ.state, A1.zip
  FROM StateZip AS SZ, AddressBook AS A1
 WHERE A1.zip BETWEEN SZ.lowzip AND SZ.highzip;
```

You need to be careful with this predicate. If one of the three columns involved has a NULL in it, the BETWEEN predicate becomes UNKNOWN and will not be recognized by the WHERE clause. If you design the table of range values with the high value in one row equal to or greater than the low value in another row, both of those rows will be returned when the test value falls on the overlap.

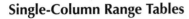

Single-Column Range Tables

If you know that you have a partitioning in the range value tables, you can write a query in SQL that will let you use a table with only the high value and the translation code. The grading system table would have ((100%, 'A'), (89%, 'B'), (79%, 'C'), (69%, 'D'), and (59%, 'F')) as its rows. Likewise, a table of the state code and the highest ZIP code in that state could do the same job as the BETWEEN predicate in the previous query.

```
CREATE TABLE StateZip2
(highzip CHAR(5) NOT NULL,
 city CHAR(20) NOT NULL,
 state CHAR(2) NOT NULL,
 PRIMARY KEY (highzip, state, city));
```

We want to write SQL code to give us the greatest lower bound or least upper bound on those values. The greatest lower bound (glb) operator finds the largest number in one column that is less than or equal to the target value in the other column. The least upper bound (lub) operator finds the smallest number greater than or equal to the target number.

Unfortunately, this is not a good trade-off, because the subquery is fairly complex and will use a lot of running time. The "high and low" columns are a better solution in most cases. Here is a second version of the AddressBook query, using only the highzip column from the StateZip2 table:

```
SELECT name, street, city, state, zip
  FROM StateZip2, AddressBook
 WHERE state =
       (SELECT state
          FROM StateZip2
         WHERE highzip =
               (SELECT MIN(highzip)
                  FROM StateZip2
                 WHERE Address.zip <= StateZip2.highzip));
```

This correlated query will take some time to execute because it is fairly complex. The original version with the BETWEEN predicate is usually better in spite of requiring more table storage space. But you do not always get to pick the way the tables are constructed. If you want to allow for multiple-row matches by not requiring that the lookup table have unique values, the equality subquery predicate should be converted to an IN predicate.

19.1.2 Partition by Functions

It is also possible to use a function that will partition the table into subsets that share a particular property. I do not include here partitionings done by JOINs, GROUP BY clauses, or search conditions within an SQL query, but rather the cases where you have to add a column with the function result to the table because the function is too complex to be reasonably written in SQL.

One common example of this technique is the Soundex function (see Section 5.3), where it is not a vendor extension; the Soundex family assigns codes to names that are phonetically alike. The complex calculations in engineering and scientific databases that involve functions that SQL does not have are another example of this technique.

SQL was never meant to be a computational language. However, many vendors allow a query to access functions in the libraries of other programming languages. You must know the cost in execution time for your product before doing this. One version of SQL uses a threaded-code approach to carry parameters over to the other language's libraries and return the results on each row—and the execution time is horrible. Some versions of SQL can compile and link another language's library into the SQL.

As a generalization, the safest technique is to unload the parameter values to a file in a standard format that can be read by the other language. Then use that file in a program to find the function results and create INSERT INTO statements that will load a table in the database with the parameters and the results. You can then use this working table to load the result column in the original table.

19.2 Relational Division

Relational division is one of the eight basic operations in Codd's relational algebra. The idea is that a divisor table is used to partition a dividend table and produce a quotient or results table. The quotient table is made up of those values of one column for which a second column had all of the values in the divisor.

This approach is easier to explain with an example. We have a table of pilots and the planes they can fly (dividend); we have a table of planes in the hangar (divisor); we want the names of the pilots who can fly every plane (quotient) in the hangar. To get this result, we divide the PilotSkills table by the planes in the hangar.

```
CREATE TABLE PilotSkills
(pilot CHAR(15) NOT NULL,
```

```
plane CHAR(15) NOT NULL,
PRIMARY KEY (pilot, plane));
```

PilotSkills

pilot	plane
'Celko'	'Piper Cub'
'Higgins'	'B-52 Bomber'
'Higgins'	'F-14 Fighter'
'Higgins'	'Piper Cub'
'Jones'	'B-52 Bomber'
'Jones'	'F-14 Fighter'
'Smith'	'B-1 Bomber'
'Smith'	'B-52 Bomber'
'Smith'	'F-14 Fighter'
'Wilson'	'B-1 Bomber'
'Wilson'	'B-52 Bomber'
'Wilson'	'F-14 Fighter'
'Wilson'	'F-17 Fighter'

```
CREATE TABLE Hangar
(plane CHAR(15) NOT NULL PRIMARY KEY);
```

Hangar

plane
'B-1 Bomber'
'B-52 Bomber'
'F-14 Fighter'

PilotSkills DIVIDED BY Hangar

pilot
'Smith'
'Wilson'

In this example, Smith and Wilson are the two pilots who can fly everything in the hangar. Notice that Higgins and Celko know how to fly a Piper Cub, but we don't have one right now. In Codd's original definition of relational division, having more rows than are called for is not a problem.

The important characteristic of a relational division is that the CROSS JOIN (Cartesian product) of the divisor and the quotient produces a valid subset of rows from the dividend. This is where the name comes from since the CROSS JOIN acts like a multiplication operator.

19.2.1 Division with a Remainder

There are several kinds of *relational division*. Division with a remainder allows the dividend table to have more values than the divisor, which was Codd's original definition. For example, if a pilot can fly more planes than just those we have in the hangar, this is fine with us. The query can be written in SQL-89 as

```
SELECT DISTINCT pilot
  FROM PilotSkills AS PS1
 WHERE NOT EXISTS
       (SELECT *
          FROM Hangar
         WHERE NOT EXISTS
               (SELECT *
                  FROM PilotSkills AS PS2
                 WHERE (PS1.pilot = PS2.pilot)
                   AND (PS2.plane = Hangar.plane)));
```

The quickest way to explain what is happening in this query is to imagine an old World War II movie where a cocky pilot has just walked into the hangar, looked over the fleet, and announced, "There ain't no plane in this hangar that I can't fly!" We are finding the pilots for whom there does not exist a plane in the hangar for which they have no skills. The NOT EXISTS( ) predicates are used for speed. Most SQL systems will look up a value in an index rather than scan the whole table. The SELECT * clause lets the query optimizer choose the column to use when looking for the index.

This query for relational division was made popular by Chris Date in his textbooks, but it is not the only method nor always the fastest. Another version of the division can be written so as to avoid three levels of nesting. While it is not original with me, I have made it popular by including it in my books.

```
SELECT PS1.pilot
  FROM PilotSkills AS PS1, Hangar AS H1
 WHERE PS1.plane = H1.plane
```

```
GROUP BY PS1.pilot
HAVING COUNT(PS1.plane) = (SELECT COUNT(plane) FROM Hangar);
```

There is a serious difference in the two methods. Suppose the hangar burns, so that the divisor is empty. Because of the NOT EXISTS() predicates in Date's query, all pilots are returned from a division by an empty set. Because of the COUNT() functions in my query, no pilots are returned from a division by an empty set.

In the sixth edition of his book *Introduction to Database Systems* (Date 1995a), Chris Date defined another operator (DIVIDEBY . . . PER), which produces the same results as my query, but with the addition of more complexity.

19.2.2 Exact Division

The second kind of relational division is *exact relational division*. The dividend table must match exactly the values of the divisor without any extra values.

```
SELECT PS1.pilot
  FROM PilotSkills AS PS1
       LEFT OUTER JOIN
       Hangar AS H1
       ON PS1.plane = H1.plane
 GROUP BY PS1.pilot
HAVING COUNT(PS1.plane) = (SELECT COUNT(plane) FROM Hangar)
   AND COUNT(H1.plane) = (SELECT COUNT(plane) FROM Hangar);
```

This says that a pilot must have the same number of certificates as there are planes in the hangar and that these certificates must all match a plane in the hangar, not something else. The "something else" is shown by a created NULL from the LEFT OUTER JOIN.

Please do not make the mistake of trying to reduce the HAVING clause with a little algebra to

```
HAVING COUNT(PS1.plane) = COUNT(H1.plane)
```

because it does not work; it will tell you that the hangar has *n* planes in it and the pilot is certified for *n* planes, but not that those two sets of planes are equal to each other.

19.2.3 Note on Performance

The nested EXISTS() predicates version of relational division was made popular by Chris Date's textbooks, while the author is associated with popularizing the COUNT(*) version of relational division. The Winter 1996 edition of *DB2 On-Line Magazine* (*www.db2mag.com/96011ar.htm*) had an article entitled "Powerful SQL: Beyond the Basics" by Sheryl Larsen, which gave the results of testing both methods. Her conclusion for DB2 was that the nested EXISTS() version is better when the quotient has less than 25% of the dividend table's rows and that the COUNT(*) version is better when the quotient is more than 25% of the dividend table.

19.2.4 Todd's Division

A relational division operator proposed by Stephen Todd is defined on two tables with common columns that are joined together, dropping the JOIN column and retaining only those non-JOIN columns that meet a criterion.

We are given a table, JobParts(jobno, partno), and another table, SupParts(supno, partno), of suppliers and the parts that they provide. We want to get the supplier-and-job pairs such that supplier sn supplies all of the parts needed for job jn. This is not quite the same thing as getting the supplier-and-job pairs such that job jn requires all of the parts provided by supplier sn.

You want to divide the JobParts table by the SupParts table. A rule of thumb: The remainder comes from the dividend, but all values in the divisor are present.

JobParts		SupParts		Result = JobSups	
job	pno	sno	pno	job	sno
'j1'	'p1'	's1'	'p1'	'j1'	's1'
'j1'	'p2'	's1'	'p2'	'j1'	's2'
'j2'	'p2'	's1'	'p3'	'j2'	's1'
'j2'	'p4'	's1'	'p4'	'j2'	's4'
'j2'	'p5'	's1'	'p5'	'j3'	's1'
'j3'	'p2'	's1'	'p6'	'j3'	's2'
		's2'	'p1'	'j3'	's3'
		's2'	'p2'	'j3'	's4'
		's3'	'p2'		
		's4'	'p2'		
		's4'	'p4'		
		's4'	'p5'		

Pierre Mullin submitted the following query to carry out the Todd division:

```
SELECT DISTINCT JP1.job, SP1.supplier
  FROM JobParts AS JP1, SupParts AS SP1
 WHERE NOT EXISTS
         (SELECT *
            FROM JobParts AS JP2
           WHERE JP2.job = JP1.job
             AND JP2.part
                  NOT IN (SELECT SP2.part
                            FROM SupParts AS SP2
                           WHERE SP2.supplier = SP1.supplier));
```

This is really a modification of the query for Codd's division, extended to use a JOIN on both tables in the outermost SELECT statement. The IN predicate for the second subquery can be replaced with a NOT EXISTS predicate; it might run a bit faster, depending on the optimizer.

Another related query looks for the pairs of suppliers who sell the same parts. In this data, that would be the pairs (s1, p2), (s3, p1), (s4, p1), (s5, p1):

```
SELECT S1.sup, S2.sup
  FROM SupParts AS S1, SupParts AS S2
 WHERE S1.sup < S2.sup      -- different suppliers
   AND S1.part = S2.part    -- same parts
 GROUP BY S1.sup, S2.sup
HAVING COUNT(*) = (SELECT COUNT (*)   -- same count of parts
                     FROM SupParts AS S3
                    WHERE S3.sup = S1.sup)
   AND COUNT(*) = (SELECT COUNT (*)
                     FROM SupParts AS S4
                    WHERE S4.sup = S2.sup);
```

This can be easily modified into Todd's division by adding the restriction that the parts must also belong to a common job.

19.2.5 Division with JOINs

SQL-92 has several JOIN operators that can be used to perform a relational division. To find the pilots who can fly the same planes as Higgins, use this query:

```
SELECT SP1.Pilot
    FROM (((SELECT plane FROM Hangar) AS H1
        INNER JOIN (SELECT pilot, plane FROM PilotSkills) AS SP1
            ON H1.plane = SP1.plane)
        INNER JOIN (SELECT *
                    FROM PilotSkills
                WHERE pilot = 'Higgins') AS H2
            ON H2.plane = H1.plane)
    GROUP BY Pilot
HAVING COUNT(*) >= (SELECT COUNT(*)
                    FROM PilotSkills
                WHERE pilot = 'Higgins');
```

The first JOIN finds all of the planes in the hangar for which we have a pilot. The next JOIN takes that set and finds which of those match up with (SELECT * FROM PilotSkills WHERE pilot = 'Higgins') skills. The GROUP BY clause will then see that the intersection we have formed with the JOINs has at least as many elements as Higgins has planes. The GROUP BY also means that the SELECT DISTINCT can be replaced with a simple SELECT. If the theta operator in the GROUP BY clause is changed from >= to =, the query finds an exact division. If the theta operator in the GROUP BY clause is changed from >= to <= or <, the query finds those pilots whose skills are a superset or a strict superset of the planes that Higgins flies.

It might be a good idea to put the divisor into a VIEW for readability in this query and as a clue to the optimizer to calculate it once. Some products will execute this form of the division query faster than the nested subquery version because they will use the PRIMARY KEY information to pre-compute the JOINs between tables.

19.2.6 Division with Set Operators

The SQL-92 set difference operator, EXCEPT, can be used to write a very compact version of Codd's relational division. The EXCEPT operator removes the divisor set from the dividend set. If the result is empty, we have a match; if there is anything left over, it has failed. Using the pilots-and-hangar-tables example, we would write

```
SELECT Pilot
    FROM PilotSkills AS P1
WHERE (SELECT plane FROM Hangar
        EXCEPT
```

```
SELECT plane
    FROM PilotSkills AS P2
WHERE P1.pilot = P2.pilot) IS NULL;
```

Again, informally, you can imagine that we got a skills list from each pilot, walked over to the hangar, and crossed off each plane he could fly. If we marked off all the planes in the hangar, we would keep this guy. Another SQL-92 trick is that an empty subquery expression returns a NULL, which is how we can test for an empty set. The WHERE clause could just as well have used a NOT EXISTS( ) predicate instead of the IS NULL predicate.

Grouping Operations

I DEAL SEPARATELY WITH partitions and grouping operations based on the idea that a group has properties that we are trying to find, so we get an answer back for each group. A partition is simply a way of subsetting the original table so that we get a table as a result.

20.1 GROUP BY Clause

SQL tries to organize data in the simplest, most portable possible fashion; hence rows are made up only of scalar values. SQL also tries to summarize data in the simplest possible fashion. That is why the only method of aggregation in the language is based on simple partitions. To repeat what was said in Section 19.1 on covering and partitions, a partition of a set divides the set into subsets such that (1) the union of the subsets returns the original set and (2) the intersection of the subsets is empty. Think of it as cutting up a pizza—each piece of pepperoni belongs to one and only one slice of pizza.

The GROUP BY clause takes the result of the FROM and WHERE clauses, then puts the rows into groups defined as having the same values for the columns listed in the GROUP BY clause. Each group is reduced to a single row in the result table. This result table is called a *grouped table,* and all operations are now defined on groups rather than on rows.

By convention, the NULLs are treated as one group. The order of the grouping columns in the GROUP BY clause does not matter, but since they have to appear in the SELECT list, you should probably use the same order in both lists to enhance readability.

Let us construct a sample table called Villes and use it to explain in detail how this works. The table is declared as

```
CREATE TABLE Villes
 (state CHAR(2) NOT NULL,
  city CHAR(25) NOT NULL,
  PRIMARY KEY (city, state));
```

and we populate it with the names of cities that end in -ville. The first problem is to find a count of the number of such cities by state. The immediate naive query might be

```
SELECT state, city, COUNT(*)
  FROM Villes
 GROUP BY state;
```

The groups for Tennessee would have the rows ('TN', 'Nashville') and ('TN', 'Knoxville'). The first position in the result is the grouping column, which has to be constant within the group. The third column in the SELECT clause is the COUNT(*) for the group, which is clearly two. The city column is a problem. Since the table is grouped by states, there can be at most 50 groups, one for each state. The COUNT(*) is clearly a single value and it applies to the group as a whole. But what possible single value could I output for a city in each group? Pick a typical city and use it? If all the cities have the same name, use that name, and otherwise output a NULL? The worst possible choice would be to output both rows with the COUNT(*) of 2, since each row would imply that there are two cities named Nashville and two cities named Knoxville in Tennessee. It is worth mentioning that Sybase and SQL Server Transaction SQL have this flaw, but that the problem was corrected in Sybase System 10 and System 11.

Each row represents a single group, so anything in it must be a characteristic of the group, not of a single row in the group. This is why there is a rule that the SELECT list must be made up only of grouping columns with optional aggregate-function expressions.

20.1.1 NULLs and Groups

SQL puts the NULLs into a single group, as if they were all equal. The other option, which was used in some of the first SQL implementations before the standard, was to put each NULL into a group by itself. That is not an unreasonable choice. But to make a meaningful choice between the two options, you would have to know the semantics of the data you are trying to model. SQL is a language based on syntax, not semantics.

For example, if a NULL is being used for a missing diagnosis in a medical record, you know that each patient will probably have a different disease when the NULLs are resolved. Putting the NULLs in one group would make sense if you wanted to consider unprocessed diagnosis reports as one group in a summary. Putting each NULL in its own group would make sense if you wanted to consider each unprocessed diagnosis report as an action item for treatment of the relevant class of diseases. Another example was a traffic ticket database that used NULL for a missing auto license tag. Obviously, there is more than one car without a tag in the database. The general scheme for getting separate groups for each NULL is straightforward:

```
SELECT x, . . .
  FROM Table1
 WHERE x IS NOT NULL
 GROUP BY x
UNION ALL
SELECT x, . . .
  FROM Table1
 WHERE x IS NULL;
```

There will also be cases, such as the traffic tickets, where you can use another GROUP BY clause to form groups where the principal grouping columns are NULL. For example, the VIN (Vehicle Identification Number) is taken when the car is missing a tag, and it would provide a grouping column.

20.1.2 GROUP BY and HAVING

One of the biggest problems in working with the GROUP BY clause is not understanding how the WHERE and HAVING clauses work. Consider the query to find all departments with fewer than five programmers:

```
SELECT deptno
  FROM Employees
 WHERE job = 'Programmer'
```

```
GROUP BY deptno
HAVING COUNT(*) < 5;
```

The result of this query does not have a row for any departments with no programmers. The order of execution of the clauses does WHERE first, so that employees whose jobs are not equal to 'Programmer' are never passed to the GROUP BY clause. You have thus missed data that you might want to trap.

It is also worth remarking that some older versions of SQL would require that the SELECT clause also have COUNT(*) in it. This is because they would materialize the grouped table and pass it to the HAVING clause in much the same way as they handled a WHERE clause. This is not standard SQL.

However, the next query will also pick up those departments that have no programmers because the COUNT(DISTINCT x) function will return a zero for an empty set:

```
SELECT DISTINCT deptno
  FROM Employees AS E1
 WHERE 5 > (SELECT COUNT(DISTINCT E2.empno)
              FROM Employees AS E2
             WHERE E1.deptno = E2.deptno
               AND E2.job ='Programmer');
```

If there is no GROUP BY clause, the HAVING clause will treat the entire table as a single group according to the SQL-89 and SQL-92 standards. In practice, however, you will find that many implementations of SQL require the HAVING clause to belong to a GROUP BY clause.

Since the HAVING clause applies only to a grouped table, it can reference only the grouping columns and aggregate functions that apply to the group. That is why this query would fail:

```
SELECT deptno          -- Invalid Query!
  FROM Employees
 GROUP BY deptno
HAVING (COUNT(*) < 5) AND (job ='Programmer');
```

When the HAVING clause is executed, job is not in the grouped table as a column—it is a property of a row, not of a group. Likewise, this query would fail for much the same reason:

```
SELECT deptno          -- Invalid Query!
  FROM Employees
 WHERE (COUNT(*) < 5) AND (job ='Programmer')
 GROUP BY deptno;
```

The COUNT(*) does not exist until after the departmental groups are formed.

20.1.3 Grouped VIEWs for Multiple Aggregation Levels

Business reports are usually based on a hierarchy of nested levels of aggregation. This type of report is so common that there are tools that perform only this sort of task. For example, sales are grouped under the salesmen who made them, then sales departments are grouped into districts, districts are grouped into regions, and so on until we have summary information at the company level. Each level is a partition of the level above it. The summary information can be constructed from the level immediately beneath it in the hierarchy.

Since SQL has no way of directly building nested hierarchies, you have to either fake it or use other tools. Frankly, using a report writer is faster and more powerful than writing SQL code to do the job.

One trick in SQL-89 is to use VIEWs with GROUP BY clauses to build the reporting levels. Using a Sales report example, the following UNIONed query will produce a report for each level, from the lowest, most detailed level (salesman), through districts and regions, to the highest level (the company).

```
SELECT reg, dist, salesman, SUM(amt)
  FROM Sales
 GROUP BY reg, dist, salesman
UNION
SELECT reg, dist, '{SALESMEN}', SUM(amt)
  FROM Sales
 GROUP BY reg, dist
UNION
SELECT reg, '{OFFICE}', '{SALESMEN}', SUM(amt)
  FROM Sales
 GROUP BY reg
UNION
SELECT '{REGION}', '{OFFICE}', '{SALESMEN}', SUM(amt)
  FROM Sales
 ORDER BY 1, 2, 3;
```

The constant strings inside the curly brackets will sort below any alphabetic strings in ASCII, and thus will appear on the end of each grouping in the hierarchy. After having shown you this trick, I need to point out its flaws.

One problem is that the columnar positional numbers in the ORDER BY clause are a deprecated feature in SQL-92; that means that the next release of the standard will not support them.

Next, running these four queries can be expensive because the base table must be scanned for each of them. A better approach would be to create VIEWs for each level and then do a SELECT * from the VIEWs:

```
CREATE VIEW Salespersons (reg, dist, salesman, amt)
AS SELECT reg, dist, salesman, SUM(amt)
     FROM Sales
      GROUP BY reg, dist, salesman;

CREATE VIEW SalesDist (reg, dist, amt)
AS SELECT reg, dist, SUM(amt)
     FROM Salespersons
     GROUP BY reg, dist;

CREATE VIEW SalesRegions (reg, amt)
AS SELECT reg, SUM(amt)
     FROM SalesDist
     GROUP BY reg;

SELECT SUM(amt)
FROM SalesRegions;
```

Most SQL implementations will materialize these VIEWs because of the GROUP BY clauses. Because each VIEW is built from the one underneath it, it does not have to reread the entire table. However, the materialized tables will have to be kept in storage, which makes this decision a classic speed-for-memory-space trade-off. Those implementations that do not materialize the VIEWs will have the opposite trade-off since they will use less main storage, but will need longer computing times to build each VIEW independently of the others.

A better approach can be found in Chapter 29 on presenting trees as nested sets in SQL.

20.1.4 Sorting and GROUP BY

Though it is not required by the standard, most implementations will automatically sort the results of a grouped query. Internally, the groups are built by first sorting the table on the grouping columns, then aggregating them. The NULL group sorts either high or low, depending on the vendor.

An ORDER BY clause whose columns are not in the same order as those in the GROUP BY clause can be expensive to execute if the optimizer does not detect the double sort request. It is also possible to sort a grouped table on an aggregate or calculated column. In the older SQL-89 standard, these columns were referenced by their position numbers; this is a deprecated feature and should not be used if possible. SQL-92 allows you to rename a column with the construct <column> AS <identifier> in the SELECT list. The most common use is to order an aggregate function column to show information.

For example, to show the sales regions in order of total sales, you would write

```
SELECT reg, dist, SUM(amt) AS dist_amt
FROM Sales
GROUP BY reg, dist
ORDER BY dist_amt DESC, reg, dist;
```

Since it is possible that two or more regions could have the same sales volume, it is always a good idea to sort by the reg column, then by the dist column. The extra sorting is cheap to execute and requires no extra storage. It is very likely that your SQL implementation is using a *nonstable sort*.

A *stable sort* preserves the original order of the rows with keys of equal value. For example, I am given a deck of playing cards to sort by rank and suit. If I first sort by rank, assuming aces high, I would get a deck with all the deuces, followed by all the treys, and so forth until I got to the aces. Within each of these groups, the suits could be in any order.

If I then sorted the deck on the suits of the cards, I would get (assuming bridge sorting order) deuces of clubs, diamonds, hearts, and finally spades, as the highest rank, followed by treys of clubs, diamonds, hearts, and spades, and so forth up to the aces.

If the second sort were a nonstable sort, it could destroy the ordering of the suits. A second sort that was a stable sort would keep the ordering in the suits.

Stable sorts are almost always slower than nonstable sorts, so nonstable sorts are preferred by most database systems. However, a smart optimizer can see an existing order in the intermediate working table and replace the usual nonstable sort with a stable sort, thereby avoiding extra work. Clustered indexes and other sources of pre-existing ordering in the data can also be used by the optimizer.

However, you should never depend on the default ordering of a particular SQL product since this will not be portable. If ordering is important, use an ORDER BY clause with all of the desired columns explicitly given in it. In

SQL-92, you will have to use an AS clause on each of the aggregate functions to give it a name that can be used in the ORDER BY clause.

20.1.5 Grouped Subqueries for Multiple Aggregation Levels

The SQL-92 standard permits you to use a table subquery in a FROM clause and a scalar subquery anywhere that you would use an expression. This lets us do some multilevel aggregation in a single query. For example, to find how each salesman did in his sales district, you can write

```
SELECT salesman, reg, dist, SUM(amt) AS salesman_tot,
          (SELECT SUM(amt)
              FROM Sales AS S1
          WHERE S1.reg = S2.reg
              AND S1.dist = S2.dist) AS dist_tot
      FROM Sales AS S2
GROUP BY salesman, reg, dist;
```

This query will work because the subquery is a constant for each group. The subquery could also be used in an expression to give the percentage of the district total each salesman contributed.

A trickier query is to find aggregates of aggregates—something like the average of the total sales of the districts for each region. Beginning SQL programmers would try to write queries like this:

```
SELECT reg, AVG(SUM(amt)) AS region_average   -- Invalid SQL
    FROM Sales
GROUP BY dist, reg;
```

and the parser would gag on AVG(SUM(amt)) and return an error message about nesting aggregate functions. SQL-92 will let you get the desired effect in exchange for a little more work. You need a subquery that will compute the sum of the sales for each district within a region.

This table then needs to be averaged for each region:

```
SELECT T1.reg, AVG(T1.district_total) AS region_average
    FROM (SELECT reg, dist, SUM(amt)
            FROM Sales
        GROUP BY reg, dist) AS T1 (reg, dist, district_total)
GROUP BY T1.reg;
```

Since this is a new SQL-92 feature, most implementations do not have it yet. However, my best guess would be that the subquery would be con-

structed once as a materialized table, then used by the SELECT statement in
the usual way. Do not think that SQL-92 would let you write

```
SELECT reg, AVG(SELECT SUM(amt)      -- Invalid SQL-92
               FROM Sales AS S1
               WHERE S1.reg = S2.reg
               GROUP BY dist) AS region_average
  FROM Sales AS S2
GROUP BY reg;
```

The parameter for an aggregate function still cannot be another aggregate
function or a subquery. The reason for this prohibition is that though this
particular subquery is scalar, other subqueries might have multiple rows
and/or multiple columns and not be able to return a single value.

20.1.6 Grouping on Computed Columns

There are implementations of SQL that allow queries that are grouped on the
result of a computed column. For example, to do a report by months on
sales, they allow you to write

```
SELECT EXTRACT(MONTH FROM saledate), SUM(amt) -- invalid SQL!
  FROM Sales
 GROUP BY EXTRACT(MONTH FROM saledate);
```

This is wrong. While it looks handy, you will pay for it in other places
with erroneous results. Besides the definition of the GROUP BY clause in the
standard allowing only column names, there is a more basic problem. The
clauses of a SELECT statement are executed in a particular order: Build a
working table in the FROM clause, remove disqualified rows in the WHERE
clause, form a new working table based on groups in the GROUP BY, remove
the disqualified groups in the HAVING clause, and finally compute the expressions in the SELECT clause. The computed columns do not exist until after
the grouping is done, so there is no way to group on them.

However, you can fake it in SQL-92 by using a subquery expression in the
FROM clause to build a working table with the computation in it.

```
SELECT salesmonth, SUM(amt)
  FROM (SELECT EXTRACT(MONTH FROM saledate) AS salesmonth,
               amt
          FROM Sales)
 GROUP BY salesmonth;
```

or by using a correlated subquery expression in the SELECT clause:

```
SELECT DISTINCT EXTRACT(MONTH FROM S1.saledate),
       (SELECT SUM(S2.amt)
          FROM Sales AS S2
         WHERE EXTRACT(MONTH FROM S2.saledate)
             = EXTRACT(MONTH FROM S1.saledate))
  FROM Sales AS S1;
```

The first version will probably run faster, since it does not have as many computations in it.

20.2 Ungrouping a Table

Sissy Kubu sent me a strange question on CompuServe. She has a table like this:

```
CREATE TABLE Inventory
(goods CHAR(10) NOT NULL PRIMARY KEY,
 pieces INTEGER NOT NULL
        CONSTRAINT zero_or_more
        CHECK (pieces >= 0));
```

She wants to deconsolidate the table; that is, get a VIEW or table with one row for each pieces. For example, given a row with ('CD-ROM', 3) in the original table, she would like to get three rows with ('CD-ROM', 1) in them. (Before you ask me, I have no idea why she wants to do this; consider it a training exercise.)

Since SQL has no "UN-COUNT(*) . . . DE-GROUP BY. . ." operators, you will have to use a cursor or the vendor's 4GL to do this. Frankly, I would do this in a report program instead of a SQL query since the results will not be a table with a key.

The obvious procedural way to do this would be to write a routine in your SQL's 4GL that reads a row from the Inventory table, and then writes the value of good to the second table in a loop driven by the value of pieces. This will be pretty slow since it will require (SELECT SUM(pieces) FROM Inventory) single-row insertions into the working table.

20.2.1 Ungrouping by Splitting a Table

I always stress the need to think in terms of sets in SQL. The way to build a better solution is to do repeated self-insertion operations, using a technique based on the "Russian peasant's algorithm," which was used for multiplication and division in early computers. You can look it up in a history of mathematics or a computer science book—it is based on binary arithmetic and can be implemented with right and left shift operators in assembly anguages.

You are still going to need a 4GL to do this, but it will not be so bad. First, let's create two working tables and one for the final answer:

```
CREATE TABLE WorkingTable1
(goods CHAR(10) NOT NULL,
 pieces INTEGER NOT NULL);

CREATE TABLE WorkingTable2
(goods CHAR(10) NOT NULL,
 pieces INTEGER NOT NULL);

CREATE TABLE Answer
(goods CHAR(10) NOT NULL,
 pieces INTEGER NOT NULL);
```

Now start by loading the goods that have only one pieces in inventory into the answer table:

```
INSERT INTO Answer
SELECT * FROM Inventory WHERE pieces = 1;
```

Now put the rest of the data into the first working table:

```
INSERT INTO WorkingTable1
SELECT * FROM Inventory WHERE pieces > 1;
```

This block of code will load the second working table with pairs of rows that each have half (or half plus 1) pieces counts of those in the first working table:

```
INSERT INTO WorkingTable2
SELECT goods, FLOOR(pieces/2.0)
 FROM WorkingTable1
WHERE pieces > 1
UNION ALL
SELECT goods, CEILING(pieces/2.0)
 FROM WorkingTable1
WHERE pieces > 1;
```

The FLOOR(x) and CEILING(x) functions return, respectively, the greatest integer that is lower than *x* and the smallest integer higher than *x*. If your SQL does not have them, you can write them with rounding and truncation functions. It is also important to divide by (2.0) and not by 2 because this will make the result into a decimal number.

Now harvest the rows that have gotten down to a pieces count of 1 and clear out the first working table:

```
INSERT INTO Answer
 SELECT *
   FROM WorkingTable2
  WHERE pieces = 1;

DELETE FROM WorkingTable1;
```

Exchange the roles of WorkingTable1 and WorkingTable2, and repeat the process until both working tables are empty. That is simple, straightforward procedural coding. The way that the results shift from table to table is interesting to follow. Think of these diagrams as an animated cartoon:

1. Load the first working table, harvesting any goods that already had a pieces count of 1.

WorkingTable1		WorkingTable2	
goods	**pieces**	**goods**	**pieces**
Alpha	4		
Beta	5		
Delta	16		
Gamma	50		

The row ('Epsilon', 1) goes immediately to Answer table.

2. Halve the pieces counts and double the rows in the second working table. Empty the first working table.

WorkingTable1		WorkingTable2	
goods	**pieces**	**goods**	**pieces**
		Alpha	2
		Alpha	2
		Beta	2
		Beta	3

Delta	8
Delta	8
Gamma	25
Gamma	25

3. Repeat the process until both working tables are empty.

WorkingTable1

goods	pieces
Alpha	1
Alpha	1
Alpha	1
Alpha	1
Beta	1
Beta	1
Beta	1
Beta	1
Beta	1
Delta	4
Delta	4
Delta	4
Delta	4
Gamma	12
Gamma	12
Gamma	13
Gamma	13

WorkingTable2

goods	pieces

Alpha and Beta are ready to harvest

The cost of completely emptying a table is usually very low. Likewise, the cost of copying sets of rows (which are in physical blocks of disk storage that can be moved as whole buffers) from one table to another is much lower than inserting one row at a time.

The code could have been written to leave the results in one of the working tables, but this approach allows the working tables to get smaller and smaller, so that you get better buffer usage. This algorithm uses (SELECT SUM(pieces) FROM Inventory) rows of storage and (log2((SELECT MAX(pieces) FROM Inventory)) + 1) moves, which is pretty good on both counts.

20.2.2 Ungrouping Using a JOIN

Peter Lawrence, president of Resolution Integration Solutions Inc., suggested another answer to the "uncount" problem, but it requires a table that contains all integers up to at least the maximum number of pieces N:

```
CREATE TABLE TallyTable (tally_nbr INTEGER NOT NULL);
INSERT INTO TallyTable VALUES (1), (2), . . . (N);
```

Given this table, you then select the "uncount" as follows:

```
SELECT goods, 1 AS tally, tally_nbr
  FROM Inventory AS I1, TallyTable AS T1
 WHERE I1.pieces >= T1.tally_nbr
   AND T1.tally_nbr >= 1;
```

The results should be

Results

goods	tally	tally_nbr
'CD-ROM'	1	1
'CD-ROM'	1	2
'CD-ROM'	1	3
'Printer'	1	1
'Printer'	1	2

. . .

This trick with the TallyTable is very useful. You can also have a Clock table containing, say, a date/time on the hour every hour. This can be used for similar queries such as selecting every hour that someone was in the office when all the database contains is the start and end times.

I like this answer and the simple JOIN should be faster than my elaborate shuffle between two working tables. The only change I would make would be to play safe as the size of the TallyTable. First of all, we need to declare it with a primary key:

```
CREATE TABLE TallyTable
(tally_nbr INTEGER NOT NULL PRIMARY KEY);
```

One method would be to see that some of the work gets done, leaving the items with a piece count greater than the highest tally number still intact:

```
SELECT DISTINCT goods,
       CASE WHEN I1.pieces > (SELECT MAX(T2.tally_nbr)
                                   FROM TallyTable AS T2)
            THEN pieces
            WHEN I1.pieces >= T1.tally_nbr
            THEN tally_nbr END AS tally_nbr
  FROM Inventory AS I1,  TallyTable AS T1
WHERE tally IS NOT NULL;
```

A second approach would be to reject the whole query if we have a piece count greater than the highest tally number:

```
SELECT goods, 1 AS tally, tally_nbr
  FROM Inventory AS I1, TallyTable AS T1
 WHERE I1.pieces >= T1.tally_nbr
   AND (SELECT MAX(I2.pieces) FROM Inventory AS I2)
      <= (SELECT MAX(T2.tally_nbr) FROM TallyTable AS T2);
```

The subquery expressions are known to be constant for the life of the query, so the optimizer can do them once, by going to an index in the case of the TallyTable and with a table scan in the case of the Inventory table, since it is not likely to be indexed on the piece count.

This method will work faster for small sets of data, but the splitting approach will work faster for large sets of data.

Vinicius Mello came up with a method of creating the working table with another version of the Russian peasant's algorithm:

```
BEGIN
DECLARE increment INTEGER;
DECLARE maxnum INTEGER;
SET increment = 2;
SET maxnum = (SELECT COUNT(*) FROM Inventory);
WHILE increment < maxnum
LOOP
  INSERT INTO TallyTable
  SELECT tally_nbr + increment
    FROM TallyTable;
  SET increment = increment + increment;
END LOOP;
END;
```

However, a better way to create the TallyTable is to first create a table of digits:

```
CREATE TABLE Digits (i INTEGER NOT NULL);
INSERT INTO Digits
VALUES (0), (1), (2), (3), (4), (5), (6), (7), (8), (9);
```

Then use that to load the TallyTable:

```
INSERT INTO TallyTable
SELECT (D1.i + (10*D2.i) + (100*D3.i) + (1000*D4.i) + 1)
  FROM Digits AS D1, Digits AS D2, Digits AS D3, Digits AS D4;
```

The CROSS JOIN will create all possible numbers from 0 to 9,999, so you need to add 1 to avoid the zero. Obviously, this method can be extended to any size number and truncated by a WHERE clause.

Aggregate Functions

THERE IS A difference between data and information. One of the major purposes of a database system is to turn data into information. This usually means doing some statistical summary from that data. Descriptive statistics measure some property of an existing data set and express it as a single number. Though there are very sophisticated measures, most applications require only basic, well-understood statistics. The most common summary functions are the count (or tally), the average (or arithmetic mean), and the sum (or total). The SQL language contains this minimal set of descriptive statistical operators, and vendors often extend these options with others. These functions are called *set functions* in the ANSI/ISO SQL standard, but vendors, textbook writers, and everyone else usually call them *aggregate functions,* so I will use that term here.

Aggregate functions first construct a column of values as defined by the parameter. The parameter is usually a single column name, but it can be an arithmetic expression with scalar functions and calculations. Pretty much the only things that cannot be parameters are other aggregate functions (e.g., SUM(AVG(x)) is illegal) and a subquery (e.g., AVG(SELECT col1 FROM SomeTable WHERE . . .) is illegal). A subquery could return more than one value, so it would not fit into a column, and an aggregate function would have to try to build a column within a column.

Once the working column is constructed, all the NULLs are removed and the function performs its operation. As you learn the definitions I am about to give, stress the words *known values* to remind yourself that the NULLs have been dropped.

There are two options, ALL and DISTINCT, that are shown as keywords inside the parameter list. The keyword ALL is optional and is never really used in practice. It says that all the rows in the working column are retained for the final calculation. The keyword DISTINCT is not optional in these functions. It removes all duplicate values from a working column before the final calculation. Let's look at the particulars of each aggregate function.

21.1 COUNT Functions

There are two forms of the COUNT( ) function, *cardinality* and *expression* counting. COUNT(*) returns the number of rows in a table (called the *cardinality of the table* in relational terms); it is the only aggregate function that uses an asterisk as a parameter. This function is very useful and usually will run quite fast since it can use system information about the table size. Remember that NULL values are also counted because this function deals with rows and not column values. An empty table has a COUNT(*) of zero, which makes sense. You would think that using the COUNT(*) would be easy, but there are a lot of subtle tricks to it. Think of a database of the presidencies of the United States, with columns for the first name, middle initial(s), and last name of each U.S. president, along with his political party and his terms in office. It would look like this:

```
CREATE TABLE Parties
(partycode CHAR(2) NOT NULL,
 partyname CHAR(25) NOT NULL);

INSERT INTO Parties VALUES ('D', 'Democratic');
INSERT INTO Parties VALUES ('DR', 'Democratic Republican');
INSERT INTO Parties VALUES ('R', 'Republican');
INSERT INTO Parties VALUES ('F', 'Federalist');
INSERT INTO Parties VALUES ('W', 'Whig');

CREATE TABLE Presidents
(firstname CHAR(11) NOT NULL,
 initial VARCHAR(4) NOT NULL DEFAULT ' ', -- one space
 lastname CHAR(11) NOT NULL,
 party CHAR(2) NOT NULL,
 startterm INTEGER NOT NULL,
 endterm INTEGER);
```

Presidents

firstname	initial	lastname	party	startterm	endterm
'George'	' '	'Washington'	'F'	1789	1797
'John'	' '	'Adams'	'F'	1797	1801
'Thomas'	' '	'Jefferson'	'DR'	1801	1809
'James'	' '	'Madison'	'DR'	1809	1817
'James'	' '	'Monroe'	'DR'	1817	1825
'John'	'Q.'	'Adams'	'DR'	1825	1829
'Andrew'	' '	'Jackson'	'D'	1829	1837
'Martin'	' '	'Van Buren'	'D'	1837	1841
'William'	'H.'	'Harrison'	'W'	1841	1841
'John'	' '	'Tyler'	'W'	1841	1845
'James'	'K.'	'Polk'	'D'	1845	1849
'Zachary'	' '	'Taylor'	'W'	1849	1850
'Millard'	' '	'Fillmore'	'W'	1850	1853
'Franklin'	' '	'Pierce'	'D'	1853	1857
'James'	' '	'Buchanan'	'D'	1857	1861
'Abraham'	' '	'Lincoln'	'R'	1861	1865
'Andrew'	' '	'Johnson'	'R'	1865	1869
'Ulysses'	'S.'	'Grant'	'R'	1869	1877
'Rutherford'	'B.'	'Hayes'	'R'	1877	1881
'James'	'A.'	'Garfield'	'R'	1881	1881
'Chester'	'A.'	'Arthur'	'R'	1881	1885
'Grover'	' '	'Cleveland'	'D'	1885	1889
'Benjamin'	' '	'Harrison'	'R'	1889	1893
'Grover'	' '	'Cleveland'	'D'	1893	1897
'William'	' '	'McKinley'	'R'	1897	1901
'Theodore'	' '	'Roosevelt'	'R'	1901	1909
'William'	'H.'	'Taft'	'R'	1909	1913
'Woodrow'	' '	'Wilson'	'D'	1913	1921
'Warren'	'G.'	'Harding'	'R'	1921	1923
'Calvin'	' '	'Coolidge'	'R'	1923	1929
'Herbert'	'C.'	'Hoover'	'R'	1929	1933
'Franklin'	'D.'	'Roosevelt'	'D'	1933	1945
'Harry'	'S.'	'Truman'	'D'	1945	1953
'Dwight'	'D.'	'Eisenhower'	'R'	1953	1961
'John'	'F.'	'Kennedy'	'D'	1961	1963

(cont.)	firstname	initial	lastname	party	startterm	endterm
	'Lyndon'	'B.'	'Johnson'	'D'	1963	1969
	'Richard'	'M.'	'Nixon'	'R'	1969	1974
	'Gerald'	'R.'	'Ford'	'R'	1974	1977
	'James'	'E.'	'Carter'	'D'	1977	1981
	'Ronald'	'W.'	'Reagan'	'R'	1981	1989
	'George'	'H.W.'	'Bush'	'R'	1989	1993
	'William'	'J.'	'Clinton'	'D'	1993	(NULL)

Your civics teacher has just asked you to tell her how many people have been president of the United States. So you write the query as SELECT COUNT(*) FROM Presidents; and get the wrong answer. For those of you who have been out of high school too long, more than one Adams, more than one John, and more than one Roosevelt have served as president. Many people have had more than one term in office, and Grover Cleveland served two discontinuous terms. In short, this database is not a simple one-row, one-person system. What you really wanted was not COUNT(*), but something that is able to look at unique combinations of multiple columns. You cannot do this in one column, so you need to construct an expression that is unique—(firstname || initial || lastname). The point is that you need to be very sure that the expression you are using as a parameter is really what you wanted to count.

The COUNT([ALL] <value expression>) returns the number of members in the <value expression> set. The NULLs were thrown away before the counting took place, and an empty set returns zero. The best way to read this is as "Count the number of known values in this expression" with stress on the word *known*.

The COUNT(DISTINCT <value expression>) returns the number of unique members in the <value expression> set. The NULLs were thrown away before the counting took place, and then all redundant duplicates are removed (i.e., we keep one copy). Again, an empty set returns a zero, just as with the other counting functions. Applying this function to a key or a unique column is the same as using the COUNT(*) function, but the optimizer may not be smart enough to spot it.

Notice that the use of the keywords ALL and DISTINCT follows the same pattern here as they did in the [ALL | DISTINCT] options in the SELECT clause of the query expressions.

21.2 SUM Functions

SUM([ALL] <value expression>) returns the numeric total of all known values. This function works only with numeric values. You should also consult your particular product's manuals to find out the precision of the results for exact and approximate numeric datatypes. An empty set returns a NULL, and since a set of only NULL values will become an empty set, it also returns a NULL.

SUM(DISTINCT <value expression>) returns the numeric total of all known, unique values. The NULLs and all redundant duplicates were removed before the summation took place. An empty set returns a NULL, not a zero. This function works only with numeric values. You should also consult your particular product's manuals to find out the precision of the results for exact and approximate numeric datatypes.

The summation of a set of numbers looks as if it should be easy, but it is not. Make two tables with the same set of positive and negative approximate numeric values, but put one in random order and have the other sorted by absolute value. The sorted table will give more accurate results. The reason is simple; positive and negative values of the same magnitude will be added together and will get a chance to cancel each other out. There is also less chance of an overflow or underflow error during calculations. Most PC SQL implementations and a lot of mainframe implementations do not bother with this trick because it would require a sort for every SUM() statement and would take a long time.

Whenever an exact or approximate numeric value is assigned to exact numeric, it may not fit into the storage allowed for it. SQL says that the database engine will use an approximation that preserves leading significant digits of the original number after rounding or truncating. The choice of whether to truncate or round is implementation-defined, however. This can lead to some surprises when you have to shift data among SQL implementations, or storage values from a host language program into an SQL table. It is probably a good idea to create the columns with one more decimal place than you think you need.

Truncation is defined as truncation toward zero; this means that 1.5 would truncate to 1, and −1.5 would truncate to −1. This is not true for all languages; everyone agrees on truncation toward zero for the positive numbers, but you will find that negative numbers may truncate away from zero (e.g., −1.5 would truncate to −2). SQL is also wishy-washy on rounding, leaving the implementation free to determine its method. There are two major types of rounding, the scientific method and the commercial method, which are discussed in Section 3.2.1 on rounding and truncation math in SQL.

21.3 AVG Functions

AVG([ALL] <value expression>) returns the average of the values in the value expression set. An empty set returns a NULL, and again a set of all NULLs will become an empty set so it also returns a NULL. Remember that in general AVG(x) is not the same as (SUM(x)/COUNT(*)); the SUM(x) function has thrown away the NULLs, but the COUNT(*) has not.

Likewise, AVG(DISTINCT <value expression>) returns the average of the distinct known values in the <value expression> set. Applying this function to a key or a unique column is the same as using the AVG(<value expression>) function, but again the optimizer may not be smart enough to spot it. Remember that in general AVG(DISTINCT x) is not the same as AVG(x) or (SUM(DISTINCT x)/COUNT(*)). The SUM(DISTINCT x) function has thrown away the duplicate values and NULLs, but the COUNT(*) has not. An empty set returns a NULL.

The SQL engine probably uses the same code for the totaling in the AVG() that it uses in the SUM() function. This leads to the same problems with rounding and truncation, so you should experiment a little with your particular product to find out what happens.

But even more troublesome than those problems is the problem with the average itself because it does not really measure central tendency and can be very misleading. Consider the chart below, from Darrell Huff's superlative little book *How to Lie with Statistics* (Huff 1954). The sample company has 25 employees, earning the following salaries:

Number of Employees	Salary	Statistic
12	$2,000	Mode, Minimum
1	$3,000	Median
4	$3,700	
3	$5,000	
1	$5,700	Average
2	$10,000	
1	$15,000	
1	$45,000	Maximum

The average salary (or, more properly, the arithmetic mean) is $5,700. When the boss is trying to make himself look good to the unions, he uses this figure. When the unions are trying to look impoverished, they use the mode, which is the most frequently occurring value, to show that the exploited workers are making $2,000 (which is also the minimum salary in this case).

A better measure in this case is the median, which will be discussed later; that is, the employee with just as many cases above him as below him. That gives us $3,000. The rule for calculating the median is that if there is no actual entity with that value, you fake it.

Most people take an average of the two values on either side of where the median would be; others jump to the higher or lower value. The mode also has a problem because not every distribution of values has one mode. Imagine a country in which there are as many very poor people as there are very rich people and nobody in between. This would be a bimodal distribution. If there are sharply defined classes of incomes, that would be a multimodal distribution.

Some SQL products have median and mode aggregate functions as extensions, but they are not part of the standard. We will discuss in detail how to write them in pure SQL in Chapter 23.

21.3.1 Averages with Empty Groups

The query used here is a bit tricky, so this section can be skipped on your first reading. Sometimes you need to count an empty set as part of the population when computing an average. This is easier to explain with an example that was posted on CompuServe. A fish and game warden is sampling different bodies of water for fish populations. Each sample falls into one or more groups (muddy bottoms, clear water, still water, and so on), and she is trying to find the average of something that is not there. This is not quite as strange as it first sounds—nor quite as simple, either. She is collecting sample data on fish in a table like this:

```
CREATE TABLE Samples
(sampleid INTEGER NOT NULL,
 fish CHAR(20) NOT NULL,
 numfound INTEGER NOT NULL,
 PRIMARY KEY (sampleid, fish));

CREATE TABLE SampleGroups
(groupid INTEGER NOT NULL,
 sampleid INTEGER NOT NULL,
 PRIMARY KEY (groupid, sampleid));
```

Assume that some of the data looks like this:

Samples

sampleid	fish	numfound
1	'Seabass'	14
1	'Minnow'	18
2	'Seabass'	19

SampleGroups

groupid	sampleid
1	1
1	2
2	2

She needs to get the average number of each species of fish in the sample groups. For example, using sample group 1 as shown, which has samples 1 and 2, we could use the parameters :myfish = 'Minnow' and :mygroup = 1 to find the average number of minnows in sample group 1, thus:

```
SELECT fish, AVG(numfound)
  FROM Samples
 WHERE sampleid IN (SELECT sampleid
                      FROM SampleGroups
                     WHERE groupid = :mygroup)
   AND fish = :myfish
 GROUP BY fish;
```

But this query will give us an average of 18 minnows, which is wrong. There were no minnows for sampleid = 2, so the average is ((18 + 0)/2) = 9. The other way is to do several steps to get the correct answer. First use a SELECT statement to get the number of samples involved, then another SELECT to get the sum, and then manually calculate the average.

The obvious answer is to enter a count of zero for each animal under each sampleid, instead of letting it be missing, so you can use the original query. You can create the missing rows with

```
INSERT INTO Samples
SELECT M1.sampleid, M2.fish, 0
  FROM Samples AS M1, Samples AS M2
 WHERE NOT EXISTS (SELECT *
                     FROM Samples AS M3
                    WHERE M1.sampleid = M3.sampleid
                      AND M2.fish = M3.fish);
```

Unfortunately, it turns out that we have over 100,000 different species of fish and thousands of samples. This trick will fill up more disk space than we have on the machine. The best trick is to use this SQL-92 statement:

```
SELECT fish, SUM(numfound)/
       (SELECT COUNT(sampleid)
           FROM SampleGroups
          WHERE groupid = :mygroup)
  FROM Samples
 WHERE fish = :myfish
 GROUP BY fish;
```

This SQL-92 query is using the rule that the average is the sum of values divided by the count of the set. Another way to do this would be to use an OUTER JOIN and preserve all the groupids, but that would create NULLs for the fish that are not in some of the sample groups and you would have to handle them.

21.4 Extrema Functions

The MIN() and MAX() functions are known as *extrema functions* in mathematics. They assume that the elements of the set have an ordering, so that it makes sense to select a first or last element based on its value. SQL provides two simple extrema functions, and you can write queries to generalize these to *n* elements.

21.4.1 Simple Extrema Functions

MAX([ALL | DISTINCT] <value expression>) returns the greatest known value in the <value expression> set. This function will also work on character and temporal values as well as numeric values. An empty set returns a NULL. Technically, you can write MAX(DISTINCT <value expression>), but it is the same as MAX(<value expression>); this form exists only for completeness and nobody ever uses it.

MIN([ALL | DISTINCT] <value expression>) returns the smallest known value in the <value expression> set. This function will also work on character and temporal values as well as numeric values. An empty set returns a NULL. Likewise, MIN(DISTINCT <value expression>) exists, but it is defined only for completeness and nobody ever uses it.

The MAX() for a set of numeric values is the largest. The MAX() for a set of temporal datatypes is the one farthest in the future or most recent. The

MAX() for a set of character strings is the last one in the ascending sort order. Likewise, the MIN() for a set of numeric values is the smallest. The MIN() for a set of temporal datatypes is the least recent one. The MIN() for a set of character strings is the first one in the ascending sort order. No surprises here.

People have a hard time understanding the MAX() and MIN() aggregate functions when they are applied to temporal datatypes. They seem to expect the MAX() to return the date closest to the current date. Likewise, if the set has no dates before the current date, they seem to expect the MIN function to return the date closest to the current date. Human psychology wants to use the current time as an origin point for temporal reasoning.

Consider the predicate billingdate < (CURRENT_DATE - INTERVAL 90 DAYS); most people have to stop and figure out that this is looking for billings that are over 90 days past due. This same thing happens with MIN() and MAX() functions.

SQL also has funny rules about comparing VARCHAR strings that can cause problems. When two strings are compared for equality, the shortest one is right-padded with blanks; then they are compared position for position. Thus, the strings 'John   ' and 'John' are equal. You will have to check your implementation of SQL to see which string is returned as the MAX() and which as the MIN(), or whether there is any pattern to it at all.

There are some tricks with extrema functions in subqueries that differ from product to product. For example, to find the current employee status in a table of salary histories, the obvious query is

```
SELECT *
  FROM SalaryHistory AS S0
 WHERE S0.changedate = (SELECT MAX(S1.changedate)
                          FROM SalaryHistory AS S1
                         WHERE S1.empid = S1.empid);
```

But you can also write the query as

```
SELECT *
  FROM SalaryHistory AS S0
 WHERE NOT EXISTS (SELECT *
                     FROM SalaryHistory AS S1
                    WHERE S0.empid = S1.empid
                      AND S0.changedate < S1.changedate);
```

The correlated subquery with a MAX() will be implemented by going to the subquery and building a working table that is grouped by empid. Then for

each group, you will keep track of the maximum and save it for the final result.

However, the NOT EXISTS version will find the first row that meets the criteria, and when found, it will return TRUE. Therefore, the NOT EXISTS() predicate should run faster.

21.4.2 Generalized Extrema Functions

This is known as the Top (or Bottom) (n) values problem and originally appeared in *Explain* magazine; it was submitted by Jim Wankowski of Hawthorne, CA (Wankowski n.d.). You are given a table of personnel and their salaries. Write a single SQL query that will display the three highest salaries from that table. It is easy to find the maximum salary with the simple query SELECT MAX(salary) FROM Personnel;, but SQL does not have a maximum function that will return a group of high values from a column. The trouble with this query is that the specification is bad for several reasons.

1. How do we define "best salary" in terms of an ordering? Is it base pay or does it include commissions? For the rest of this section, assume that we are using a simple table with a column that has the salary for each employee.

2. What if we have three or fewer personnel in the company? Do we report all the personnel we do have? Or do we return a NULL, empty result set or error message? This is the equivalent of calling the contest for lack of entries.

3. How do we handle two personnel who tied? Include them all and allow the result set to be bigger than three? Pick an arbitrary subset and exclude someone? Or do we return a NULL, empty result set, or error message?

To make these problems more explicit, consider this table:

Personnel

name	salary
'Able'	1000.00
'Baker'	900.00
'Charles'	900.00
'Delta'	800.00
'Eddy'	700.00
'Fred'	700.00
'George'	700.00

Able, Baker, and Charles are the three highest-paid employees in Personnel, but $1,000.00, $900.00, and $800.00 are the three highest salaries. The highest salaries belong to Able, Baker, Charles, and Delta—a set with four elements.

The way that most new SQL programmers do this in other SQL products is produce a result with an ORDER BY clause, then read the first so many rows from that cursor result. Remember, only cursors have the ORDER BY clause. Sybase has a SET ROWCOUNT n option that clips the result set at exactly n rows. The results depend completely on the order that the rows were constructed, and that can change from query to query. Oracle and other applications have a row number that is in effect a sequential number in a system-generated column that you can use to clip out the first n rows. Both suffer from the same problem; your results depend completely on the order in which the rows were constructed, and that can change from one execution of the query to the next.

All these problems still exist in a procedural programming language. The first thought of a novice procedural-language programmer is to sort the table in descending order by salary, then print the first three records from the table. Ties do not get handled very well, however, since you never see them in the final results.

This problem is better done with an algorithm due to C. A. R. Hoare. It is the partition function in QuickSort, crippled to avoid sorting the whole file, which would take $(n*log2(n))$ time. Assuming that on the average it splits the current sublist in half, this one will run in only $(2 * n)$ time.

In practice, it is a good idea to start with a pivot at or near position n because real data tends to have some ordering already in it. If the file is already in sorted order, this trick will return an answer in one pass:

```
CONST
    listlength = { some large number };
    . . .
TYPE
    LIST = ARRAY [1..listlength] OF REAL;
    . . .
PROCEDURE FindTopK (Kth : INTEGER, records : LIST);
VAR pivot, left, right, start, finish: INTEGER;
BEGIN
start := 1;
finish := listlength;
WHILE (start < finish)
```

```
DO BEGIN
    pivot := records[Kth];
    left := start;
    right := finish;
    REPEAT
        WHILE (records[left] > pivot) DO left := left + 1;
        WHILE (records[right] < pivot) DO right := right - 1;
        IF (left >= right)
        THEN BEGIN   { swap right and left elements }
                Swap (records[left], records[right]);
                left := left + 1;
                right := right - 1;
                END;
    UNTIL (left < right);
    IF (right < Kth) THEN start := left;
    IF (left > Kth) THEN finish := right;
    END;

{ the first k numbers are in positions 1 through kth,
  in no  particular order except that the kth highest number
  is in position k }
END.
```

The naive SQL programmer's approach is to mimic the naive procedural-language programmer's approach. This is not too surprising since they are often the same people. They write a query that sorts the results like this:

```
SELECT DISTINCT salary
   FROM Personnel
 ORDER BY salary;
```

They then just look at the top three numbers. This is actually the way that most people do it since they can scroll results on a terminal screen from an interactive SQL tool, but it is not valid SQL. The ORDER BY can only appear on a DECLARE CURSOR statement; the results of a query are not sorted. Oh, yes, did I mention that the whole table has to be sorted and that this can take some time if the table is large? The original articles in *Explain* magazine gave several solutions (Murchison n.d.; Wankowski n.d.).

One involved UNION operations on nested subqueries. The first result table was the maximum for the whole table, the second result table was the maximum for the table entries less than the first maximum, and so forth. The pattern is extensible. It looked like this:

```
SELECT MAX(salary) FROM Personnel
 UNION
SELECT MAX(salary) FROM Personnel
 WHERE salary < (SELECT MAX(salary)
                      FROM Personnel)
 UNION
SELECT MAX(salary)
  FROM Personnel
 WHERE salary < (SELECT MAX(salary)
                    FROM Personnel
                    WHERE salary
                      < (SELECT MAX(salary) FROM Personnel));
```

This answer can give you a pretty serious performance problem because of the subquery nesting and the UNION operations. Every UNION will trigger a sort to remove duplicate rows from the results since salary is not a UNIQUE column.

A special case of the use of the scalar subquery with the MAX() function is finding the last two values in a set to look for a change. This is most often done with date values for time series work. For example, to get the last two salary reviews for an employee:

```
SELECT :somename, MAX(P1.review_date), P2.review_date
  FROM Personnel AS P1, Personnel AS P2
 WHERE P1.review_date < P2.review_date
   AND P1.name = :somename
   AND P2.review_date = (SELECT MAX(review_date) FROM Personnel)
 GROUP BY P2.review_date;
```

The scalar subquery is not correlated, so it should run pretty fast and be executed only once.

An improvement on the UNION approach is to find the third highest salary with a subquery, then return all the records with salaries that were equal or higher. This will handle ties; it looked like this:

```
SELECT DISTINCT salary
  FROM Personnel
 WHERE salary >=
       (SELECT MAX(salary)
          FROM Personnel
          WHERE salary < (SELECT MAX(salary)
```

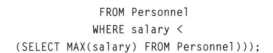

```
                    FROM Personnel
                   WHERE salary <
          (SELECT MAX(salary) FROM Personnel)));
```

Another answer is to use correlation names and return a single-row result table. This pattern is more easily extensible to larger groups; it will also present the results in sorted order without requiring the use of an ORDER BY clause. The disadvantage of this answer is that it will return a single row and not a column result. That might make it unusable for JOINing to other queries. It looked like this:

```
SELECT MAX(P1.salary), MAX(P2.salary), MAX(P3.salary)
  FROM Personnel AS P1, Personnel AS P2, Personnel AS P3
 WHERE P1.salary > P2.salary
   AND P2.salary > P3.salary;
```

This approach will return the three highest salaries.

The best variation on the single-row approach is done with the scalar subquery expressions in SQL-92. The query becomes

```
SELECT (SELECT MAX (salary)
          FROM Personnel) AS s1,
       (SELECT MAX (salary)
          FROM Personnel
         WHERE salary NOT IN (s1)) AS s2,
       (SELECT MAX (salary)
          FROM Personnel
         WHERE salary NOT IN (s1, s2)) AS s3,
          . . .
       (SELECT MAX (salary)
          FROM Personnel
         WHERE salary NOT IN (s1, s2, . . .  s[n-1])) AS sn,
  FROM Dummy;
```

where the table Dummy is anything, even an empty table. This is the fastest solution I have found as of this writing, but not all SQL products have SQL-92 scalar subquery expressions.

There are single-column answers based on the fact that SQL is a set-oriented language, so we ought to use a set-oriented specification. We want to get a subset of salary values that has a count of n, has the greatest value from the original set as an element, and includes all values greater than its least element.

The idea is to take each salary and build a group of other salaries that are greater than or equal to it—this value is the boundary of the subset. The groups with three or fewer rows are what we want to see. The third element of an ordered list is also the maximum or minimum element of a set of three unique elements, depending on the ordering. Think of concentric sets, nested inside each other. This query gives a columnar answer, and the query can be extended to other numbers by changing the constant in the HAVING clause.

```
SELECT MIN(P1.salary)    -- the element on the boundary
  FROM Personnel AS P1,  -- P2 gives the elements of the subset
       Personnel AS P2   -- P1 gives the boundary of the subset
 WHERE P1.salary >= P2.salary
 GROUP BY P2.salary
HAVING COUNT(DISTINCT P1.salary) <= 3;
```

If you would like to see the ranking next to the employees, here is another version using a GROUP BY.

```
SELECT P1.name,
       SUM (CASE WHEN (P1.salary || P1.name)
                    < (P2.salary || P1.name)
                THEN 1 ELSE 0 END) + 1 AS rank
  FROM Personnel AS P1, Personnel AS P2
 WHERE P1.name <> P2.name
 GROUP BY P1.name
HAVING (CASE WHEN (P1.salary || P1.name)
                 < (P2.salary || P1.name)
             THEN 1 ELSE 0 END) <= (:n - 1);
```

The concatenation makes ties in salary different by adding the key to a string conversion.

Here is another version that will produce the ties on separate lines with the names of the personnel who made the cut. Pierre Boutquin is the source for this answer.

```
SELECT P1.name, P1.salary
  FROM Personnel AS P1, Personnel AS P2
 WHERE P1.salary >= P2.salary
 GROUP BY P1.name, P1.salary
HAVING (SELECT COUNT(*) FROM Personnel) - COUNT(*) + 1 <= :n;
```

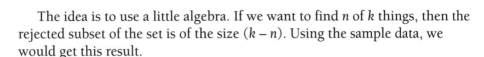

The idea is to use a little algebra. If we want to find n of k things, then the rejected subset of the set is of the size $(k - n)$. Using the sample data, we would get this result.

Result

name	salary
'Able'	1000.00
'Baker'	900.00
'Charles'	900.00

If we add a new employee at $900, we would also get him, but not a new employee at $800 or less. In many ways this is the most satisfying answer.

As an aside, if you were awake during your college set theory course, you will remember that John von Neumann's definition of ordinal numbers is based on nested sets. You can get a lot of ideas for self-JOINs from set theory theorems. This is the John von Neumann who was one of the greatest mathematicians of this century before he invented the modern stored program computer and game theory. Know your nerd heritage!

It should be obvious that 3 can be replaced by any cardinal number, but let's just leave it. A subtle point is that the predicate "P1.salary <= P2.salary" will include the boundary value and so implies that if we have three or fewer personnel, then we still have a result. If you want to call off the competition for lack of a quorum, then change the predicate to "P1.salary < P2.salary" instead.

Another way to express the query would be

```
SELECT Elements.name, Elements.salary
  FROM Personnel AS Elements
 WHERE (SELECT COUNT(*)
          FROM Personnel AS Boundary
         WHERE Elements.salary < Boundary.salary) < 3;
```

You can reverse the terms in the WHERE comparison in SQL-92, but not in SQL-89. Likewise, the COUNT(*) and comparisons in the scalar subquery expression can be changed to give slightly different results.

You might want to test each version to see which one runs faster on your particular SQL product. If you want to swap the subquery and the constant for readability, that is legal in SQL-92, but not in SQL-89.

What if I want to allow ties? Then just change COUNT( ) to a COUNT-(DISTINCT) function in the HAVING clause:

```
SELECT Elements.name, Elements.salary
  FROM Personnel AS Elements, Personnel AS Boundary
 WHERE Elements.salary <= Boundary.salary
 GROUP BY Elements.name, Elements.salary
HAVING COUNT(DISTINCT Boundary.salary) <= 3;
```

This says that I want to count the values of salary, not the salespersons, so that if two or more of the crew hit the same total, I will include them in the report as tied for a particular position. This also means that the results can be more than three rows because I can have ties. As you can see, it is easy to get a subtle change in the results with just a few simple changes in predicates.

Notice that you can change the comparisons from "<=" to "<" and the "COUNT(*)" to "COUNT(DISTINCT P2.salary)" to change the specification.

You can get other aggregate functions by using this query with the IN predicate. Assume that I have SalaryHistory table from which I wish to determine the average pay for the three most recent pay changes of each employee. I am going to further assume that if you had three or fewer old salaries, you would still want to average the one, two, or three values you have on record.

```
SELECT SO.empno, AVG(SO.lastsalary)
  FROM SalaryHistory AS SO
WHERE SO.changedate
      IN (SELECT P1.changedate
            FROM SalaryHistory AS P1, SalaryHistory AS P2
           WHERE P1.changedate <= P2.changedate
           GROUP BY P1.changedate
          HAVING COUNT(*) <= 3)
 GROUP BY SO.empno;
```

21.4.3 Multiple-Criteria Extrema Functions

Since the generalized extrema functions are based on sorting the data, it stands to reason that you could further generalize them to use multiple columns in a table. This can be done by changing the WHERE search condition. For example, to locate the Top(n) tall and heavy employees for the basketball team, we could write

```
SELECT P1.empid
  FROM Parts as P1, Parts AS P2
 WHERE (P2.height < P1.height) -- major sort term
   OR  (P2.height = P1.height -- next sort term
        AND (P2.weight <= P1.weight))
 GROUP BY P1.empid
HAVING COUNT(*) <= :n;
```

Procedural programmers will recognize this predicate because it is what they used to write to do a sort on more than one field in a file system. Now it becomes very important to look at the predicates at each level of nesting to be sure that you have the right theta operator. The ordering of the predicates is also critical—there is a difference in ordering by height within weight or by weight within height.

One improvement would be to use the SQL-92 feature of row comparisons when it becomes more available to make the code simpler and probably faster:

```
SELECT P1.empid
  FROM Personnel as P1, Personnel AS P2
 WHERE (P2.height, P2.weight) <= (P1.height, P1.weight)
 GROUP BY P1.empid
HAVING COUNT(*) <= 4;
```

The downside of this approach is that you cannot easily mix ascending and descending comparisons in the same comparison predicate. The trick is to make numeric columns negative to reverse the sense of the theta operator.

Before you attempt it, here is the scalar subquery version of the multiple extrema problem:

```
SELECT
  (SELECT MAX(P0.height)
     FROM Personnel AS P0
    WHERE P0.weight = (SELECT MAX(weight)
                         FROM Personnel AS P1)) AS s1,
  (SELECT MAX(P0.height)
     FROM Personnel AS P0
    WHERE height NOT IN (s1)
      AND P0.weight = (SELECT MAX(weight)
                         FROM Personnel AS P1
                        WHERE height NOT IN (s1))) AS s2,
```

```
(SELECT MAX(PO.height)
   FROM Personnel AS PO
  WHERE height NOT IN (s1, s2)
    AND PO.weight = (SELECT MAX(weight)
                       FROM Personnel AS P1
                      WHERE height NOT IN (s1, s2))) AS s3
 FROM Dummy;
```

Again, multiple criteria and their ordering would be expressed as multiple levels of subquery nesting. This picks the tallest people and decides ties with the greatest weight within that subset of personnel. While this looks awful and is hard to read, it does run fairly fast because the predicates are repeated and can be factored out by the optimizer.

21.5 Other Aggregate Functions

Many vendors have added additional aggregate functions to their products, such as median, standard deviation, and other statistical functions. Even with vendor extensions that allow the programmer to add his own user-defined functions to SQL, most products will not allow you to create an aggregate function of your own. We will discuss how to write queries to do some of the more common descriptive statistics in Chapter 23, but here are two useful aggregates not provided by standard SQL.

21.5.1 The LIST( ) Aggregate Function

The LIST([DISTINCT] <string expression>) is part of Sybase's SQL Anywhere (formerly WATCOM SQL). It is the only aggregate function to work on character strings. It takes a column of strings, removes the NULLs, and merges them into a single result string having commas between each of the original strings. The DISTINCT option removes duplicates as well as NULLs before concatenating the strings together. This function is a generalized version of concatenation, just as SUM( ) is a generalized version of addition.

This is handy when you use SQL to write SQL queries. As one simple example, you can apply it against the schema tables and obtain the names of all the columns in a table, then use that list to expand a SELECT * into the current column list.

One way of doing this query without the WATCOM extension is with scalar subquery expressions. Assume we have these two tables:

```
CREATE TABLE People
(id INTEGER NOT NULL PRIMARY KEY,
 name CHAR(10) NOT NULL);

INSERT INTO People
VALUES (1, 'John'), (2, 'Mary'), (3, 'Fred'), (4, 'Jane');

CREATE TABLE Clothes
(id INTEGER NOT NULL,
 seq INTEGER NOT NULL,
 item CHAR(10) NOT NULL,
 worn CHAR(1) NOT NULL
      CONSTRAINT worn_yes_no
      CHECK (worn IN ('Y', 'N')),
 PRIMARY KEY (id, seq));

INSERT INTO Clothes
VALUES (1, 1, 'Hat', 'Y');
       (1, 2, 'Coat', 'N'),
       (1, 3, 'Glove','Y'),
       (2, 1, 'Hat', 'Y'),
       (2, 2, 'Coat', 'Y'),
       (3, 1, 'Shoes', 'N'),
       (4, 1, 'Pants', 'N'),
       (4, 2, 'Socks', 'Y');
```

Using the LIST() function, we could get an output of the outfits of the people with the simple query

```
SELECT PO.id, PO.name, LIST(item) AS fashion
  FROM People AS PO, Clothes AS CO
 WHERE PO.id = CO.id
   AND CO.worn = 'Y'
 GROUP BY PO.id, PO.name;
```

Result

id	name	fashion
1	'John'	'Hat,Glove'
2	'Mary'	'Hat,Coat'
4	'Jane'	'Socks'

The LIST( ) Function with a Procedure

To do this without an aggregate function, you must first know the highest sequence number so you can create the query. This is a simple "SELECT MAX(seq) FROM Clothes" statement in this case, but you might have to use a COUNT(*) for other tables.

```
SELECT DISTINCT PO.id, PO.name,
    SUBSTRING ((SELECT CASE WHEN C1.worn = 'Y'
                      THEN (', ' || item) ELSE '' END
          FROM Clothes as C1
          WHERE C1.id = CO.id
            AND C1.seq = 1)  ||
        (SELECT CASE WHEN C2.worn = 'Y'
                      THEN (', ' || item) ELSE '' END
          FROM Clothes as C2
          WHERE C2.id = CO.id
            AND C2.seq = 2) ||
        (SELECT CASE WHEN C3.worn = 'Y'
                      THEN (', ' || item) ELSE '' END
          FROM Clothes as C3
          WHERE C3.id = CO.id
            AND C3.seq = 3) FROM 3) AS list
      FROM People AS PO, Clothes AS CO
    WHERE PO.id = CO.id;
```

id	name	list
1	John	Hat, Glove
2	Mary	Hat, Coat
3	Fred	
4	Jane	Socks

Again, the CASE expression on "worn" can be replaced with an IS NULL to replace NULLs with an empty string. If you don't want to see that Fred is naked—has an empty string of clothing—then change the outermost WHERE clause to read

```
    . . .
  WHERE PO.id = CO.id AND CO.worn = 'Y';
```

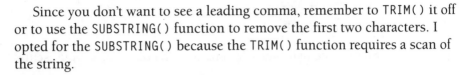

Since you don't want to see a leading comma, remember to TRIM( ) it off or to use the SUBSTRING( ) function to remove the first two characters. I opted for the SUBSTRING( ) because the TRIM( ) function requires a scan of the string.

The LIST( ) Function by Crosstabs

Carl Federl used the ideas described in Section 23.6.1, on crosstabs by CROSS JOIN, to get a similar result:

```
CREATE TABLE Crosstabs
(seq INTEGER NOT NULL PRIMARY KEY,
 seq_1 INTEGER NOT NULL,
 seq_2 INTEGER NOT NULL,
 seq_3 INTEGER NOT NULL,
 seq_4 INTEGER NOT NULL,
 seq_5 INTEGER NOT NULL);
INSERT INTO Crosstabs VALUES (1, 1, 0, 0, 0, 0);
INSERT INTO Crosstabs VALUES (2, 0, 1, 0, 0, 0);
INSERT INTO Crosstabs VALUES (3, 0, 0, 1, 0, 0);
INSERT INTO Crosstabs VALUES (4, 0, 0, 0, 1, 0);
INSERT INTO Crosstabs VALUES (5, 0, 0, 0, 0, 1);

SELECT Clothes.id,
    TRIM (MAX(SUBSTRING(item FROM 1 FOR seq_1 * 10))
 || ' ' || MAX(SUBSTRING(item FROM 1 FOR seq_2 * 10))
 || ' ' || MAX(SUBSTRING(item FROM 1 FOR seq_3 * 10))
 || ' ' || MAX(SUBSTRING(item FROM 1 FOR seq_4 * 10))
 || ' ' || MAX(SUBSTRING(item FROM 1 FOR seq_5 * 10)))
  FROM Clothes, Crosstabs
 WHERE Clothes.seq = Crosstabs.seq
   AND Clothes.worn = 'Y'
 GROUP BY Clothes.id;
```

21.5.2 The PROD( ) Aggregate Function

In January, Bob McGowan sent me a message on CompuServe asking for help with a problem. His client, a financial institution, tracks investment performance with a table something like this:

```
CREATE TABLE Performance
(portfolio_id CHAR(7) NOT NULL,
```

```
execute_date DATE NOT NULL,
rate_of_return DECIMAL(13,7) NOT NULL);
```

In order to calculate a rate of return over a date range, you use the formula

```
(1 + rate_of_return [day_1])
* (1 + rate_of_return [day_2])
* (1 + rate_of_return [day_3])
* (1 + rate_of_return [day_4])
  . . .
* (1 + rate_of_return [day_N])
```

How would you construct a query that would return one row for each portfolio's return over the date range? What McGowan really wants is an aggregate function in the SELECT clause to return a columnar product, like the SUM( ) returns a columnar total.

If you are a math major, you would write these functions as capital sigma (Σ) for summation and capital pi for product (Π). If such an aggregate function existed in SQL, the syntax for it would look something like

```
PROD ([DISTINCT] <expression>)
```

While I am not sure that there is any use for the DISTINCT option, the new aggregate function would let us write his problem simply as

```
SELECT portfolio_id, PROD(1 + rate_of_return)
  FROM Performance
 WHERE execute_date BETWEEN start_date AND end_date
 GROUP BY portfolio_id;
```

PROD( ) Function by Expressions

There is a trick for solving the problem using the PROD( ) function, but you need a second table that looks like this to cover a period of five days:

```
CREATE TABLE BigPi
(execute_date DATE NOT NULL,
 day_1 INTEGER NOT NULL,
 day_2 INTEGER NOT NULL,
 day_3 INTEGER NOT NULL,
 day_4 INTEGER NOT NULL,
 day_5 INTEGER NOT NULL);
```

Let's assume we want to look at January 6 to 10, so we need to update the execute_date column to that range:

```
INSERT INTO BigPi VALUES ('1996-01-06', 1, 0, 0, 0, 0);
INSERT INTO BigPi VALUES ('1996-01-07', 0, 1, 0, 0, 0);
INSERT INTO BigPi VALUES ('1996-01-08', 0, 0, 1, 0, 0);
INSERT INTO BigPi VALUES ('1996-01-09', 0, 0, 0, 1, 0);
INSERT INTO BigPi VALUES ('1996-01-10', 0, 0, 0, 0, 1);
```

The idea is that there is a 1 in the column when `BigPi.execute_date` is equal to the *n*th date in the range and 0 otherwise. The query for this problem is

```
SELECT portfolio_id,
 (SUM((1.00 + P1.rate_of_return) * M1.day_1) *
  SUM((1.00 + P1.rate_of_return) * M1.day_2) *
  SUM((1.00 + P1.rate_of_return) * M1.day_3) *
  SUM((1.00 + P1.rate_of_return) * M1.day_4) *
  SUM((1.00 + P1.rate_of_return) * M1.day_5)) AS product
  FROM Performance AS P1, BigPi AS M1
 WHERE M1.execute_date = P1.execute_date
   AND P1.execute_date BETWEEN'1996-01-06' AND '1996-01-10'
 GROUP BY portfolio_id;
```

If anyone is missing a `rate_of_return` entry on a date in that range, their product will be zero. That might be fine, but if you needed to get a NULL when you have missing data, then replace each SUM( ) expression with a CASE expression like this:

```
CASE WHEN SUM((1.00 + P1.rate_of_return) * M1.day_N) = 0
     THEN NULL
     ELSE SUM((1.00 + P1.rate_of_return) * M1.day_N)
END
```

or if your SQL has the full SQL-92 set of expressions, with this version:

```
NULLIF (SUM((1.00 + P1.rate_of_return) * M1.day_N), 0)
```

The PROD( ) Aggregate Function by Logarithms

Roy Harvey, another SQL guru who answers questions on CompuServe, found a different solution; perhaps he is old enough to remember slide rules and that we can multiply by adding logs. The nice part of this solution is that you can also use the DISTINCT option in the SUM() function.

But a lot of warnings must accompany this approach. Some older SQL implementations might have trouble with using an aggregate function result as a parameter. This has always been part of the standard, but some SQL products use very different mechanisms for the aggregate functions.

Another, more fundamental problem is that the log of zero or less is undefined, so your SQL application might return a NULL or an error message. You will also see some SQL products that use LN() for the natural log and LOG10() for the logarithm base 10, and others that use LN (<parameter>, <base>) for a general logarithm function.

Within all those warnings, examine the expression for the product of a column from logarithm and exponential functions:

```
SELECT ((EXP (SUM (LN (CASE WHEN nbr = 0.00
                            THEN NULL
                            ELSE ABS(nbr) END))))
  * (CASE WHEN MIN (ABS (nbr)) = 0.00
          THEN 0.00
          ELSE 1.00 END)
  * (CASE WHEN MOD (SUM (CASE WHEN SIGN(nbr) = -1
                              THEN 1
                              ELSE 0 END), 2) = 1
          THEN -1.00
          ELSE 1.00 END) AS Prod
FROM NumberTable;
```

The nice part of this method is that you can also use the SUM (DISTINCT <expression>) option to get the equivalent of PROD (DISTINCT <expression>).

You should watch the data type of the column involved and use either integer 0 and 1 or decimal 0.00 and 1.00, as is appropriate in the CASE statements. It is worth studying the three CASE expressions that make up the terms of the PROD calculation.

The first CASE expression is to ensure that all zeros and negative numbers are converted to a nonnegative or NULL for the SUM() function, just in case your SQL product raises an exception.

The second CASE expression will return zero as the answer if there was a zero in the nbr column of any selected row. The MIN(ABS(nbr)) is a handy trick for detecting the existence of a zero in a list of both positive and negative numbers with an aggregate function.

The third CASE expression will return −1 if there was an odd number of negative numbers in the nbr column. The innermost CASE expression uses a SIGN( ) function that returns +1 for a positive number, −1 for a negative number, and 0 for a zero. The SUM( ) counts the −1 results, then the MOD( ) function determines if the count was odd or even.

In addition, you may want to check Z. A. Melzak's book *A Simple Approach to Complexity* (Melzak 1983), a short mathematical book on the general principle of *conjugacy*. This is the method of using a transform and its inverse to reduce the complexity of a calculation.

Auxiliary Tables

A UXILIARY TABLES ARE a way of building functions that would be difficult if not impossible to build with the limited computational power of SQL-92. They should not appear on the E-R diagrams for the database because they are not really a part of the model, but serve as adjuncts to all the tables and queries in the database that can use them. Sequence tables and calendar tables are the two most common examples of such auxiliary tables.

22.1 The Sequence Table

This table has the general declaration

```
CREATE TABLE Sequence
(nbr INTEGER NOT NULL PRIMARY KEY
     CONSTRAINT non_negative_nbr
     CHECK (nbr > 0)
 cardinal VARCHAR(100) NOT NULL,
 ordinal VARCHAR(100) NOT NULL,

 . . .
 CONSTRAINT numbers_are_complete
 CHECK ((SELECT COUNT(*) FROM Sequence) =
        (SELECT MAX(nbr) FROM Sequence));
```

with data like

nbr	cardinal	ordinal . . .
1	'one'	'first'
2	'two'	'second'
3	'three'	'third'
. . .	. . .	. . .
101	'One hundred and one'	'One hundredth and first'
. . .	. . .	. . .

This table is a list of all the integers from 1 to (SELECT MAX(nbr) FROM Sequence). The other columns are simply examples of handy things that you might want to do with an integer, such as turn it into English words, something that would be difficult in pure SQL.

I have found that it is a bad idea to start with zero, though that seems more natural for computer programmers. The reason for omitting zero is that this auxiliary table is often used to provide row numbering by being CROSS JOIN-ed to another table, and the zero would throw off the one-to-one mapping.

22.1.1 An Example of the Sequence Table

Start with a table with the monthly sales data shown as an attribute (the monthly amounts have to be NULL-able to hold missing values for the future):

```
CREATE TABLE AnnualSales1
(salesman CHAR(15) NOT NULL PRIMARY KEY,
 jan DECIMAL(5,2),
 feb DECIMAL(5,2),
 mar DECIMAL(5,2),
 apr DECIMAL(5,2),
 may DECIMAL(5,2),
 jun DECIMAL(5,2),
 jul DECIMAL(5,2),
 aug DECIMAL(5,2),
 sep DECIMAL(5,2),
 oct DECIMAL(5,2),
 nov DECIMAL(5,2),
 "dec" DECIMAL(5,2));
```

The goal is to "flatten" it out so that it looks like this:

```
CREATE TABLE AnnualSales2
(salesman CHAR(15) NOT NULL PRIMARY KEY,
 month CHAR(3) NOT NULL
        CONSTRAINT valid_month_code
        CHECK (month IN ('Jan', 'Feb', 'Mar', 'Apr',
                          'May', 'Jun', 'Jul', 'Aug',
                          'Sep', 'Oct', 'Nov', 'Dec')),
 amount DECIMAL(5,2) NOT NULL,
 PRIMARY KEY(salesman, month));
```

The trick is to build a VIEW of the original table with a number beside each month:

```
CREATE VIEW NumberedSales
AS SELECT salesman,
           1 AS M01, jan,
           2 AS M02, feb,
           3 AS M03, mar,
           4 AS M04, apr,
           5 AS M05, may,
           6 AS M06, jun,
           7 AS M07, jul,
           8 AS M08, aug,
           9 AS M09, sep,
          10 AS M10, oct,
          11 AS M11, nov,
          12 AS M12, "dec"
    FROM AnnualSales1;
```

Now you can use the auxiliary table of sequential numbers or you can use a VALUES table constructor to build one. The "flattened" VIEW is

```
CREATE VIEW AnnualSales2 (salesman, month, amount)
AS SELECT S1.salesman,
         (CASE WHEN A.nbr = M01 THEN 'Jan'
               WHEN A.nbr = M02 THEN 'Feb'
               WHEN A.nbr = M03 THEN 'Mar'
               WHEN A.nbr = M04 THEN 'Apr'
               WHEN A.nbr = M05 THEN 'May'
               WHEN A.nbr = M06 THEN 'Jun'
               WHEN A.nbr = M07 THEN 'Jul'
```

```
                WHEN A.nbr = M08 THEN 'Aug'
                WHEN A.nbr = M09 THEN 'Sep'
                WHEN A.nbr = M10 THEN 'Oct'
                WHEN A.nbr = M11 THEN 'Nov'
                WHEN A.nbr = M12 THEN 'Dec'
                ELSE NULL END),
        (CASE WHEN A.nbr = M01 THEN jan
                WHEN A.nbr = M02 THEN feb
                WHEN A.nbr = M03 THEN mar
                WHEN A.nbr = M04 THEN apr
                WHEN A.nbr = M05 THEN may
                WHEN A.nbr = M06 THEN jun
                WHEN A.nbr = M07 THEN jul
                WHEN A.nbr = M08 THEN aug
                WHEN A.nbr = M09 THEN sep
                WHEN A.nbr = M10 THEN oct
                WHEN A.nbr = M11 THEN nov
                WHEN A.nbr = M12 THEN "dec"
                ELSE NULL END)
   FROM AnnualSales AS S1
        CROSS JOIN
        (SELECT nbr FROM Sequence WHERE nbr <= 12) AS A(nbr);
```

If your SQL product has derived tables, this can be written as a single VIEW query.

22.2 The Calendar Table

The calendar table has two general forms. The first form maps single dates into some value and has the general declaration

```
CREATE TABLE Calendar
(cal_date DATE NOT NULL PRIMARY KEY,
 julian_day INTEGER NOT NULL
            CONSTRAINT valid_julian_day
            CHECK (julian_day BETWEEN 1 AND 366),
 business_day INTEGER NOT NULL CHECK (business_day IN (0,1)),
 three_business_days DATE NOT NULL,
 fiscal_month INTEGER NOT NULL
            CONSTRAINT valid_month_nbr
            CHECK (fiscal_month BETWEEN 1 AND 12),
```

```
fiscal_year INTEGER NOT NULL,
 . . . );
```

The second form maps an interval into some value and has the general declaration

```
CREATE TABLE EventCalendar
(event VARCHAR(30) NOT NULL PRIMARY KEY,
 start_date DATE NOT NULL,
 end_date DATE NOT NULL,
 . . . ,
 CONSTRAINT started_before_ended
 CHECK (start_date <= end_date));
```

This is the most useful auxiliary table because the calendar is so irregular and there are so many different fiscal calendars in use.

As a demonstration of the irregularity, consider the Security and Exchange Commission's rule that a brokerage transaction must close within three business days. A business day does *not* include Saturdays, Sundays, or holidays declared by the New York Stock Exchange. You can compute the occurrences of Saturdays and Sundays with a library function in many SQL products, but not the holidays. In fact, the New York Stock Exchange can be closed by a declared national emergency.

The data for the calendar table can be built with the help of a good spreadsheet since spreadsheets usually have more temporal functions than databases.

22.2.1 An Example of the Calendar Table

Let's assume that we have a table of sales slips that looks like this:

```
CREATE TABLE SalesSlips
(salesman CHAR(15) NOT NULL PRIMARY KEY,
 sales_date DATE NOT NULL,
 item_nbr INTEGER NOT NULL REFERENCES Inventory(item_nbr),
 amount DECIMAL(10,2) NOT NULL,
 . . . );
```

and we want to get a report based on the fiscal year:

```
SELECT S1.salesman, C1.fiscal_year, SUM(S1.amount)
  FROM SalesSlips AS S1. Calendar AS C1
```

```
WHERE S1.sales_date = C1.cal_date
GROUP BY S1.salesman, C1.fiscal_year;
```

If you want to see why this is a good technique, try to write this simple query using function calls and CASE expressions.

22.3 Interpolation with Auxiliary Function Tables

SQL is not a functional programming language, so you often have to depend on vendor extensions providing a good library or on being able to write the functions with the limited power in standard SQL. However, SQL is good at handling tables, and you can often set up auxiliary tables of the general form

```
CREATE TABLE SomeFunction
(parameter <datatype> NOT NULL,
 result <datatype> NOT NULL);
```

when the range of the function is relatively small. Thus, the pseudocode expression

```
SELECT SomeFunction(T1.x), . . .
  FROM TableOne AS T1
 WHERE . . .
```

is replaced by

```
SELECT F1.result,
  FROM TableOne AS T1, SomeFunction AS F1
 WHERE T1.x = F1.parameter
   AND . . .
```

However, if the function has a large range, the SomeFunction table can become huge or completely impractical.

A technique that has fallen out of favor since the advent of cheap, fast computers is interpolation. It consists of using two known functional values, a and b, and their results in the function $f(a)$ and $f(b)$, to find the result of a value, x, between them.

Linear interpolation is the easiest method, and if the table has a high precision, it will work quite well for most applications. It is based on the idea that a straight line drawn between two function values $f(a)$ and $f(b)$ will approximate the function well enough that you can take a proportional increment of x relative to (a,b) and get a usable answer for $f(x)$.

The algebra looks like this:

$$f(x) = f(a) + (x - a) * ((f(b) - f(a))/(b - a))$$

where ($a <= x <= b$) and x is not in the table. This can be translated into SQL-92 where x is :myparameter, F1 is related to the variable a, and F2 is related to the variable b:

```
SELECT :myparameter AS input,
       (F1.result
       + (:myparameter - F1.parameter)
       * ((F2.result - F1.result)
          / (CASE WHEN F1.parameter = F2.parameter
                  THEN 1.00
                  ELSE F2.parameter - F1.parameter END)))
       AS answer
  FROM SomeFunction AS F1, SomeFunction AS F2
 WHERE F1.parameter     -- establish a and f(a)
       = (SELECT MAX(parameter)
            FROM SomeFunction
           WHERE parameter <= :myparameter)
   AND F2.parameter     -- establish b and f(b)
       = (SELECT MIN(parameter)
            FROM SomeFunction
           WHERE parameter >= :myparameter);
```

The CASE expression in the divisor is to avoid division-by-zero errors when $f(x)$ is in the table.

The rules for interpolation methods are always expressible in four-function arithmetic, which is good for standard SQL-92. In the old days, the function tables gave an extra value with each parameter and result pair, called delta squared, which was based on finite differences. Delta squared was like a second derivative and could be used in a formula to improve the accuracy of the approximation.

This is not a book on numerical analysis, so you will have to go to a library to find details—or ask an old engineer.

Statistics in SQL

SQL IS NOT a statistical programming language. However, there are some tricks that will let you do simple descriptive statistics. Many vendors also include other descriptive statistics besides the required ones. Other sections of this book give portable queries for computing some of the more common statistics. Before using any of these queries, you should check to see if they already exist in your SQL product. Built-in functions will run far faster than these queries, so you should use them if portability is not vital. The most common extensions are the median, the mode, the standard deviation, and the variance.

If you need to do a detailed statistical analysis, you can extract data with SQL and pass it along to a statistical programming language, such as SAS, SPSS, or Osiris.

23.1 The Mode

The *mode* is the most frequently occurring value in a set. If there are two such values in a set, statisticians call it a bimodal distribution; three such values make it trimodal, and so forth. Most SQL implementations do not have a mode function since it is easy to calculate. A simple frequency table can be written as a single query in SQL-92.

This version is from Shepard Towindo and will handle multiple modes.

```
SELECT salary, COUNT(*) AS frequency
  FROM Payroll
 GROUP BY salary
HAVING COUNT(*) >= ALL (SELECT COUNT(*)
                         FROM Payroll
                        GROUP BY salary);
```

For a more accurate picture, you can allow for a 5% difference among frequencies that are near the mode, but would otherwise not technically qualify.

```
SELECT AVG(salary) AS mode
  FROM Payroll
 GROUP BY salary
HAVING COUNT(*) >= ALL (SELECT COUNT(*) * 0.95
                         FROM Payroll
                        GROUP BY salary);
```

The mode is a weak descriptive statistic because it can be changed by small amounts of additional data. For example, if we have 100,000 cases where the value of the color variable is 'red' and 99, 999 cases where the value is 'green', the mode is 'red'. But when two more 'green's are added to the set, the mode switches to 'green'. A better idea is to allow for some variation, k, in the values. In general, the best way to compute k is probably as a percentage of the total number of occurrences. Of course, knowledge of the actual situation could change this. For $k = 2\%$ error, the query would look like this:

```
SELECT var_col AS mode, occurs
  FROM ModeFinder
WHERE occurs
      BETWEEN (SELECT MAX(occurs) - (.02 * SUM(occurs))
             FROM ModeFinder))
         AND (SELECT MAX(occurs) + (.02 * SUM(occurs))
             FROM ModeFinder));
```

This would return the result set ('red', 'green') for the example table and would not change to ('green') until the ratio of 'red' to 'green' tipped by 2 percentage points.

23.2 The Median

The median is defined as the value for which there are just as many cases with a value below it as above it. If such a value exists in the data set, this value is called the *statistical median* by some authors. If no such value exists in the data set, the usual method is to divide the data set into two halves of equal size such that all values in one half are lower than any value in the other half. The median is then the average of the highest value in the lower half and the lowest value in the upper half, and is called the *financial median* by some authors. The financial median is the most common term used for this median, so we will stick to it. Let us use Date's famous Parts table from several of his textbooks (Date 1983, 1995a), which has a column for weight in it, like this:

Parts

pno	pname	color	weight	city
'p1'	'Nut'	'Red'	'12'	'London'
'p2'	'Bolt'	'Green'	'17'	'Paris'
'p3'	'Cam'	'Blue'	'12'	'Paris'
'p4'	'Screw'	'Red'	'14'	'London'
'p5'	'Cam'	'Blue'	'12'	'Paris'
'p6'	'Cog'	'Red'	'19'	'London'

First sort the table by weights and find the three rows in the lower half of the table. The greatest value in the lower half is 12; the smallest value in the upper half is 14; their average, and therefore the median, is 13. If the table had an odd number of rows, we would have looked at only one row after the sorting.

The median is a better measure of central tendency than the average, but it is also harder to calculate without sorting. This is a disadvantage of SQL as compared with procedural languages. This might be the reason that the median is not a common vendor extension in SQL implementations. However, the variance and standard deviation are quite common, probably because they are much easier to calculate since they require no sorting, but they are less useful to commercial users.

23.2.1 Date's First Median

Date proposed two different solutions for the median (Date 1992a, Celko and Date 1993). His first solution was based on the fact that if you duplicate every row in a table, the median will stay the same. The duplication will guarantee that you always work with a table that has an even number of rows. The first version that appeared in his column was wrong and drew some mail from me and from others who had different solutions. Here is a corrected version of his first solution:

```
CREATE VIEW Temp1
AS SELECT weight FROM Parts
     UNION ALL
   SELECT weight FROM Parts;

CREATE VIEW Temp2
AS SELECT weight
     FROM Temp1
   WHERE (SELECT COUNT(*) FROM Parts)
          <= (SELECT COUNT(*)
                FROM Temp1 AS T1
                WHERE T1.weight >= Temp1.weight)
     AND (SELECT COUNT(*) FROM Parts)
          <= (SELECT COUNT(*)
                FROM Temp1 AS T2
                WHERE T2.weight <= Temp1.weight);

SELECT AVG(DISTINCT weight) AS median
  FROM Temp2;
```

This involves the construction of a doubled table of values, which can be expensive in terms of both time and storage space. You will also find that this requires a good implementation of the SQL-92 standard that allows you to use a correlated scalar subquery in place of a scalar value expression. Most SQL implementations are not yet that sophisticated.

The use of AVG(DISTINCT x) is important because leaving it out would return the simple average instead of the median. Consider the set of weights (12, 17, 17, 14, 12, 19). The doubled table, Temp1, is then (12, 12, 12, 12, 14, 14, 17, 17, 17, 17, 19, 19). But because of the duplicated values, Temp2 becomes (14, 14, 17, 17, 17, 17), not just (14, 17). The simple average is (96 / 6.0) = 16; it should be (31 / 2.0) = 15.5 instead.

23.2.2 Celko's First Median

A slight modification of Date's solution will avoid the use of a doubled table, but it depends on an SQL-92 implementation that has a CEILING( ) function or particular vendor implementation of rounding and truncation.

```
SELECT MIN(weight)    -- smallest value in upper half
  FROM Parts
 WHERE weight IN (SELECT P1.weight
                    FROM Parts AS P1, Parts AS P2
                   WHERE P2.weight >= P1.weight
                   GROUP BY P1.weight
                   HAVING COUNT(*) <=
                          (SELECT CEILING(COUNT(*) / 2.0)
                             FROM Parts))
UNION
SELECT MAX(weight)    -- largest value in lower half
  FROM Parts
 WHERE weight IN (SELECT P1.weight
                    FROM Parts AS P1, Parts AS P2
                   WHERE P2.weight <= P1.weight
                   HAVING COUNT(*) <=
                          (SELECT CEILING(COUNT(*) / 2.0)
                             FROM Parts));
```

Older SQL products allow a HAVING clause only with a GROUP BY; this may not work with your SQL. The CEILING( ) function ensures that if there is an odd number of rows in Parts, the two halves will overlap on that value. Again, truncation and rounding in division are implementation-defined, so you will need to experiment with your product.

A safer way to do this in SQL-89 is to use VIEWs for the levels of nesting.

```
CREATE VIEW UpperHalf
AS SELECT P1.pno, P1.weight
     FROM Parts AS P1, Parts AS P2
    WHERE P1.weight <= P2.weight
    GROUP BY P1.pno, P1.weight
   HAVING COUNT(*) <= (SELECT CEILING(COUNT(*) / 2.0)
                         FROM Parts);
```

```
CREATE VIEW LowerHalf
AS SELECT P1.pno, P1.weight
     FROM Parts AS P1, Parts AS P2
    WHERE P1.weight >= P2.weight
    GROUP BY P1.pno, P1.weight
   HAVING COUNT(*) <= (SELECT CEILING(COUNT(*) / 2.0)
                         FROM Parts);

CREATE VIEW MiddleHalf (weight)
AS SELECT *
     FROM Parts
    WHERE weight = (SELECT MIN(weight) FROM LowerHalf)
    UNION ALL
    SELECT *
     FROM Parts
    WHERE weight = (SELECT MAX(weight) FROM UpperHalf);

SELECT AVG(weight) FROM MiddleHalf;
```

Again, the way your implementation handles truncation and rounding will determine whether you need the "+ 0.5" or not. The two VIEWs that are created are the upper and lower halves of the original table. The middle element, if any, will appear in both VIEWs. There are two major advantages in this approach. The VIEW MiddleHalf has all the information about the median entities, so we can see if the median is a true measure of central tendency or if the distribution is bimodal. If the bimodal distribution is a population that has extremes at both ends of its range, the median won't mean much. As I noted earlier, a simple example of this would be a country where there are very rich people and very poor people but no middle class.

23.2.3 Date's Second Median

Date's second solution (Date 1995b) was based on Celko's median, folded into one query:

```
SELECT AVG(DISTINCT Parts.weight) AS median
  FROM Parts
 WHERE Parts.weight IN
         (SELECT MIN(weight)
            FROM Parts
           WHERE Parts.weight IN
                 (SELECT P2.weight
```

```
            FROM Parts AS P1, Parts AS P2
           WHERE P2.weight <= P1.weight)
           GROUP BY P2.weight
      HAVING COUNT(*)
            <= (SELECT CEILING(COUNT(*) / 2.0)
                 FROM Parts))
    UNION
 (SELECT MAX(weight)
   FROM Parts
WHERE Parts.weight IN
        (SELECT P2.weight
            FROM Parts AS P1, Parts AS P2
         WHERE P2.weight >= P1.weight)
         GROUP BY P2.weight
         HAVING COUNT(*)
               <= (SELECT CEILING(COUNT(*) / 2.0)
                    FROM Parts)));
```

Date mentions that this solution will return a NULL for an empty table and that it assumes there are no NULLs in the column. If there are NULLs, the WHERE clauses should be modified to remove them.

23.2.4 Murchison's Median

Rory Murchison of the Aetna Institute has a solution that modifies Date's first method by concatenating the key to each value to make sure that every value is seen as a unique entity. Selecting the middle values is then a special case of finding the nth item in the table.

```
SELECT AVG(weight)
  FROM Parts AS P1
 WHERE EXISTS
     (SELECT COUNT(*)
        FROM Parts AS P2
       WHERE CAST(weight AS CHAR(5)) || P2.pno >=
             CAST(weight AS CHAR(5)) || P1.pno
      HAVING COUNT(*) = (SELECT FLOOR(COUNT(*) / 2.0)
                           FROM Parts)
          OR COUNT(*) = (SELECT CEILING((COUNT(*) / 2.0)
                           FROM Parts));
```

This method depends on being able to use a HAVING clause without a GROUP BY, which is part of the ANSI standard but not always part of vendor implementations.

Another handy trick if you don't have FLOOR() and CEILING() functions is to use (COUNT(*) + 1) / 2.0 and COUNT(*) / 2.0 + 1 to handle the odd-and-even-elements problem. Just to work it out, consider the case where the COUNT(*) returns 8 for an answer: $(8 + 1) / 2.0 = (9 / 2.0) = 4.5$ and $(8 / 2.0) + 1 = 4 + 1 = 5$. The 4.5 will round to 4 in DB2 and other SQL implementations. The case where the COUNT(*) returns 9 would work like this: $(9 + 1) / 2.0 = (10 / 2.0) = 5$ and $(9 / 2.0) + 1 = 4.5 + 1 = 5.5$, which will likewise round to 5 in DB2.

23.2.5 Celko's Second Median

Celko's second median is another method for finding the median that does not depend on SQL-92 features. The trick is to build a working table with the values and a tally of their occurrences from the original table. This working table should be quite a bit smaller than the original table and very fast to construct if there is an index on the target column. The Parts table will serve as an example:

```
-- construct Working table of occurrences by weight
CREATE TABLE Working
    (weight REAL NOT NULL,
    occurs INTEGER NOT NULL);

INSERT INTO Working (weight, occurs)
SELECT weight, COUNT(*)
  FROM Parts
 GROUP BY weight;
```

Now that we have this table, we want to use it to construct a summary table that has the number of occurrences of each weight and the total number of data elements before and after we add them to the working table.

```
-- construct table of cumulative tallies
CREATE TABLE Summary
(weight REAL NOT NULL,
 occurs INTEGER NOT NULL, -- number of occurrences
 pretally INTEGER NOT NULL, -- cumulative tally before
   posttally INTEGER NOT NULL);
```

```
-- cumulative tally after
INSERT INTO Summary
SELECT S2.weight, S2.occurs, SUM(S1.occurs)-S2.occurs, SUM(S1.occurs)
  FROM Working AS S1, Working AS S2
 WHERE S1.weight <= S2.weight
 GROUP BY S2.weight, S2.occurs;
```

Let $(n / 2.0)$ be the middle position in the table. There are two mutually exclusive situations. In the first case, the median lies in a position between the pretally and posttally of one weight value. In the second case, the median lies on the pretally of one row and the posttally of another. The middle position can be calculated by the scalar subquery (SELECT MAX(posttally) / 2.0 FROM Summary). Remember that in SQL-89, there can be a scalar subquery on only one side of a theta operator, not on both.

```
SELECT AVG(S3.weight) AS median
  FROM Summary AS S3
 WHERE (S3.posttally > (SELECT MAX(posttally) / 2.0 FROM Summary)
   AND S3.pretally < (SELECT MAX(posttally) / 2.0 FROM Summary))
    OR S3.pretally = (SELECT MAX(posttally) / 2.0 FROM Summary)
    OR S3.posttally = (SELECT MAX(posttally) / 2.0 FROM Summary);
```

This is such "vanilla" SQL that it will run on any implementation. The first predicate, with the AND operator, handles the case where the median falls inside one weight value; the other two predicates handle the case where the median is between two weights. A BETWEEN predicate will not work in this query.

These tables can be used to compute percentiles, deciles, and quartiles simply by changing the scalar subquery. For example, to find the highest tenth (first decile), use the subquery (SELECT 9 * MAX(posttally) / 10 FROM Summary); to find the highest two-tenths, (SELECT 8 * MAX(posttally) / 10 FROM Summary); and in general to find the highest n-tenths, (SELECT (10 - n) * MAX(posttally) / 10 FROM Summary).

23.2.6 Vaughan's Median with VIEWs

A simple median technique based on all of these methods was proposed by Philip Vaughan of San Jose, CA. It derives a VIEW with unique weights and number of occurrences and then a VIEW of the middle weights.

```
CREATE VIEW ValueSet(weight, occurs)
AS SELECT weight, COUNT(*)
```

```
   FROM Parts
 GROUP BY weight;
```

The MiddleValues VIEW is used to get the median by taking an average. The clever part of this code is the way that it handles empty result sets in the outermost WHERE clause that result from having only one value for all weights in the table. Empty sets sum to NULL because there is no element to map the index.

```
CREATE VIEW MiddleValues(weight)
AS SELECT weight
     FROM ValueSet AS VS1
   WHERE (SELECT SUM(VS2.occurs)/2.0 + 0.25
            FROM ValueSet AS VS2) >
         (SELECT SUM(VS2.occurs)
            FROM ValueSet AS VS2
           WHERE VS1.weight <= VS2.weight) - VS1.occurs
     AND (SELECT SUM(VS2.occurs)/2.0 + 0.25
            FROM ValueSet AS VS2) >
         (SELECT SUM(VS2.occurs)
            FROM ValueSet AS VS2
           WHERE VS1.weight >= VS2.weight) - VS1.occurs;

SELECT AVG(weight) AS median FROM MiddleValues;
```

23.2.7 Median with Characteristic Function

Anatoly Abramovich, Yelena Alexandrova, and Eugene Birger presented a series of articles in *SQL Forum* magazine on computing the median (*SQL Forum* 1993, 1994). They define a characteristic function, which they call delta, using the Sybase SIGN( ) function. The delta or characteristic function accepts a Boolean expression as an argument and returns 1 if it is TRUE and 0 if it is FALSE or UNKNOWN.

In SQL-92 we have a CASE expression, which can be used to construct the delta function. This is new to SQL-92, but you can find vendor functions of the form IF . . . THEN . . . ELSE that behave like the condition expression in Algol or like the "question mark and colon" operator in C.

The authors also distinguish between the statistical median, whose value must be a member of the set, and the financial median, whose value is the average of the middle two members of the set. A statistical median exists when there is an odd number of items in the set. If there is an even number of items, you must decide if you want to use the highest value in the lower half (they call this the *left median*) or the lowest value in the upper half (they call this the *right median*).

The left statistical median of a unique column can be found with this query, if you assume that we have a column called bin that represents the storage location of a part.

```
SELECT P1.bin
  FROM Parts AS P1, Parts AS P2
 GROUP BY P1.bin
HAVING SUM(CASE WHEN (P2.bin <= P1.bin) THEN 1 ELSE 0 END)
       = (COUNT(*) / 2.0);
```

Changing the direction of the theta test in the HAVING clause will allow you to pick the right statistical median if a central element does not exist in the set. You will also notice something else about the median of a set of unique values: It is usually meaningless. What does the median bin number mean, anyway? A good rule of thumb is that if it does not make sense as an average, it does not make sense as a median.

The statistical median of a column with duplicate values can be found with a query based on the same ideas, but you have to adjust the HAVING clause to allow for overlap; thus, the left statistical median is found by

```
SELECT P1.weight
  FROM Parts AS P1, Parts AS P2
 GROUP BY P1.weight
HAVING SUM(CASE WHEN P2.weight <= P1.weight
               THEN 1 ELSE 0 END)
           >= (COUNT(*) / 2.0)
   AND SUM(CASE WHEN P2.weight >= P1.weight
               THEN 1 ELSE 0 END)
           >= (COUNT(*) / 2.0);
```

Notice that here the left and right medians can be the same, so there is no need to pick one over the other in many of the situations where you have an even number of items. Switching the comparison operators in the two CASE expressions will give you the right statistical median.

The author's query for the financial median depends on some Sybase features that cannot be found in other products, so I would recommend using a combination of the right and left statistical medians to return a set of values about the center of the data and then averaging them. Using the derived table feature in SQL-92, we can write the query as

```
SELECT AVG(DISTINCT weight)
  FROM (SELECT P1.weight
          FROM Parts AS P1, Parts AS P2
         GROUP BY P1.weight
        HAVING (SUM(CASE WHEN P2.weight <= P1.weight
                         THEN 1 ELSE 0 END)
               >= ((COUNT(*)) / 2.0)
            AND SUM(CASE WHEN P2.weight >= P1.weight
                         THEN 1 ELSE 0 END)
               >= (COUNT(*)/2.0)));
```

and we can gain some additional control over the calculations. This version
will use one copy of the left and right median to compute the statistical
median. However, by simply changing the AVG(DISTINCT weight) to
AVG(weight), the median will favor the direction with the most occurrences.
This might be easier to see with an example. Assume that we have weights
(13, 13, 13, 14) in the Parts table. A pure statistical median would be
(13 + 14) / 2.0 = 13.5; however, weighting it would give (13 + 13 + 13 + 14)
/ 4.0 = 13.25, a number that is more representative of central tendency.

23.2.8 Celko's Third Median

Another approach made easier with SQL-92 involves looking at a picture of a
line of sorted values and seeing where the median would fall. Every value in
column weight of the table partitions the table into three sections, the values
that are less than weight, equal to weight, or greater than weight. We can get
a profile of each value with a tabular subquery expression.

Now the question is how to define a median in terms of the partitions.
Clearly, the definition of a median means that if (lesser = greater), then
weight is the median.

Now look at Figure 23.1 for the other situations. If there are more
greater values than half the size of the table, weight cannot be a median.
Likewise, if there are more lesser values than half the size of the table, weight
cannot be a median. If (lesser + equal) = greater, weight is a left-hand
median. Likewise, if (greater + equal) = lesser, weight is a right-hand median.
However, if weight is the median, both lesser and greater must have tallies
less than half the size of the table. That translates into the following SQL:

Fig. 23.1

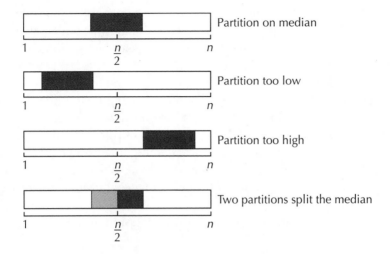

```
SELECT AVG(DISTINCT weight)
   FROM (SELECT F1.pno, F1.weight,
                  SUM(CASE WHEN F2.weight < F1.weight
                       THEN 1 ELSE 0 END),
                  SUM(CASE WHEN F2.weight = F1.weight
                       THEN 1 ELSE 0 END),
                  SUM(CASE WHEN F2.weight > F1.weight
                       THEN 1 ELSE 0 END)
            FROM Parts AS F1, Parts AS F2
            GROUP BY F1.pno, F1.weight)
              AS Partitions (pno, weight, lesser, equal, greater)
   WHERE lesser = greater
      OR (lesser <= (SELECT COUNT(*) FROM Parts)/2.0
          AND greater <= (SELECT COUNT(*) FROM Parts)/2.0);
```

The reason for not expanding the VIEW in the FROM clause into a tabular subquery expression is that the table can be used for other partitions of the table, such as quintiles.

It is also worth noting that you can use either AVG(DISTINCT i) or AVG(i) in the SELECT clause. The AVG(DISTINCT i) will return the usual median when there are two values. This happens when you have an even number of rows and a partition in the middle, such as (1, 2, 2, 3, 3, 3), which has (2, 3) in the middle, giving us 2.5 for the median. The AVG(i) will return the weighted median instead. A weighted median includes the number of times the two values in the middle of a table each appear. The table with (1, 2, 2, 3, 3, 3) would return (2, 2, 3, 3, 3) in the middle, which gives us 2.6 for the weighted median. The weighted median is a more accurate description of the data.

I sent this first attempt to Richard Romley, who invented the method of first working with groups when designing a query. It simplified the process, but let me take you through the steps so you can see the reasoning.

Look at the WHERE clause. It could use some algebra, and since it deals only with aggregate functions and scalar subqueries, you could move it into a HAVING clause. Moving things from the WHERE clause into the HAVING clause in a grouped query is important for performance, but it is not always possible.

But first let's do some algebra on the expression in the WHERE clause.

```
lesser <= (SELECT COUNT(*) FROM Parts)/2.0
```

Since we already have lesser, equal, and greater for every row in the derived table Partitions, and since the sum of lesser, equal, and greater must always be exactly equal to the total number of rows in the Parts table, we can replace the scalar subquery with this expression:

```
lesser <= (lesser + equal + greater)/2.0
```

But this is the same as

```
2.0 * lesser <= lesser + equal + greater
```

which becomes

```
2.0 * lesser - lesser <= equal + greater
```

which becomes

```
lesser <= equal + greater
```

So the query becomes

```
SELECT AVG(DISTINCT weight)
  FROM (SELECT F1.pno, F1.weight,
               SUM(CASE WHEN F2.weight < F1.weight
                    THEN 1 ELSE 0 END),
               SUM(CASE WHEN F2.weight = F1.weight
                    THEN 1 ELSE 0 END),
               SUM(CASE WHEN F2.weight > F1.weight
```

```
              THEN 1 ELSE 0 END)
       FROM Parts AS F1, Parts AS F2
       GROUP BY F1.pno, F1.weight)
          AS Partitions (pno, weight, lesser, equal, greater)
WHERE lesser = greater
   OR (lesser <= equal + greater
       AND greater <= equal + lesser);
```

We can rewrite the WHERE clause with DeMorgan's law.

```
WHERE lesser = greater
   OR (equal >= lesser - greater
       AND equal >= greater - lesser)
```

But this is the same as

```
WHERE lesser = greater
   OR equal >= ABS(lesser - greater)
```

But if the first condition was true (lesser = greater), the second must necessarily also be true (i.e., equal >= 0), so the first clause is redundant and can be eliminated completely.

```
WHERE equal >= ABS(lesser - greater)
```

So much for algebra. Instead of a WHERE clause operating on the columns of the derived table, why not perform the same test as a HAVING clause on the inner query, which derives Partitions? This eliminates all but one column from the derived table, it will run much faster, and it simplifies the query down to this:

```
SELECT AVG(DISTINCT weight)
  FROM (SELECT F1.weight
          FROM Parts AS F1, Parts AS F2
         GROUP BY F1.pno, F1.weight
        HAVING SUM(CASE WHEN F2.weight = F1.weight
                        THEN 1 ELSE 0 END)
        >= ABS(SUM(CASE WHEN F2.weight < F1.weight THEN 1
                        WHEN F2.weight > F1.weight THEN -1
                        ELSE 0 END)))
       AS Partitions;
```

23.3 Variance and Standard Deviation

The standard deviation is a measure of how far away from the average the values in a normally distributed population are. It is hard to calculate in SQL because it involves a square root and standard SQL has only the basic four arithmetic operators. Many vendors will allow you to use other math functions, but in all fairness, most SQL databases are in commercial applications and have little or no need for engineering or statistical calculations.

The usual trick is to load the raw data into an appropriate host language, such as Fortran, and do the work there. The formula for the standard deviation is

$$\sqrt{((\Sigma x^2 - ((\Sigma x)^2/n))/(n-1))}$$

where n is the number of items in the sample set and the x's are the values of the items.

The variance is defined as the standard deviation squared, so we can avoid taking a square root and keep the calculations in pure SQL. The queries look like this:

```
CREATE TABLE SomeTable (x REAL NOT NULL);
INSERT INTO SomeTable (x)
VALUES (64.0), (48.0), (55.0), (68.0), (72.0),
       (59.0), (57.0), (61.0), (63.0), (60.0),
       (60.0), (43.0), (67.0), (70.0), (65.0),
       (55.0), (56.0), (64.0), (61.0), (60.0);

SELECT ((COUNT(*) * SUM(x*x)) - (SUM(x) * SUM(x)))
       /(COUNT(*) * (COUNT(*)-1)) AS variance
  FROM SomeTable;
```

If you want to check this on your own SQL product, the correct answer is 48.9894. . . or just 49, depending how you handle rounding. If your SQL product has a standard deviation operator, use it instead.

23.4 Average Deviation

If you have an SQL product with an absolute value function, ABS(), you can also compute the average deviation following this pattern:

```
BEGIN
SELECT AVG(x) INTO :average FROM SomeTable;
```

```
SELECT SUM(ABS(x - :average)) / COUNT(x) AS AverDeviation
   FROM SomeTable;
END;
```

This is a measure of how much data values drift away from the average without any consideration of the direction of the drift.

23.5 Cumulative Statistics

A cumulative or running statistic looks at each data value and how it is related to the whole data set. The most common examples involve changes in an aggregate value over time or on some other well-ordered dimension. A bank balance, which changes with each deposit or withdrawal, is a running total over time. The total weight of a delivery truck as we add packages is a running total over the set of packages, but since two packages can have the same weight, we need a way to break ties—for example, use the arrival dates of the packages, and if that fails, use the alphabetical order of the last names of the shippers. In SQL, this means that we need a table with a key that we can use to order the rows.

Computer people classify reports as one-pass reports or two-pass reports, a terminology that comes from the number of times the computer used to have to read the data file to produce the desired results. These are really cumulative aggregate statistics.

Most report writers can produce a listing with totals and other aggregated descriptive statistics after each grouping ("Give me the total amount of sales broken down by salesmen within territories"). Such reports are called *banded reports* or *control-break reports,* depending on the vendor. The closest thing to such reports that the SQL language has is the GROUP BY clause used with aggregate functions, which was discussed in Chapter 20.

The two-pass report involves finding out something about the group as a whole in the first pass, then using it in the second pass to produce the results for each row in the group. The most common two-pass reports order the groups against each other ("Show me the total sales in each territory, ordered from high to low") or show the cumulative totals or cumulative percentages within a group ("Show me what percentage each customer contributes to total sales").

23.5.1 Running Totals

Running totals keep track of changes, which usually occur over time, but these could be changes on some other well-ordered dimension. A common example we all know is a bank account, for which we record withdrawals and deposits in a checkbook register. The running total is the balance of the account after each transaction. The query for the checkbook register is simply

```
SELECT B0.transaction, B0.transdate, SUM(B1.amount) AS balance
   FROM BankAccount AS B0, BankAccount AS B1
  WHERE B1.transdate <= B0.transdate
  GROUP BY B0.transaction, B0.transdate;
```

In SQL-92, you can use a scalar subquery instead:

```
SELECT B0.transaction, B0.transdate,
   (SELECT SUM(B1.amount)
      FROM BankAccount AS B1
    WHERE B1.transdate <= B0.transdate) AS balance
FROM BankAccount AS B0;
```

Which version will work better is dependent on your SQL product. Notice that this query handles both deposits (positive numbers) and withdrawals (negative numbers). There is a problem with running totals when two items occur at the same time. In this example, the transaction code keeps the transactions unique, but it is possible to have a withdrawal and a deposit on the same day that will be aggregated together.

If we showed the withdrawals before the deposits on that day, the balance could fall below zero, which might trigger some actions we don't want. The rule in banking is that deposits are credited before withdrawals on the same day, so simply extend the transaction date to show all deposits with a time before all withdrawals to fool the query. But remember that not all situations have a clearly defined policy like this.

23.5.2 Running Differences

Another kind of statistic, related to running totals, is running differences. In this case, we have the actual amount of something at various points in time and we want to compute the change since the last reading. Here is a quick scenario: We have a clipboard and a paper form on which we record the quantities of a chemical in a tank at different points in time from a gauge. We need to report the time, the gauge reading, and the difference between each reading and the preceding one. Here is some sample result data, showing the calculation we need:

tank	reading	quantity	difference	
'50A'	'1994-02-01-07:30'	300	NULL	starting data
'50A'	'1994-02-01-07:35'	500	200	
'50A'	'1994-02-01-07:45'	1200	700	
'50A'	'1994-02-01-07:50'	800	-400	
'50A'	'1994-02-01-08:00'	NULL	NULL	
'50A'	'1994-02-01-09:00'	1300	500	
'51A'	'1994-02-01-07:20'	6000	NULL	starting data
'51A'	'1994-02-01-07:22'	8000	2000	
'51A'	'1994-02-01-09:30'	NULL	NULL	
'51A'	'1994-02-01-00:45'	5000	-3000	
'51A'	'1994-02-01-01:00'	2500	-2500	

The NULL values mean that we missed taking a reading. The trick is a correlated subquery expression that computes the difference between the quantity in the current row and the quantity in the row with the largest known time value that is less than the time in the current row on the same date and on the same tank. We can do that in SQL-92:

```
SELECT tank, time, (quantity -
   (SELECT quantity
    FROM Deliveries AS D1
WHERE D1.tank = D0.tank -- same tank
    AND D1.time = (SELECT MAX (D2.time) -- most recent delivery
         FROM Deliveries AS D2
      WHERE D2.tank = D0.tank -- same tank
        AND D2.time < D0.time))) AS difference
   FROM Deliveries AS D0;
```

This is a modification of the running-totals query, but it is more elaborate since it cannot use the sum of the prior history.

23.5.3 Cumulative Percentages

Cumulative percentages are a bit more complex than running totals or differences. They show what percentage of the whole set of data values the current subset of data values is. Again, this is easier to show with an example than to say in words. You are given a table of the sales made by your sales force, which looks like this:

```
CREATE TABLE Sales
(salesman CHAR(10),
 client CHAR(10),
 amount DECIMAL (5, 2) NOT NULL,
PRIMARY KEY (salesman, client));
```

The problem is to show each salesman, his client, the amount of that sale, what percentage of his total sales volume that one sale represents, and the cumulative percentage of his total sales we have reached at that point.   We will sort the clients from the largest amount to the smallest. This problem is based on a salesman's report originally written for a small commercial printing company. The idea was to show the salesmen where their business was coming from and to persuade them to give up their smaller accounts (defined as the lower 20%) to new salesmen. The report lets each salesman run his finger down the page and see which customers represented the top 80% of his income.

This solution was given by L. Carl Pedersen of Hanover, NH. It is dependent on your SQL implementation, so check it out carefully before using it. The first step is to compute the total amount of sales for each salesman.

```
DELETE FROM SalesTot; -- clear out working table
INSERT INTO SalesTot (salesman, totamt)
    SELECT salesman, SUM(amount)
    FROM Sales
    GROUP BY salesman;
```

In XDB or DB2, we must have a temporary table to hold the totals for the salesmen. In Oracle Version 6 and more recent SQLs, you can use a VIEW instead of these two statements. The working SQL-89 query is

```
SELECT S1.salesman, S1.client, S1.amount,
       (S1.amount*100.00/ST1.totamt) AS percentage_of_total,
       (SUM(S2.amount)*100.00/ST1.totamt) AS cum_percent
    FROM Sales AS S1, SalesTot AS ST1, Sales AS S2
WHERE S1.salesman = ST1.salesman AND ST1.salesman = S2.salesman
    AND (S2.amount > S1.amount
       OR (S2.amount = S1.amount AND S2.client >= S1.client))
GROUP BY S1.salesman, S1.client, S1.amount, ST1.totamt
ORDER BY S1.salesman, S1.amount DESC, cum_percent DESC;
```

Notice the logic, which will alphabetize clients that place orders for the same amount. This linear ordering is important in running statistics. An SQL-92 solution can put the view creation into the FROM clause:

```
SELECT S0.salesman, S0.client, S0.amount,
       ((S0.amount * 100.00)/ ST.salesman_total
         AS percent_of_total,
       (SUM(S1.amount)/((S0.amount * 100)/ ST.salesman_total))
         AS cum_percent
  FROM Sales AS S0
       INNER JOIN
       Sales AS S1
       ON (S0.salesman, S0.client) <= (S1.salesman, S1.client)
         INNER JOIN
         (SELECT S2.salesman, SUM(S1.amount)
            FROM Sales AS S2
          GROUP BY S2.salesman) AS ST(salesman, salesman_total)
         ON S0.salesman = ST.salesman
GROUP BY S0.salesman, S0.client, S0.amount
ORDER BY S0.salesman, S0.amount DESC;
```

23.5.4 Rankings and Related Statistics

Martin Tillinger posted this problem on the MSACCESS forum of Compu-Serve in early 1995. How do you rank your salespeople in each territory, given a SalesReport table that looks like this?

```
CREATE TABLE SalesReport
(salesman CHAR(20) NOT NULL PRIMARY KEY
     REFERENCES Salesforce(salesman),
 territory INTEGER NOT NULL,
 totalsales DECIMAL (8,2) NOT NULL);
```

This statistic is called a ranking. A ranking is shown as integers that represent the ordinal values (first, second, third, and so on) of the elements of a set based on one of the values. In this case, sales personnel are ranked by their total sales within a territory. The one with the highest total sales is in first place, the next highest is in second place, and so forth.

The hard question is how to handle ties. The rule is that if two salespersons have the same value, they have the same ranking and there are no gaps in the rankings. This is the nature of ordinal numbers—there cannot be a third place without a first and a second place. A query that will do this for us is

```
SELECT S1.salesman, S1.territory, S1.totalsales,
       (SELECT COUNT(DISTINCT totalsales)
          FROM SalesReport AS S2
         WHERE S2.totalsales >= S1.totalsales
           AND S2.territory = S1.territory) AS rank
  FROM SalesReport AS S1;
```

You might also remember that this is really a version of the generalized extrema functions we have already discussed. Here is another way to write this query:

```
SELECT S1.salesman, S1.territory, MAX(S1.totalsales),
       SUM (CASE
               WHEN (S1.totalsales || S1.name)
                  <= (S2.totalsales || S2.name)
               THEN 1 ELSE 0 END) AS rank
  FROM SalesReport AS S1, SalesReport AS S2
 WHERE S1.salesman <> S2.salesman
   AND S1.territory = S2.territory
 GROUP BY S1.salesman, S1.territory;
```

This query uses the MAX() function on the nongrouping columns in the SalesReport to display them so that the aggregation will work.

It is worth looking at the four possible variations on this basic query to see what each change does to the result set.

Version 1: COUNT(DISTINCT) and >= yields a ranking:

```
SELECT S1.salesman, S1.territory, S1.totalsales,
       (SELECT COUNT(DISTINCT totalsales)
          FROM SalesReport AS S2
         WHERE S2.totalsales >= S1.totalsales
           AND S2.territory = S1.territory) AS rank
  FROM SalesReport AS S1;
```

salesman	territory	totalsales	rank
Wilson	1	990.00	1
Smith	1	950.00	2
Richards	1	800.00	3
Quinn	1	700.00	4
Parker	1	345.00	5
Jones	1	345.00	5
Hubbard	1	345.00	5
Date	1	200.00	6
Codd	1	200.00	6
Blake	1	100.00	7

Version 2: COUNT(DISTINCT) and > yields a ranking, but it starts at zero:

```
SELECT S1.salesman, S1.territory, S1.totalsales,
    (SELECT COUNT(DISTINCT totalsales)
       FROM SalesReport AS S2
       WHERE S2.totalsales > S1.totalsales
       AND S2.territory = S1.territory) AS rank
    FROM SalesReport AS S1;
```

salesman	territory	totalsales	rank
Wilson	1	990.00	0
Smith	1	950.00	1
Richards	1	800.00	2
Quinn	1	700.00	3
Parker	1	345.00	4
Jones	1	345.00	4
Hubbard	1	345.00	4
Date	1	200.00	5
Codd	1	200.00	5
Blake	1	100.00	6

Version 3: COUNT(ALL) and >= yields a standing that starts at 1:

```
SELECT S1.salesman, S1.territory, S1.totalsales,
    (SELECT COUNT(totalsales)
       FROM SalesReport AS S2
       WHERE S2.totalsales >= S1.totalsales
```

```
        AND S2.territory = S1.territory) AS standing
FROM SalesReport AS S1;
```

salesman	territory	totalsales	standing
Wilson	1	990.00	1
Smith	1	950.00	2
Richards	1	800.00	3
Quinn	1	700.00	4
Parker	1	345.00	7
Jones	1	345.00	7
Hubbard	1	345.00	7
Date	1	200.00	9
Codd	1	200.00	9
Blake	1	100.00	10

Version 4: COUNT(ALL) and > yields a standing that starts at zero:

```
SELECT S1.salesman, S1.territory, S1.totalsales,
     (SELECT COUNT(totalsales)
        FROM SalesReport AS S2
      WHERE S2.totalsales > S1.totalsales
        AND S2.territory = S1.territory) AS standing
  FROM SalesReport AS S1;
```

salesman	territory	totalsales	standing
Wilson	1	990.00	0
Smith	1	950.00	1
Richards	1	800.00	2
Quinn	1	700.00	3
Parker	1	345.00	4
Jones	1	345.00	4
Hubbard	1	345.00	4
Date	1	200.00	7
Codd	1	200.00	7
Blake	1	100.00	9

A third system used in British schools will also leave gaps in the numbers, but in a different direction. For example, consider this set of marks:

marks	class_standing
100	1
90	2
90	2
70	4

Both students with 90 were second because only one person had a higher mark. The student with 70 was fourth because there were three people ahead of him. With our data that would be

```
SELECT S1.salesman, S1.territory, S1.totalsales,
     (SELECT COUNT(S2. totalsales)
         FROM SalesReport AS S2
       WHERE S2.totalsales > S1.totalsales
         AND S2.territory = S1.territory) + 1 AS british
   FROM SalesReport AS S1;
```

salesman	territory	totalsales	British
Wilson	1	990.00	1
Smith	1	950.00	2
Richards	1	800.00	3
Quinn	1	700.00	4
Parker	1	345.00	5
Jones	1	345.00	5
Hubbard	1	345.00	5
Date	1	200.00	8
Codd	1	200.00	8
Blake	1	100.00	10

An aside for the mathematicians among the readers: I always use the heuristic that it helps solve a SQL problem to think in terms of sets. What we are looking for in these ranking queries is how to assign an ordinal number to a subset of the SalesReport table. This subset is the rows that have an equal or higher sales volume than the salesman at whom we are looking. Or in other words, one copy of the SalesReport table provides the elements of the subsets, and the other copy provides the boundary of the subsets. This count is really a sequence of nested subsets.

If you happen to have had a good set theory course, you'll remember John von Neumann's definition of the *n*th ordinal number; it is the set of all ordinal numbers less than the *n*th number.

23.6 Cross Tabulations

A *cross tabulation,* or crosstab for short, is a common statistical report. It can be done in IBM's QMF tool, using the ACROSS summary option, and in many other SQL-based reporting packages. SPSS, SAS, and other statistical packages have library procedures or language constructs for crosstabs. Many spreadsheets can load the results of SQL queries and perform a crosstab within the spreadsheet.

If you can use a reporting package on the server in a client/server system instead of the following method, do so. It will run faster and in less space than the method discussed here. However, if you have to use the reporting package on the client side, the extra time required to transfer data will make these methods on the server side much faster.

A one-way crosstab "flattens out" a table to display it in a report format. Assume that we have a table of sales by product and the dates the sales were made. We want to print out a report of the sales of products by years for a full decade. The solution is to create a table and populate it to look like an identity matrix (all elements on the diagonal are 1, all others 0), then JOIN the Sales table to it.

```
CREATE TABLE Sales
(product CHAR(15) NOT NULL,
 price DECIMAL(5, 2) NOT NULL,
 qty INTEGER NOT NULL,
 salesyear INTEGER NOT NULL);

CREATE TABLE crosstabs
(year INTEGER NOT NULL,
 year1 INTEGER NOT NULL,
 year2 INTEGER NOT NULL,
 year3 INTEGER NOT NULL,
 year4 INTEGER NOT NULL,
 year5 INTEGER NOT NULL,
 year6 INTEGER NOT NULL,
 year7 INTEGER NOT NULL,
 year8 INTEGER NOT NULL,
 year9 INTEGER NOT NULL,
 year10 INTEGER NOT NULL);
```

The table would be populated as follows:

year	year1	year2	year3	year4	year5	. . .	year10
1990	1	0	0	0	0	. . .	0
1991	0	1	0	0	0	. . .	0
1992	0	0	1	0	0	. . .	0
1993	0	0	0	1	0	. . .	0
1994	0	0	0	0	1	. . .	0
⋮							
1999	0	0	0	0	0	. . .	1

The query to produce the report table is

```
SELECT S2.product,
    SUM(S2.qty * price * C1.year1),
    SUM(S2.qty * price * C1.year2),
    SUM(S2.qty * price * C1.year3),
    SUM(S2.qty * price * C1.year4),
    SUM(S2.qty * price * C1.year5),
    . . .
    SUM(S2.qty * price * C1.year10)
FROM Sales AS S2, crosstabs AS C1
WHERE S2.year = C1.year
GROUP BY S2.product;
```

Obviously, (price * qty) is the total dollar amount of each product in each year. The yearN column will be either a 1 or a 0. If it is a 0, the total dollar amount in the SUM() is 0; if it is a 1, the total dollar amount in the SUM() is unchanged. This solution lets you adjust the time frame being shown in the report by replacing the values in the year column to whatever consecutive years you wish.

A two-way crosstab takes two variables and produces a spreadsheet with all values of one variable on the rows and all values of the other represented by the columns. Each cell in the table holds the COUNT of entities that have those values for the two variables. NULLs will not fit into a crosstab very well unless you decide to make them a group of their own or to remove them.

There are also totals for each column and each row and a grand total. Crosstabs of n variables are defined by building an n-dimensional spreadsheet. But you cannot easily print n dimensions on two-dimensional paper. The usual trick is to display the results as a two-dimensional grid with one or both axes as a tree structure. The way the values are nested on the axis is usually under program control; thus, "race within sex" shows sex broken down by race, whereas "sex within race" shows race broken down by sex.

Assume that we have a table, Personnel (empno, sex, race, jobno, salary), keyed on employee number, with no NULLs in any columns. We wish to write a crosstab of employees by sex and race that would look like this:

	Asian	Black	Caucasian	Hispanic	Other	TOTALS
Male	3	2	12	5	5	27
Female	1	10	20	2	9	42
TOTAL	4	12	32	7	14	69

The first thought is to use a GROUP BY and write a simple query:

```
SELECT sex, race, COUNT(*)
  FROM Personnel
 GROUP BY sex, race;
```

This approach works fine for two variables and would produce a table that could be sent to a report writer program to give a final version. But where are your column and row totals? This means you also need to write these two queries:

```
SELECT race, COUNT(*) FROM Personnel GROUP BY race;
SELECT sex, COUNT(*) FROM Personnel GROUP BY sex;
```

However, what I wanted was a table with a row for males and a row for females, with columns for each of the racial groups, just as I drew it.

But let us assume that we want to get this information broken down within a third variable, say, job code. I want to see the jobno and the total by sex and race within each job code. Our query set starts to get bigger and bigger. A crosstab can also include other summary data, such as total or average salary within each cell of the table.

23.6.1 Crosstabs by CROSS JOIN

A solution proposed by John M. Baird of Datapoint, in San Antonio, Texas, involves creating a matrix table for each variable in the crosstabs:

SexMatrix

sex	Male	Female
'M'	1	0
'F'	0	1

RaceMatrix

race	Asian	Black	Caucasian	Hispanic	Other
Asian	1	0	0	0	0
Black	0	1	0	0	0
Caucasian	0	0	1	0	0
Hispanic	0	0	0	1	0
Other	0	0	0	0	1

The query then constructs the cells by using a CROSS JOIN (Cartesian product) and summation for each one:

```
SELECT jobno,
       SUM(asian * male) AS AsianMale,
       SUM(asian * female) AS AsianFemale,
       SUM(black * male) AS BlackMale,
       SUM(black * female) AS BlackFemale,
       SUM(cauc * male) AS CaucMale,
       SUM(cauc * female) AS CaucFemale,
       SUM(hisp * male) AS HispMale,
       SUM(hisp * female) AS HispFemale,
       SUM(other * male) AS OtherMale,
       SUM(other * female) AS OtherFemale
  FROM Personnel, SexMatrix, RaceMatrix
 WHERE (RaceMatrix.race = Personnel.race)
   AND (SexMatrix.sex = Personnel.sex)
 GROUP BY jobno;
```

Numeric summary data can be obtained from this table. For example, the total salary for each cell can be computed by SUM(<race> * <sex> * salary) AS <cell name> in place of what we have here.

23.6.2 Crosstabs by OUTER JOINs

Another method, due to Jim Panttaja, uses a series of temporary tables or VIEWs and then combines them with OUTER JOINs.

```
CREATE VIEW Guys (race, maletally)
AS SELECT race, COUNT(*)
     FROM Personnel
    WHERE sex = 'M'
    GROUP BY race;
```

Correspondingly, you could have written

```
CREATE VIEW Dolls (race, femaletally)
AS SELECT race, COUNT(*)
     FROM Personnel
    WHERE sex = 'F'
    GROUP BY race;
```

But the tables can be combined for a crosstab, without column and row totals, like this:

```
SELECT Guys.race, maletally, femaletally
   FROM Guys LEFT OUTER JOIN Dolls
        ON Guys.race = Dolls.race;
  WHERE Personnel.sex = 'F'
  GROUP BY Guys.race, maletally;
```

The idea is to build a starting column in the crosstab, then progressively add columns to it. You use the LEFT OUTER JOIN to avoid missing-data problems.

23.6.3 Crosstabs by Subquery

Another method takes advantage of the orthogonality of correlated subqueries in SQL-92. Think about what each row or column in the crosstab wants:

```
SELECT race,
       (SELECT COUNT(*)
          FROM Personnel AS P1
         WHERE P0.race = P1.race
           AND sex = 'M') AS MaleTally,
       (SELECT COUNT(*)
          FROM Personnel AS P2
         WHERE P0.race = P2.race
           AND sex = 'F') AS FemaleTally
FROM Personnel AS P0;
```

An advantage of this approach is that you can attach another column to get the row tally by adding

```
(SELECT COUNT(*)
    FROM Personnel AS P3
  WHERE PO.race = P3.race) AS RaceTally
```

Likewise, to get the column tallies, UNION the previous query with

```
SELECT' Summary',
          (SELECT COUNT(*)
              FROM Personnel
            WHERE sex = 'M') AS GrandMaleTally,
          (SELECT COUNT(*)
              FROM Personnel
            WHERE sex = 'F') AS GrandFemaleTally,
          (SELECT COUNT(*)
              FROM Personnel) AS GrandTally
FROM Personnel;
```

CHAPTER 24

Regions, Runs, and Sequences

REGIONS, RUNS, AND sequences form a general class of queries that assumes a table with at least two columns. One of them is an identifier drawn from a sequence that is the primary key. The other has a value we want to search for, based on the ordering imposed by the first column. A *sequence* has consecutive unique identifiers without any gaps in the numbering. Examples of this sort of data would be ticket numbers, time series data taken at fixed intervals, and the like. The ordering of those identifiers carries some information content, such as physical or temporal location.

A *subsequence* is a set of consecutive unique identifiers within a larger, containing sequence. For example, given the data (99, 1, 2, 3, 4, 5, 0), you can find subsequences of size 3—(1, 2, 3), (2, 3, 4), and (3, 4, 5)—but the longest sequence is (1, 2, 3, 4, 5), and it is of size 5.

A *run* is like a sequence, but the numbers don't have to be consecutive, just increasing and contiguous. For example, given the run (1, 2, 12, 15, 23), you can find subruns of size 3: (1, 2, 12), (2, 12, 15), and (12, 15, 23).

A *region* is contiguous and all the values are the same. For example, (1, 0, 0, 0, 25) has a region of zeros that is three items long.

In procedural languages, you would simply sort the data and scan it. In SQL, you have to define everything in terms of sets and nested sets. None of these queries will run very fast, but they do demonstrate that such things are possible in SQL.

24.1 Finding Subregions of Size *n*

This example is adapted from *SQL and Its Applications* (Lorie and Daudenarde 1991). You are given a table of theater seats, defined by

```
CREATE TABLE Theater
(seat INTEGER NOT NULL PRIMARY KEY,
 status CHAR(1) NOT NULL
        CONSTRAINT valid_status
        CHECK (status IN ('A', 'S')));
```

where a status code of 'A' means *available* and 'S' means *sold*. Your problem is to write a query that will return the subregions of *n* consecutive seats still available. Assume that *consecutive seat numbers* means that the seats are also consecutive for a moment, ignoring rows of seating where seat *n* and seat $(n + 1)$ might be in different physical theater rows. For $n = 3$, we can write a self-JOIN query:

```
SELECT S1.seat, S2.seat, S3.seat
  FROM Theater AS S1, Theater AS S2, Theater AS S3
 WHERE S1.status = 'A'
   AND S2.status = 'A'
   AND S3.status = 'A'
   AND S2.seat = S1.seat + 1
   AND S3.seat = S2.seat + 1;
```

The trouble with this answer is that it works only for $n = 3$ and for nothing else. This pattern can be extended for any *n*, but what we really want is a generalized query where we can use *n* as a parameter to the query.

The solution given by Lorie and Daudenarde starts with a given seat number and looks at all the available seats between it and $(n - 1)$ seats further up. The real trick is switching from the English-language statement "All seats between here and there are available" to the passive-voice version, "Available is the status of all the seats between here and there," so that you can see the query.

```
SELECT seat, ' thru ', (seat + (:n - 1))
  FROM Theater AS T1
 WHERE status = 'A'
   AND 'A' = ALL (SELECT status
                    FROM Theater AS T2
```

```
    WHERE T2.seat > T1.seat
      AND T2.seat <=  T1.seat + (:n - 1));
```

Please note that this returns subregions. That is, if seats (1, 2, 3, 4, 5) are available, this query will return (1, 2, 3), (2, 3, 4), and (3, 4, 5) as its answer.

24.2 Finding Regions of Maximum Size

A query to find a region of seats, rather than a subregion of known size, was presented in *SQL Forum* (Rozenshtein, Abramovich, and Birger 1993).

```
SELECT T1.seat, ' thru ', T2.seat
  FROM Theater AS T1, Theater AS T2
 WHERE T1.seat < T2.seat
   AND NOT EXISTS
          (SELECT *
             FROM Theater AS T3
            WHERE (T3.seat BETWEEN T1.seat AND T2.seat
                  AND T3.status <> 'A')
               OR (T3.seat = T2.seat + 1 AND T3.status = 'A')
               OR (T3.seat = T1.seat - 1 AND T3.status = 'A'));
```

The trick here is to look for the starting and ending seats in the region. The starting seat of a region is to the right of a sold seat, and the ending seat is to the left of a sold seat. No seat between the start and the end has been sold.

If you keep only the available seat numbers in a table, the solution is a bit easier. It is also a more general problem that applies to any table of sequential, possibly noncontiguous, data:

```
CREATE TABLE Seatings
 (seat INTEGER NOT NULL
       CONSTRAINT valid_seat_nbr
       CHECK (seat BETWEEN 001 AND 999));
INSERT INTO Seatings VALUES (199);
INSERT INTO Seatings VALUES (200);
INSERT INTO Seatings VALUES (201);
INSERT INTO Seatings VALUES (202);
INSERT INTO Seatings VALUES (204);
INSERT INTO Seatings VALUES (210);
INSERT INTO Seatings VALUES (211);
INSERT INTO Seatings VALUES (212);
```

```
INSERT INTO Seatings VALUES (214);
INSERT INTO Seatings VALUES (218);
```

where you need to create a result that will show the start and finish values of each sequence in the table, thus:

199 202
204 204
210 212
214 214
218 218

This is a common way of checking to see if all the tickets in a series have been sold, if all the invoices are accounted for, or whatever else you do that assumes a sequence of some sort in a numbering scheme.

Let's draw a number line with Xs for the numbers that are in the table and Os for the numbers that are not. The test data would look something like this:

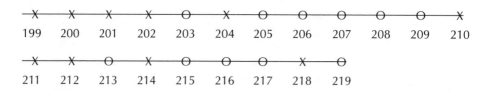

What do you see about a sequence? Well, we can start with a fact that anyone who has done inventory knows. The number of elements in a sequence is equal to the ending value minus the starting value plus one. This is a basic property of ordinal numbers:

```
(finish - start + 1) = Length of Seatings
```

This tells us that we need to have a self-JOIN with two copies of the table, one for the starting value and one for the ending value of each sequence. Once we have those two items, we can compute the length with our formula and see if it is equal to the count of the items between the start and finish.

```
SELECT S1.seat, MAX(S2.seat) -- start and rightmost item
  FROM Seatings AS S1
       INNER JOIN
       Seatings AS S2  -- self-JOIN
       ON S1.seat <= S2.seat
```

```
                  AND (S2.seat - S1.seat + 1) -- formula for length
                     = (SELECT COUNT(*)  -- items in the sequence
                            FROM Seatings AS S3
                           WHERE S3.seat BETWEEN S1.seat AND S2.seat)
                         AND NOT EXISTS (SELECT *
                                            FROM Seatings AS S4
                                           WHERE S1.seat - 1 = S4.seat)
      GROUP BY S1.seat;
```

Finally, we need to be sure that we have the furthest item to the right as
the end item. Each sequence of n items has n subsequences that all start with
the same item. So we finally do a GROUP BY on the starting item and use a
MAX( ) to get the rightmost value.

However, there is a faster three-table version. This solution is based on
looking at other properties of a sequence. Let's look at a subsequence in the
original data:

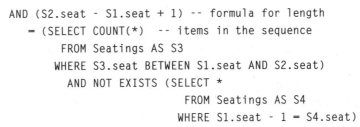

If you look to the right of the last item, you do not find anything.
Likewise, if you look to the left of the first item, you do not find anything.
These missing items, which are "just over the border," define a sequence by
framing it. Nor can there be any "gaps"—missing items—inside those borders. That translates into SQL as

```
SELECT S1.seat, MIN(S2.seat) --start and leftmost border
  FROM Seatings AS S1, Seatings AS S2
 WHERE S1.seat <= S2.seat
   AND NOT EXISTS  -- border items of the sequence
       (SELECT *
          FROM Seatings AS S3
         WHERE S3.seat NOT BETWEEN S1.seat AND S2.seat
           AND (S3.seat = S1.seat - 1 OR S3.seat = S2.seat + 1))
 GROUP BY S1.seat;
```

We do not have to worry about getting the rightmost item in the sequence, but we do have to worry about getting the leftmost border. Once again we do a GROUP BY, but use a MIN( ) to get what we want.

Since the second approach uses only three copies of the original table, it should be a bit faster. Also, the EXISTS( ) predicates can often take advantage of indexing and thus run faster than subquery expressions, which require a table scan.

24.3 Bound Queries

Another form of query asks if there was an overall trend between two points in time bounded by a low value and a high value in the sequence of data. This is easier to show with an example. Let us assume that we have data on the selling prices of a stock in a table. We want to find periods of time when the price was generally increasing. Consider this data:

MyStock

saledate	price
'1994-12-01'	10.00
'1994-12-02'	15.00
'1994-12-03'	13.00
'1994-12-04'	12.00
'1994-12-05'	20.00

The stock was generally increasing in all the periods that began on December 1 or ended on December 5—that is, it finished higher at the ends of those periods, in spite of the slump in the middle. A query for this problem is

```
SELECT S1.saledate, ' thru ', S2.saledate
  FROM MyStock AS S1, MyStock AS S2
 WHERE S1.saledate < S2.saledate
   AND NOT EXISTS
       (SELECT *
          FROM MyStock AS S3
         WHERE S3.saledate BETWEEN S1.saledate AND S2.saledate
           AND S3.price NOT BETWEEN S1.price AND S2.price);
```

24.4 Run and Sequence Queries

Runs are informally defined as sequences with gaps. That is, we have a set of unique numbers whose order has some meaning, but the numbers are not all consecutive. Time series information where the samples are taken at irregular intervals is an example of this sort of data. Runs can be constructed in the same manner as the sequences by making a minor change in the search condition. Let's do these queries with an abstract table made up of a sequence number and a value:

```
CREATE TABLE Sequences
(seq INTEGER NOT NULL PRIMARY KEY,
 val INTEGER NOT NULL);
```

Sequences

seq	val
1	6
2	41
3	12
4	51
5	21
78	70
79	79
80	62
81	30
82	31
83	32
84	34
85	35
86	57
87	19
88	84
89	80
90	90
91	63
92	53
93	3
94	59
95	69
96	27
97	33

One of the problems is that we don't want to get back all the runs and sequences of length 1. Ideally, the length *n* of the run should be adjustable. This query will find runs of length *n* or greater; if you want runs of exactly *n*, change the "greater than" to an equal sign.

```
SELECT S1.seq, ' thru ', S2.seq
  FROM Sequences AS S1, Sequences AS S2
 WHERE S1.seq < S2.seq        -- start and end points
   AND (S2.seq - S1.seq) > (:n - 1)  -- length restrictions
   AND NOT EXISTS    -- ordering within the end points
       (SELECT *
           FROM Sequences AS S3, Sequences AS S4
          WHERE S4.seq BETWEEN S1.seq AND S2.seq
          AND S3.seq BETWEEN S1.seq AND S2.seq
          AND S3.seq < S4.seq
          AND S3.val > S4.val);
```

What this query does is set up the S1 sequence number as the starting point and the S2 sequence number as the ending point of the run. The monster subquery in the NOT EXISTS predicate is looking for a row in the middle of the run that violates the ordering of the run. If there is none, the run is valid. The best way to understand what is happening is to draw a linear diagram (Figure 24.1). This shows that as the ordering, seq, increases, so must the corresponding values, val.

A sequence has the additional restriction that every value increases by 1 as you scan the run from left to right. This means that in a sequence, the highest value minus the lowest value, plus 1, is the length of the sequence.

```
SELECT S1.seq, ' thru ', S2.seq
    FROM Sequences AS S1, Sequences AS S2
WHERE S1.seq < S2.seq
    AND (S2.seq - S1.seq) = (S2.val - S1.val)  -- order condition
    AND (S2.seq - S1.seq) > (:n - 1)  -- length restrictions
    AND NOT EXISTS
        (SELECT *
            FROM Sequences AS S3
          WHERE S3.seq BETWEEN S1.seq AND S2.seq
            AND((S3.seq - S1.seq) <> (S3.val - S1.val)
                OR (S2.seq - S3.seq) <> (S2.val - S3.val)));
```

Fig. 24.1

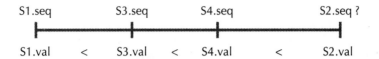

The subquery in the NOT EXISTS predicate says that there is no point in between the start and the end of the sequence that violates the ordering condition.

Obviously, any of these queries can be changed from increasing to decreasing, from strictly increasing to simply increasing or simply decreasing, and so on, by changing the comparison predicates. You can also change the query for finding sequences in a table by altering the size of the step from 1 to *k*, by observing that the difference between the starting position and the ending position should be *k* times the difference between the starting value and the ending value.

Array Structures in SQL

ARRAYS CANNOT BE represented directly in standard SQL, but this is a common vendor language extension. Arrays violate the rules of First Normal Form (1NF) required for a relational database, which say that the tables have no repeating groups in any column. A repeating group is a data structure that is not scalar; examples of repeating groups include linked lists, arrays, records, and even tables within a column.

The reason they are not allowed is that a repeating group would have to fit into a column as a datatype. There is no obvious way to JOIN a column that contains an array to other columns since there are no comparison operators or conversion rules. There is no obvious way to display or transmit a column that contains an array as a result set. Different languages and different compilers for the same language store arrays in column-major or row-major order, so there is no standard.

The goal of SQL was to be a database language that would operate with a wide range of host languages. To meet that goal, the scalar datatypes are as varied as possible to match the host language datatypes, but as simple in structure as possible to make the transfer of data to the host language as easy as possible.

25.1 Representing Arrays in SQL

An array in other programming languages has a name and subscripts by which the array elements are referenced. The array elements are all of the same datatype and the subscripts are all integers. Some languages start numbering at zero, some start numbering at one, and some let the user set the upper and lower bounds. For example, a Pascal array declaration would look like this:

```
foobar : ARRAY [1..5] OF INTEGER;
```

It would have elements foobar[1], foobar[2], foobar[3], foobar[4], and foobar[5]. The same structure is most often mapped into a SQL declaration as

```
CREATE TABLE Foobar1
(element1 INTEGER NOT NULL,
 element2 INTEGER NOT NULL,
 element3 INTEGER NOT NULL,
 element4 INTEGER NOT NULL,
 element5 INTEGER NOT NULL);
```

The elements cannot be accessed by the use of a subscript in this table as they can in a true array. That is, to set all the array elements equal to zero in Pascal takes one statement with a FOR loop in it:

```
FOR i := 1 TO 5 DO foobar[i] := 0;
```

The same action in SQL would be performed with the statement

```
UPDATE Foobar1
    SET element1 = 0,
        element2 = 0,
        element3 = 0,
        element4 = 0,
        element5 = 0;
```

because there is no subscript that can be iterated in a loop. In fact, there is no loop control structure at all in SQL-92. Any access has to be based on column names and not on subscripts.

Let's assume that we design an Employee table with separate columns for the names of four children, and we start with an empty table and then try to use it.

1. What happens if we hire a man with fewer than four children? We can fire him immediately or make him have more children. We can restructure the table to allow for fewer children. The usual, and less drastic, solution is to put NULLs in the columns for the nonexistent

children. We then have all of the problems associated with NULLs to handle.

2. What happens if we hire a man with five children? We can fire him immediately or order him to kill one of his children. We can restructure the table to allow five children. We can add a second row to hold the information on children 5 through 8; however, this destroys the uniqueness of the empno, so it cannot be used as a key. We can overcome that problem by adding a new column for record number, which will form a two-column key with the empno. This leads to needless duplication in the table.

3. What happens if the employee dies? We will delete all his children's data along with his, even if the company owes benefits to the survivors.

4. What happens if the child of an employee dies? We can fire him or order him to get another child immediately. We can restructure the table to allow only three children. We can overwrite the child's data with NULLs and get all of the problems associated with NULL values. This last one is the most common decision. But what if we had used the multiple-row trick and this employee had a fifth child—should that child be brought into the vacant slot in the current row and the second row of the set deleted?

5. What happens if the employee replaces a dead child with a new one? Should the new child's data overwrite the NULLs in the dead child's data? Should the new child's data be put in the next available slot and overwrite the NULLs in those columns?

Some of these choices involve rebuilding the database. Others are simply absurd attempts to restructure reality to fit the database. The real point is that each insertion or deletion of a child involves a different procedure, depending on the size of the group to which he belongs. Consider instead a table of employees and another table for their children:

```
CREATE TABLE Employees
(empno INTEGER NOT NULL,
 empname CHAR(30) NOT NULL,
   . . .);

CREATE TABLE Children
(empno INTEGER NOT NULL,
```

```
child CHAR(30) NOT NULL,
birthday DATE NOT NULL,
sex CHAR(1) NOT NULL);
```

To add a child, you insert a row into Children. To remove a child, you delete a row from Children. There is nothing special about the fourth or fifth child that requires the database system to use special procedures. There are no NULLs in either table.

The trade-off is that the number of tables in the database schema increases, but the total amount of storage will be smaller because you will keep data only on children who exist rather than using NULLs to hold space. The goal is to have data in the simplest possible format so that any host program can use it.

In her excellent DB2 classes, Gabrielle Wiorkowski uses an example of a table for tracking the sales made by salespersons during the past year. That table could be defined as

```
CREATE TABLE AnnualSales1
(salesman CHAR(15) NOT NULL,
 jan DECIMAL(5,2),
 feb DECIMAL(5,2),
 mar DECIMAL(5,2),
 apr DECIMAL(5,2),
 may DECIMAL(5,2),
 jun DECIMAL(5,2),
 jul DECIMAL(5,2),
 aug DECIMAL(5,2),
 sep DECIMAL(5,2),
 oct DECIMAL(5,2),
 nov DECIMAL(5,2),
 "dec" DECIMAL(5,2));
```

We have to allow for NULLs in the monthly amounts in the first version of the table, but the table is actually quite a bit smaller than it would be if we were to declare it as

```
CREATE TABLE AnnualSales2
(salesman CHAR(15) NOT NULL PRIMARY KEY,
 month CHAR(3)
      CONSTRAINT valid_month_abbrev
      CHECK (month IN ('Jan', 'Feb', 'Mar', 'Apr',
                       'May', 'Jun', 'Jul', 'Aug',
```

```
                       'Sep', 'Oct', 'Nov', 'Dec'),
amount DECIMAL(5,2) NOT NULL,
PRIMARY KEY(salesman, month));
```

In Wiorkowski's actual example in DB2, the break-even point for DASD storage was April; that is, the storage required for AnnualSales1 and AnnualSales2 is the same in April of the given year. Queries that deal with individual salespersons will run much faster against the AnnualSales1 table than queries based on the AnnualSales2 table because all the data is in one row in the AnnualSales1 table. They may be a bit messy and may have to have function calls to handle possible NULL values, but they are not very complex.

Another approach to faking a multidimensional array is to map arrays into a table with an integer column for each subscript:

```
CREATE TABLE Foobar2
(i INTEGER NOT NULL
    CONSTRAINT valid_index
    CHECK(i BETWEEN 1 AND 5),
 element INTEGER NOT NULL,
 PRIMARY KEY (i));
```

This looks more complex than the first approach, but it is closer to what the original Pascal declaration was doing behind the scenes. Subscripts resolve to unique physical addresses, so it is not possible to have two values for foobar[i]; hence, i is a key. The Pascal compiler will check to see that the subscripts are within the declared range; hence the CHECK() clause.

The first advantage of this approach is that multidimensional arrays are easily handled by adding another column for each subscript. The Pascal declaration

```
ThreeD : ARRAY [1..3, 1..4, 1..5] OF REAL;
```

is mapped over to

```
CREATE TABLE ThreeD
(i INTEGER NOT NULL
    CONSTRAINT valid_i
    CHECK(i BETWEEN 1 AND 3),
 j INTEGER NOT NULL
    CONSTRAINT valid_j
    CHECK(j BETWEEN 1 AND 4),
 k INTEGER NOT NULL
```

```
   CONSTRAINT valid_k
   CHECK(k BETWEEN 1 AND 5),
element REAL NOT NULL,
PRIMARY KEY (i, j, k));
```

Obviously, SELECT statements with GROUP BY clauses on the subscript columns will produce row and column totals:

```
SELECT i, j, SUM(element) -- sum across the k columns
    FROM ThreeD
GROUP BY i, j;

SELECT i, SUM(element) -- sum across the j and k columns
    FROM ThreeD
GROUP BY i;

SELECT SUM(element) -- sum the entire array
    FROM ThreeD;
```

If the original one element/one column approach were used, the table declaration would have 120 columns, named "element111" through "element345." This would be too many names to handle in any reasonable way; in addition, you would not be able to use the GROUP BY clauses for array projection.

Another advantage of this approach is that the subscripts can be datatypes other than integers. DATE and TIME datatypes are often useful, but CHARACTER and approximate numerics can have their uses, too.

25.2 Matrix Operations in SQL

A matrix is not quite the same thing as an array. Matrices are mathematical structures with particular properties that we cannot take the time to discuss here. You can find that information in an algebra book. Though it is possible to do many matrix operations in SQL, it is not a good idea because such queries and operations will eat up resources and run much too long. SQL was never meant to be a language for calculations.

Let us assume that we have two-dimensional arrays that are declared as tables, using two columns for subscripts, and that all columns are declared with a NOT NULL constraint.

The presence of NULLs is not defined in linear algebra, and I have no desire to invent a three-valued linear algebra of my own. Another problem is that a matrix has rows and columns that are not the same as the rows and columns of an SQL table; as you read the rest of this section, be careful not to confuse the two.

```
CREATE TABLE MyMatrix
(element INTEGER NOT NULL, -- could be any numeric datatype
 i INTEGER NOT NULL CHECK (i>0),
 j INTEGER NOT NULL CHECK (j>0);
CHECK ((SELECT MAX(i) FROM MyMatrix)
       = (SELECT COUNT (i) FROM MyMatrix)),
CHECK ((SELECT MAX(j) FROM MyMatrix)
       = (SELECT COUNT (j) FROM MyMatrix));
```

The constraints limit the subscripts of each element to a proper range. I am starting my subscripts at one, but a little change in the logic would allow any value.

25.2.1 Matrix Equality

This test for matrix equality is from an article in *Database Programming & Design* (Mrdalj, Vujovic, and Jovanovic 1996). Two matrices are equal if (1) their cardinalities are equal, and (2) their intersection is also equal.

```
SELECT COUNT(*) FROM MatrixA
UNION ALL
SELECT COUNT(*) FROM MatrixB
UNION ALL
SELECT COUNT(*)
  FROM MatrixA AS A, MatrixB AS B
 WHERE A.i = B.i
   AND A.j = B.j
   AND A.element = B.element;
```

25.2.2 Matrix Addition

Matrix addition and subtraction are possible only between matrices of the same dimensions. The obvious way to do the addition is simply

```
SELECT A.i, A.j, (A.element + B.element) AS total
  FROM MatrixA AS A, MatrixB AS B
 WHERE A.i = B.i
   AND A.j = B.j;
```

But you ought to add some checking:

```
SELECT A.i, A.j, (A.element + B.element) AS total
  FROM MatrixA AS A, MatrixB AS B
 WHERE A.i = B.i
   AND A.j = B.j
   AND (SELECT COUNT(*) FROM MatrixA) =
       (SELECT COUNT(*) FROM MatrixB)
   AND (SELECT MAX(i) FROM MatrixA) =
       (SELECT MAX(i) FROM MatrixB)
   AND (SELECT MAX(j) FROM MatrixA) =
       (SELECT MAX(j) FROM MatrixB));
```

Likewise, to make the addition permanent, you can use the same basic query in an UPDATE statement:

```
UPDATE MatrixA
  SET element = element + (SELECT element
                            FROM MatrixB
                           WHERE MatrixB.i = MatrixA.i
                             AND MatrixB.j = MatrixA.j)
 WHERE (SELECT COUNT(*) FROM MatrixA) =
       (SELECT COUNT(*) FROM MatrixB)
   AND (SELECT MAX(i) FROM MatrixA) =
       (SELECT MAX(i) FROM MatrixB)
   AND (SELECT MAX(j) FROM MatrixA) =
       (SELECT MAX(j) FROM MatrixB));
```

25.2.3 Matrix Multiplication

Multiplication by a scalar constant is direct and easy:

```
UPDATE MyMatrix
  SET element = element * :constant;
```

Matrix multiplication is not as big a mess as might be expected. Remember that the first matrix must have the same number of rows as the second matrix has columns. That means $A[i,k] * B[k,j] = C[i,j]$, which we can show with an example:

```
CREATE TABLE MatrixA
(i INTEGER NOT NULL,
```

```
k INTEGER NOT NULL,
element INTEGER NOT NULL,
PRIMARY KEY (i,k));
```

MatrixA

i	k	element
1	1	2
1	2	-3
1	3	4
2	1	-1
2	2	0
2	3	2

```
CREATE TABLE MatrixB
(k INTEGER NOT NULL,
 j INTEGER NOT NULL,
 element INTEGER NOT NULL,
 PRIMARY KEY (k,j));
```

MatrixB

k	j	element
1	1	-1
1	2	2
1	3	3
2	1	0
2	2	1
2	3	7
3	1	1
3	2	1
3	3	-2

```
CREATE VIEW MatrixC(i, j, element)
AS SELECT i, j, SUM(MatrixA.element * MatrixB.element)
       FROM  MatrixA, MatrixB
    WHERE MatrixA.k = MatrixB.k
       GROUP BY i, j;
```

25.2.4 Other Matrix Operations

The transpose of a matrix is easy to do:

```
CREATE VIEW TransA (i, j, element)
AS SELECT j, i, element FROM MatrixA;
```

Again, you can make the change permanent with an UPDATE statement:

```
UPDATE MatrixA
  SET i = j, j = i;
```

Multiplication by a column or row vector is just a special case of matrix multiplication, but a bit easier. Given the vector V and MatrixA:

```
SELECT i, SUM(A.element * V.element)
  FROM MatrixA AS A, VectorV AS V
 WHERE V.j = A.i
 GROUP BY A.i;
```

Crosstabs and other statistical functions traditionally use an array to hold data. Some of these operations are covered in the sections in Chapter 23 on cross tabulations and statistics.

It is possible to do other matrix operations in SQL, but the code becomes so complex and the execution time so long that it is simply not worth the effort. If a reader would like to submit queries for eigenvalues and determinants, I will be happy to put them in future editions of this book.

25.3 Flattening a Table into an Array

Reports often want to see an array laid horizontally across a line. The original one element/one column approach to mapping arrays was based on seeing such reports and duplicating that structure in a table. A subscript is often an enumeration, denoting a month or another time period, rather than an integer. For example, a row in a Salesmen table might have a dozen columns, one for each month of the year, each of which holds the total commission earned in a particular month. The year is really an array, subscripted by the month.

The subscripts-and-value approach requires more work to produce the same results. It is often easier to explain a technique with an example. Let us imagine a company that collects time cards from its truck drivers, each with the driver's name, the week within the year (numbered 0 to 51 or 52, depending on the year), and his total hours. We want to produce a report

with one line for each driver and six weeks of his time across the page. The
Timecards table looks like this:

```
CREATE TABLE Timecards
(driver CHAR(25) NOT NULL,
 week INTEGER NOT NULL
        CONSTRAINT valid_week_nbr
        CHECK(week BETWEEN 0 AND 52)
 hours INTEGER
        CONSTRAINT zero_or_more_hours
        CHECK(hours >= 0),
 PRIMARY KEY (driver, week));
```

We need to "flatten out" this table to get the desired rows for the report.
First create a working storage table from which the report can be built. In
SQL-92, this could be a CREATE TEMPORARY TABLE statement instead.

```
CREATE TABLE TimeReportWork    -- working storage
(driver CHAR(25) NOT NULL,
 wk1 INTEGER, -- important that these columns are NULL-able
 wk2 INTEGER,
 wk3 INTEGER,
 wk4 INTEGER,
 wk5 INTEGER,
 wk6 INTEGER);
```

Notice two important points about this table. First, there is no primary
key; second, the weekly data columns are NULL-able. This table is then filled
with time card values:

```
BEGIN
INSERT INTO TimeReportWork (driver, wk1)
    SELECT driver, hours
        FROM Timecards
    WHERE 0 = week MOD 52;

INSERT INTO TimeReportWork (driver, wk2)
    SELECT driver, hours
        FROM Timecards
    WHERE 1 = week MOD 52;
```

```
INSERT INTO TimeReportWork (driver, wk3)
    SELECT driver, hours
        FROM Timecards
    WHERE 2 = week MOD 52;

INSERT INTO TimeReportWork (driver, wk4)
    SELECT driver, hours
        FROM Timecards
    WHERE 3 = week MOD 52;

INSERT INTO TimeReportWork (driver, wk5)
    SELECT driver, hours
        FROM Timecards
    WHERE 4 = week MOD 52;

INSERT INTO TimeReportWork (driver, wk6)
    SELECT driver, hours
        FROM Timecards
    WHERE 5 = week MOD 52;
END;
```

The number of the weeks in the WHERE clauses will vary with the period covered by the report. The parameter :n is the current week, and the report is for the prior six weeks. A row with NULLs in all but one of the weekly columns is being inserted for each time card entry. The actual report is done with a grouped VIEW, which hides the summary functions. That VIEW looks like this:

```
CREATE VIEW TimeReport (driver, wk1tot, wk2tot, wk3tot, wk4tot,
wk5tot, wk6tot)
AS
SELECT driver, SUM(wk1), SUM(wk2), SUM(wk3), SUM(wk3), SUM(wk5),
SUM(wk6)
FROM TimeReportWork
WHERE week BETWEEN :N AND :N-5
GROUP BY driver;
```

If a driver did not work in a particular week, the corresponding weekly column gets no row to represent it. However, if the driver has not worked at all in the last six weeks, we could lose him completely (no time cards, no summary). Depending on the nature of the report, you might consider using

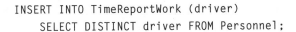

```
INSERT INTO TimeReportWork (driver)
   SELECT DISTINCT driver FROM Personnel;
```

to load all the names into the table first. All the weekly columns will default to NULL, and every driver will have at least one row. The SUM( ) of a column of NULLs is always NULL.

The NULLs are thrown out and the set is left empty, so the SUM( ) of an empty set is NULL. This lets you tell the difference between a driver who was missing for the reporting period and a driver who worked zero hours and turned in a time card for that during the period. That difference could be important for computing the payroll.

25.4 Comparing Arrays in Table Format

It is often necessary to compare one array or set of values with another when the data is represented in a table. Remember that comparing a set with a set does not involve ordering the elements, whereas an array does. For this discussion, let us create two tables, one for employees and one for their dependents. The children are subscripted in the order of their births—that is, 1 is the oldest living child, and so forth.

```
CREATE TABLE Employees
(empno INTEGER PRIMARY KEY,
 empname CHAR(15) NOT NULL,
 . . . );

CREATE TABLE Dependents
(empno INTEGER NOT NULL -- the parent
  kid  CHAR(15) NOT NULL,   -- the array element
  birthorder INTEGER NOT NULL, -- the array subscript
  PRIMARY KEY (empno, kid));
```

The query "Find pairs of employees whose children have the same set of names" is very restrictive, but we can make it more so by requiring that the children be named in the same birth order. Both Mr. X and Mr. Y must have exactly the same number of dependents; both sets of names must match. We can assume that no parent has two children with the same name (George

Foreman does not work here) or born at the same time (we will order twins). Let us begin by inserting test data into the Dependents table:

Dependents

empno	kid	birthorder
1	'Dick'	2
1	'Harry'	3
1	'Tom'	1
2	'Dick'	3
2	'Harry'	1
2	'Tom'	2
3	'Dick'	2
3	'Harry'	3
3	'Tom'	1
4	'Harry'	1
4	'Tom'	2
5	'Curly'	2
5	'Harry'	3
5	'Moe'	1

In this test data, employees 1, 2, and 3 all have dependents named Tom, Dick, and Harry. The birth order is the same for the children of employees 1 and 3, but not for employee 2. For testing purposes, you might consider adding an extra child to the family of employee 3, and so forth, to play with this data.

Though there are many ways to solve this query, this approach will give us some flexibility that others would not. Construct a VIEW that gives us the number of dependents for each employee:

```
CREATE VIEW Familysize (empno, tally)
AS SELECT empno, COUNT(*)
      FROM Dependents
   GROUP BY empno;
```

Create a second VIEW that holds pairs of employees who have families of the same size. This VIEW is also useful for other statistical work, but that is another topic.

```
CREATE VIEW Samesize (empno1, empno2, tally)
AS SELECT F1.empno, F2.empno, F1.tally
      FROM Familysize AS F1, Familysize AS F2
```

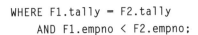

```
      WHERE F1.tally = F2.tally
        AND F1.empno < F2.empno;
```

We will test for set equality by doing a self-JOIN on the dependents of employees with families of the same size. If one set can be mapped onto another with no children left over, and in the same birth order, then the two sets are equal.

```
SELECT D1.empno, ' named his ',
       S1.tally, ' kids just like ',
       D2.empno
  FROM Dependents AS D1, Dependents AS D2, Samesize AS S1
 WHERE S1.empno1 = D1.empno
   AND S1.empno2 = D2.empno
   AND D1.kid = D2.kid
   AND D1.birthorder = D2.birthorder
 GROUP BY D1.empno, D2.empno, S1.tally
HAVING COUNT(*) = S1.tally;
```

If birth order is not important, then drop the predicate D1.birthorder = D2.birthorder from the query.

Set Operations

BY SET OPERATIONS, I mean union, intersection, and set differences where the sets in SQL are tables. (Operations that define subsets from another set will be covered in the next chapter.) These are the basic operators used in elementary set theory, which has been taught in the U.S. public school systems for decades. Since the relational model is based on sets of tuples, you would expect that SQL would have had a good variety of set operators from the start. But this was not the case. The SQL-92 standard has added what was missing in the SQL-86 and SQL-89 standards, but you should look for vendor extensions that provide the same functions with different syntax.

There is another problem in SQL that you did not have in high school set theory. SQL tables are *multisets* (also called *bags*), which means that, unlike sets, they allow duplicate elements (rows or tuples). Codd's relational model is stricter and uses only true sets. SQL handles these duplicate rows with an `ALL` or `DISTINCT` modifier in different places in the language; `ALL` preserves duplicates and `DISTINCT` removes them.

So that we can discuss the result of each operator formally, let R be a row that is a duplicate of some row in TableA, or of some row in TableB, or of both. Let m be the number of duplicates of R in TableA and let n be the number of duplicates of R in TableB, where $m >= 0$ and $n >= 0$. Informally, the decision in the SQL-92 standard was to pair off the two tables on a row-per-row basis in set operations. We will see how this works for each operator. In SQL-92, we introduced the shorthand TABLE <table name> for the query or subquery SELECT * FROM <table name>, which lets us refer to a table as a whole without referring to its columns.

26.1 UNION and UNION ALL

UNIONs are supported in SQL-86, SQL-89, and SQL-92, but the other set operations have to be constructed by the programmer in SQL-89. That limits us to single-column tables, but this can still be useful. The SQL-92 syntax for the UNION statement is

<query> UNION [ALL] <query> [ORDER BY <sort specification>]

The UNION statement takes two result tables and builds a new table from them. The two tables must be UNION-compatible, which means that they have the same number of columns, and that each column in the first table has the same datatype (or automatically cast to it) as the column in the same position in the second table. That is, their rows have the same structure, so they can be put in the same final result table. Most implementations will do some datatype conversions to create the result table, but this capability is very implementation-dependent and you should check it out for yourself.

The ORDER BY clause is very common and was part of the SQL-89 standard, but it may not be available in all SQL implementations. This is because only cursors are supposed to be ordered in SQL, so many earlier implementations did not have this feature. There are two forms of the UNION statement: the UNION and the UNION ALL. The simple UNION is the same operator you had in high school set theory. It returns the rows that appear in either or both tables and removes duplicates from the result table. In most implementations, this removal is done by merge-sorting the two tables and discarding duplicates during the sorting. This has the side effect that the result table is sorted, but you cannot depend on that. This also explains why the ORDER BY clause is a common feature—as long as the engine is sorting anyway, why not let the programmer decide the ordering?

The UNION ALL preserves the duplicates from both tables in the result table. In most implementations, this statement is done by appending one table to the other, giving you a predictable ordering. If an ORDER BY clause is used, a merge-sort is often used by the SQL engine. But, again, you cannot depend on any ordering in the results of either version of the UNION statement. Each SQL implementation could use a different sorting algorithm within the engine, or could even use a hashing algorithm to find duplicates. The UNION and UNION ALL operators are infixed operators that appear between query expressions—for example,

```
(SELECT a, b, c FROM TableA WHERE city = 'Boston')
UNION
(SELECT x, y, z FROM TableB WHERE city = 'New York');
```

The parentheses around the SELECT statements are an option in the SQL-92 syntax, but not in the SQL-89 standard, which would see them as subqueries. If your implementation has the parentheses, use them for safety and clarity. The columns in the result table do not have names, only position numbers, in SQL-89. The reason for the lack of names is that there is no way to decide which existing columns to use—should it be (a, b, c) or (x, y, z) in the above example? This is a deprecated feature in SQL-92, however, and will not appear in the next version of the standard. In SQL-92, you can assign names to the columns by using the AS operator to name both the result and the columns of the result:

```
((SELECT a, b, c FROM TableA WHERE city = 'Boston')
UNION
(SELECT x, y, z FROM TableB WHERE city = 'New York'))
AS Cities (tom, dick, harry)
```

SQL-92 will also let you use UNIONs in the FROM clause. If your SQL does not have these features, then you may need to create a VIEW with the UNION in it to give names to columns.

26.1.1 Duplicates and Union Operators

The UNION removes all duplicate rows from the results and does not care from which table the duplicate rows came. We could use this feature to write a query to remove duplicates from a table:

```
(TABLE TableA)
UNION
(TABLE TableA);
```

But this is the same as

```
SELECT DISTINCT * FROM TableA;
```

The second query will probably run faster and preserve the column names as well. Most SQL products implement UNION and SELECT DISTINCT with a sorting algorithm that throws away duplicates while it sorts. The UNION operator is expecting two result tables, which it loads into working storage with a merge-sort, usually without checking to see that they are identical. SELECT DISTINCT loads working storage with only one result table, and it is freer to pick a sort algorithm. Sort algorithms vary from product to product, but most work from left to right, using the columns in the SELECT clause list when they cannot find an index to help match up duplicates. If the result table has to be materialized, the indexes will be lost. This means that it is usually a good idea to put keys to the left to speed up the sort.

The UNION ALL operator keeps the duplicate rows and is often implemented as a file append algorithm, without any sorting. The number of duplicates of R in the result table will be the number of duplicates of R in TableA plus the number of duplicates of R in TableB.

26.1.2 Order of Execution

UNION and UNION ALL operators are executed from left to right unless parentheses change the order. Since the UNION operator is associative and commutative, the order of a chain of UNIONs will not affect the results. However, order and grouping can affect performance. Consider two small tables that have many duplicates between them. If the optimizer does not consider table sizes, this query

```
(TABLE SmallTable1)
UNION
(TABLE BigTable)
UNION
(TABLE SmallTable2);
```

will merge SmallTable1 into BigTable, then merge SmallTable2 into that first result. If the rows of SmallTable1 are spread out in the first result table, locating duplicates from SmallTable2 will take longer than if we had written the query thus:

```
(TABLE SmallTable1)
UNION
(TABLE SmallTable2))
UNION
(TABLE BigTable);
```

Optimization of UNIONs is highly product-dependent, so you should experiment with it.

26.1.3 Mixed UNION and UNION ALL Operators

If you know that there are no duplicates, or that duplicates are not a problem in your situation, use the UNION ALL operator instead of UNION for speed. For example, if we are sure that BigTable has no duplicates in common with SmallTable1 and SmallTable2, this query will produce the same results as before but should run much faster:

```
((TABLE SmallTable1)
UNION
(TABLE SmallTable2))
UNION ALL
(TABLE BigTable);
```

But be careful when mixing UNION and UNION ALL operators. The left-to-right order of execution will cause the last operator in the chain to have an effect on the results. Microsoft introduced its Access database product in 1992, after five years and tens of millions of dollars' worth of development work. The first complaints Microsoft got on its CompuServe user support forum involved the lack of a UNION operator. UNION is a very important tool in relational database work. For the rest of this discussion, let us create two tables with the same structure, which we can use for examples.

```
CREATE TableA
(col1 INTEGER NOT NULL);
INSERT INTO TableA VALUES (1), (1), (2), (3), (4), (5);

CREATE TableB
(col1 INTEGER NOT NULL);
INSERT INTO TableB VALUES (1), (2), (2), (3);
```

will yield

```
(SELECT col1 FROM TableA)
UNION
(SELECT col1 FROM TableB)
```

```
1
2
3
4
5
```

```
(SELECT col1 FROM TableA)
UNION ALL
(SELECT col1 FROM TableB)
```

```
1
1
1
2
2
2
3
3
4
5
```

26.2 Set Difference Operator

Set difference is part of the SQL-92 standard, and a few versions of SQL have implemented it as of this writing. However, they may use a different term from the EXCEPT keyword in SQL-92, such as MINUS in Oracle. The set difference is the rows in the first table, except for those that also appear in the second table. It answers questions like "Give me all the employees except the salesmen" in a natural manner.

The SQL-92 EXCEPT operator discards duplicate rows from the first table, then removes all rows that also occur in the second table. This is a pure set operator:

```
(SELECT col1 FROM TableA)
EXCEPT
(SELECT col1 FROM TableB)
```

```
4
5
```

To do this in SQL-89, you would need to use this query:

```
SELECT DISTINCT col1
  FROM TableA
 WHERE NOT EXISTS (SELECT *
```

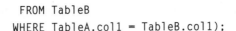

```
FROM TableB
WHERE TableA.col1 = TableB.col1);
```

which is fairly straightforward. As you would expect, the EXCEPT ALL operator is more of a problem. The number of duplicates of a row in the result table is the maximum of the number of duplicates of R in the left-hand table minus the number of duplicates of R in the right-hand table and zero. To do the UNION statement, you need to know the row counts in both tables:

```
(SELECT col1 FROM TableA)
EXCEPT ALL
(SELECT col1 FROM TableB)
```

```
1
4
5
```

Duplicating this in SQL-89 is difficult. First, construct a VIEW to hold the row counts:

```
CREATE VIEW RowCountView (col1, t1tally, t2tally)
AS SELECT col1, COUNT(*), 0
          FROM TableA
        GROUP BY col1
    UNION
    SELECT col1, 0, COUNT(*)
          FROM TableB
        GROUP BY col1;
```

This view can in turn construct a final view:

```
CREATE VIEW ExceptView (col1, dups)
AS SELECT col1, (SUM(t1tally) - SUM(t2tally)) AS dups
    FROM RowCountView
    GROUP BY col1
    HAVING (SUM(t1tally) - SUM(t2tally)) > 0;
```

This is not quite the same thing as the EXCEPT ALL result, but the degree of duplication is clearly shown as a column.

26.2.1 Set Difference with OUTER JOIN

The set difference can also be written in SQL with an OUTER JOIN operator, as well as the NOT EXISTS( ) predicate we've just shown. Jim Panttaja reports that this approach requires about one-fourth of the logical I/O operations of the EXISTS( ) approach that is involved when you are using Sybase, but this proportion may vary.

```
SELECT DISTINCT TableA.*
  FROM (TABLE TableA LEFT OUTER JOIN TABLE TableB
        ON TableA.keycol = TableB.keycol)
 WHERE TableB.keycol IS NULL;
```

The idea is that rows in TableB that match to TableA rows will not be NULL-padded in the OUTER JOIN.

26.3 Intersection

An *intersection* is defined as the elements that are common members of two sets. Intersection is associative, commutative, and idempotent, just like the UNION operator. If your algebra is weak, *associative* means that the way you group the operations does not change the results; in symbols, $((x \text{ R } y) \text{ R } z) = (x \text{ R } (y \text{ R } z))$. *Commutative* means that the order in which you do a chain of operations does not change the results; in symbols, $x \text{ R } y = y \text{ R } x$. *Idempotent* means that if you do the operation to the same set, you get the same set back as a result; in symbols, $x \text{ R } x = x$.

Intersection is part of the SQL-92 standard, but it has not been implemented in most SQL products today. There are two flavors of intersection in SQL-92, INTERSECT and INTERSECT ALL. As you would expect from the UNION and EXCEPT operators, INTERSECT removes any duplicate rows between the two tables involved.

The INTERSECT [ALL] operators also have a higher precedence than UNION, so intersection is done first in a chain of set operations:

```
(SELECT col1 FROM TableA)
INTERSECT
(SELECT col1 FROM TableB)
```

1

2

3

To do this in SQL-89, we need to test all of the columns in both tables against their corresponding matches in the other table. The table from which we work also needs to have duplicates removed from it, which means we use a SELECT DISTINCT. We can either write this query

```
-- TableA on the outer correlation level and remove duplicates

SELECT DISTINCT col1
  FROM TableA AS T1
 WHERE EXISTS (SELECT *
                 FROM TableB AS T2
                WHERE T1.col1 = T2.col1);
```

or this query

```
-- TableB on the outer correlation level and remove duplicates

SELECT DISTINCT col1
  FROM TableB AS T2
 WHERE EXISTS (SELECT *
                 FROM TableA AS T1
                WHERE T1.col1 = T2.col1);
```

The difference in performance will vary with the quality of the optimizer in your SQL product and the degree of duplication in the tables. Try both versions to see if there is any difference in the order of the tables involved.

INTERSECT ALL preserves duplicate rows between the two tables, keeping the minimum of the number of duplicate rows in the first table and the number of duplicate rows in the second table in its result table. For the data in TableA and TableB, the results of INTERSECT and INTERSECT ALL are the same:

```
(SELECT col1 FROM TableA)
INTERSECT ALL
(SELECT col1 FROM TableB)
```

1

2

3

Writing this in SQL-89 is harder than you would think. The obvious approach is to simply change SELECT DISTINCT to SELECT in the query proposed for INTERSECT to get an SQL-89 query that is equivalent to the SQL-92 INTERSECT ALL. This approach sounds promising, but it does not work. Rewriting the first query, we get

```
-- this version will keep duplicates, but only from TableA
SELECT col1
   FROM TableA AS T1
 WHERE EXISTS (SELECT *
                 FROM TableB AS T2
                WHERE T1.col1 = T2.col1);
```

col1
1
1
2
3

and, likewise, rewriting the second query,

```
-- this version will keep duplicates, but only from TableB
SELECT col1
   FROM TableB AS T2
 WHERE EXISTS (SELECT *
                 FROM TableA AS T1
                WHERE T1.col1 = T2.col1);
```

col1
1
2
3

So we have the same problem we had with the EXCEPT operator: SQL-92 defines the number of duplicates of a row in the result table to be the minimum of the number of duplicate rows in the first table and the number of duplicate rows in the second table. First construct a VIEW to hold the row counts for each value:

```
CREATE VIEW RowCountView (col1, tally)
AS SELECT col1, COUNT(*)
     FROM TableA
    GROUP BY col1
```

```
UNION
SELECT col1, COUNT(*)
  FROM TableB
  GROUP BY col1;
```

This view can in turn construct a final view:

```
CREATE VIEW IntersectView (col1, mindups)
AS SELECT col1, MIN(tally)
    FROM RowCountView
  GROUP BY col1
  HAVING COUNT(*) > 1;
```

The HAVING clause will find those columns that were represented in both tables. This is not quite the same thing as the INTERSECT ALL result, but the degree of duplication is clearly shown as a column.

26.4 A Note on ALL and SELECT DISTINCT

Here is a series of observations about the relationship between the ALL option in set operations and the SELECT DISTINCT options in a query from Beught Gunne.

Given two tables with duplicate values:

```
CREATE TABLE A (i INTEGER NOT NULL);
INSERT INTO A VALUES (1), (1), (4), (4), (4), (4);

CREATE TABLE B (i INTEGER NOT NULL);
INSERT INTO B VALUES (2), (2), (3), (3);
```

The UNION and INTERSECT operations have regular behavior in that

```
(A UNION B) = SELECT DISTINCT (A UNION ALL B) = ((1), (2), (3))
```

and

```
(A INTERSECT B) = SELECT DISTINCT (A INTERSECT ALL B) = (2)
```

However,

```
(A EXCEPT B) <> SELECT DISTINCT (A EXCEPT ALL B)
```

Or more literally, (1) <> ((1), (2)) for the tables given in the example. And likewise, we have

(B EXCEPT A) = SELECT DISTINCT (B EXCEPT ALL A) = (3)

by a coincidence of the particular values used in these tables.

CHAPTER 27

Subsets

I DEFINE SUBSET OPERATIONS as queries, which extract a particular subset from a given set, as opposed to set operations, which work between sets. The obvious way to extract a subset from a table is just to use a WHERE clause, which will pull out the rows that meet that criterion. But not all the subsets we want are easily defined by such a simple predicate. This chapter is a collection of tricks for constructing useful, but not obvious, subsets from a table. You should also look in Section 21.4.2 for the generalized extrema functions.

27.1 Every *n*th Item in a Table

This problem was presented in *Explain* magazine by Rory Murchison, DB2 instructor at the Aetna Institute (Murchison n.d.). SQL is a set-oriented language, and so cannot identify individual rows by their positions in a table. Instead, a unique key is detected by logical expressions. If you are given a file of employees in a non-SQL system and you want to pick out every *n*th employee for a survey where the ordering is based on employee identification numbers, the job is easy. You write a procedure with nested loops that reads the records and writes every *n*th one to a second file.

The immediate thought of how to do this in SQL is that you can simply compute MOD(empno, :n), where MOD is the modulo function found in most SQL implementations, and save those employee rows where this function is zero. The trouble is that employees are not issued consecutive identification numbers. The identification numbers are unique, however.

Vendor extensions often, but not always, include a row identifier that can be used by procedural extension to perform these functions. Informix/SQL is one product with this feature. This makes the code easy to write in SQL. It will look something like this:

```
SELECT *
  FROM Personnel
 WHERE MOD(RowNumber, :n) = 0
 ORDER BY empno;
```

Yes, this query can be done when RowNumber is not supplied by the database engine. It requires a self-JOIN on the Personnel table to partition it into a nested series of grouped tables. You then pick out the largest value in each group. There may be an index or a uniqueness constraint on the empno column to ensure uniqueness, so the EXISTS predicate will get a performance boost. Incidentally, row numbers are not just nonstandard; they are also prone to create problems when you use them in any query with a sort because you do not know if the row number is the position in the table before or after the sort. Users logged on and looking at the same base table through different VIEWs may or may not get the same row number for the same physical row. Another set of problems involves deleting and inserting rows. Exactly what happens when a user deletes a row and inserts another? What if he tried to insert a row well past the last row of the table—are deleted rows created as needed, or what?

```
SELECT empno
  FROM Personnel AS P1
 WHERE EXISTS (SELECT MAX(empno)
                 FROM Personnel AS P2
                WHERE P1.empno >= P2.empno
                HAVING MOD (COUNT(*), :n) = 0);
```

A nonnested version of the same query looks like this:

```
SELECT P1.empno
  FROM Personnel AS P1, Personnel AS P2
 WHERE P1.empno >= P2.empno
 GROUP BY P1.empno
HAVING MOD (COUNT(*), :n) = 0;
```

27.2 Picking Random Rows from a Table

You cannot pick a set of random rows from a table in SQL. There is no randomize operator in the standard, and you don't often find a pseudorandom number generator function as a vendor extension either.

Picking random rows from a table for a statistical sample is a handy thing, and you can do it in other languages with a random number generator. There are two kinds of random drawings from a set, those with, or without, replacement. If SQL had a random number function, I suppose these would be shown as RANDOM(x) and RANDOM(DISTINCT x). But there is no such function in SQL and none is planned. The problem is that SQL is a set-oriented language and wants to do an operation "all at once" on a well-defined set of rows. Random sets are not well-defined; that is, you have to use a procedure to construct them instead of a logic expression.

The best way to do this is to add a column to the table to hold a random number, then use a procedural language with a good pseudorandom number generator in its function library to load the new column with random values with a cursor in a host language. You have to do it this way because random number generators work differently from other function calls. They start with an initial value called a "seed" provided by the user or the system clock. The seed is used to create the first number in the sequence, Random(1). Then each call, Random(n), to the function uses the previous number to generate the next one, Random($n + 1$). There is no way to do a sequence of actions in SQL without a cursor, so you are in procedural code.

The term *pseudorandom number generator* is often referred to just as a *random number generator,* but this is technically wrong. All of the generators will eventually return a value that appeared in the sequence earlier, and the procedure will hang in a cycle. Procedures are deterministic, and we are living in a mathematical contradiction when we try to use them to produce truly random results. However, if the sequence has a very long cycle and meets some other tests for randomness over the range of the cycle, then we can use it.

There are many kinds of generators. The linear congruence pseudorandom number generator family has formulas of the form

```
Random(n + 1) := MOD ((x * Random(n) + y), m);
```

where

r is the number of bits in the result
x is 3 or 5

y is an integer constant
m is any integer (2^n)
you have picked *x* and *r* such that $(r + \log2(x) + 1) < r$

For example, some old favorites that many C programmers use from this family are

```
Random(n + 1) := (Random(n) * 1103515245) + 12345;
Random(n + 1) := MOD ((16807 * Random(n)), ((2^31) - 1));
```

The first formula has the advantage of not requiring a MOD function, so it can be written in standard SQL. However, the simplest generator that can be recommended (Park and Miller 1988) uses

```
Random(n + 1) := MOD ((48271 * Random(n)), ((2^31) - 1));
```

Notice that the modulus is a prime number; this is important. The period of this generator is $((2^{31}) - 2)$, which is 2,147,483,646, or over 2 billion numbers before this generator repeats. You must determine if this is long enough for your application.

If you have an XOR function in your SQL, then you can also use shift register algorithms. The XOR is the bitwise exclusive OR that works on an integer as it is stored in the hardware; I would assume 32 bits on most small computers. Some usable shift register algorithms are

```
Random(n + 1) := Random(n - 103) XOR Random(n - 250);
Random(n + 1) := Random(n - 1063) XOR Random(n - 1279);
```

But what if you just want to generate something on the fly in a query? One trick in some SQL implementations is to use the SOUNDEX() and SIMILAR() functions. Both these functions take a string and convert it in to a number.

Be sure that the SOUNDEX() function that comes with your SQL is not the original Soundex, which would produce a four-place character string that began with a letter. If it is, then you have to truncate it and convert it to an integer.

The SIMILAR() function is a little different, but it is also a string function used mostly with names. It compares two strings and scores them as to how well they match, with 100 being an exact match of characters and their positions and 0 for no matches at all.

You can mix these two functions to produce a crude random number on the fly. The trick is to use a CHAR(n) column that contains a name or other string that is unique—do not use a column that holds an alphabetic code! It will be full of duplicate values. For example, you might write this query against the Personnel table:

```
SELECT empnum, empname, ABS(SOUNDEX(empname) +
                     SIMILAR(empname, 'etoin') +
                     SIMILAR(empname, 'shurld') +
                     SIMILAR(empname, 'kpml')) AS random
  FROM Personnel;
```

Using the WATCOM 4.0 implementation of SQL, this will give us

Results

empnum	empname	random
1	'Tom'	788
5	'Dick'	367
12	'Harry'	872
13	'Melvin'	22913
14	'Mary'	877
23	'George'	2923
27	'Brad'	3943
30	'Seymour'	6910
32	'Lucy'	370
39	'Wendy'	3840
42	'Sally'	632
43	'Janet'	3833

Since some SOUNDEX() implementations can return a negative result, I used an absolute value function to guarantee only positive integer results. If you need a particular range of values, you can use the MIN() and some algebra to adjust the values in the random column. Also, do not use a multiplication in the formula between the SIMILAR() function calls—you are too apt to get a zero from several of the rows and skew your distribution.

The choice of nonsense words in the second parameter of the SIMILAR() function calls is not random. These strings contain the most common letters in English. The idea to guarantee some scoring for almost any word that appears in the "seed" column.

Frankly, there is probably a better way to pick nonsense words for any particular "seed" column if you have a known distribution of letters.

Likewise, several columns could be used in a formula. The reader can probably come up with some other versions of this, depending on his data.

Another method is to use a PRIMARY KEY or UNIQUE column(s) and apply a hashing algorithm. You can pick one of the random number generator functions already discussed and use the unique values as if it were the seed as a quick way to get a hashing function. Hashing algorithms try to be uniformly distributed, so if you can find a good one, you will approach nearly unique random selection. The trick is that the hashing algorithm has to be simple enough to be written in the limited math available in SQL.

27.3 The CONTAINS Operators

Set theory has two symbols for subsets. One, $\subset$, means that set A is contained within set B; this is sometimes said to denote a proper subset. The other, $\subseteq$, means "is contained in or equal to" and is sometimes called just a subset or containment operator.

Standard SQL has never had an operator to compare tables against each other for equality or containment. Several college textbooks on relational databases mention a CONTAINS predicate, which does not exist in SQL-89 or SQL-92. This predicate existed in the original System R, IBM's first experimental SQL system, but it was dropped from later SQL implementations because of the expense of running it.

27.3.1 Proper Subset Operators

The IN predicate is a test for membership. For those of you who remember your high school set theory, membership is shown with a stylized epsilon with the containing set on the right side: $a \in A$. Membership is for one element, whereas a subset is itself a set, not just an element. As an example of a subset predicate, consider a query to tell you the names of each employee who works on all of the projects in department 5. Using the System R syntax,

```
SELECT name    -- Not valid SQL!
  FROM Personnel
 WHERE (SELECT projectno
          FROM WorksOn
         WHERE Personnel.employeeno = WorksOn.employeeno)
       CONTAINS
         (SELECT projectno
            FROM Projects
           WHERE deptno = 5);
```

In the second SELECT statement of the CONTAINS predicate, we build a table of all the projects in department 5. In the first SELECT statement of the CONTAINS predicate, we have a correlated subquery that will build a table of all the projects each employee works on. If the table of the employee projects is equal to or a superset of the department 5 table, the predicate is TRUE.

You must first decide what you are going to do about duplicate rows in either or both tables. That is, does the set { a, b, c } contain the multiset { a, b, b } or not? Some SQL set operations, such as SELECT and UNION, have options to remove or keep duplicates from the results, as in UNION ALL and SELECT DISTINCT. I would argue that duplicates should be ignored and that the multiset is a subset of the other. For our example, let us use a table of employees and another table with the names of the company bowling team members, which should be a proper subset of the Personnel table. For the bowling team to be contained in the set of employees, each bowler must be an employee, or, to put it another way, there must be no bowler who is not an employee.

```
NOT EXISTS (SELECT *
      FROM Bowling AS B1
          WHERE B1.empno NOT IN (SELECT empno FROM Personnel))
```

27.3.2 Set Equality

When two sets, A and B, are equal, we know that

1. Both have the same number of elements.

2. No elements in A are not in B.

3. No elements in B are not in A.

4. Set A is equal to the intersection of A and B.

5. Set B is equal to the intersection of A and B.

6. Set B is a subset of A.

7. Set A is a subset of B.

If you look at items 1 and 3 in this list, then you will probably try to solve this problem using NOT EXISTS( ) predicates:

```
. . .
WHERE NOT EXISTS (SELECT *
              FROM A
```

```
                WHERE A.keycol
                    NOT IN (SELECT keycol
                                FROM B
                                WHERE A.keycol = B.keycol))
        AND NOT EXISTS (SELECT *
                    FROM B
                    WHERE B.keycol
                        NOT IN (SELECT keycol
                                FROM A
                                WHERE A.keycol = B.keycol))
```

However, if you look at 1, 4, and 5, you might come up with this answer:

```
 . . .
WHERE (SELECT COUNT(*)
        FROM A) = (SELECT COUNT(*)
                        FROM A INNER JOIN B
                            ON A.keycol = B.keycol)
        AND
        (SELECT COUNT(*)
            FROM B) = (SELECT COUNT(*)
                        FROM A INNER JOIN B
                            ON A.keycol = B.keycol)
```

Consider the problem of using a suppliers-and-parts table to find pairs of suppliers who provide exactly the same parts. That is, the set of parts from one supplier is equal to the set of parts from the other supplier.

```
CREATE TABLE SupParts
(sno CHAR(2) NOT NULL,
 pno CHAR(2) NOT NULL,
 PRIMARY KEY (sno, pno));
```

The usual way of proving that two sets are equal is to show that set A contains set B and set B contains set A.

What you would usually do in standard SQL would be to show that there exists no element in set A that is not in set B, and therefore A is a subset of B. Instead, consider another approach. First JOIN one supplier to another on their common parts, eliminating the situation where supplier 1 is the same as supplier 2, so that you have the intersection of the two sets. If the intersection has the same number of pairs as each of the two sets has elements, the two sets are equal.

```
SELECT SP1.sno AS Supplier1, SP2.sno AS Supplier2
  FROM SupParts AS SP1
       INNER JOIN
       SupParts AS SP2
         ON (SP1.pno = SP2.pno
             AND SP1.sno < SP2.sno)
 GROUP BY Supplier1, Supplier2
HAVING COUNT(*) = (SELECT COUNT(*)
                     FROM SupParts AS SP3
                    WHERE SP3.sno = SP1.sno)
   AND COUNT(*) = (SELECT COUNT(*)
                     FROM SupParts AS SP4
                    WHERE SP4.sno = SP2.sno);
```

This solution uses some SQL-92 features, but can easily be written in SQL-89. If there is an index on the supplier number in the SupParts table, it can provide the counts directly as well as helping with the JOIN operation.

I am glossing over the problems with NULLs and redundant duplicate values. If two tables hold the same values, but a different number of each, are they equal or not? That is, do you need an ALL and a DISTINCT version of the equality test?

Eventually, you will be able to handle this with the INTERSECT and UNION operators in SQL-92 and tune the query to whatever definition of equality you wish to use.

Adjacency List Model
of Trees in SQL

A TREE IS A special kind of directed graph. *Graphs* are data structures that are made up of nodes (usually shown as boxes) connected by edges (usually shown as lines with arrowheads). Each edge represents a one-way relationship between the two nodes it connects. In an organizational chart, the nodes are employees, and each edge is the "reports to" relationship. In a parts explosion (also called a bill of materials), the nodes are assembly units (eventually resolving down to individual parts), and each edge is the "is made of" relationship.

The top of the tree is called the root. In an organizational chart, it is the highest authority; in a parts explosion, it is the final assembly. The number of edges coming out of the node are its *outdegree,* and the number of edges entering it are its *indegree.* A binary tree is one in which a parent can have at most two children; more generally, an *n*-ary tree is one in which a node can have at most outdegree *n*.

The nodes of the tree that have no subtrees beneath them are called the *leaf nodes.* In a parts explosion, they are the individual parts, which cannot be broken down any further. The descendants, or children, of a node (called the *parent*) are every node in the subtree that has the parent node as its root.

There are several ways to define a tree: It is a graph with no cycles; it is a graph where all nodes except the root have indegree 1 and the root has indegree 0. Another defining property is that a path can be found from the root to any other node in the tree by following the edges in their natural direction.

Trees are often drawn as charts. In the United States, we like to put the root at the top and grow the tree downward; Europeans will often put the root at the bottom and grow the tree upward, or grow the tree from left to right across the page. Another way of representing trees is to show them as nested sets; this is the basis for the nested sets representation in SQL, which will be discussed in Chapter 29 on trees.

Since the two most common examples of trees in the real world and in SQL textbooks are parts explosions and organizational charts, these are the two we will use for the rest of this chapter.

It should be no surprise that hierarchies were very easy to represent in hierarchical databases, where the structure of the data and the structure of the database were the same. In fact, one reason that hierarchical databases were created was to accommodate existing hierarchical data structures.

Unfortunately, SQL provides poor support for such data. It does not directly map hierarchical data into tables because tables are based on sets rather than on graphs. SQL directly supports neither the retrieval of the raw data in a meaningful recursive or hierarchical fashion nor computation of recursively defined functions that commonly occur in these types of applications.

Support for such structures was discussed in the proposed SQL3 standard in the form of the RECURSIVE UNION operator, but it was removed from consideration in 1996. Recursive sets are now derived using the WITH operator, which was put into the SQL-99 specifications by IBM (the only product that has it).

In the meantime, most programmers use 3GL host languages or report writers, which can better handle tree structures. The SQL programmer has to remember that any relationship in the data must be shown explicitly in SQL as data. This means that we will have to add columns to represent tree components.

28.1 Adjacency List in a Single Table

Since the nodes contain the data, we can add columns to represent the edges of a tree. This is usually done in one of two ways in SQL: a single table or two tables. In the single-table representation, the edge connection appears in the same table as the node. In the two-table format, one table contains the nodes of the graph and the other table contains the edges, represented as pairs of end points. The two-table representation can handle generalized

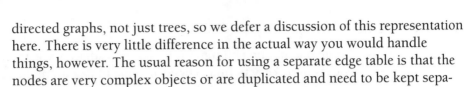

directed graphs, not just trees, so we defer a discussion of this representation here. There is very little difference in the actual way you would handle things, however. The usual reason for using a separate edge table is that the nodes are very complex objects or are duplicated and need to be kept separately for normalization.

In the single-table representation of hierarchies in SQL, there has to be one column for the identifier of the node and one column of the same datatype for the parent of the node. In the organizational chart, the linking column is usually the employee identification number of the immediate boss of each employee. The single table works best for organizational charts because each employee can appear only once (assuming each employee has one and only one manager), whereas a parts explosion can have many occurrences of the same part within many different assemblies. Let us define a simple Personnel table:

```
CREATE TABLE Personnel
(emp CHAR(20) PRIMARY KEY,
 boss CHAR(20),  -- he has to be NULL-able!
 salary DECIMAL(6,2) NOT NULL);
```

Personnel

emp	boss	salary
'Albert'	NULL	1000.00
'Bert'	'Albert'	900.00
'Chuck'	'Albert'	900.00
'Donna'	'Chuck '	800.00
'Eddie'	'Chuck'	700.00
'Fred'	'Chuck'	600.00

28.2 Finding the Root Node

The root of the tree has a boss that is NULL—the root has nothing over it:

```
SELECT *
  FROM Personnel
 WHERE boss IS NULL;
```

28.3 Finding Leaf Nodes

A leaf node is one that has no children under it. In an adjacency list model, this set of nodes is fairly easy to find. They are going to be the employees who are not bosses to anyone else in the company:

```
SELECT *
  FROM Personnel AS E1
WHERE NOT EXISTS (SELECT *
                    FROM Personnel AS E2
                    WHERE E1.emp = E2.boss);
```

28.4 Finding Levels in a Tree

The length of a path from one node to another is measured by the number of levels of the hierarchy that you have to travel to get from the start to the finish. This is handy for queries such as "Does Mr. King have any authority over Mr. Jones?" or "Does a gizmo use a frammistat?" which are based on paths. To find the name of the boss for each employee, the query is a self-JOIN, like this:

```
SELECT B1.emp, ' bosses ', E1.emp
  FROM Personnel AS B1, Personnel AS E1
 WHERE B1.emp = E1.boss;
```

But something is missing here. These are only the immediate bosses of the employees. Your boss's boss also has authority over you, and so forth up the tree until we find someone who has no subordinates. To go two levels deep in the tree, we need to do a more complex self-JOIN:

```
SELECT B1.emp, ' bosses ', E2.emp
  FROM Personnel AS B1, Personnel AS E1, Personnel AS E2
 WHERE B1.emp = E1.boss
   AND E1.emp = E2.boss;
```

To go more than two levels deep in the tree, just extend the pattern:

```
SELECT B1.emp, ' bosses ', E3.emp
  FROM Personnel AS B1, Personnel AS E1,
       Personnel AS E2, Personnel AS E3
 WHERE B1.emp = E1.boss
   AND E1.emp = E2.boss
   AND E2.emp = E3.boss;
```

Unfortunately, you have no idea just how deep the tree is, so you must keep extending this query until you get an empty set back as a result. The practical problem is that most SQL compilers will start having serious problems optimizing queries with a large number of tables. Typically, these problems start with five or more tables.

The other method is to declare a CURSOR and traverse the tree procedurally. This is usually very slow, but it will work for any depth of tree.

28.5 Functions in the Adjacency List Model

Tree functions are queries that answer questions based on sets of nodes defined by hierarchical relationships. For example, what is the total of the salaries of the subordinates of a given boss? The Transitive Closure table (see Section 28.8) is vital for most of these functions, such as

```
SELECT :mymanager, ' salary budget is ', SUM(salary)
   FROM Personnel
 WHERE emp IN (SELECT finish
                 FROM TransClosure
                WHERE start = :mymanager);
```

You can add "OR emp = :mymanager" to the WHERE if you want to include the boss in his own budget. Our sample table would produce these results:

Result

:mymanager	SUM(salary)
'Mr. King'	3900.00
'Mr. Duke'	2100.00

Another common function involves using quantity columns in the nodes to compute an accumulated total. This usually occurs in parts explosions, where one assembly may contain several occurrences of a subassembly. This sort of relationship is usually shown in the two-table graph representation because the quantity can be put in the second table, which holds the edges, rather than in the nodes, which hold the parts descriptions.

28.6 Tree Operations

Tree operations are those that alter the size and shape of a tree, not the contents of the nodes of the tree. Some of these operations can be very complex, such as balancing a binary tree, but we will deal only with deletion and insertion of a whole subtree.

28.6.1 Subtree Deletion

Deleting a subtree is hard in the adjacency list model. You have to find all of the subordinates, then remove that subset from the table. One way of doing this is with a cursor, but you can also mark the subordinates, then delete them:

```
BEGIN ATOMIC
UPDATE Personnel
   SET boss = '???????"   -- deletion marker
 WHERE boss = :subtree_root;

WHILE EXISTS (SELECT *           -- There are unmarked nodes
                FROM Personnel
               WHERE boss = '???????'
                 AND emp <> '???????')
 LOOP UPDATE Personnel          -- mark subordinates
         SET emp = '???????'
       WHERE boss = '???????';
         AND emp <> '???????';
 END LOOP;

DELETE FROM Personnel       -- delete marked nodes
   WHERE boss = '???????';
END;
```

Obviously, you do not want to use a marker that has any real meaning in the table.

28.6.2 Subtree Insertion

Inserting a subtree under a given node is easy. Given a table with the subtree that is to be made subordinate to a given node, you simply write

```
BEGIN
-- subordinate the subtree to his new boss
INSERT INTO Personnel VALUES (:subtree_root, :new_boss, . . .);
-- insert the subtree
INSERT INTO Personnel SELECT * FROM Subtree;
END;
```

28.7 Vendor Tree Extensions

As you can see from the examples above, you very quickly get into recursive or procedural code in handling trees. Since the single-table adjacency list model is popular, several vendors have added extensions to SQL to handle this approach. Here are descriptions of some vendor extensions.

28.7.1 Oracle Tree Extensions

Oracle added CONNECT BY PRIOR and START WITH clauses in the SELECT statement to provide partial support for reachability and path enumeration queries. The START WITH clause tells the engine which value the root of the tree has. The CONNECT BY PRIOR clause establishes the edges of the graph. The function LEVEL gives the distance from the root to the current node, starting at 1 for the root. Let us use a list of parts and subcomponents as the example database table. The query "Show all subcomponents of part A1, including the substructure" can be handled by the following Oracle SQL statement:

```
SELECT LEVEL AS pathlength, assemblyno, subassemblyno
  FROM Blueprint
 START WITH assemblyno = 'A1'
CONNECT BY PRIOR subassemblyno = assemblyno;
```

The query produces the following result:

Result1

pathlength	assemblyno	subassemblyno
1	'A1'	'A2'
2	'A2'	'A5'
2	'A2'	'A6'
3	'A6'	'A8'
3	'A6'	'A9'
1	'A1'	'A3'
2	'A3'	'A6'
3	'A6'	'A8'
3	'A6'	'A9'
2	'A3'	'A7'
1	'A1'	'A4'

The output is an adequate representation of the query result because it is possible to construct the path enumeration tree of Figure 29.2 from it. The CONNECT BY PRIOR clause provides traversal but not support for recursive functions. For example, it is not possible to sum the weights of all subcomponents of part A1 to find the weight of A1. The only recursive function supported by the CONNECT BY PRIOR clause is the LEVEL function. Another limitation of the CONNECT BY PRIOR clause is that it does not permit the use of JOINs. The reason for disallowing JOINs is that the order in which the rows are returned in the result is important. The parent nodes appear before their children, so you know that if the pathlength increases, these are children; if it does not, they are new nodes at a higher level.

This also means that an ORDER BY can destroy any meaning in the results. This means, moreover, that the CONNECT BY PRIOR result is not a true table since a table by definition does not have an internal ordering. In addition, this means that it is not always possible to use the result of a CONNECT BY query in another query. A trick for working around this limitation, which makes indirect use of the CONNECT BY PRIOR clause, is to hide it in a subquery that is used to make a JOIN at the higher level. For example, to attach a product category description, form another table to the parts explosion:

```
SELECT partno, categoryname
  FROM Parts, ProductCategory
 WHERE Parts.categoryid = ProductCategory.categoryid
   AND partno IN  (SELECT subassemblyno
                     FROM Blueprint
                    START WITH assemblyno = 'A1'
                    CONNECT BY PRIOR subassemblyno = assemblyno);
```

The subquery has only one table in the FROM clause and complies with the restriction that there must be no JOINs in any query block that contains a CONNECT BY PRIOR. On the other hand, the main query involves a JOIN of two tables, which would not be possible with direct use of the CONNECT BY PRIOR clause.

Another query that cannot be processed by direct use of the CONNECT BY PRIOR clause is one that displays all parent–child relationships at all levels. A technique to process this query is illustrated by the following SQL:

```
SELECT DISTINCT PX.partno, PX.pname, PY.partno, PY.pname
  FROM Parts AS PX, Parts AS PY
 WHERE PY.partno IN (SELECT Blueprint.subassemblyno
                       FROM Blueprint
```

```
            START WITH assemblyno = PX.partno
            CONNECT BY PRIOR subassemblyno = assemblyno)
ORDER BY PX.partno, PY.partno;
```

Again, the outer query includes a JOIN, which is not allowed with the CON-
NECT BY PRIOR clause. Note that the correlated subquery references
PX.partno.

28.7.2 XDB Tree Extension

XDB has a set of extensions similar to those in Oracle, but this product uses
functions rather than clauses to hide the recursion. The PREVIOUS(<col-
umn>) function finds the parent node value of the <column>. The keyword
LEVEL is a system constant for each row, which gives its pathlength from the
root; the root is at LEVEL = 0. There is a special value for the pathlength of a
leaf node, called BOTTOM. For example, to find all of the subcomponents of
A1, you would write this query:

```
SELECT assemblyno
  FROM Blueprint
 WHERE PREVIOUS(subassemblyno) = assemblyno
   AND assemblyno = 'A1'
   AND LEVEL <= BOTTOM;
```

Other vendors do similar things, but they are all based on establishing a
root and a relationship to join the original table to a correlated copy of itself.
Indexing can help, but such queries are still very expensive.

28.7.3 DB2's WITH Operator

IBM added the WITH operator, or common table expression, to its DB2 product line to handle the need to factor out common subquery expressions and
give them a name for the duration of the query. The other alternatives have
been to repeat the code (hoping that the optimizer would do the factoring),
or to create a VIEW and use it. However, the VIEW will be persistent in the
schema after the query is done unless you explicitly drop it.

However, instead of being a simple temporary VIEW mechanism, IBM
made the WITH clause handle recursive queries by allowing self-references.
This is useful for tree structures in particular. You define a special form of the
temporary VIEW query that has an initial subquery and a recursive subquery.
These two parts have to be connected by a UNION ALL operator—no other set
operation will do. The VIEW is initialized with the results of the initial

subquery, then the result of the recursive subquery is added to the VIEW over and over as it is used.

This might be easier to explain with an example, taken from the usual adjacency list model Personnel table. To find the immediate subordinates of boss 'Albert' you would write

```
SELECT *
  FROM Personnel
 WHERE boss = 'Albert';
```

To find all of his subordinates, you add this WITH clause to the query:

```
WITH Subordinates (emp, salary)
  AS (SELECT emp, salary
        FROM Personnel AS P0
       WHERE boss = 'Albert') -- initial set
      UNION ALL
      (SELECT emp, salary
         FROM Personnel AS P1, Subordinates AS S1
        WHERE P1.boss = S1.emp) -- recursive set
SELECT emp
  FROM Subordinates;
```

Each time you fetch a row from Subordinates, the WITH clause is executed using the current rows of the temporary VIEW table. First I fetch 'Albert' and his immediate subordinates. I then UNION ALL the personnel that have those subordinates as bosses, and so forth until the subquery is empty. Then the VIEW table is passed to the main SELECT clause to which the WITH clause is attached.

28.7.4 Date's EXPLODE Operator

In his book *Relational Database: Selected Writings* (Date 1986), Chris Date proposed an EXPLODE(<table name>) operator that would convert a table into another table with four columns: the level number, the current node, the subordinate node, and the sequence number. The sequence number was included to get around the problem of the ordering's having meaning in the hierarchy. The EXPLODE results are derived from simple tree-traversal rules.

28.7.5 Tillquist and Kuo's Proposals

John Tillquist and Feng-Yang Kuo proposed an extension wherein a tree is viewed as a special kind of GROUP BY clause (Tillquist and Kuo 1989). They would add a GROUP BY LEAVES (<major column>, <minor column>) that would find the set of all rows where the <minor column> value does not appear in the <major column>. This operator can be approximated with the query

```
SELECT *
  FROM TreeTable AS T1
WHERE NOT EXISTS (SELECT *
                    FROM TreeTable AS T2
                   WHERE T1.major = T2.minor)
GROUP BY boss;
```

The idea is that you get groups of leaf nodes, with their immediate parent as the single grouping column. Other extensions in Tillquist and Kuo's paper include a GROUP BY NODES (<major column>, <minor column>), which would use each node only once to prevent problems with cycles in the graph and would find all of the descendants of a given parent node. They then extend the aggregate functions with a COMPOUND function modifier (along the lines of DISTINCT) that carries the aggregation up the tree.

28.8 The Transitive Closure Model

You can extend the idea of the adjacency list by constructing a table that shows the start and finish of all paths in the tree along with their lengths. This table is called the *path enumeration* or the *transitive closure* of the tree. It is called the transitive closure because it is built from repeating a transitive operation, traversal, over and over until the set of paths is complete. Let us build a working table, called TransClosure, to hold the start and finish values of each path along with its length:

```
CREATE TABLE TransClosure
(start CHAR(20) NOT NULL
       REFERENCES Personnel(emp),
 finish CHAR(20) NOT NULL
       REFERENCES Personnel(emp),
 pathlength INTEGER NOT NULL DEFAULT 1
         CONSTRAINT positive_pathlength
         CHECK (pathlength > 0),
```

```
CONSTRAINT no_cycles
    CHECK (start <> finish),
PRIMARY KEY (start, finish));
```

Begin by inserting the adjacency list paths into the table. Now repeat the following statement until you are inserting zero rows:

```
BEGIN
DECLARE old_size INTEGER;
DECLARE new_size INTEGER;

INSERT INTO TransClosure (start, finish, pathlength)
SELECT B1.emp, E1.emp, 1
  FROM Personnel AS B1, Personnel AS E1
 WHERE B1.emp = E1.boss;

SET old_size = (SELECT COUNT(*) FROM TransClosure);
SET new_size = old_size - 1;

WHILE old_size < new_size
LOOP
INSERT INTO TransClosure (start, finish, pathlength)
SELECT DISTINCT P1.start, P2.finish, (P1.pathlength + 1)
  FROM TransClosure AS P1, TransClosure AS P2
 WHERE P2.pathlength = 1
   AND P1.finish = P2.start
   AND P1.pathlength = (SELECT MAX(pathlength) FROM TransClosure);
SET old_size = new_size;
SET new_size = (SELECT COUNT(*) FROM TransClosure);
END LOOP;
END;
```

I know of no way to do this in a single standard SQL statement or without a loop in a procedural host language. Another version of the insertion constructs the missing paths by inserting all combinations of pairs of existing paths.

```
INSERT INTO TransClosure (start, finish, pathlength)
SELECT DISTINCT P1.start, P2.finish,
                (P1.pathlength + P2.pathlength)
  FROM TransClosure AS P1, TransClosure AS P2
 WHERE P1.finish = P2.start        -- connect paths
   AND NOT EXISTS (SELECT *     -- this path not in tree
```

```
FROM TransClosure AS P3
WHERE P3.start = P1.start
  AND P3.finish = P2.finish);
```

The problem is that the query generates a lot of candidates and then rejects most of them as the table gets larger and larger. The SELECT DISTINCT is needed to avoid constructing the same path in two different ways, such as $(a)(bc) = (ab)(c)$.

While I have shown how to construct the transitive closure as a table in its own right, you could also keep several VIEWs. Each of these VIEWs would have an ancestor and its descendants for a particular generation or level in the tree.

There are good reasons for separating the Personnel table (nodes) from the hierarchy (edges). The first and most important reason is normalization. Nodes are entities, and edges are relationships; a table should model one or the other but not both. From a more practical viewpoint, it makes it easier to update personnel records if they are in one table, and likewise to change the company organizational chart when it is in another table.

28.8.1 Estimating Table Size

The problem with the transitive closure is that the table gets larger as the tree increases in size. Obviously a tree that is one level deep will have n rows in its table. At the other extreme, a tree that has a single chain of nodes will have $(n * (n - 1))/2$ rows. In between, the number of ways to arrange n nodes into a binary tree is given by a series called the Catalan numbers, which are given by the recursive formula

$$C(1) = 1$$
$$C(2) = 2$$
$$C(3) = 5$$
$$C(4) = 14$$
$$\ldots$$
$$C(n - 1) = (C(n) * (4*n - 6)) / n$$

I do not know of a formula for trees in general.

28.8.2 Deleting Nodes

Deleting a leaf node is simple. Remove the subset of rows that contain it.

```
DELETE FROM TransClosure
 WHERE finish = :mynode;
```

Likewise, removing a subtree is also simple:

```
DELETE FROM TransClosure
 WHERE start = :mynode;
```

Since all possible paths are in the table, there is no need to recalculate the pathlengths.

28.8.3 Subtree Insertion

Inserting a subtree consists of inserting the subtree table, which is also in transitive closure format, and running the routine for building the Trans-Closure table again.

28.8.4 Summary Functions

The adjacency list model is very difficult to use for hierarchical summary functions, and you need to use a vendor extension or write code with cursors. The transitive closure model is much easier to use: Simply summarize all the ending nodes on all paths that start from the root of the subtree.

```
SELECT T1.start, SUM(P1.salary)
  FROM TransClosure AS T1, TransClosure AS T2,
       Personnel AS P1
 WHERE T1.start = T2.finish
   AND T2.finish = P1.emp
 GROUP BY T1.start;
```

28.8.5 The Transitive Closure Model with Fixed Depth

If you know that the hierarchy will always have a fixed number of levels, then you can use this to model all of the paths in it. To use an actual example, an Internet marketing firm classifies its media-related products by store, metacategory, category, subcategory, and product. The highest level is the table itself, which represents the entire virtual shopping mall, stores are the next level down, and so forth.

```
CREATE TABLE VirtualMall
(store CHAR(15) NOT NULL,
 metacategory CHAR(15) NOT NULL,
```

```
category CHAR(15) NOT NULL,
subcategory CHAR(15) NOT NULL,
product CHAR(15) NOT NULL,
PRIMARY KEY (store, metacategory,
                category, subcategory, product));
```

Sample data would look like this:

```
INSERT INTO VirtualMall
VALUES ('Xena', 'Media', 'Audio', 'CD', 'Music from Xena'),
       ('Xena', 'Media', 'Audio', 'Tape', 'Music from Xena'),
       ('Xena', 'Media', 'Video', 'DVD', 'Episode #1'),
       ('Xena', 'Media', 'Video', 'Tape', 'Episode #1'),
          . . . ;
```

This leads to a bit of redundancy in the columns, but since the table is all key columns, we know it is in Fifth Normal Form.

Finding items of the same category is easy; for example, all CDs in the mall use this query:

```
SELECT *
  FROM VirtualMall
 WHERE subcategory = 'CD';
```

You might also consider adding CHECK( ) or REFERENCES constraint clauses that attach each level to a list or table of allowed values for that level.

The real use for this model comes when you have a second table with NULL-able columns. Each customer can fill out a form that lists their preferences, and they will only see merchandise from the stores they choose and then only within the metacategories, categories, or subcategories they've selected. The NULLs are used as wildcards to match anything in that level. That is, they can ask for or exclude a subtree or a level in the inventory. The customer's table looks like this:

```
CREATE TABLE Preferences
(customer CHAR(20) NOT NULL,
 store CHAR(15),
 metacategory CHAR(15),
 category CHAR(15),
 subcategory CHAR(15),
 prefers CHAR(4) NOT NULL CHECK (prefers IN ('show', 'hide')));
```

Thus, someone who wants to see only Xena audio products would add in this row in his profile:

```
INSERT INTO Preferences
VALUES ('Eddy Ears', 'Xena', 'Audio', NULL, NULL, 'show'),
       ('Eddy Ears', 'Xena', NULL, NULL, NULL, 'hide'),
```

The query to return the current offering that a customer wants to see is simply this:

```
SELECT :mycustomer, V1.*
  FROM VirtualMall AS V1, Preferences AS P1
 WHERE P1.customer = :mycustomer
   AND P1.prefers = 'show'
   AND V1.store = COALESCE (P1.store, V1.store)
   AND V1.metacategory = COALESCE (P1.metacategory, V1.metacategory)
   AND V1.category = COALESCE (P1.category, V1.category)
   AND V1.subcategory = COALESCE (P1.subcategory, V1.subcategory)
```

Another trick is to force the customer to build his preferences as proper subtrees in the hierarchy. That can be done with this CHECK() constraint:

```
CHECK (CASE WHEN store IS NULL)
           THEN COALESCE (metacategory, category, subcategory)
           WHEN metacategory IS NULL
           THEN COALESCE (category, subcategory)
           WHEN category IS NULL
           THEN COALESCE (subcategory)
           ELSE NULL END IS NULL)
```

The trade-off with this method is that the hierarchy must always have a fixed number of levels, but this is often true in many situations.

Nested Set Model
of Trees in SQL

IF YOU NEED a general discussion of trees, read the first section of Chapter 28 on the adjacency list model. Trees are often drawn as "boxes-and-arrows" charts, as I have done in this chapter. Another way of representing trees is to show them as nested sets. Since SQL is a set-oriented language, this is a better model for the approach discussed here. Let us define a simple Personnel table to represent the hierarchy in some organization. The first three columns explain themselves. Ignore the lft and rgt columns for now, but note that their names are abbreviations for "left" and "right," which are reserved words in SQL-92.

```
CREATE TABLE Personnel
(emp CHAR(10) NOT NULL PRIMARY KEY,
 boss CHAR(10), -- this has to be nullable for the root node!!
 salary DECIMAL(6, 2) NOT NULL,
 lft INTEGER NOT NULL,
 rgt INTEGER NOT NULL);
```

Personnel

emp	boss	salary	lft	rgt
'Albert'	NULL	1000.00	1	12
'Bert'	'Albert'	900.00	2	3
'Chuck'	'Albert'	900.00	4	11
'Donna'	'Chuck'	800.00	5	6
'Eddie'	'Chuck'	700.00	7	8
'Fred'	'Chuck'	600.00	9	10

This would look like Figure 29.1 as a graph.

To show a tree as nested sets, replace the boxes with ovals, then nest subordinate ovals inside their parents. Containment represents subordination. The root will be the largest oval and will contain every other node. The leaf nodes will be the innermost ovals, with nothing else inside them, and the nesting will show the hierarchical relationship. This is a natural way to model a parts explosion, since a final assembly is made of physically nested assemblies that finally break down into separate parts. The tree shown in Figure 29.2 translates into the nesting of sets shown in Figure 29.3.

Using this approach, we can model a tree with lft and rgt nested sets with number pairs. These number pairs will always contain the pairs of their subordinates, so that a child node is within the bounds of its parent. Figure 29.4 is a version of the nested sets, flattened onto a number line.

If that mental model does not work for you, then visualize the nested sets model as a little worm with a Bates automatic numbering stamp crawling along the "boxes-and-arrows" version of the tree. The worm starts at the top, the root, and makes a complete trip around the tree. When he comes to a node, he puts a number in the cell on the side he is visiting and his number-

Fig. 29.1

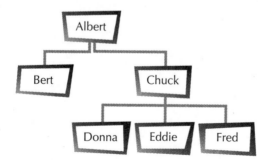

Fig. 29.2

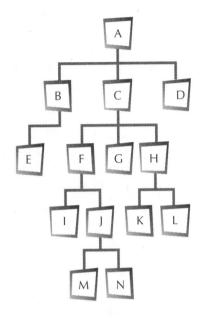

Fig. 29.3

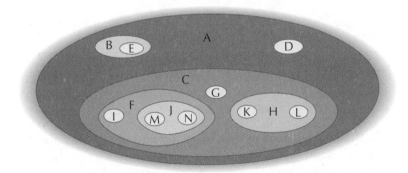

Fig. 29.4

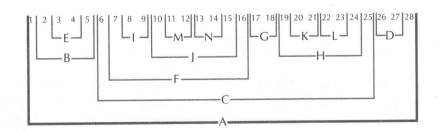

ing stamp increments itself. Each node will get two numbers, one for the right (rgt) side and one for the left (lft) side. Computer science majors will recognize this as a modified preorder tree traversal algorithm. This numbering has some predictable results that we can use for building queries.

29.1 Finding Root and Leaf Nodes

The root will always have a 1 in its lft column and twice the number of nodes in its rgt column. This is easy to understand; the worm has to visit each node twice, once for the lft side and once for the rgt side, so the final count has to be twice the number of nodes in the whole tree. The root of the tree is found with the query

```
SELECT *
  FROM Personnel
 WHERE lft = 1;
```

This query will take advantage of the index on the lft value. A leaf node is one that has no children under it. In an adjacency matrix model, it is not that easy to find all the leaf nodes since you have to use a correlated subquery:

```
SELECT *
  FROM Personnel AS P1
 WHERE NOT EXISTS (SELECT *
                     FROM Personnel AS P2
                    WHERE E1.emp = P2.boss);
```

In the nested set table, the difference between the lft and rgt values of leaf nodes is always 1. Think of the little worm turning the corner as he crawls along the tree. That means you can find all leaf nodes with the extremely simple query

```
SELECT *
  FROM Personnel
 WHERE (rgt - lft) = 1;
```

There is a further trick you can use to speed up queries. Build a unique index on either the lft column or on the pair of columns (lft, rgt) and then you can rewrite the query to take advantage of the index. The previous query will also benefit.

```
SELECT *
 FROM Personnel
 WHERE lft = (rgt - 1);
```

The reason this improves performance is that the SQL engine can use the index on the lft column when it does not appear in an expression. Don't use (rgt − lft) = 1, since that will prevent the index from being used.

29.2 Finding Subtrees

Trees have a lot of special properties, and those properties are very useful to us.

A tree is a graph that has no cycles in it. That is, no path folds back on itself to catch you in an endless loop when you follow it. Another defining property is that there is always a path from the root to any other node in the tree.

Another very useful property is that any node in the tree is the root of a subtree (the leaf nodes are a degenerate case). In the nested sets table, all the descendants of a node can be found by looking for the nodes with a rgt and lft number between the lft and rgt values of their parent node. For example, to find all the subordinates of each boss in the corporate hierarchy, you would write

```
SELECT Mangers.emp, ' is a boss of ', Workers.emp
   FROM Personnel AS Managers, Personnel AS Workers
 WHERE Workers.lft BETWEEN Managers.lft AND Managers.rgt
   AND Workers.rgt BETWEEN Managers.lft AND Managers.rgt;
```

Look at the way the numbering was done and you can convince yourself that this search condition is too strict. We can drop the last predicate and simply use

```
SELECT Mangers.emp, ' is a boss of ', Workers.emp
   FROM Personnel AS Managers, Personnel AS Workers
 WHERE Workers.lft BETWEEN Managers.lft AND Managers.rgt;
```

This would tell you that everyone is also his own superior, so in some situations you would also add the predicate

```
. . . AND Workers.lft <> Managers.lft
```

This simple self-JOIN query is the basis for almost everything that follows in the nested set model.

29.3 Finding Levels and Paths in a Tree

The level of a node in a tree is the number of edges between the node and the root, where the larger the depth number, the farther away the node is from the root. A path is a set of edges that directly connect two nodes.

The nested set model uses the fact that each containing set is wider (where width = (rgt − lft)) than the sets it contains. Obviously, the root will always be the widest row in the table. The level function is the number of edges between two given nodes; it is fairly easy to calculate. For example, to find the level of each worker, you would use

```
SELECT P2.emp, (COUNT(P1.emp) - 1) AS level
  FROM Personnel AS P1, Personnel AS P2
 WHERE P2.lft BETWEEN P1.lft AND P1.rgt;
```

The reason for using the expression (COUNT(*) - 1) is to remove the duplicate count of the node itself because a tree starts at level 0. If you prefer to start at 1, drop the extra arithmetic.

29.3.1 Finding the Height of a Tree

The height of a tree is the length of the longest path in the tree. We know that this path runs from the root to a leaf node, so we can write a query to find it like this:

```
SELECT MAX(level) AS height
  FROM (SELECT P2.emp, (COUNT(P1.emp) - 1)
          FROM Personnel AS P1, Personnel AS P2
         WHERE P2.lft BETWEEN P1.lft AND P1.rgt
         GROUP BY P2.emp) AS L(emp, level);
```

Other queries can be built from this tabular subquery expression of the nodes and their level numbers.

29.3.2 Finding Immediate Subordinates

The adjacency model allows you to easily find the immediate subordinates of a node; you simply look in the column that gives the parent of every node in the tree.

This becomes complicated in the nested set model. You have to prune the subtree rooted at the node of the boss we are looking at to one level. Another way to find his subordinates is to define them as personnel who have no other employee between themselves and the boss in question.

```
CREATE VIEW Immediate_Subordinates (boss, worker, lft, rgt)
AS SELECT Managers.emp, Workers.emp, Workers.lft, Workers.rgt
     FROM Personnel AS Managers, Personnel AS Workers
    WHERE Workers.lft BETWEEN Managers.lft AND Managers.rgt
      AND NOT EXISTS  -- no middle manager between the boss and us!
          (SELECT *
             FROM Personnel AS MidMgr
            WHERE MidMgr.lft BETWEEN Managers.lft
                                 AND Managers.rgt
              AND Workers.lft BETWEEN MidMgr.lft
                                  AND MidMgr.rgt
              AND MidMgr.emp NOT IN (Workers.emp, Managers.emp));
```

There is a reason for setting this up as a VIEW and including the lft and rgt numbers of the children. The lft and rgt numbers for the parent can be reconstructed by

```
SELECT boss, MIN(lft) - 1, MAX(rgt) + 1
  FROM Immediate_Subordinates AS S1
 GROUP BY boss;
```

This query can be generalized to any distance (:n) in the hierarchy, thus:

```
SELECT Workers.emp, ' is ', :n,  ' levels down from', :myemployee
  FROM Personnel AS Managers, Personnel AS Workers
 WHERE Managers.emp = :myemployee
   AND Workers.lft BETWEEN Managers.lft
                       AND Managers.rgt
   AND :n = (SELECT COUNT(MidMgr.emp)
               FROM Personnel AS MidMgr
              WHERE MidMgr.lft BETWEEN Managers.lft
                                   AND Managers.rgt
                AND Workers.lft BETWEEN MidMgr.lft
                                    AND MidMgr.rgt
                AND MidMgr.emp
                    NOT IN (Workers.emp, Managers.emp));
```

This illustrates a general principle of the nested set model; it is easier to work with subtrees than to work with individual nodes or other subsets of the tree.

29.3.3 Finding Oldest and Youngest Subordinates

The nested set model usually assumes that the subordinates are ranked by age, seniority, or in some way from left to right among the immediate subordinates of a node. The adjacency model does not have a concept of such rankings, so the following queries are not possible without extra columns to hold the rankings in the adjacency list model.

The most senior subordinate is found by this query:

```
SELECT Workers.emp, ' is the oldest child of ', :myemployee
  FROM Personnel AS Managers, Personnel AS Workers
 WHERE Managers.emp = :myemployee
   AND Workers.lft - 1 = Managers.lft; -- leftmost child
```

Most junior subordinate:

```
SELECT Workers.emp, ' is the youngest child of ', :myemployee
  FROM Personnel AS Managers, Personnel AS Workers
 WHERE Managers.emp = :myemployee
   AND Workers.rgt = Managers.rgt - 1; -- rightmost child
```

The real trick is to find the *n*th sibling of a parent in a tree. If you remember the old Charlie Chan movies: Detective Chan always referred to his sons by number, such as "Number one son," "Number two son," and so forth. This becomes a self-JOIN on the set of immediate subordinates of the parent under consideration. That is why I created a VIEW for telling us the immediate subordinates before introducing this problem. The query is much easier to read using the VIEW.

```
SELECT S1.worker, ' is the number ', :n, ' son of ', S1.boss
  FROM Immediate_Subordinates AS S1,
 WHERE S1.boss = :myemployee
   AND 1 = (SELECT COUNT(S2.lft) - 1
              FROM Immediate_Subordinates AS S2
             WHERE S2.boss = S1.boss
               AND S2.boss <> S1.worker
               AND S2.lft BETWEEN 1 AND S1.lft);
```

Notice that you have to subtract 1 to avoid counting the parent as its own child.

29.3.4 Finding a Path

To find and number the nodes in the path from a `:start_node` to a `:finish_node`, you can repeat the nested set "BETWEEN predicate trick" twice to form an upper and a lower boundary on the set:

```
SELECT T2.node,
       (SELECT COUNT(*)
          FROM Tree AS T4
         WHERE T4.lft BETWEEN T1.lft AND T1.rgt
           AND T2.lft BETWEEN T4.lft AND T4.rgt) AS path_nbr
  FROM Tree AS T1, Tree AS T2, Tree AS T3
 WHERE T1.node = :start_node
   AND T3.node = :finish_node
   AND T2.lft BETWEEN T1.lft AND T1.rgt
   AND T3.lft BETWEEN T2.lft AND T2.rgt;
```

Using the Parts explosion tree, this query would return the following table for the path from `'C'` to `'N'`, with 1 being the highest starting node and the other nodes numbered in the order they must be traversed.

node	path_nbr
C	1
F	2
J	3
N	4

However, if you just need a column to use in a sort for outputting the answer in a host language, then replace the subquery expression with "(T2.rgt - T2.lft) AS sort_col" and use an ORDER BY clause in a cursor.

29.4 Functions in the Nested Set Model

JOINs and ORDER BY clauses will not interfere with the nested set model, as they will with the adjacency graph model. Nor are the results dependent on the order in which the rows are displayed, as in vendor extensions. The LEVEL function for a given employee node is a matter of counting how many lft and rgt groupings (superiors) this employee node's lft or rgt is within.

You can get this by modifying the sense of the BETWEEN predicate in the query for subtrees:

```
SELECT COUNT(Managers.emp) AS level
   FROM Personnel AS Managers, Personnel AS Workers
 WHERE Workers.lft BETWEEN Managers.lft AND Managers.rgt
   AND Workers.emp = :myemployee;
```

A simple total of the salaries of the subordinates of a supervising employee works out the same way. Notice that this total will include the boss's salary, too.

```
SELECT SUM (Workers.salary) AS payroll
   FROM Personnel AS Managers, Personnel AS Workers
 WHERE Workers.lft BETWEEN Managers.lft AND Managers.rgt
   AND Managers.emp = :myemployee;
```

A slightly trickier function involves using quantity columns in the nodes to compute an accumulated total. This usually occurs in parts explosions, where one assembly may contain several occurrences of a subassembly.

```
SELECT SUM (Subassem.qty * Subassem.price) AS totalcost
   FROM Blueprint AS Assembly, Blueprint AS Subassem
 WHERE Subassem.lft
       BETWEEN Assembly.lft AND Assembly.rgt
   AND Assembly.partno = :thispart;
```

We will do something with this in more detail in Section 29.7 shortly.

29.5 Deleting Nodes and Subtrees

Another interesting property of this representation is that the subtrees must fill from lft to rgt. In other tree representations, it is possible for a parent node to have a rgt child and no lft child. This lets you assign some significance to being the leftmost child of a parent. For example, the node in this position might be the next in line for promotion in a corporate hierarchy.

29.5.1 Deleting Subtrees

This query will take a downsized employee as a parameter and remove the subtree rooted under him. The trick in this query is that we are using the key, but we need to get the lft and rgt values to do the work. The answer is scalar subqueries:

```
DELETE FROM Personnel
 WHERE lft BETWEEN
   (SELECT lft FROM Personnel WHERE emp = :downsized)
    AND
   (SELECT rgt FROM Personnel WHERE emp = :downsized);
```

The problem is that this will result in gaps in the sequence of nested set numbers. You can still do most tree queries on a table with such gaps, but you will lose the properties that let you find leaf nodes and the root, and which make other operations easier. Unfortunately, you just lost some information that would be very useful in closing those gaps, namely the rgt and lft numbers of the root of the subtree. Let's forget the query and write a procedure instead:

```
CREATE PROCEDURE DropTree (downsized IN CHAR(10) NOT NULL)
BEGIN ATOMIC
DECLARE dropemp CHAR(10), droplft INTEGER, droprgt INTEGER;

-- save the dropped subtree data with a singleton SELECT
SELECT emp, lft, rgt
  INTO dropemp, droplft, droprgt
  FROM Personnel
 WHERE emp = downsized;

-- the deletion is easy
DELETE FROM Personnel
 WHERE lft BETWEEN droplft and droprgt;

-- close up the gap
UPDATE Personnel
   SET lft = CASE
             WHEN lft > droplft
             THEN lft - (droprgt - droplft + 1)
             ELSE lft END,
       rgt = CASE
             WHEN rgt > droplft
             THEN rgt - (droprgt - droplft + 1)
             ELSE rgt END;
END;
```

A real procedure should have some error handling, but I am leaving that as an exercise for the reader.

29.5.2 Deleting a Single Node

Deleting a single node in the middle of the tree is harder than removing whole subtrees. When you remove a node in the middle of the tree, you have to decide how to fill the hole. There are two ways. The first method is to promote one of the children to the original node's position—Dad dies and the oldest son takes over the business, as shown in Figure 29.5. The oldest child is always shown as the leftmost child node under its parent.

There is a problem with this operation, however. If the older child has children of his own, then you have to decide how to handle them, and so on down the tree until you get to a leaf node.

The second method is to connect the children to the parent of the original node—Mom dies and the kids are adopted by Grandma, as shown in Figure 29.6.

This happens automatically in the nested set model; you just delete the node and its children are already contained in their ancestor nodes. However, you have to be careful when you try to close the gap left by the deletion. There is a difference in renumbering the descendants of the deleted node and renumbering other nodes to the right. Here is a procedure for doing that:

```
CREATE PROCEDURE DropNode (downsized IN CHAR(10))
BEGIN ATOMIC
DECLARE dropemp CHAR(10), droplft INTEGER, droprgt INTEGER;

-- save the dropped node data with a singleton SELECT
SELECT emp, lft, rgt
  INTO dropemp, droplft, droprgt
  FROM Personnel
 WHERE emp = downsized;

-- the deletion is easy
DELETE FROM Personnel
 WHERE emp = downsized;

-- close up the gap
UPDATE Personnel
   SET lft = CASE
             WHEN lft BETWEEN droplft AND droprgt THEN lft - 1
             WHEN lft > droprgt THEN lft - 2
             ELSE lft END,
       rgt = CASE
```

Fig. 29.5

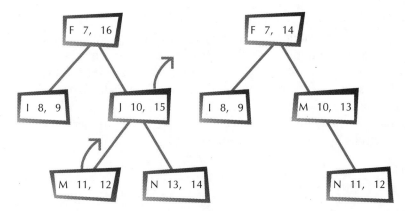

Filling the gap by promotion of the oldest child

Fig. 29.6

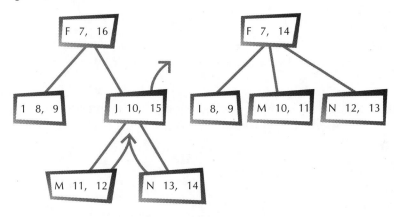

Filling the gap by promotion of the subtree

```
            WHEN rgt BETWEEN droplft AND droprgt THEN rgt - 1
            WHEN rgt > droprgt THEN rgt - 2
            ELSE rgt END
    WHERE lft > droplft;
 END PROCEDURE;
```

29.6 Closing Gaps in the Tree

The important thing is to preserve the nested subsets based on lft and rgt numbers. As you remove nodes from a tree, you create gaps in the nested set numbers. These gaps do not destroy the subset property, but they can present other problems and should be closed. This is like garbage collection in other languages. The easiest way to understand the code is to break it up into a series of meaningful VIEWs, then use the VIEWs to UPDATE the tree table. This VIEW "flattens out" the whole tree into a list of nested sets numbers, regardless of whether they are lft or rgt numbers:

```
CREATE VIEW FlatTree (visit)
AS SELECT lft FROM Personnel
   UNION
   SELECT rgt FROM Personnel;
```

This VIEW finds the lft numbers in gaps instead of in the tree:

```
CREATE VIEW Firstvisit (visit)
AS SELECT (visit + 1)
   FROM FlatTree
  WHERE (visit + 1) NOT IN (SELECT visit FROM FlatTree)
   AND (visit + 1) > 0;
```

The final predicate is to keep you from going past the leftmost limit of the root node, which is always 1. Likewise, this VIEW finds the rgt nested sets numbers in gaps:

```
CREATE VIEW Lastvisit (visit)
AS SELECT (visit - 1)
   FROM Personnel
  WHERE (visit - 1) NOT IN (SELECT visit FROM FlatTree)
   AND (visit - 1) < 2 * (SELECT COUNT (*) FROM Personnel);
```

The final predicate is to keep you from going past the rightmost limit of the root node, which is twice the number of nodes in the tree. You then use these two VIEWs to build a table of the gaps that have to be closed:

```
CREATE VIEW Gaps (start, finish, size)

AS SELECT F1.visit, L1.visit, ((L1.visit - F1.visit) + 1)
   FROM Firstvisit AS F1, Lastvisit AS L1
```

```
WHERE L1.visit = (SELECT MIN (L2.visit)
                    FROM Lastvisit AS L2
                   WHERE F1.visit <= L2.visit);
```

This query will tell you the start and finish nested set numbers of the gaps, as well as their size. It makes a handy report in itself, which is why I have shown it with the redundant finish and size columns. But that is not why we created it. It can be used to "slide" everything over to the left:

```
BEGIN
-- This will have to be repeated until gaps disappear
WHILE EXISTS (SELECT * FROM Gaps)
LOOP UPDATE Frammis
        SET rgt = CASE
                    WHEN rgt > (SELECT MIN(start) FROM Gaps)
                    THEN rgt - 1 ELSE rgt END,
            lft = CASE
                    WHEN lft > (SELECT MIN(start) FROM Gaps)
                    THEN lft - 1 ELSE lft END;
END WHILE;
```

The actual number of iterations is given by the pre-closure value of the rgt nested set number of the root SELECT rgt FROM Frammis WHERE lft = 1 minus the number of nodes remaining in the tree SELECT COUNT(*) FROM Frammis. This method keeps the code fairly simple at this level, but the VIEWs under it are pretty tricky and could take a lot of execution time. It would seem reasonable to use the gap size to speed up the closure process, but that can get tricky when more than one node has been dropped.

29.7 Summary Functions on Trees

There are tree queries that deal strictly with the nodes themselves and have nothing to do with the tree structure at all. For example, what is the name of the president of the company? How many people are in the company? Are there two people with the same name working here? These queries are handled with the usual SQL queries and there are no surprises.

Other types of queries do depend on the tree structure. For example, what is the total weight of a finished assembly (i.e., the total of all of its sub-assembly weights)? Do Harry and John report to the same boss? And so forth. Let's consider a sample database that shows a parts explosion for a frammis again, but this time in nested set representation. The leaf nodes are the basic parts, the root node is the final assembly, and the nodes in between are subassemblies. Each part or assembly has a unique catalog number (in this case a single letter), a weight, and the quantity of this unit that is required to make the next unit above it. The declaration looks like this:

```
CREATE TABLE Frammis
(part CHAR (2) PRIMARY KEY,
 qty INTEGER NOT NULL
      CONSTRAINT non_negative_qty
      CHECK (qty >= 0),
 wgt INTEGER NOT NULL
      CONSTRAINT non_negative_wgt
      CHECK (wgt >= 0),
 lft INTEGER NOT NULL UNIQUE
      CONSTRAINT valid_lft
      CHECK (lft > 0),
 rgt INTEGER NOT NULL UNIQUE
      CONSTRAINT valid_rgt
      CHECK (rgt > 1),
 CONSTRAINT valid_range_pair
 CHECK (lft < rgt));
```

We initially load it with this data:

Frammis

part	qty	wgt	lft	rgt
'A'	1	0	1	28
'B'	1	0	2	5
'C'	2	0	6	19
'D'	2	0	20	27
'E'	2	12	3	4
'F'	5	0	7	16
'G'	2	6	17	18
'H'	3	0	21	26
'I'	4	8	8	9
'J'	1	0	10	15
'K'	5	3	22	23
'L'	1	4	24	25
'M'	2	7	11	12
'N'	3	2	13	14

Fig. 29.7

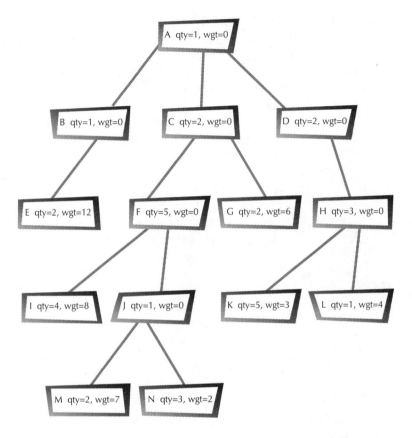

Notice that the weights of the subassemblies are initially set to zero and only parts (leaf nodes) have weights. You can easily ensure this is true with this statement:

```
UPDATE Frammis
   SET wgt = 0
 WHERE lft < (rgt - 1);
```

The weight of an assembly will be calculated as the total weight of all its subassemblies. The tree initially looks like Figure 29.7.

Look at the M and N leaf nodes. The table says that we need two M units weighing 7 kilograms each, plus three N units weighing 2 kilograms each, to make one J assembly. So that is $((2 * 7) + (3 * 2)) = 20$ kilograms per J assembly. The weight of a nonleaf node is thus the sum of the products of the weights and quantities of its immediate subordinates.

The problem is that the nested set model is good at finding subtrees, but not at finding a single level within the tree. The immediate subordinates of a node can be found with this view:

```
CREATE VIEW Immediate_Kids (parent, child, wgt)
AS SELECT F2.part, F1.part, F1.wgt
    FROM Frammis AS F1, Frammis AS F2
   WHERE F1.1ft BETWEEN F2.1ft AND F2.rgt
     AND F1.part <> F2.part
     AND NOT EXISTS
            (SELECT *
               FROM Frammis AS F3
              WHERE F3.1ft BETWEEN F2.1ft+ 1 AND F2.rgt - 1
                AND F1.1ft BETWEEN F3.1ft+ 1 AND F3.rgt - 1);
```

The query says that F2 is the parent, and F1 is one of its children. The EXISTS( ) checks to see that there are no other descendants strictly between F1 and F2. This VIEW can then be used with this UPDATE statement to calculate the weights of each level of the Frammis.

```
BEGIN ATOMIC
UPDATE Frammis -- set nonleaf nodes to zero
   SET wgt = 0
 WHERE 1ft = rgt - 1;
WHILE (SELECT wgt FROM Frammis WHERE 1ft = 1) = 0
LOOP UPDATE Frammis
       SET wgt
           = (SELECT SUM(F1.qty * F1.wgt)
                FROM Frammis AS F1
               WHERE EXISTS
                     (SELECT *
                        FROM Immediate_kids AS I1
                       WHERE parent = Frammis.part
                         AND I1.child = F1.part))
     WHERE wgt = 0 -- weight is missing
       AND NOT EXISTS -- subtree rooted here is completed
             (SELECT *
                FROM Immediate_kids AS I2
               WHERE I2.parent = Frammis.part
                 AND I2.wgt = 0);
END LOOP;
END;
```

This is a bit tricky, but in English we are calculating the weights of the Frammis by moving up the tree until we get to the root. A node is filled in with a weight when all of its children have a weight assigned to them. The EXISTS() predicate in the WHERE clause says that this part in Frammis is a parent and the NOT EXISTS() predicate says that no sibling has a zero (i.e., unknown) weight. This query works from the leaf nodes up to the root and has to be applied repeatedly.

If we change the weight of any part, we must correct the whole tree. Simply set the weight of all nonleaf nodes to zero first and redo this procedure. Once the proper weights and quantities are in place, it is fairly easy to find averages and other aggregate functions within a subtree.

Here is how the table changes after each execution:

First iteration (seven rows affected)

part	qty	wgt	lft	rgt
'A'	1	0	1	28
'B'	1	24	2	5
'C'	2	0	6	19
'D'	2	0	20	27
'E'	2	12	3	4
'F'	5	0	7	16
'G'	2	6	17	18
'H'	3	19	21	26
'I'	4	8	8	9
'J'	1	20	10	15
'K'	5	3	22	23
'L'	1	4	24	25
'M'	2	7	11	12
'N'	3	2	13	14

Second iteration (four rows affected)

part	qty	wgt	lft	gt
'A'	1	0	1	28
'B'	1	24	2	5
'C'	2	0	6	19
'D'	2	57	20	27
'E'	2	12	3	4
'F'	5	52	7	16

(cont.)

part	qty	wgt	lft	gt
'G'	2	6	17	18
'H'	3	19	21	26
'I'	4	8	8	9
'J'	1	20	10	15
'K'	5	3	22	23
'L'	1	4	24	25
'M'	2	7	11	12
'N'	3	2	13	14

Third iteration (two rows affected)

part	qty	wgt	lft	rgt
'A'	1	0	1	28
'B'	1	24	2	5
'C'	2	272	6	19
'D'	2	57	20	27
'E'	2	12	3	4
'F'	5	52	7	16
'G'	2	6	17	18
'H'	3	19	21	26
'I'	4	8	8	9
'J'	1	20	10	15
'K'	5	3	22	23
'L'	1	4	24	25
'M'	2	7	11	12
'N'	3	2	13	14

Fourth iteration (one row, the root, is affected and looping halts)

part	qty	wgt	lft	rgt
'A'	1	682	1	28
'B'	1	24	2	5
'C'	2	272	6	19
'D'	2	57	20	27
'E'	2	12	3	4
'F'	5	52	7	16
'G'	2	6	17	18
'H'	3	19	21	26

'I'	4	8	8	9
'J'	1	20	10	15
'K'	5	3	22	23
'L'	1	4	24	25
'M'	2	7	11	12
'N'	3	2	13	14

29.8 Inserting and Updating Trees

Updates to the nodes are done by searching for the key of each node; there is nothing special about them. Rearranging the structure of the tree is best done by drawing a picture of the desired tree and figuring out the lft and rgt nested set numbers for yourself. As a programming project, you might want to build a tool that takes a "boxes-and-arrows" graphic and converts it into a series of UPDATE and INSERT statements. Inserting a subtree or a new node involves finding a place in the tree for the new nodes, spreading the other nodes apart by incrementing their nested set numbers, then renumbering the subtree to fit. This is basically the deletion procedure in reverse. First determine the parent for the node, then spread the nested set numbers out two positions to the rgt. For example, let's insert a new node, G1, under part G. We can insert one node at a time like this:

```
BEGIN
INSERT INTO Frammis (part, qty, wgt, lft, rgt)
VALUES ('G1', 3, 4, 0, 0);

UPDATE Frammis
   SET lft = CASE WHEN lft > (SELECT F1.lft
                                FROM Frammis AS F1
                               WHERE F1.part = 'G')
                  THEN lft + 2
                  WHEN lft = 0
                  THEN (SELECT F1.lft + 1
                          FROM Frammis AS F1
                         WHERE F1.part = 'G')
                  ELSE lft END,
       rgt = CASE WHEN lft > (SELECT F1.lft
                                FROM Frammis AS F1
                               WHERE F1.part = 'G')
                  THEN rgt + 2
```

```
            WHEN lft = 0
            THEN (SELECT     F2.lft + 2
                     FROM     Frammis AS F2
                    WHERE     F2.part = 'G')
            ELSE rgt END;
END;
```

We really need to explain this monster. The first WHEN clause in the updates for the lft and rgt numbers spreads a space for two numbers if the node in question is to the right of the insertion point. The second WHEN clause updates the new node under its parent. The ELSE clause leaves the nodes on the left of the new node unchanged.

This procedure will add the new node to the leftmost child position. The code could be modified to add the new node to the rightmost child position or between existing children, but it is more difficult.

29.9 The Linear Version of the Nested Set Model

If you look at the diagram that shows the left and right numbers on a number line (Figure 29.4), you will realize that this diagram can be used directly to represent a tree in a nested set model. The numbers appear once, but the nodes appear exactly twice—once for the lft number and once for their rgt number. The table can be defined like this.

```
CREATE TABLE Personnel
(emp CHAR(10) NOT NULL,
 nbr INTEGER NOT NULL UNIQUE,
 CONSTRAINT natural_numbers
      CHECK(nbr > 0),
 CONSTRAINT got_all_numbers
 CHECK ((SELECT COUNT(*) FROM Personnel)
        = (SELECT MAX(nbr) FROM Personnel)),
 CONSTRAINT exactly_twice
 CHECK (NOT EXISTS (SELECT *
                    FROM Personnel
                    GROUP BY emp
                    HAVING COUNT(*) <> 2)),
 PRIMARY KEY (emp, nbr));
```

In fairness, the got_all_numbers and exactly_twice constraints will be hard to implement in most SQL products today, but they are legal in full SQL-92. Our Personnel tree is represented by this data:

Personnel

emp	nbr
'Albert'	1
'Albert'	12
'Bert'	2
'Bert'	3
'Chuck	4
'Chuck'	11
'Donna'	5
'Donna'	6
'Eddie'	7
'Eddie'	8
'Fred'	9
'Fred'	10

The standard nested set model can be constructed using this nonupdatable VIEW for queries:

```
CREATE VIEW PersonnelChart (emp, lft, rgt)
AS SELECT emp, MIN(nbr), MAX(nbr)
     FROM Personnel
    GROUP BY emp;
```

The major advantage of this model is that insertion and deletion are much easier than in the standard nested sets model. For example, to remove a subtree rooted at :myemployee, you would use

```
PROCEDURE RemoveSubtree (IN myemployee CHAR(10))
LANGUAGE SQL
BEGIN ATOMIC
 DECLARE INTEGER leftmost;
 DECLARE INTEGER rightmost;
 -- remember where the subtree root was
 SET leftmost = (SELECT MIN(nbr)
                 FROM Personnel
                WHERE emp = myemployee);
```

```
          SET rightmost = (SELECT MAX(nbr)
                             FROM Personnel
                            WHERE emp = myemployee);
-- remove the subtree
DELETE FROM Personnel
 WHERE nbr BETWEEN leftmost AND rightmost;
-- compute the size of the subtree & close the gap
UPDATE Personnel
   SET nbr = nbr - (rightmost - leftmost + 1) / 2
 WHERE nbr > leftmost;
END;
```

Insertion is the reverse of this operation. You must create a gap, then add the new subtree to the table.

```
PROCEDURE InsertSubtree (IN myboss CHAR(10))
LANGUAGE SQL
BEGIN ATOMIC
-- assume that the new subtree is held in NewTree
-- and is in linear nested set format
 DECLARE INTEGER treesize;
 DECLARE INTEGER boss_right;
 -- get size of the subtree
 SET treesize = (SELECT (MAX(nbr) - MIN(nbr) + 1)
                   FROM NewTree;
 -- place new tree to right of siblings
 SET boss_right = (SELECT MAX(nbr)
                     FROM Personnel
                    WHERE emp = myboss);
 -- move everyone over to the right
 UPDATE Personnel
    SET nbr = nbr + treesize
  WHERE nbr >= bossright;
 -- re-number the subtree and insert it
 INSERT INTO Personnel
 SELECT emp, (nbr + boss_right) FROM NewTree;
 -- clear out subtree table
 DELETE FROM SubTree;
END;
```

29.10 Converting Adjacency List to Nested Set Model

Most SQL databases have used the adjacency list model for two reasons. The first reason is that Dr. Codd came up with it in the early days of the relational model and nobody thought about it after that. The second reason is that the adjacency list is a way of "faking" pointer chains, the traditional programming method in procedural languages for handling trees.

However, after seeing the advantages of the nested set model, we know that we need a way to convert adjacency lists into nested sets in SQL. It would be fairly easy to load an adjacency list model table into a host language program, then use a recursive preorder tree traversal program from a college freshman data structures textbook to build the nested set model.

The pseudocode for the algorithm is based on having a procedure to read the top of the stack and extract a column from it.

1. Set the numbering counter to zero.

2. Push the root of the adjacency list tree on a stack, setting its lft and rgt numbers to 1 and twice the count of the original adjacency list table (Personnel in these examples).

3. Find the eldest immediate subordinate (alphabetical order will be fine) and repeat the process until you run out of subordinates.

4. Now start popping the stack and inserting the rgt numbers as the nodes leave the stack.

5. Repeat steps 2 and 3 based on the top of the stack until the Personnel table is empty, which means that the counter is equal to twice the count of the original table.

The code might look like this:

```
BEGIN
DECLARE counter INTEGER;
SET counter = 0;

INSERT INTO Stack    -- push the root node
SELECT emp, 1, NULL
  FROM Personnel
 WHERE boss IS NULL;
DELETE FROM Personnel -- remove root from original table
 WHERE boss IS NULL;
```

```
WHILE counter <= 2 * (SELECT COUNT(*) - 1 FROM Personnel)
 LOOP
 WHILE EXISTS (SELECT *         -- push on the stack
                  FROM Personnel
                  WHERE boss = STACK_TOP (emp))
 LOOP
 INSERT INTO Stack
 SELECT MIN(emp), counter, NULL  -- push leftmost children
   FROM Personnel
  WHERE boss = STACK_TOP (emp);
 DELETE FROM Personnel    -- remove node from original table
  WHERE emp = (SELECT MIN(emp)
                  FROM Personnel
                  WHERE boss = STACK_TOP (emp));
 SET counter = counter + 1;
 END LOOP;

 WHILE NOT EXISTS (SELECT *    -- pop the stack
                     FROM Personnel
                     WHERE boss = STACK_TOP (emp))
 LOOP
 UPDATE Stack
    SET rgt = counter + 1
  WHERE emp = STACK_TOP(emp);
 SET counter = counter + 1;
 END LOOP;

END LOOP;
END;
```

Graphs in SQL

THE TERMINOLOGY IN graph theory pretty much explains itself; if it does not, you can read some of the books suggested in the *Appendix: Readings and Resources*. Graphs are important because they are a general way to represent many different types of data and their relationships. Here is a quick review of terms.

A *graph* is a data structure made up of *nodes* connected by *edges*. Edges can be directed (permit travel in only one direction) or undirected (permit travel in both directions). The number of edges entering a node is its *indegree*; likewise, the number of edges leaving a node is its *outdegree*. A set of edges that allow you to travel from one node to another is called a *path*. A *cycle* is a path that comes back to the node from which it started without crossing itself (this means that a big *O* is fine but a figure 8 is not).

Recursively structured data relationships are either trees (hierarchies) or generalized directed graphs. A *tree* is a type of directed graph that is important enough to have its own terminology (see Chapters 28 and 29 on trees in SQL). Its special properties and frequent use have made it important enough to be covered in a separate chapter. The following section stresses other useful kinds of generalized directed graphs. Generalized directed graphs are classified into nonreconvergent and reconvergent graphs. In a reconvergent graph there are multiple paths between at least one pair of nodes. Reconvergent graphs are either cyclic or acyclic.

30.1 Two-Table Representation of a Graph

In the two-table representation of a graph, one table holds the nodes of the graph and the other table holds the edges. The edges are shown by their starting and ending nodes, which will be keys in the nodes table. The edge table might also contain other information about the relationships it represents. Let us begin with a two-table version of a parts explosion database:

```
CREATE TABLE Parts -- this holds the nodes, which are parts
(assemblyno CHAR(2) PRIMARY KEY,
 pname CHAR(10) NOT NULL,
 wgt INTEGER NOT NULL
      CONSTRAINT non_negative_wgt
      CHECK(wgt >= 0),
 color CHAR(6) NOT NULL);

CREATE TABLE Blueprint -- the edges; how parts are assembled
(assemblyno CHAR(2) NOT NULL,
 subassemblyno CHAR(2) NOT NULL,
 quantity INTEGER
         CONSTRAINT non_negative_qty
         CHECK(qty >= 0),
    PRIMARY KEY(assemblyno, subassemblyno),
    FOREIGN KEY assemblyno REFERENCES Parts(assemblyno),
    FOREIGN KEY subassemblyno REFERENCES Parts(assemblyno));
```

with the following data for constructing a frammis:

Parts

assemblyno	pname	wgt	color
'A1'	'frammis'	5	'Yellow'
'A2'	'gizmo'	6	Green'
'A3'	'cam'	7	'Red'
'A4'	'clip'	8	'Red'
'A5'	'gear'	9	'Yellow'
'A6'	'jack'	10	'Red'
'A7'	'nut'	11	'Yellow'
'A8'	'pin'	12	'Red'
'A9'	'plug'	13	'Green'

Blueprint

assemblyno	subassemblyno	qty
'A1'	'A2'	2
'A1'	'A3'	2
'A1'	'A4'	2
'A2'	'A5'	3
'A2'	'A6'	2
'A3'	'A6'	1
'A3'	'A7'	3
'A6'	'A8'	2
'A6'	'A9'	1

The relationships between the parts are shown in the Blueprint table, which simulates the traversal of a directed graph in which the Parts rows are the nodes and the Blueprint rows are the edges of the graph. We will assume that the normal direction of traversal is from assemblies to subassemblies. For example, the Blueprint row (A1, A2, 2) connects part A1 to part A2 and also carries the additional information that two units of A2 (i.e., two gizmos) go into making each A1 (frammis). Please remember that a special assumption has been made here. We are assuming that each assembly is a part in its own right and not just the result of putting together all of its components. That is why a gizmo (A2) needs to have gears (A5) and jacks (A6) added to it. Think of each nonleaf node in the graph as a holder for the parts subordinate to it, like a circuit board that needs chips to become complete. The data relationships are illustrated graphically in Figure 30.1. The graph is reconvergent because there are two paths connecting node A1 to any one of nodes A6, A8, and A9. For example, A1 and A6 are connected by a path that goes through A2 and another that goes through A3. The graph illustrates the hierarchical relationships between the various rows in the Parts table. For example, part A1 is made up of parts A2, A3, and A4. Part A2, in turn, is made up of parts A5 and A6. Part A3 is made up of parts A6 and A7. Notice that part A6 is a subcomponent of both part A2 and part A3. This is not a true tree structure, so it could not be represented by the single-table approaches used in Chapter 29 on trees.

30.2 Path Enumeration in a Graph

Reachability means finding all nodes that can be reached from one or more starting nodes. You have to assume that the graph can be traversed in only

Fig. 30.1

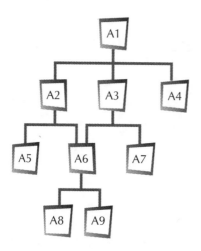

one direction, which in our case is from assemblies to subassemblies. Reachability can be found by first building a path enumeration table. This table has the start and end nodes of all possible paths in the graph. This is a generalization of the edge table, extended to hold paths. A cycle will have a row with the same value for the start and end nodes, but the pathlength will be greater than zero. In fact, one of the problems with a cycle is deciding when to stop going around it when enumerating it. This is one reason that this section does not deal with cycles and that they are not often used. At this point, you must decide whether you will include paths of length zero to represent the traversal from a node to itself. This can be handy for certain queries, since it means that the starting node will appear as a path of length zero when we are following paths that lead out of it. In other queries, however, you can find yourself with cycle problems. The program to build the path enumeration table can be implemented using any procedural language that has SQL access capabilities. Ideally, the language should support recursion, because this is generally helpful in implementing graph traversal algorithms. Here is a pseudocode program using SQL inside a simple 4GL language and with no recursion:

```
PROCEDURE BuildPathEnum
BEGIN
DECLARE pathlength, oldsize, newsize INTEGER NOT NULL;

-- start with an empty table, no primary key
CREATE TABLE PathEnum
```

```
(assemblyno CHAR(2) NOT NULL,
 subassemblyno CHAR(2) NOT NULL,
 pathlength INTEGER
            CONSTRAINT non_negative_pathlength
            CHECK(pathlength >= 0);

-- path of node to itself - this is optional and not used in the results
BEGIN ATOMIC
INSERT INTO PathEnum

SELECT DISTINCT subassemblyno, subassemblyno, 0
  FROM Blueprint;

-- load paths of length = 1 into table
INSERT INTO PathEnum

SELECT assemblyno, subassemblyno, 1
  FROM Blueprint;

-- insert rows only while table grows
SET oldsize = 0;

SET newsize = (SELECT COUNT(*) FROM PathEnum);

WHILE (oldsize < newsize)
LOOP
     INSERT INTO PathEnum

SELECT P1.assemblyno, B1.subassemblyno, (P1.pathlength + 1)
  FROM PathEnum AS P1, Blueprint AS B1
     -- advance existing paths by one level
  WHERE EXISTS (SELECT *
                FROM PathEnum AS P2
                WHERE B1.assemblyno = P2.subassemblyno)
     -- insert only new rows into table
    AND NOT EXISTS (SELECT *
                    FROM PathEnum AS P3
                    WHERE P1.assemblyno = P3.assemblyno
                    AND B1.subassemblyno = P3.subassemblyno);
     SET oldsize = newsize;
     SET newsize = (SELECT COUNT(*) FROM PathEnum)
     END LOOP;
END;
END;
```

The result is

PathEnum

assemblyno	subassemblyno	pathlength
'A1'	'A2'	1
'A1'	'A3'	1
'A1'	'A4'	1
'A1'	'A5'	2
'A1'	'A6'	2
'A1'	'A7'	2
'A1'	'A8'	3
'A1'	'A8'	3
'A1'	'A9'	3
'A1'	'A9'	3
'A2'	'A5'	1
'A2'	'A6'	1
'A2'	'A8'	2
'A2'	'A9'	2
'A3'	'A6'	1
'A3'	'A7'	1
'A3'	'A8'	2
'A3'	'A9'	2
'A6'	'A8'	1
'A6'	'A9'	1

The reachability query "Where can I get to from here?" is now simply

```
SELECT DISTINCT assemblyno, subassemblyno
  FROM PathEnum
 WHERE assemblyno = :startnode;
```

The path enumeration table should be indexed for efficiency. Notice that in our example we could index on columns (assemblyno), (sub-assemblyno), (assemblyno, subassemblyno), or (subassemblyno, assemblyno); the choice would be determined by the most common direction of traversal and the sort of reports needed. In some applications it might be worth the effort to keep the information that the pathlength from a node to itself is zero in the table. That can then force the node to show up in queries that start with it. Another approach is to develop a table of named

paths that run from the root to the leaf nodes, using a slight modification of
the procedural code. You have to capture the path identification number and
the position of the step along the path. The procedural code for doing this
will vary quite a bit from product to product and according to how well a
given product supports cursors, an SQL topic that is not discussed in this
book at all. Attach the weight and quantity to it since that information is useful for computing other functions. This will give us a table of simple paths
that has the path identification number, the step within the path, and the
start (assemblyno) and end (subassemblyno) of each step. Using this table,
we can build a complete path information table with a query like this:

```
CREATE TABLE Paths
(path INTEGER NOT NULL,   -- path id number
 step INTEGER NOT NULL,   -- step within the path
 assemblyno CHAR(2) NOT NULL,      -- assembly part number
 subassemblyno CHAR(2) NOT NULL,   -- subassembly part number
 wgt INTEGER NOT NULL,    -- weight of assembly
 subwgt INTEGER NOT NULL,  -- weight of subassembly
 qty INTEGER NOT NULL,    -- quantity of subassembly in assembly
 PRIMARY KEY (path, step));
```

The results should look like this:

Paths

path	step	assemblyno	subassemblyno	wgt	subwgt	qty
1	1	'A1'	'A2'	5	6	2
1	2	'A2'	'A5'	6	9	3
2	1	'A1'	'A2'	5	6	2
2	2	'A2'	'A6'	6	10	2
2	3	'A6'	'A8'	10	12	2
3	1	'A1'	'A2'	5	6	2
3	2	'A2'	'A6'	6	10	2
3	3	'A6'	'A9'	10	13	1
4	1	'A1'	'A3'	5	7	2
4	2	'A3'	'A6'	7	10	1
4	3	'A6'	'A8'	10	12	2
5	1	'A1'	'A3'	5	7	2
5	2	'A3'	'A6'	7	10	1
5	5	'A6'	'A9'	10	13	1

(cont.)	path	step	assemblyno	subassemblyno	wgt	subwgt	qty
	6	1	'A1'	'A3'	5	7	2
	6	2	'A3'	'A7'	7	11	3
	7	1	'A1'	'A4'	5	8	2

The reachability query is now more complex, but not bad. For node Y to be reachable from node X, they must be on the same path and Y must be "downhill" from X. The query is

```
SELECT P2.subassemblyno
  FROM Paths AS P1, Paths AS P2
 WHERE P1.assemblyno = :startnode
   AND P1.path = P2.path
   AND P1.step <= P2.step;
```

Though reachability became complex, finding all the paths that go through a given node regardless of their direction became very simple. (If the graph represented a transportation network instead of a parts explosion, this could be quite handy.) This query is

```
SELECT DISTINCT path
  FROM Paths
 WHERE assemblyno = :startnode
    OR subassemblyno = :startnode;
```

Using both the assemblyno and the subassemblyno is important. This will take care of both root and leaf node situations. In the example of A6, we would get the result set of paths (2 → 3 → 4 → 5). To find the paths that do not go through a particular node, use this query:

```
SELECT *
  FROM Paths AS P1
 WHERE NOT EXISTS (SELECT *
                     FROM Paths AS P2
                    WHERE (assemblyno = :startnode
                       OR subassemblyno = :startnode)
                      AND P1.path = P2.path);
```

These techniques have several obvious drawbacks. First, the path information tables require procedural code to construct. Second, the path information tables can be very large, depending on the sizes of the underlying base tables and the degree of reconvergence in the data relationships. Just compare the sizes of the sample tables to that of either the Parts or Blueprint table. Third, the tables represent a snapshot of the database at some particular point in time and have to be rebuilt procedurally whenever the underlying node and edge tables are changed, unlike a VIEW within the schema. In practice, this is not really a big problem, because such data often tends to be relatively static; you do not redesign organizational charts or manufactured products on a regular basis. If it is a problem, you can store procedural code that automatically repopulates the graph tables.

30.3 Path Aggregation in a Graph

Path aggregation in a tree attempts to "flatten out" the tree structure of a path enumeration to come up with totals for each subtree in the graph. The most common example for a parts explosion problem is finding the total weight or cost of an assembly when you know the weight of each part and how many of them are used in each of its subassemblies. The problem is that a subassembly may occur in several places in a reconvergent graph structure. This is particularly true for common parts, such as screws or connectors in mechanical assemblies. In our example, part A6 is a subassembly of both part A2 and part A3. So the total quantity of part A6 required to assemble part A1 must take into account the quantity of part A6 required to assemble both parts A2 and A3.

There is no straightforward way to handle a convergent graph in a table as there is in tree path enumeration. The best that can be done is to list the nodes reachable from a given start node, along with the aggregate function value associated with the node. The result of the query "What are the subparts of A1 and the total quantity of each in it?" is

Explosion

assemblyno	subassemblyno	qty	
'A1'	'A2'	2	
'A1'	'A3'	2	
'A1'	'A4'	2	
'A1'	'A5'	6	$= (2 * 3)$
'A1'	'A6'	4	$= (2 * 2)$
'A1'	'A7'	6	$= (2 * 3)$
'A1'	'A8'	12	$= (2 * 2 * 2) + (2 * 1 * 2)$
'A1'	'A9'	6	$= (1 * 2 * 2) + (1 * 1 * 2)$

What this table says is that an A1 part is made with two A2, two A3, and two A4 subassemblies. But in turn, each of the A2 assemblies uses three A5 subassemblies, which would give us a total of (2 * 3) or 6 A5s in the A1 unit. The problem becomes worse when we have to count the A8 and A9 parts, which are shared by more than one subassembly. This can be done with procedural code that uses the path and step columns to guide itself through the graph. However, the best technique seems to be to use node splitting, which we will discuss in the next section.

30.4 Node Splitting

An example of a path enumeration query where a portion of the resulting tree must be pruned is the following: "Show all subparts of part A1, excluding part A3 and its subcomponents." This query sounds as if we should prune the subtree rooted at node A3 with an SQL statement like this:

```
SELECT PE1.subassemblyno, SUM(qty)
  FROM PathEnum AS PE1, Blueprint AS B1
 WHERE PE1.assemblyno ='A1'  -- the final assembly
   AND subassemblyno
       NOT IN
       (SELECT subassemblyno
          FROM PathEnum AS PE2
         WHERE PE2.assemblyno ='A3'   -- root of subtree
           OR PE2.subassemblyno ='A3')
          AND B1.subassemblyno = PE1.subassemblyno  -- JOIN gets qty
GROUP BY PE1.assemblyno, PE1.subassemblyno;
```

However, this will work only for a tree and not for a convergent graph. Our query would first construct a subquery result table like this:

Subquery results

assemblyno	subassemblyno	pathlength
'A3'	'A6'	1
'A3'	'A7'	1
'A3'	'A8'	2
'A3'	'A9'	2
'A1'	'A3'	1

which would then reduce to

```
SELECT PE1.assemblyno, PE1.subassemblyno, SUM(qty)
  FROM PathEnum AS PE1
 WHERE assemblyno = 'A1'  -- the final assembly
   AND subassemblyno NOT IN ('A3', 'A6', 'A7', 'A8', 'A9')
 GROUP BY PE1.assemblyno, PE1.subassemblyno;
```

This in turn reduces, before JOINing and GROUPing, to

PE1 Result

assemblyno	subassemblyno	pathlength
'A1'	'A2'	1
'A1'	'A4'	1
'A1'	'A5'	2

The reconvergent nature of this graph means that our query also removed A6 from under A2 as well as from under A3. This would have worked fine with a tree, but it is not what we wanted. To support these kinds of queries in a graph, we must change the path enumeration table to differentiate among the paths that connect two nodes. That is why there are duplicate rows— (A1, A9), (A1, A8), and (A1, A6)—in the PathEnum table.

One trick is to duplicate (or split) the nodes to convert the convergent graph into a tree. The nodes that need splitting are those that have an indegree greater than 1; they can be found with this query:

```
SELECT subassemblyno, COUNT(*)
  FROM Blueprint
 GROUP BY subassemblyno
HAVING COUNT(*) > 1;
```

In the example graph, we will get A6, with a count of 2. Using a mix of SQL and procedural code, update the two rows with A6 as their subassembly with two new subassemblies; call them A6a and A6b, which are subordinate to A2 and A3, respectively.

And they both link to A8 and to A9. Oops, that makes nodes A8 and A9 convergent because they now have indegree 2, and the same process has to be done again until the graph is a tree. As you can see, the tree that is developed this way can get fairly big and have a lot of synonyms for common parts in it.

Blueprint with split node A6

subassemblyno	qty	left	right
'A1'	1	1	24
'A2'	2	2	11
'A3'	2	12	21
'A4'	2	22	23
'A5'	3	3	4
'A6a'	2	5	10
'A6b'	1	13	18
'A7'	3	19	20
'A8a'	2	6	7
'A8b'	2	14	15
'A9a'	1	8	9
'A9b'	1	16	17

Optimizing Code

THERE IS NO set of rules for writing code that will take the best advantage of every query optimizer. The query optimizers are simply too different for universal rules; however, we can make some general statements. What would improve performance in one SQL implementation might not do anything at all in another—or could even make performance worse.

There are two kinds of optimizers: *rule-based* and *cost-based*. A rule-based optimizer looks at the syntax of the query and plans how to execute without any consideration of the size of the tables or the statistical distribution of the data. A rule-based optimizer (such as Oracle before Version 7.0) will parse a query and execute it in the order in which it was written, perhaps doing some reorganization of the query into an equivalent form using some syntax rules. Basically, it is no optimizer at all.

A cost-based optimizer looks at both the query and the statistical data about the database itself and decides on the best way to execute the query. These decisions involve whether to use indexes, whether to use hashing, which tables to bring into main storage, what sorting technique to use, and so forth. Most of the time (but not all!), it will make better decisions than a human programmer would have simply because it has more information. Ingres has one of the best optimizers, which extensively reorders a query before executing it. It is one of the few products that can find most semantically identical queries and reduce them to the same internal form. Rdb, from Oracle, uses a searching method (taken from an AI [artificial intelligence] game-playing program) to inspect the costs of several different approaches before making a decision. DB2 has a system table with a statistical profile of the base tables. In short, no two products use exactly the same optimization techniques.

The fact that each SQL engine uses a different internal storage scheme and access methods for its data makes some optimizations nonportable. Likewise, some optimizations depend on the hardware configuration, and a technique that was excellent for one product on one hardware configuration could be a disaster in another product or on another hardware configuration.

31.1 Access Methods

For this discussion, let us assume that there are four basic methods of getting to data: table scans or sequential reads of all the rows in the table, access via some kind of index, hashing, and bit vector indexes.

31.1.1 Sequential Access

The table scan is a sequential read of all the data in the order in which it appears in physical storage, grabbing one page of memory at a time. Most databases do not physically remove deleted rows, so a table can use a lot of physical space and yet hold little data. Depending on just how dynamic the database is, you may want to run a utility program to reclaim storage and compress the database. The performance can suddenly improve drastically after a database reorganization.

31.1.2 Indexed Access

Indexed access returns one row at a time. The index is probably going to be a B tree of some sort, but it could be a hashed index, inverted file structures, or other format. Obviously, if you don't have an index on a table, then you cannot use indexed access on it.

An index can be clustered or unclustered. A clustered index is in the same order as the physical storage. Obviously, there can be only one clustered index on a table. Clustered indexes keep the table in sorted order, so a table scan will often produce results in that order. A clustered index will also tend to put duplicates of the indexed column values on the same page of physical memory, which may speed up access.

31.1.3 Hashed Indexes

A hashed index divides the data into "buckets" that have the same hashing value. If the index is on a unique column, the ideal situation is what is called a *minimal perfect hashing function*—every value hashes to one physical storage address and there are no empty spaces. The next best situation for a unique column is what is called a *perfect hashing function*—every value hashes to one physical storage address, but there are some empty spaces in the physical storage.

A hashing function for a nonunique column should hash to a bucket small enough to fit into main storage.

31.1.4 Bit Vector Indexes

The fact that a particular occurrence of an entity has a particular value for a particular attribute is represented as a single bit in a vector or array. These techniques are very fast for large amounts of data and are used by the Nucleus database engine from Sand Technology and Foxpro's Rushmore indexes.

31.2 Expressions and Unnested Queries

Although this book is devoted to fancy queries and programming tricks, the truth is that most real work is done with very simple logic. The better the design of the database schema, the easier the queries will be to write.

Here are some tips for keeping your queries as simple as possible. Like all general statements, these tips will not be valid for all products in all situations, but they are how the smart money bets.

31.2.1 Use Simple Expressions

Where possible, avoid JOIN conditions in favor of simple search arguments, called SARGs in the jargon. For example, let's match up students with rides back to Atlanta.

```
SELECT *
  FROM Students AS S1, Rides AS R1
 WHERE S1.town = R1.town
   AND S1.town = 'Atlanta';
```

Clearly, a little algebra shows you that this is true:

```
SELECT *
  FROM Students AS S1, Rides AS R1
 WHERE R1.town = 'Atlanta'
   AND S1.town = 'Atlanta';
```

However, the second version will guarantee that the two tables involved will be projected to the smallest size, then the CROSS JOIN will be done. Since each of these projections should be fairly small, the JOIN will not be expensive.

Assume that there are 10 students out of 100 going to Atlanta and 5 people offering rides to Atlanta out of 100. If the JOIN is done first, you would have (100 * 100) = 10,000 rows in the CROSS JOIN to prune with the predicates. This is why no product does the CROSS JOIN first. Instead, many products would do the (S1.town = 'Atlanta') predicate first and get a working table of 10 rows to join to the Rides table, which would give us (10 * 100) = 1,000 rows for the CROSS JOIN to prune. But in the second version, we would have a working table of 10 students and another working table of 5 rides to CROSS JOIN, or merely (5 * 10) rows in the result set.

Another rule of thumb is that given a chain of ANDed predicates that test for constant values, put the most restrictive ones first. For example,

```
SELECT *
  FROM Students
 WHERE sex = 'female'
   AND grade = 'A';
```

This will probably run slower than:

```
SELECT *
  FROM Students
 WHERE grade = 'A'
   AND sex = 'female';
```

because there are fewer 'A' students than the number of female students. There are several ways that this query can be executed:

1. Assuming an index on grades, fetch a row from the Students table where grade = 'A'; if sex = 'female' then put it into the final results. The index on grades is called the driving index of the loop thorough the Students table.

2. Assuming an index on sex, fetch a row from the Students table where sex = 'female'; if grade = 'A' then put it into the final

results. The index on sex is now the driving index of the loop through the Students table.

3.   Assuming indexing on both grades and sex, scan the index on sex and put pointers to the rows where sex = 'female' into results working file R1. Scan the index on grades and put pointers to the rows where grade = 'A' into results file R2. Sort and merge R1 and R2, keeping the pointers that appear twice. Use this result to fetch the rows into the final result. If the hardware can support parallel access, this can be quite fast.

Another application of the same principle is a trick with predicates that involve two columns to force the choice of the index that will be used. Place the table with the smallest number of rows last in the FROM clause and the expression that uses that table first in the WHERE clause. For example, consider two tables, one for orders and one that translates a code number into English, each with an index on the JOIN column:

```
SELECT *
  FROM Orders AS O1, Codes AS C1
 WHERE C1.code = O1.code;
```

where the Codes table is noticeably smaller than the Orders table. This query will probably use a strategy of merging the index values. However, if you add a dummy expression, you can force a loop over the index on the smaller table. For example assume that all the order type codes are greater than or equal to '00' in our code translation example, so that the first predicate of this query is always TRUE:

```
SELECT *
  FROM Orders AS O1, Codes AS C1
 WHERE O1.ordertype >= '00'
   AND C1.somecode = O1.ordertype;
```

The dummy predicate will force the SQL engine to use an index on Orders. This same trick can also be used to force the sorting in an ORDER BY clause to be done with an index.

Since SQL is not a computational language, implementations do not tend to do even simple algebra:

```
SELECT *
  FROM Sales
 WHERE quantity = 500 + 1/2;
```

is the same thing as quantity = 500.50, but some dynamic SQL products will take a little extra time to compute and add a half as they check each row of the Sales table. The extra time adds up when the expression involves complex math and/or type conversions. However, this can have another effect that we will discuss in Section 31.11 on expressions that contain indexed columns.

The <> comparison has some unique problems. Most optimizers assume that this comparison will return more rows than it rejects, so they prefer a sequential scan and will not use an index on a column involved in such a comparison. This is not always true, however. For example, to find someone in Ireland who is not a Catholic, you would normally write

```
SELECT *
  FROM Ireland
 WHERE religion <> 'Catholic';
```

The way around this is to break up the inequality:

```
SELECT *
  FROM Ireland
 WHERE religion < 'Catholic'
    OR religion > 'Catholic';
```

and force the use of an index. However, without an index on religion, the ORed version of the predicate could take longer to run.

Another trick is to avoid the x IS NOT NULL predicate and use x >= <minimal constant> instead. The NULLs are kept in different ways in different implementations, but almost never in the same physical storage area as their columns. As a result, the SQL engine has to do extra searching. For example, if we have a CHAR(3) column that holds a NULL or three letters, we could look for missing data with

```
SELECT *
  FROM Sales
 WHERE alphacode IS NOT NULL;
```

but it would be better written as

```
SELECT *
  FROM Sales
 WHERE alphacode >= 'AAA';
```

because this avoids the extra reads.

Another trick that will often work is to use an index to get a COUNT() since the index itself may have the number of rows already worked out. For example,

```
SELECT COUNT(*)
  FROM Sales;
```

might not be as fast as

```
SELECT COUNT(sale_id)
  FROM Sales;
```

where sale_id is the PRIMARY KEY (or any other unique non-NULL column) of the Sales table. Being the PRIMARY KEY means that there is a unique index on sale_id. A smart optimizer knows to look for indexed columns automatically when it sees a COUNT(*), but it is worth testing on your product.

31.2.2 String Expressions

Likewise, string expressions can be recalculated each time. A particular problem for strings is that the optimizer will often stop at the '%' or '_' in the pattern of a LIKE predicate, so that it does not have a string it can use with an index. For example, consider this table with a fixed-length CHAR(5) column:

```
SELECT *
  FROM Students
 WHERE homeroom LIKE 'A-1__'; -- two underscores in pattern
```

It may or may not use an index on the homeroom column. However, if we know that the last two positions are always numerals, then we can replace this query with

```
SELECT *
  FROM Students
 WHERE homeroom BETWEEN 'A-100' AND 'A-199';
```

This query can use an index on the homeroom column. Notice that this trick assumes that the homeroom column is CHAR(5), and not a VARCHAR(5) column. If it were VARCHAR(5), then the second query would pick 'A-1' while the original LIKE predicate would not. String equality and BETWEEN predicates pad the shorter string with blanks on the right before comparing them; the LIKE predicate does not pad either the string or the pattern.

31.3 Give Extra JOIN Information in Queries

Optimizers are not always able to draw conclusions that a human being can draw. The more information contained in the query, the better the chance that the optimizer will be able to find an improved execution plan. For example, to JOIN three tables together on a common column, you might write

```
SELECT *
  FROM Table1, Table2, Table3
 WHERE Table2.common = Table3.common
   AND Table3.common = Table1.common;
```

or, alternately,

```
SELECT *
  FROM Table1, Table2, Table3
 WHERE Table1.common = Table2.common
   AND Table1.common = Table3.common;
```

Some optimizers will JOIN pairs of tables based on the equi-JOIN conditions in the WHERE clause in the order in which they appear. Let us assume that Table1 is a very small table and that Table2 and Table3 are large. In the first query, doing the Table2–Table3 JOIN first will return a large result set, which is then pruned by the Table1–Table3 JOIN. In the second query, doing the Table1–Table2 JOIN first will return a small result set, which is then matched to the small Table1–Table3 JOIN result set.

The best bet, however, is to provide all the information so that the optimizer can decide for itself when the table sizes change. This leads to redundancy in the WHERE clause:

```
SELECT *
  FROM Table1, Table2, Table3
 WHERE Table1.common = Table2.common
   AND Table2.common = Table3.common
   AND Table3.common = Table1.common;
```

Do not confuse this redundancy with needless logical expressions that will be recalculated and can be expensive. For example,

```
SELECT *
  FROM Sales
 WHERE alphacode BETWEEN 'AAA' AND 'ZZZ'
   AND alphacode LIKE 'A_C';
```

will redo the BETWEEN predicate for every row. It does not provide any information that can be used for a JOIN, and, clearly, if the LIKE predicate is TRUE, then the BETWEEN predicate also has to be TRUE.

A final tip that does not always work with every product is to order the tables with the fewest rows in the result set last in the FROM clause. This is helpful because as the number of tables increases, many optimizers do not try all the combinations of possible JOIN orderings; the number of combinations is factorial. Instead the optimizer falls back on the order in the FROM clause.

31.4 Index Tables Carefully

You should create indexes on the tables of your database to optimize query search time, but do not create any more indexes than you absolutely need. Indexes have to be updated and possibly reorganized when you INSERT, UPDATE, or DELETE rows in a table. Too many indexes can result in extra time spent tending indexes that are seldom used. But even worse, the presence of an index can fool the optimizer into using it when it should not. For example, given the simple query

```
SELECT *
  FROM Warehouse
 WHERE quantity = 500
   AND color = 'Purply Green';
```

with an index on color, but not on quantity, most optimizers will first search for rows with color = 'Purply Green' via the index, then apply the quantity = 500 test. However, if you were to add an index on quantity, the optimizer would likely take the tests in order, doing the quantity test first. I assume that very few items are 'Purply Green', so it would have been better to test for color first. A smart optimizer with detailed statistics would do this right, but to play it safe, order the predicates from the most restricting (i.e., the smallest number of qualifying rows in the final result) to the least.

You might also remember that an index will not be used if the column is in an expression. If you want to avoid an index, then put the column in a "do nothing" expression, such as

```
SELECT *
  FROM Warehouse
 WHERE quantity = 500 + 0
   AND color = 'Purply Green';
```

or

```
SELECT *
  FROM Warehouse
 WHERE quantity + 0 = 500
   AND color = 'Purply Green';
```

This will stop the optimizer from using an index on quantity. Likewise, the epxression (`color || '' = 'Purply Green'`) will avoid the index on color.

Consider an actual example of indexes making trouble, in a database for a small club membership list that was indexed on the members' names as the `PRIMARY KEY`. There was a column in the table that had one of five status codes (paid member, free membership, expired, exchange newsletter, and miscellaneous). The report query on the number of people by status was

```
SELECT M1.status, C1.codetext, COUNT(*)
  FROM Members AS M1, Codes AS C1
 WHERE M1.status = C1.status
 GROUP BY M1.status, C1.codetext;
```

In a PC SQL database product, it ran an order of magnitude slower with an index on the status column than without one. The optimizer saw the index on the Members table and used it to search for each status code text. Without the index, the much smaller Codes table was brought into main storage and five buckets were set up for the `COUNT(*)`; then the Members table was read once in sequence.

An index that is used to ensure uniqueness on a column or set of columns is called a *primary index*; those used to speed up queries on nonunique column(s) are called *secondary*. SQL implementations automatically create a primary index on a `PRIMARY KEY` or `UNIQUE` constraint. Implementations may or may not create indexes that link `FOREIGN KEYs` within the table to their targets in the referenced table. This link can be very important since a lot of `JOINs` are done from `FOREIGN KEY` to `PRIMARY KEY`.

You also need to know something about the queries to run against the schema. Obviously, if all queries are asked on only one column, that is all you need to index. The query information is usually given as a statistical model of the expected inputs. For example, you might be told that 80% of the queries will use the PRIMARY KEY and 20% will use another column, picked at random. This is pretty much what you would know in a real-world situation, since most of the accesses will be done by production programs with embedded SQL in them, and only a small percentage will be ad hoc queries.

Without giving you a computer science lecture, a computer problem is called NP-complete if it gets so big, so fast, that it is not practical to solve it for a reasonable-sized set of input values. Usually this means that you have to try all possible combinations to find the answer. Finding the optimal indexing arrangement is known to be NP-complete (Comer 1978; Paitetsky-Shapiro 1983). This does not mean that you cannot optimize indexing for a particular database schema and set of input queries, but it does mean that you cannot write a program that will do it for all possible relational databases and query sets.

31.5 Watch the IN Predicate

The IN predicate is really shorthand for a series of ORed equality tests. There are two forms: either an explicit list of values is given or a subquery is used to make such a list of values.

The database engine has no statistics about the relative frequency of the values in a list of constants, so it will assume that the list is in the order in which the values are to be used. People like to order lists alphabetically or by magnitude, but it would be better to order the list from most frequently occurring values to least frequent. It is also pointless to have duplicate values in the constant list, since the predicate will return TRUE if it matches the first duplicate it finds and will never get to the second occurrence. Likewise, if the predicate is FALSE for that value, the program wastes computer time traversing a needlessly long list.

Many SQL engines perform an IN predicate with a subquery by building the result set of the subquery first as a temporary working table, then scanning that result table from left to right. This can be expensive in many cases; for example,

```
SELECT P1.*
  FROM Personnel AS P1, BowlingTeam AS B1
 WHERE P1.lastname IN (SELECT lastname
                         FROM BowlingTeam AS B1
                        WHERE P1.emp_nbr = B1.emp_nbr)
   AND P1.firstname IN (SELECT firstname
```

```
             FROM BowlingTeam AS B2
            WHERE P1.emp_nbr = B2.emp_nbr);
```

will not run as fast as

```
SELECT *
  FROM Personnel AS P1
 WHERE firstname || lastname IN
        (SELECT firstname || lastname
          FROM BowlingTeam AS B1
         WHERE P1.emp_nbr = B1.emp_nbr);
```

which can be further simplified to

```
SELECT *
  FROM Personnel AS P1
 WHERE firstname || lastname IN
        (SELECT firstname || lastname
           FROM BowlingTeam);
```

since there can be only one row with a complete name in it.

The first version of the query may make two passes through the Bowling Team table to construct two separate result tables. The second version makes only one pass to construct the concatenation of the names in its result table.

The optimizer is supposed to figure out when two queries are the same and will not be fooled by two queries with the same meaning and different syntax. For example, the SQL standard defines

```
SELECT *
  FROM Warehouse AS W1
 WHERE quantity IN (SELECT quantity FROM Sales);
```

as identical to

```
SELECT *
  FROM Warehouse
 WHERE quantity = ANY (SELECT quantity FROM Sales);
```

but you will find that some SQL engines prefer the first version to the second because they do not convert the expressions into a common internal form. Very often, things like the choice of operators and their order make a large performance difference. The first query can be converted to this "flattened" JOIN query:

```
SELECT W1.*
  FROM Warehouse AS W1, Sales AS S1
 WHERE W1.quantity = S1.quantity;
```

This form will often be faster if there are indexes to help with the JOIN.

31.6 Avoid UNIONs

Unions are often done by constructing the two result sets, then merge-sorting them together. The optimizer works only within a single SELECT statement or subquery. For example,

```
SELECT *
  FROM Personnel
 WHERE work = 'New York'
UNION
SELECT *
  FROM Personnel
 WHERE home = 'Chicago';
```

is the same as

```
SELECT DISTINCT *
  FROM Personnel
 WHERE work = 'New York'
    OR home = 'Chicago';
```

which will run faster.

Another trick is to use UNION ALL in place of UNION whenever duplicates are not a problem. A UNION ALL is implemented as an append operation without the need for a sort to aid duplicate removal.

31.7 Prefer JOINs over Nested Queries

A nested query is hard to optimize. Optimizers try to "flatten" nested queries so that they can be expressed as JOINs and the best order of execution can be determined. Consider the database

```
CREATE TABLE Authors
(authorno INTEGER NOT NULL PRIMARY KEY,
 authorname CHAR(50) NOT NULL);
```

```
CREATE TABLE Titles
(bookno INTEGER NOT NULL PRIMARY KEY,
 title CHAR(50) NOT NULL,
 advance DECIMAL (8,2) NOT NULL);

CREATE TABLE TitleAuthors
(authorno INTEGER NOT NULL REFERENCES Authors(authorno),
 bookno INTEGER NOT NULL REFERENCES Titles(bookno),
 royalty DECIMAL (5,4) NOT NULL,
 PRIMARY KEY (authorno, bookno));
```

This query finds authors who are getting less than 50% royalties:

```
SELECT authorno
  FROM Authors
 WHERE authorno IN
        (SELECT authorno
           FROM TitleAuthors
          WHERE royalty < 0.50)
```

which could also be expressed as

```
SELECT DISTINCT Author.authorno
  FROM Authors, TitleAuthors
 WHERE (Authors.authorno = TitleAuthors.authorno)
    AND (royalty < 0.50);
```

The SELECT DISTINCT is important. Each author's name will occur only once in the Authors table. Therefore, the IN predicate query should return one occurrence of O'Leary. Assume that O'Leary wrote two books; with just a SELECT, the second query would return two O'Leary rows, one for each book.

31.8 Avoid Expressions on Indexed Columns

If a column appears in a mathematical or string expression, its indexes cannot be used by the optimizer. For example, given a table of tasks and their start and finish dates, to find the tasks that took three days to complete in 1994, we could write

```
SELECT taskno
  FROM Tasks
 WHERE (finish - start) = 3
   AND start >= DATE '1994-01-01';
```

But since most of the reports deal with the finish dates, we have an index on that column.

This means that the query will run faster if it is rewritten as

```
SELECT taskno
  FROM Tasks
 WHERE finish = (start + 3)
   AND start >= DATE '1994-01-01';
```

This same principle applies to columns in string functions and, very often, to LIKE predicates.

However, this can be a good thing for queries with small tables since it will force those tables to be loaded into main storage instead of being searched by an index.

31.9 Avoid Sorting

The SELECT DISTINCT, UNION, INTERSECT, and EXCEPT clauses can do sorts to remove duplicates; the exception is when an index exists that can be used to eliminate the duplicates without sorting. The GROUP BY often uses a sort to cluster groups together, do the aggregate functions, and then reduce each group to a single row, based on duplicates in the grouping columns. Each sort will cost you $(n*\log2(n))$ operations, which is a lot of extra computer time that you can save if you do not need to use these clauses.

If a SELECT DISTINCT clause includes a set of key columns in it, then all the rows are already known to be unique. Since SQL-92 now has the ability to declare a set of columns to be a PRIMARY KEY in the table declaration, an optimizer can spot such a query and automatically change SELECT DISTINCT to just SELECT. However, SQL-89 implementations do not have this advantage, and it is up to the programmer to do the optimization by hand.

You can often replace a SELECT DISTINCT clause with an EXISTS subquery, in violation of another rule of thumb that says to prefer unnested queries to nested queries.

For example, a query to find the students who are majoring in the sciences would be

```
SELECT DISTINCT S1.name
  FROM Students AS S1, ScienceDepts AS D1
 WHERE S1.dept = D1.dept;
```

This can be replaced with a better query

```
SELECT S1.name
  FROM Students AS S1
 WHERE EXISTS (SELECT *
                 FROM ScienceDepts AS D1
                WHERE S1.dept = D1.dept);
```

Another problem is that the DBA might not declare all candidate keys or might declare superkeys instead. Consider a table for a school schedule:

```
CREATE TABLE Schedule
(room INTEGER NOT NULL,
 course CHAR(7) NOT NULL,
 teacher CHAR(20) NOT NULL,
    period INTEGER NOT NULL,
 PRIMARY KEY (room, period));
```

This says that if I know the room and the period, I can find a unique teacher and course—"Third-period Freshman English in Room 101 is taught by Ms. Jones." However, I might have also added the constraint UNIQUE (teacher, period) since Ms. Jones can be in only one room and teach only one class during a given period. If the table was not declared with this extra constraint, the optimizer could not use it in parsing a query. Likewise, if the DBA decided to declare PRIMARY KEY (room, course, teacher, period), the optimizer could not break down this superkey into candidate keys and optimize SELECT DISTINCT teacher, period FROM Schedule; by removing DISTINCT.

Avoid using a HAVING or a GROUP BY clause if the SELECT or WHERE clause can do all the needed work. One way to avoid grouping is in situations where you know the group criterion in advance and make it a constant. This example is a bit extreme, but you can convert

```
SELECT project, AVG(cost)
  FROM Tasks
 GROUP BY project
HAVING project = 'bricklaying';
```

to the simpler and faster

```
SELECT 'bricklaying', AVG(cost)
  FROM Tasks
 WHERE project = 'bricklaying';
```

Both queries have to scan the entire table to inspect values in the project column. The first query will simply throw each row into a bucket based on its project code, then look at the HAVING clause to throw away all but one of the buckets before computing the average. The second query rejects those unneeded rows and arrives at one subset of projects when it scans.

SQL-92 has ways of removing GROUP BY clauses that SQL-89 did not because it can use a subquery in a SELECT statement. This is easier to show with an example in which you are now in charge of the Widget-Only Company inventory. You get requisitions that tell how many widgets people are putting into or taking out of the warehouse on a given date. Sometimes that quantity is positive (returns); sometimes it is negative (withdrawals).

The table of requisitions looks like this:

```
CREATE TABLE Requisitions
(reqdate DATE NOT NULL,
 qty INTEGER NOT NULL
    CONSTRAINT non_zero_qty
    CHECK (qty <> 0));
```

Your job is to provide a running balance of the quantity on hand with a query. We want something like

RESULT

reqdate	qty	qty_on_hand
'1994-07-01'	100	100
'1994-07-02'	120	220
'1994-07-03'	−150	70
'1994-07-04'	50	120
'1994-07-05'	−35	85

The classic SQL-89 solution would be

```
SELECT R1.reqdate, R1.qty, SUM(R2.qty) AS qty_on_hand
  FROM Requisitions AS R1, Requisitions AS R2
 WHERE R2.reqdate <= R1.reqdate
 GROUP BY R1.reqdate, R1.qty;
```

SQL-92 can use a subquery in the SELECT list, even a correlated query. The rule is that the result must be a single value, hence the name *scalar subquery*; if the query results are an empty table, the result is a NULL.

In this problem, we need to do a summation of all the requisitions posted up to and including the date we are looking at. The query is a nested self-JOIN:

```
SELECT R1.reqdate, R1.qty,
     (SELECT SUM(R2.qty)
        FROM Requisitions AS R2
        WHERE R2.reqdate <= R1.reqdate) AS qty_on_hand
  FROM Requisitions AS R1
 ORDER BY R1.reqdate, R1.qty;
```

Frankly, both solutions will run slowly compared to a procedural solution that could build the current quantity on hand from the previous quantity on hand from a sorted file of records. Both queries must build the subquery from the self-JOINed table based on dates. However, the first query will also probably sort rows for each group it has to build. The earliest date will have one row to sort, the second earliest date will have two rows, and so forth, until the most recent date will sort all the rows. The second query has no grouping, so it just proceeds to the summation without the sorting.

31.10 Avoid CROSS JOINs

It is much easier to avoid unintentional CROSS JOINs in SQL-92 than in the older SQL-89 standard. Consider a three-table JOIN in SQL-89:

```
SELECT P1.color
  FROM Paints AS P1, Warehouse AS W1, Sales AS S1
 WHERE W1.quantity + S1.quantity =
       P1.gallons/2.5;
```

Because all of the columns involved in the JOIN are in a single expression, their indexes cannot be used. The SQL engine will construct the CROSS JOIN of all three tables first, then prune that temporary working table to get the final answer. In SQL-92, you can first do a subquery with a CROSS JOIN to get one side of the equation:

```
(SELECT (W1.quantity + S1.quantity) AS stuff
   FROM Warehouse AS W1 CROSS JOIN Sales AS S1)
```

and push it into the WHERE clause, like this:

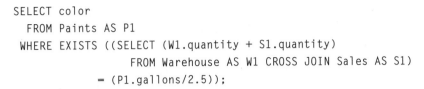

```
SELECT color
  FROM Paints AS P1
 WHERE EXISTS ((SELECT (W1.quantity + S1.quantity)
                  FROM Warehouse AS W1 CROSS JOIN Sales AS S1)
               = (P1.gallons/2.5));
```

The SQL engine, we hope, will do the two-table CROSS JOIN subquery and put the results into a temporary table. That temporary table will then be filtered using the Paints table, but without generating a three-table CROSS JOIN as the first form of the query did. With a little algebra, the original equation can be changed around and different versions of this query built with other combinations of tables.

A good rule of thumb is that the FROM clause should have only those tables that provide columns to its matching SELECT clause.

31.11 Learn to Use Indexes Carefully

To review: Most indexes are tree structures and consist of a page or node that has values, from the columns of the table from which the index is built, and pointers. The pointers point to other nodes of the tree and eventually point to rows in the table that has been indexed. The idea is that searching the index is much faster than searching the table itself in a sequential fashion (called a *table scan*).

The index is also ordered on the columns used to construct it; the rows of the table may or may not be in that order. When the index and the table are sorted on the same columns, the index is called a *clustered index*. The best example of this in the physical world is a large dictionary with a thumb-notch index—the index and the words in the dictionary are both in alphabetical order.

For obvious physical reasons, you can use only one clustered index on a table. The decision as to which columns to use in the index can be important to performance. There is a superstition among older DBAs who have worked with ISAM files and network and hierarchical databases that the primary key must be done with a clustered index. This stems from the fact that in the older file systems, files had to be sorted or hashed on their keys. All searching and navigation was based on this.

This is not true in SQL systems. The primary key's uniqueness will probably be preserved by a unique index, but it does not have to be a clustered unique index. Consider a table of employees keyed by a unique employee identification number. Updates are done with the employee ID number, of course, but very few queries use it. Updating individual rows in a table will actually be about as fast with a clustered or a nonclustered index. Both tree structures will be the same, except for the final physical position to which they point.

However, it might be that the most important corporate unit for reporting purposes is the department, not the employee. A clustered index on the employee ID number would sort the table in order of employee ID numbers. There is no inherent meaning in the ID number ordering; in fact, I would be more likely to sort a list of employees by their last names than by their ID numbers. However, a clustered index on the (nonunique) department code would sort the table in department order and put employees in the same department on the same physical page of storage. The result would be that fewer pages would have to be read to answer queries.

31.12 Order Indexes Carefully

Consider the Employees table again. There may be a difference among these CREATE INDEX statements:

1. ```
   CREATE INDEX XDeptDiv
   ON Employees (dept, division):
   ```

2. ```
   CREATE INDEX XDivDept
   ON Employees (division, dept);
   ```

3. ```
   CREATE CLUSTERED INDEX XCDeptDiv
   ON Employees (dept, division);
   ```

4. ```
   CREATE CLUSTERED INDEX XCDivDept
   ON Employees (division, dept);
   ```

In cases 1 and 2, some products build an index only on the first column and ignore the second column. This is because their SQL engine is based on an older product that allows only single-column indexing, and the parser is throwing out the columns it cannot handle. Other products use the first column to build the index tree structure and the secondary columns in such a way that they are searched much more slowly. Both types of SQL engine are like an alphabetic accordion file. Each pocket of an accordion file locates a letter of the alphabet, but within each pocket you have to do a manual search for a particular paper.

If your implementation suffers from this problem, the best thing to do is to order the columns by their granularity; that is, put the column with the most values first and the column with the fewest values last. In our example, assume that we have a few divisions located in major cities, and within each division we have lots of departments. An indexed search that stops at the division will leave us with a scan over the many departments. An indexed search that stops at the department will leave us with a scan over the few divisions.

In some products, you may find that the order will not matter or that separate, nonunique indexes will do as well as or better than a unique compound index. The reason is that they use hashing or bit-map indexes. Foxpro and Nucleus are two examples of products that use different bit-map schemes, but they have some basic features in common. Imagine an array with table row numbers or pointers on its columns and values for that column on its rows.

If a table row has that value in that position, then the bit is set; if not, the bit is zeroed. A search is done by doing bitwise ANDs, ORs, and NOTs on the bit vectors.

This might be easier to explain with an example of the technique. Assume we have a table of Parts, which has columns for the attributes color and weight.

Parts

pno	pname	color	weight	city	
p1	Nut	Red	12	London	-- Physical row # 3
p2	Bolt	Green	17	Paris	-- Physical row # 4
p3	Cam	Blue	12	Paris	-- Physical row # 7
p4	Screw	Red	14	London	-- Physical row # 9
p5	Cam	Blue	12	Paris	-- Physical row # 11
p6	Cog	Red	19	London	-- Physical row # 10

The bit indexes are built by using the physical row and the values of the attributes in an array:

INDEX Parts(color)

Rows	1	2	3	4	5	6	7	8	9	10	11
Blue	0	0	0	0	0	0	1	0	0	0	1
Green	0	0	0	1	0	0	0	0	0	0	0
Red	0	0	1	0	0	0	0	0	1	1	0

INDEX Parts(weight)

Rows	1	2	3	4	5	6	7	8	9	10	11
12	0	0	1	0	0	0	1	0	0	0	1
17	0	0	0	1	0	0	0	0	0	0	0
14	0	0	0	0	0	0	0	0	1	0	0
19	0	0	0	0	0	0	0	0	0	1	0

To find a part that weighs 12 units and is red, you would perform a bitwise AND and get a new bit vector as the answer:

Red	0	0	1	0	0	0	0	0	1	1	0

AND

12	0	0	1	0	0	0	1	0	0	0	1
answer	0	0	1	0	0	0	0	0	0	0	0

To find a part that weighs 12 units or is colored red, you would perform a bitwise OR and get a new bit vector as the answer:

Red	0	0	1	0	0	0	0	0	1	1	0

OR

12	0	0	1	0	0	0	1	0	0	0	1
answer	0	0	1	0	0	0	1	0	1	1	0

Searches become a combination of bitwise operators on the indexes before any physical access to the table is done.

31.13 Recompile Static SQL after Schema Changes

In most implementations, static SQL is compiled in a host program with a fixed execution plan. If a database schema object is altered, execution plans based on that object have to be changed. In the old SQL-89 standard, if a schema object was dropped, the programmer had to recompile the queries that referred to it. The SQL engine was not required to do any checking and most implementations did not. Instead, you could get a runtime error. Even worse, you could have a scenario like this:

1. Create table A.

2.   Create view VA on table A

3.   Use view VA.

4.   Drop table A.

5.   Create a new table A.

6.   Use view VA.

What happens in step 6? That depended on your SQL product, but the results were not good. The worst result was that the entire schema could be hopelessly messed up. The best result was that the VIEW VA in step 3 was not the VIEW VA in step 6, but was still usable.

The SQL-92 standard has added the option of specifying the behavior of any of the DROP statements as either CASCADE or RESTRICT. The RESTRICT option is the default, and it will disallow the dropping of any schema object that is being used to define another object. For example, you cannot drop a base table that has VIEWs defined on it or is part of a referential integrity constraint if RESTRICT is used. The CASCADE option will drop any of the dependent objects from the schema when the original object is removed. Be careful with this! Some products will automatically recompile static SQL when an index is dropped and some will not. However, few products automatically recompile static SQL when an index is added. Furthermore, few products automatically recompile static SQL when the statistical distribution within the data has changed. DEC's Rdb is an exception to this since it investigates possible execution paths when each query is invoked.

The DBA usually has to update the statistical information explicitly and ask for a recompilation. What usually happens is that one person adds an index and then compiles his program. The new index could either hinder or help other queries when they are recompiled, so it is hard to say whether the new index is a good or a bad thing for the overall performance of the system.

However, a situation that is always bad is when two programmers build indexes that are identical in all but name and never tell each other. Most SQL implementations will not detect this. The duplication will waste both time and space. Whenever one index is updated, the other one will have to be updated also. This is one reason that only the DBA should be allowed to create schema objects.

31.14 Temporary Tables Are Handy

Another trick is to use temporary tables to hold intermediate results to avoid CROSS JOINs and excessive recalculations. A materialized VIEW is also a form of temporary table, but you cannot index it. In this problem, we want to find the total amount of the latest balances in all our accounts.

Assume that the Payments table holds the details of each payment and that the payment numbers are increasing over time. The Accounts table shows the account identification number and the balance after each payment is made. The query might be done like this:

```
SELECT SUM(A1.balance)
  FROM Accounts AS A1, Payments AS P1
 WHERE P1.acct = A1.acct
       AND P1.payment_number = (SELECT MAX(payment_number)
                                  FROM Payments AS P2
                                 WHERE P2.acct = A1.acct);
```

Since this uses a correlated subquery with an aggregate function, it will take a little time to run for each row in the answer. It would be faster to create a temporary working table or VIEW like this:

```
BEGIN
CREATE TABLE LastPayments
(acct INTEGER NOT NULL,
 last_payment_number INTEGER NOT NULL,

CREATE INDEX LPX ON LastPayment(acct, payment_number);

INSERT INTO LastPayments
SELECT acct, MAX(payment_number)
  FROM Payments
 GROUP BY acct;

SELECT SUM(A1.balance) -- final answer
  FROM Accounts AS A1, LastPayments AS LP1
 WHERE LP1.acct = A1.acct
   AND LP1.payment_number = A1.payment_number;

DROP TABLE LastPayments;

END;
```

Consider this three-table query that creates a list of combinations of items and all the different packages for which the selling price (price and box cost) is 10% of the warranty plan cost. Assume that any item can fit into any box we have and that any item can be put on any warranty plan.

```
SELECT I1.item
  FROM Inventory AS I1, Packages AS P1, Warranty AS W1
 WHERE I1.price + P1.box = W1.plancost * 10;
```

Since all the columns appear in an expression, the engine cannot use indexes, so the query will become a large CROSS JOIN in most SQL implementations. This query can be broken down into a temporary table that has an index on the calculations, thus:

```
BEGIN
CREATE TABLE SellingPrices
(item CHAR(15) NOT NULL,
 sellprice DECIMAL (8,2) NOT NULL);

-- optional index on the calculation
CREATE INDEX SPX ON SellingPrices(sellprice);

-- do algebra and get everything on one side of an equation
INSERT INTO SellingPrices (item, sellprice)
SELECT DISTINCT I1,item, (P1.box + I1.price) * 0.1
  FROM Inventory AS I1, packages AS P1;

-- do the last join
SELECT DISTINCT SP1. item
  FROM SellingPrices AS SP1, Warranty AS W1
 WHERE SP1.sellprice = W1.plancost;
END;
```

Readings and Resources

General References

Adams, Douglas. 1979. *Hitchhiker's Guide to the Galaxy*. New York: Harmony Books. *ISBN 0-517-54209-9.*

Babbage, Charles. *For information on Charles Babbage, contact the Charles Babbage Institute, University of Minnesota.*

Logic

Boole, George. 1854, 1951. *An Investigation of the Laws of Thought, on Which are Founded the Mathematical Theories of Logic and Probabilities.* New York: Macmillan and Co., 1854. New York: Dover, 1951. *The original is a rare collector's piece, but you can get a reprint of the original 1854 edition (Dover Books, 1951). ISBN 0-486-60028-9.*

Bole, Leonard, and Piotr Borowik. 1993. *Many-Valued Logics.* New York: Springer-Verlag. *ISBN 0-387-55926-4. This book has a whole chapter devoted to three-valued logic systems.*

Celko, Joe. 1992b. "SQL Explorer: Voting Systems." *DBMS* (November).

Mathematical Techniques

Gardner, Martin. 1983. *Wheels, Life, and Other Mathematical Amusements.* New York: W. H. Freeman. *ISBN 0-716-71589-9.*

Huff, Darrell. 1954. *How to Lie with Statistics.* New York: Norton.

Melzak, Z. A. 1983. *Bypasses: A Simple Approach to Complexity.* New York: Wiley-InterScience. *ISBN 0-471-86854-X.*

Mrdalj, Stevan, Branislav Vujovic, and Vladan Jovanovic. 1996. "SQL Matrix Processing." *Database Programming & Design* (August).

Random Numbers

Bays, Carter, and W. E. Sharp. 1992. "Improved Random Numbers for Your Personal Computer or Workstation." *Geobyte* 7(2):25.

Carta, David G. 1990. "Two Fast Implementations of the 'Minimal Standard' Random Number Generator." *Communications of the ACM* 33(1):87.

Chambers, W. G., and Z. D. Dai. 1991. "Simple But Effective Modification to a Multiplicative Congruential Random Number Generator." *IEEE Proceedings: Computers and Digital Technology* 138(3):121.

Chassing, P. 1989. "An Optimal Random Number Generator Zp." *Statistics & Probability Letters* 7(4):307.

Elkins, T.A. 1989. "A Highly Random Number Generator." *Computer Language* 6(12):59.

Hulquist, Paul F. 1991. "A Good Random Number Generator for Microcomputers." *Simulation* 57(4):258.

Kao, Chiang. 1989. "A Random Number Generator for Microcomputers." *OR: The Journal of the Operation Research Society* 40(7):687.

Knuth, Donald. 1981. *Art of Computer Programming, Vol. 2: Seminumeral Algorithms.* 2d ed. Reading, MA: Addison-Wesley, page 29.

Komo, John J. 1991. "Decimal Pseudo-Random Number Generator." *Simulation* 57(4)228.

Lancaster, Don. 1977. *CMOS Cookbook.* Indianapolis, IN: Sams Publishing, page 318.

Leva, Joseph L. 1992a. "A Fast Normal Random Number Generator." *ACM Transactions on Mathematical Software* 18(4):449.

———. 1992b. "Algorithm 712: A Normal Random Number Generator." *ACM Transactions on Mathematical Software* 18(4):454.

Macomber, James H., and Charles S. White. 1990. "An N-Dimensional Uniform Random Number Generator Suitable for IBM-Compatible Microcomputers." *Interfaces* 20(3):49.

Maier, W.L. 1991. "A Fast Pseudo Random Number Generator." *Dr. Dobb's Journal* 17(5):152.

Marsaglia, G., B. Narasimhan, and A. Zaman. 1990. "A Random Number Generator for PCs." *Computer Physics Communications* (60):345-349.

Marsaglia, G., and A. Zaman. 1990. "Toward a Universal Random Number Generator." *Statistics & Probability Letters* (8):35-39.

Morton, Mike. 1985. "A Digital Dissolve for Bit-Mapped Graphics Screens." *Dr. Dobb's Journal* (November):48.

Press, William H., Brian P. Flannery, and William T. Vetterling. 1989. *Numerical Recipes in Pascal: The Art of Scientific Computing.* Cambridge, UK: Cambridge University Press, page 233.

Sezgin, Fatin. 1990. "On a Fast and Portable Uniform Quasi-Random Number Generator." *Simulation* Digest 21(2):30.

Scales and Measurements

Crocker, Linda, and James Algina. 1986. *Introduction to Classical and Modern Test Theory.* Austin, TX: Holt, Rinehart & Winston. *ISBN 0-030-61634-4.*

Missing Values

Codd, E. F. 1975. "Understanding Relations." *FDT* 7:3–4.

Grahne, G. 1989. "Horn Tables—An Efficient Tool for Handling Incomplete Information in Databases." *ACM SIGACT/SIGMOD/SIGART Symposium on Principles of Database Systems:*75–82.

Grant, J. 1977. "Null Values in a Relational Database." *Information Processing Letters* 6(5):156–157.

————. 1979. "Partial Values in a Tabular Database Model." *Information Processing Letters* 9(2):97–99.

Honeyman. 1980. "Functional Dependencies and the Universal Instance Property in the Relational Model of Database Systems." (Ph.D dissertation, Princeton University).

Lien. 1979. "Multivalued Dependencies with Null Values in Relational Databases." *Proceedings of the Fifth International Conference on Very Large Databases.* New York: ACM; Piscataway, NJ: IEEE.

Lipski, W. 1981."On Databases with Incomplete Information." *Journal of the ACM* 28 (1):41–70.

————. 1981. "On Semantic Issues Connected with Incomplete Information." *ACM Transactions on Database Systems* (September):262–296.

McGoveran, David. 1993. "Nothing from Nothing Part I (or, What's Logic Got to Do with It?)." *Database Programming & Design* 6(12):32. *A four-part series on missing values that argues against the SQL style* NULL *in favor of indicators.*

————. 1994a. "Nothing from Nothing Part II: Classical Logic: Nothing Compares 2 U." *Database Programming & Design* 7(1):54.

————. 1994b. "Nothing from Nothing Part III: Can't Lose What You Never Had." *Database Programming & Design* 7(2):42.

————. 1994c. "Nothing from Nothing Part IV: It's in the Way That You Use It." *Database Programming & Design* 7(3):54.

Rozenshtein, David. 1981. "Implementing Null Values in Relations." (unpublished, May).

————. 1995. *Optimizing Transact-SQL: Advanced Programming Techniques.* Fremont, CA: SQL Forum Press. *ISBN 0-964-98120-3.*

SPARC Study Group on Database Management Systems. 1975. "Interim Report 75-02-08 to the ANSI X3." *FDT-Bulletin* ACM SIGMOD 7(2).

Vassiliou, Y. 1979. "Null Values in Database Management—A Denotational Semantics Approach." *ACM SIGMOD Conference Proceedings*:162–169.

————. 1980. "Functional Dependencies and Incomplete Information." *Proceedings of the Sixth International Conference on Very Large Databases.* New York: ACM; Piscataway, NJ: IEEE.

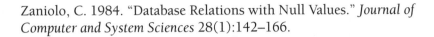

Zaniolo, C. 1984. "Database Relations with Null Values." *Journal of Computer and System Sciences* 28(1):142–166.

Graph Theory

Eve, Shimon. 1979. *Graph Algorithms.* New York: Computer Science Press. *ISBN 0-914-89421-8.*

Fulkerson, D. R., ed. 1975. *Studies in Graph Theory, Vols. 1 & 2.* Providence, RI: American Mathematical Association. *ISBN 0-883-58111-3* and *ISBN 0-883-58112-3.*

Harary, Frank. 1972. *Graph Theory.* Reading, MA: Addison-Wesley. *ISBN 0-201-02787-9.*

McHugh, James A. 1990. *Algorithmic Graph Theory.* Englewood Cliffs, NJ: Prentice Hall. *ISBN 0-130-23615-2.*

Ore, Oystein (revised by Robin J. Wilson). 1990. *Graphs and Their Uses.* Providence, RI: American Mathematical Association. *ISBN 0-883-58635-2.*

Introductory SQL Books

Atzeni, Paolo, and Valeria De Antonellis. 1993. *Relational Database Theory.* Redwood City, CA: Benjamin/Cummings. *ISBN 0-805-30261-1.*

Codd, E. F. 1990. *The Relational Model for Database Management: Version 2.* Reading, MA: Addison-Wesley.

Date, C. J. 1983. *Database, A Primer.* Reading, MA: Addison-Wesley. *ISBN 0-201-11358-9.*

———. 1995. *An Introduction to Database Systems, Vols. 1 & 2.* 6th ed. Reading, MA: Addison-Wesley. *ISBN 0-201-51381-1* and *ISBN 0-201-14474-3.*

Groff, James R., and Paul N. Weinberg. 1994. *LAN Times Guide to SQL.* New York: McGraw-Hill. *ISBN 0-078-82026-X.*

Gruber, Martin. 1990. *Understanding SQL.* Alameda, CA: Sybex. *ISBN 0-895-88644-8.*

Lorie, Raymond A., and Jean-Jacques Daudenarde. 1991. *SQL and Its Applications.* Englewood Cliffs, NJ: Prentice Hall. *ISBN 0-138-37956-4.*

Lusardi, Frank. 1988. *The Database Expert's Guide to SQL.* New York: McGraw-Hill. *ISBN 0-070-39002-9.*

Pascal, Fabian. 1989. *SQL and Relational Basics.* New York: M&T Books.

————. 1993. *Understanding Relational Databases.* New York: M&T Books. *ISBN 0-471-58538-6.*

Shasha, Dennis E. 1992. *Database Tuning: A Principled Approach.* Englewood Cliffs, NJ: Prentice Hall. *ISBN 0-132-05246-6.*

Stonebraker, Michael. 1998. *Readings in Database Systems.* 3d ed. San Francisco: Morgan Kaufmann. *ISBN 1-55860-523-1.*

Trimble, Harvey, and David Chappel. 1989. *A Visual Introduction to SQL.* New York: John Wiley. *ISBN 0-471-61684-2.*

van der Lans, Rick F. 1989. *The SQL Standard: A Complete Reference Guide.* Englewood Cliffs, NJ: Prentice Hall International. Schoonhaven: Academic Service. *ISBN 0-138-40059-8.*

Wellesley Software Group. 1991. *Learning SQL.* Englewood Cliffs, NJ: Prentice Hall. *ISBN 0-135-28704-9.*

————. 1992. *Learning Advanced SQL.* Englewood Cliffs, NJ: Prentice Hall. *ISBN 0-135-28712-X.*

Optimizing Queries

Gulutzan, Peter, and Trudy Pelzer. 1994. *Optimizing SQL: Embedded SQL in C.* Lawrence, KS: R&D Publications. *ISBN 0-131-00215-5.*

Shasha, Dennis E. 1992. *Database Tuning: a Principled Approach.* Englewood Cliffs, NJ: Prentice Hall. *ISBN 0-132-05246-6.*

Temporal Data and the Year 2000 Problem

ANSI X3. 1985, 1991. "Representation for Calendar Date and Ordinal Date for Information Interchange." 30-1985 (R-1991). New York: American National Standards Institute. *This publication is two pages and costs $14 plus $4 handling.*

————. 1994. "Information Systems—Representations of Universal Time, Local Time Differentials, and United States Time Zone References for Information Interchange." *51-1994.* New York: American National Standards Institute. *This publication costs $15 plus $4 handling.*

Arnold, Robert S. 1995a. "Millennium Now: Solutions for Century Data Change Impact." *Application Development Trends* (January).

———. 1995b. "Resolving Year 2000 Problems in Legacy Software." Presentation at Software Quality Week, June, San Francisco.

Associated Press. 1995. "Troubled Time" (May 25).

Celko, Joe. 1981. "Father Time Software Secrets Allows Updating of Dates." *Information Systems News* (February).

Cini, Al. 1995. "System Bug of the Apocalypse." *Internetwork* (January).

Cohn, Michael B. "No Need to Fear the Year 2000." *ComputerWorld*.

Fine, Doug. 1995. "Companies Brace for Millennium." *Infoworld* (April 10).

Furman, Jeff, Albert Marotta, and Cliff Candiotti. 1995. "Party When It's 1999." *Software Magazine* (April).

Hayes, Brian. 1995. "Waiting for 01-01-00." *American Scientist* 83 (January-February).

Hitchens, Randall L. 1991. "Viewpoint." *ComputerWorld* (January).

ISO. 1988. "Data Elements and Interchange Formats—Information Interchange—Representation of Dates and Times." *ISO 8601:1988.* New York: American National Standards Institute. *This publication is 14 pages and costs $48 plus $5 handling.*

Ross, Noah. 1995. "The End of the Century is Nearer than You Think." *Application Development Trends* (April).

Rubin, Howard, and Jim Woodward. [n.d.] "Millennium: A Billion Dollar Software Crisis." Videotape. The Computer Channel Inc.

Sullivan, R. Lee. 1995. "Ghosts in the Machines." *Forbes* (June 19).

Tantzen, Robert G. 1980. "Algorithm 199: Conversion between Calendar Date and Julian Day Number." *Collected Algorithms from the ACM.* New York: Association for Computing Machinery.

Xenakis, John. 1995. "The Millenium Bug: The Fin De Siecle Computer Virus." *CFO Magazine* (July).

Books

Murray, Jerome T., and Marilyn J. Murray. 1984. *Computers in Crisis: How to Avert the Coming Worldwide Computer Systems Collapse.* New York: Petrocelli Books. *ISBN 0-894-33223-6. A solution, with code, for the Year 2000 problem.*

Zerubavel, Eviatar. 1985. *The Seven Day Circle.* New York: The Free Press. ISBN 0-029-34680-0. *A history of the week in different calendar systems.*

Newsletters

Tick, Tick, Tick Newsletter. Box #020538, Brooklyn, NY 11202.

SQL Programming Techniques

Celko, Joe. 1992a. "Implementing T-Joins in SQL Queries." *DBMS* (March).

————. 1993. "Views: More than Meets the Eye." *Database Programming & Design* (September). Citing Nelson Mattos, from an ANSI X3H2 paper.

Celko, Joe, and C. J. Date. 1993. "Access Path: Lauds and Lectures, Kudos and Critiques." *Database Programming & Design* (September):9 (letter to the editor).

Classics

Codd, E. F. 1970. "A Relational Model of Data for Large Shared Data Banks." *Communications of the ACM* 13(6):377-87. New York: Association for Computing Machinery.

Comer, D. 1978. "The Difficulty of Optimum Index Selection." *ACM Transactions on Database Systems* 3(4):440-5.

Damerau, F. J. 1964. "A Technique for Computer Detection of Correction of Spelling Errors." *Communications of the ACM* 7(3).

Date, C. J. 1992a. "According to Date: Shedding Some Light." *Database Programming & Design* (February):15-7.

Goodman, Nathan. 1990. "VIEW Update is Practical." *InfoDB* 5(2).

Information Systems Week (ISW). 1987. "Code Overload Plagues NYC Welfare System." *Information Systems Week* (December).

Limeback, Rudy. [n.d.] "SQL Workshop Challenge." *Explain* (18). Undated publication; no.18 issued 1991-1993.

Lorie, Raymond A., and Jean-Jacques Daudenarde. 1991. *SQL and Its Applications.* Englewood Cliffs, NJ: Prentice Hall.

Martinis, Miljenko. 1992. *DBMS* (May) (letters column).

Melton, Jim, and Alan R. Simon. 1993. *Understanding the New SQL: A Complete Guide.* San Francisco: Morgan Kaufmann. *ISBN 1-55860-245-3.*

Murchison, Rory. [n.d.] "SQL Workshop Challenge." *Explain* (16). Undated publication; no.16 issued 1991-1993.

Paitetsky-Shapiro, G. 1983. "The Optimal Selection of Secondary Indexes in NP-Complete." *SIGMOD Record* 13(2):72-75.

Palmer, Roger. 1994. *The Bar Code Book.* Peterborough, NH: Helmer's Publishing. *ISBN 0-911-261-09-5.*

Philips, Lawrence. 1990. "Hanging on the Metaphone. (A Phonetic Text-Retrieval Algorithm Better than Soundex)." *Computer Language* 7(12):38.

Rozenshtein, David, Anatoly Abramovich, and Eugene Birger. 1993. "Loop-Free SQL Solutions for Finding Continuous Regions." *SQL Forum* 2(6).

Smithwick, Terry. 1991. Pascal version of Lawrence Philips' Metaphone. CompuServe. *CLMFORUM.* Originally published by Lawrence Philips. 1990. "Hanging on the Metaphone. (A Phonetic Text-Retrieval Algorithm Better than Soundex)." *Computer Language* 7(12):38.

SQL Forum. 1993, 1994. *SQL Forum.* See articles by Anatoly Abramovich, Yelena Alexandrova, and Eugene Birger (July/August 1993, March/April 1994).

Stevens, S. S. 1957. "On the Psychophysical Law." *Psychological Review* 64:153-81.

Tillquist, John, and Feng-Yang Kuo. 1989. "An Approach to the Recursive Retrieval Problem in the Relational Database." *Communications of the ACM* 32(2):239.

van der Lans, Rick F. 1991. "SQL Portability." *The Relational Journal* 2(6).

Verhoeff, J. 1969. "Error Detecting Decimal Codes." *Mathematical Centre Tract #29.* Amsterdam: The Mathematical Centre.

Vicik, Rick. 1993. "Advanced Transact SQL." *SQL Forum* (July/August).

Wankowski, Jim. [n.d.] "SQL Workshop Solutions." *Explain* (17). Undated publication; no.17 issued 1991-1993.

Yozallinas, J. R. 1981. *Tech Specialist* (May) (letters column).

Updatable Views

Codd, E. F. 1990. "RV-6 VIEW Updating." *The Relational Model for Database Management: Version 2.* Reading, MA: Addison-Wesley. *ISBN 0-201-14192-2.*

Date, C. J. 1986. "Updating VIEWs." *Relational Database: Selected Writings.* Reading, MA: Addison-Wesley. *ISBN 0-201-14196-5.*

Date, C. J., and Hugh Darwen. 1992. "Role of Functional Dependencies in Query Decomposition." *Relational Database: Writings, 1989–1991.* Reading, MA: Addison-Wesley. *ISBN 0-201-54303-6.*

Goodman, Nathan. 1990. "VIEW Update is Practical." *InfoDB* 5(2).

Umeshar, Dayal, and P. A. Bernstein. 1982. "On the Correct Translation of Update Operations on Relational VIEWs." *ACM Transactions on Database Systems* 7(3).

Theory, Normalization, and Advanced Database Topics

Bernstein, P. A. 1976. "Synthesizing Third Normal Form Relations from Functional Dependencies." *ACM Transactions on Database Systems* 1(4):277-298.

Codd. E. F. 1990. *The Relational Model for Database Management: Version 2.* Reading, MA: Addison-Wesley.

Date, C. J. 1986. *Relational Database: Selected Writings.* Reading, MA: Addison-Wesley. *ISBN 0-201-14196-5.*

———. 1990. *Relational Database: Writings, 1985-1989.* Reading, MA: Addison-Wesley. *ISBN 0-201-50881-8.*

———. 1992. *Relational Database: Writings, 1989-1991.* Reading, MA: Addison-Wesley. *ISBN 0-201-54303-6.*

———. 1995. *Relational Database: Writings, 1991-1994.* Reading, MA: Addison-Wesley. *ISBN 0-201-82459-0.*

Dutka, Alan, and Howard Hanson. 1989. *Fundamentals of Data Normalization.* Reading, MA: Addison-Wesley. *ISBN 0-201-06645-9.*

Fagin, Ron. 1979. "Normal Forms and Relational Database Operators." *Proceedings ACM SIGMOD International Conference on Management of Data* (May). *This is the definitive paper on the five normal forms.*

Fleming, Candace C., and Barbara von Halle. 1989. *Handbook for Relational Database Design.* Reading, MA: Addison-Wesley. *ISBN 0-201-11434-8.*

Kent, William. 1983. "A Simple Guide to Five Normal Forms in Relational Database Theory." *Communications of the ACM* 26(2).

Maier, David. 1983. *The Theory of Relational Databases.* New York: Computer Science Press. *ISBN 0-914-89442-0.*

Teorey, Toby J. 1994. *Database Modeling and Design: The Fundamental Principles.* 2d ed. San Francisco: Morgan Kaufmann. *ISBN 1-55860-294-1.*

Books on SQL-92

Cannan, Stephen, and Gerard Otten. 1992. SQL: *The Standard Handbook.* New York: McGraw-Hill. *ISBN 0-077-07664-8.*

Date, C. J., and Hugh Darwen. 1993. *A Guide to the SQL Standard.* Reading, MA: Addison-Wesley. *ISBN 0-201-55822-X.*

Gruber, Martin. 1990. *Understanding SQL.* Alameda, CA: Sybex. *ISBN 0-895-88644-8.*

————. 1994. SQL *Instant Reference.* Alameda, CA: Sybex. *ISBN 0-782-11148-3.*

Melton, Jim, and Alan R. Simon. 1993. *Understanding the New SQL: A Complete Guide.* San Francisco: Morgan Kaufmann. *ISBN 1-55860-245-3.*

Standards and Related Groups

For ANSI and ISO standards

American National Standards Institute
1430 Broadway
New York, NY 10018
phone: (212) 354-3300

Director of Publications
American National Standards Institute
11 West 42nd Street
New York, NY 10036
phone: (212) 642-4900

Copies of the SQL-92 document and other ANSI documents can be purchased from

> Global Engineering Documents Inc.
> 2805 McGaw Avenue
> Irvine, CA 92714
> phone: (800) 854-7179

Other consortiums are

> X/Open
> 1010 El Camino Real #380
> Menlo Park, CA 94025
> phone : (415) 323-7992

> NIST (National Institute for Standards and Technology)
> Technology A-266
> Gaithersberg, MD 20899
> Attn: FIPS-127 test suites
> phone: (301) 975-2000

> TPC Council
> c/o Shanley Public Relations
> 777 North First Street #600
> San Jose, CA 95112-6113
> phone: (408) 295-8894

> Object Management Group
> 492 Old Connecticut Path
> Framingham, MA 01701
> phone: (508) 820-4300

Web Sites Related to SQL

The SQL home page is maintained by one of the X3H2 Committee members at

> *www.jjc.com/sql_stnd.html*

You can also get help with queries and technical stuff at

> *www.inquiry.com/techtips/thesqlpro/index.html*

REFERENCES

ACM (Association for Computing Machinery). 1980. "Algorithm 199." *Collected Algorithms from the ACM.* New York: Association for Computing Machinery.

Adams, Douglas. 1979. *Hitchhiker's Guide to the Galaxy.* New York: Harmony Books. ISBN 0-517-54209-9.

ANSI X3. 1985, 1991. "Representation for Calendar Date and Ordinal Date for Information Interchange." *30-1985* (R-1991). New York: American National Standards Institute.

———. 1994. "Information Systems—Representations of Universal Time, Local Time Differentials, and United States Time Zone References for Information Interchange." *51–1994.* New York: American National Standards Institute.

Arnold, Robert S. 1995a. "Millennium Now: Solutions for Century Data Change Impact." *Application Development Trends* (January).

———. 1995b. "Resolving Year 2000 Problems in Legacy Software." Presentation at Software Quality Week, June, San Francisco.

Associated Press. 1995. "Troubled Time" (May 25).

Atzeni, Paolo, and Valeria De Antonellis. 1993. *Relational Database Theory.* Menlo Park, CA: Benjamin/Cummings. ISBN 0-805-30261-1.

Bays, Carter, and W. E. Sharp. 1992. "Improved Random Numbers for Your Personal Computer or Workstation." *Geobyte* 7(2):25.

Beech, David. 1989. "New Life for SQL." *Datamation* (January).

Bernstein, P. A. 1976. "Synthesizing Third Normal Form Relations from Functional Dependencies." *ACM Transactions on Database Systems* 1(4):277-298.

Bole, Leonard, and Piotr Borowik. 1993. *Many-Valued Logics.* New York: Springer-Verlag. ISBN 0-387-55926-4.

Boole, George. 1854, 1951. *An Investigation of the Laws of Thought, on Which are Founded the Mathematical Theories of Logic and Probabilities.* New York: Macmillan and Co., 1854. New York: Dover, 1951 (reprint of 1854 edition—ISBN 0-486-60028-9).

Cannan, Stephen, and Gerard Otten. *1992. SQL: The Standard Handbook.* New York: McGraw-Hill. ISBN 0-077-07664-8.

Carta, David G. 1990. "Two Fast Implementations of the 'Minimal Standard' Random Number Generator." *Communications of the ACM* 33(1):87.

Celko, Joe. 1981. "Father Time Software Secrets Allows Updating of Dates." *Information Systems News* (February).

———. 1992a. "Implementing T-Joins in SQL Queries." *DBMS* (March).

———. 1992b. "SQL Explorer: Voting Systems." *DBMS* (November).

———. 1993. "Views: More than Meets the Eye." *Database Programming & Design* (September). Citing Nelson Mattos, from an ANSI X3H2 paper.

———. 1997. *Joe Celko's SQL Puzzles and Answers.* San Francisco: Morgan Kaufmann. ISBN 1-55860-453-7.

———. 1999. *Joe Celko's Data and Databases: Concepts in Practice.* San Francisco: Morgan Kaufmann. ISBN 1-55860-452-4.

Celko, Joe, and C. J. Date. 1993. "Access Path: Lauds and Lectures, Kudos and Critiques." *Database Programming & Design* (September):9 (letter to the editor).

CFO. 1991. *CFO* (July): editorial.

Chambers, W. G., and Z. D. Dai. 1991. "Simple But Effective Modification to a Multiplicative Congruential Random Number Generator." *IEEE Proceedings: Computers and Digital Technology* 138(3):121.

Chassing, P. 1989. "An Optimal Random Number Generator Zp." *Statistics & Probability Letters* 7(4):307.

Cini, Al. 1995. "System Bug of the Apocalypse." *Internetwork* (January).

Codd, E. F. 1970. "A Relational Model of Data for Large Shared Data Banks." *Communications of the ACM* 13(6):377-387. New York: Association for Computing Machinery.

————. 1975. "Understanding Relations." FDT 7:3–4.

————. 1989. "The Need for Duplicate Rows in Tables." *Datamation* (January).

————. 1990. "RV-6 VIEW Updating." *The Relational Model for Database Management: Version 2.* Reading, MA: Addison-Wesley. ISBN 0-201-14192-2.

Cohn, Michael B. [n.d.] "No Need to Fear the Year 2000." *ComputerWorld.*

Comer, D. 1978. "The Difficulty of Optimum Index Selection." *ACM Transactions on Database Systems* 3(4):440–445.

Crocker, Linda, and James Algina. 1986. *Introduction to Classical and Modern Test Theory.* Austin, TX: Holt, Rinehart & Winston. ISBN 0-030-61634-4.

Damerau, F. J. 1964. "A Technique for Computer Detection of Correction of Spelling Errors." *Communications of the ACM* 7(3).

Date, C. J. 1983. *Database, A Primer.* Reading, MA: Addison-Wesley. ISBN 0-201-11358-9.

————. 1986. "Updating VIEWs." *Relational Database: Selected Writings.* Reading, MA: Addison-Wesley. ISBN 0-201-14196-5.

————. 1990. *Relational Database: Writings, 1985-1989.* Reading, MA: Addison-Wesley, page 227. ISBN 0-201-50881-8.

————. 1992a. "According to Date: Shedding Some Light." *Database Programming & Design* (February):15–17.

————. 1992b. *Relational Database: Writings, 1989-1991.* Reading, MA: Addison-Wesley. ISBN 0-201-54303-6.

————. 1995a. *An Introduction to Database Systems, Vols. 1 & 2.* 6th ed. Reading, MA: Addison-Wesley. ISBN 0-201-51381-1 & ISBN 0-201-14474-3.

————. 1995b. *Relational Database: Writings, 1991-1994.* Reading, MA: Addison-Wesley. ISBN 0-201-82459-0.

Date, C. J., and Hugh Darwen. 1992. "Role of Functional Dependencies in Query Decomposition." *Relational Database: Writings, 1989–1991.* Reading, MA: Addison-Wesley. ISBN 0-201-54303-6.

————. 1993. *A Guide to the SQL Standard.* Reading, MA: Addison-Wesley. ISBN 0-201-55822-X.

Dutka, Alan, and Howard Hanson. 1989. *Fundamentals of Data Normalization.* Reading, MA: Addison-Wesley. ISBN 0-201-06645-9.

Elkins, T.A. 1989. "A Highly Random Number Generator." *Computer Language* 6(12):59.

Eve, Shimon. 1979. *Graph Algorithms*. New York: Computer Science Press. ISBN 0-914-89421-8.

Fagin, Ronald. 1979. "Normal Forms and Relational Database Operators." *Proceedings ACM SIGMOD International Conference on Management of Data* (May).

————. 1981. "A Normal Form for Relational Databases That Is Based on Domains and Keys." *ACM TODS* 6(3).

Fine, Doug. 1995. "Companies Brace for Millennium." *Infoworld* (April 10).

Fleming, Candace C., and Barbara von Halle. 1989. *Handbook for Relational Database Design*. Reading, MA: Addison-Wesley. ISBN 0-201-11434-8.

Fulkerson, D. R., ed. 1975. *Studies in Graph Theory, Vols. 1 & 2*. Providence, RI: American Mathematical Association. ISBN 0-883-58111-3 and ISBN 0-883-58112-3.

Furman, Jeff, Albert Marotta, and Cliff Candiotti. 1995. "Party When It's 1999." *Software Magazine* (April).

Gallagher, Len. 1993. "Access Path." *Database Programming & Design* (May):11–13.

————. 1996. Internal X3H2 paper. New York: American National Standards Institute.

Gardner, Martin. 1983. *Wheels, Life, and Other Mathematical Amusements*. New York: W. H. Freeman. ISBN 0-716-71589-9.

Goodman, Nathan. 1990. "VIEW Update is Practical." *InfoDB* 5(2).

Grahne, G. 1989. "Horn Tables—An Efficient Tool for Handling Incomplete Information in Databases." *ACM SIGACT/SIGMOD/SIGART Symposium on Principles of Database Systems*:75–82.

Grant, J. 1977. "Null Values in a Relational Database." *Information Processing Letters* 6(5):156–157.

————. 1979. "Partial Values in a Tabular Database Model." *Information Processing Letters* 9(2):97–99.

Groff, James R., and Paul N. Weinberg. 1994. *LAN Times Guide to SQL*. New York: McGraw-Hill. ISBN 0-078-82026-X.

Gruber, Martin. 1990. *Understanding SQL*. Alameda, CA: Sybex. ISBN 0-895-88644-8.

————. 1994. *SQL Instant Reference*. Alameda, CA: Sybex. ISBN 0-782-11148-3.

Gulutzan, Peter, and Trudy Pelzer. 1994. *Optimizing SQL: Embedded SQL in C*. Lawrence, KS: R&D Publications. ISBN 0-131-00215-5.

Harary, Frank. 1972. *Graph Theory*. Reading, MA: Addison-Wesley. ISBN 0-201-02787-9.

Hayes, Brian. 1995. "Waiting for 01-01-00." *American Scientist* 83 (January–February).

Hitchens, Randall L. 1991. "Viewpoint." *ComputerWorld* (January).

Honeyman. 1980. "Functional Dependencies and the Universal Instance Property in the Relational Model of Database Systems." (Ph.D dissertation, Princeton University).

Huff, Darrell. 1954. *How to Lie with Statistics.* New York: Norton.

Hulquist, Paul F. 1991. "A Good Random Number Generator for Microcomputers." *Simulation* 57(4):258.

Information Systems Week (ISW). 1987. "Code Overload Plagues NYC Welfare System." *Information Systems Week* (December).

ISO. 1988. "Data Elements and Interchange Formats—Information Interchange—Representation of Dates and Times." *ISO 8601:1988.* New York: American National Standards Institute.

Kao, Chiang. 1989. "A Random Number Generator for Microcomputers." *OR: The Journal of the Operation Research Society* 40(7):687.

Kent, William. 1983. "A Simple Guide to Five Normal Forms in Relational Database Theory." *Communications of the ACM* 26(2).

Knuth, Donald. 1981. *Art of Computer Programming, Vol. 2: Seminumeral Algorithms.* 2d ed. Reading, MA: Addison-Wesley, page 29.

Komo, John J. 1991. "Decimal Pseudo-Random Number Generator." *Simulation* 57(4)228.

Lancaster, Don. 1977. *CMOS Cookbook.* Indianapolis, IN: Sams Publishing, page 318.

Lardner, Dionysus. 1834. *A Treatise on Arithmetic, Practical and Theoretical.* London: Longman, Rees, Orme, Brown, Green, & Longman.

Larsen, Sheryl. 1996. "Powerful SQL: Beyond the Basics." *DB-2 On-Line Magazine* (Winter). *www.db2mag.com/9601lar.htm.*

Leva, Joseph L. 1992a. "A Fast Normal Random Number Generator." *ACM Transactions on Mathematical Software* 18(4):449.

———. 1992b. "Algorithm 712: A Normal Random Number Generator." *ACM Transactions on Mathematical Software* 18(4):454.

Lien. 1979. "Multivalued Dependencies with Null Values in Relational Databases." *Proceedings of the Fifth International Conference on Very Large Databases.* New York: ACM; Piscataway, NJ: IEEE.

Limeback, Rudy. [n.d.] "SQL Workshop Challenge." *Explain* (18). Undated publication; no.18 issued 1991–1993.

Lipski, W. 1981a. "On Databases with Incomplete Information." *Journal of the ACM* 28 (1):41–70.

———. 1981b. "On Semantic Issues Connected with Incomplete Information." *ACM Transactions on Database Systems* (September):262–296.

Lorie, Raymond A., and Jean-Jacques Daudenarde. 1991. *SQL and Its Applications.* Englewood Cliffs, NJ: Prentice Hall. ISBN 0-138-37956-4.

Lusardi, Frank. 1988. *The Database Expert's Guide to SQL.* New York: McGraw-Hill. ISBN 0-070-39002-9.

Macomber, James H., and Charles S. White. 1990. "An *N*-Dimensional Uniform Random Number Generator Suitable for IBM-Compatible Microcomputers." *Interfaces* 20(3):49.

Maier, David. 1983. *The Theory of Relational Databases.* New York: Computer Science Press. ISBN 0-914-89442-0.

Maier, W. L. 1991. "A Fast Pseudo Random Number Generator." *Dr. Dobb's Journal* 17(5):152.

Marsaglia, G., B. Narasimhan, and A. Zaman. 1990. "A Random Number Generator for PCs." *Computer Physics Communications* (60):345-349.

Marsaglia, G., and A. Zaman. 1990. "Toward a Universal Random Number Generator." *Statistics & Probability Letters* (8):35–39.

McFadden, F., J. Hoffer, and M. Prescott. 1998. *Modern Database Management.* 5th ed. Reading, MA: Addison-Wesley.

McGoveran, David. 1993. "Nothing from Nothing Part I (or, What's Logic Got to Do with It?)." *Database Programming & Design* 6(12):32.

———. 1994a. "Nothing from Nothing Part II: Classical Logic: Nothing Compares 2 U." *Database Programming & Design* 7(1):54.

———. 1994b. "Nothing from Nothing Part III: Can't Lose What You Never Had." *Database Programming & Design* 7(2):42.

———. 1994c. "Nothing from Nothing Part IV: It's in the Way That You Use It." *Database Programming & Design* 7(3):54.

McGoveran, David, and C. J. Date. 1992. *Guide to Sybase and SQL Server.* Reading, MA: Addison-Wesley.

McHugh, James A. 1990. *Algorithmic Graph Theory.* Englewood Cliffs, NJ: Prentice Hall. ISBN 0-130-23615-2.

Melton, Jim. 1998. *Understanding SQL's Stored Procedures: A Complete Guide to SQL/PSM*. San Francisco: Morgan Kaufmann. ISBN 1-55860-461-8.

Melton, Jim, and Alan R. Simon. 1993. *Understanding the New SQL: A Complete Guide*. San Francisco: Morgan Kaufmann. ISBN 1-55860-245-3.

Melzak, Z. A. 1983. *Bypasses: A Simple Approach to Complexity*. New York: Wiley-InterScience. ISBN 0-471-86854-X.

Miljenko, Martinis. 1992. *DBMS* (May): letters column.

Morton, Mike. 1985. "A Digital Dissolve for Bit-Mapped Graphics Screens." *Dr. Dobb's Journal* (November):48.

Mrdalj, Stevan, Branislav Vujovic, and Vladan Jovanovic. 1996. "SQL Matrix Processing." *Database Programming & Design* (August).

Murchison, Rory. [n.d.] "SQL Workshop Challenge." *Explain* (16). Undated publication; no.16 issued 1991–1993.

Murray, Jerome T., and Marilyn J. Murray. 1984. *Computers in Crisis: How to Avert the Coming Worldwide Computer Systems Collapse*. New York: Petrocelli Books. ISBN 0-894-33223-6.

Ore, Oystein (revised by Robin J. Wilson). 1990. *Graphs and Their Uses*. Providence, RI: American Mathematical Association. ISBN 0-883-58635-2.

Paitetsky-Shapiro, G. 1983. "The Optimal Selection of Secondary Indexes in NP-Complete." *SIGMOD Record* 13(2):72–75.

Palmer, Roger. 1994. *The Bar Code Book*. Peterborough, NH: Helmer's Publishing. ISBN 0-911-261-09-5.

Park, S. K., and K. W. Miller. 1988. "Random Number Generators: Good Ones Are Hard to Find." *CACM* 31(10):1201.

Pascal, Fabian. 1989. *SQL and Relational Basics*. New York: M&T Books.

———. 1993. *Understanding Relational Databases*. New York: M&T Books. ISBN 0-471-58538-6.

Philips, Lawrence. 1990. "Hanging on the Metaphone. (A Phonetic Text-Retrieval Algorithm Better than Soundex)." *Computer Language* 7(12):38.

Press, William H., Brian P. Flannery, and William T. Vetterling. 1989. *Numerical Recipes in Pascal: The Art of Scientific Computing*. Cambridge, UK: Cambridge University Press, page 233.

Ross, Noah. 1995. "The End of the Century is Nearer than You Think." *Application Development Trends* (April).

Rozenshtein, David. 1981. "Implementing Null Values in Relations." (unpublished, May).

———. 1995. *Optimizing Transact-SQL: Advanced Programming Techniques*. Fremont, CA: SQL Forum Press. ISBN 0-964-98120-3.

Rozenshtein, David, Anatoly Abramovich, and Eugene Birger. 1993. "Loop-Free SQL Solutions for Finding Continuous Regions." *SQL Forum* 2(6).

Rubin, Howard, and Jim Woodward. [n.d.] "Millennium: A Billion Dollar Software Crisis." Videotape. The Computer Channel Inc.

Sezgin, Fatin. 1990. "On a Fast and Portable Uniform Quasi-Random Number Generator." *Simulation Digest* 21(2):30.

Shasha, Dennis E. 1992. *Database Tuning: A Principled Approach*. Englewood Cliffs, NJ: Prentice Hall. ISBN 0-132-05246-6

Smithwick, Terry. 1991. Pascal version of Lawrence Philips' Metaphone. CompuServe. *CLMFORUM*. Originally published by Lawrence Philips. 1990. "Hanging on the Metaphone. (A Phonetic Text-Retrieval Algorithm Better than Soundex)." *Computer Language* 7(12):38.

SPARC Study Group on Database Management Systems. 1975. "Interim Report 75-02-08 to the ANSI X3." *FDT-Bulletin ACM SIGMOD* 7(2).

SQL Forum. 1993, 1994. *SQL Forum*. See articles by Anatoly Abramovich, Yelena Alexandrova, and Eugene Birger (July/August 1993, March/April 1994).

Stevens, S. S. 1957. "On the Psychophysical Law." *Psychological Review* 64:153-181.

Stonebraker, Michael. 1998. *Readings in Database Systems*. 3d ed. San Francisco: Morgan Kaufmann. ISBN: 1-55860-523-1.

Sullivan, R. Lee. 1995. "Ghosts in the Machines." *Forbes* (June 19).

Tantzen, Robert G. 1980. "Algorithm 199: Conversion between Calendar Date and Julian Day Number." *Collected Algorithms from the ACM*. New York: Association for Computing Machinery.

Teorey, Toby J. 1994. *Database Modeling and Design: The Fundamental Principles*. 2d ed. San Francisco: Morgan Kaufmann. ISBN 1-55860-294-1.

Tillquist, John, and Feng-Yang Kuo. 1989. "An Approach to the Recursive Retrieval Problem in the Relational Database." *Communications of the ACM* 32(2):239.

Trimble, Harvey, and David Chappel. 1989. *A Visual Introduction to SQL*. New York: John Wiley. ISBN 0-471-61684-2.

Umeshar, Dayal, and P. A. Bernstein. 1982. "On the Correct Translation of Update Operations on Relational VIEWs." *ACM Transactions on Database Systems* 7(3).

van der Lans, Rick F. 1989. *The SQL Standard: A Complete Reference Guide.* Englewood Cliffs, NJ: Prentice Hall International. Schoonhaven: Academic Service. ISBN 0-138-40059-8.

————. 1991. "SQL Portability." *The Relational Journal* 2(6).

Vassiliou, Y. 1979. "Null Values in Database Management—A Denotational Semantics Approach." *ACM SIGMOD Conference Proceedings*:162–169.

————. 1980. "Functional Dependencies and Incomplete Information." *Proceedings of the Sixth International Conference on Very Large Databases*. New York: ACM; Piscataway, NJ: IEEE.

Verhoeff, J. 1969. "Error Detecting Decimal Codes." *Mathematical Centre Tract #29.* Amsterdam: The Mathematical Centre.

Vicik, Rick. 1993. "Advanced Transact SQL." *SQL Forum* (July/August).

Wankowski, Jim. [n.d.]. "SQL Workshop Solutions." *Explain* (17). Undated publication; no.17 issued 1991-1993.

Wellesley Software Group. 1991. *Learning SQL.* Englewood Cliffs, NJ: Prentice Hall. ISBN 0-135-28704-9.

————. 1992. *Learning Advanced SQL.* Englewood Cliffs, NJ: Prentice Hall. ISBN 0-135-28712-X.

Xenakis, John. 1995. "The Millenium Bug: The Fin De Siecle Computer Virus." *CFO Magazine* (July).

Yozallinas, J. R. 1981. *Tech Specialist* (May): letters column.

Zaniolo, C. 1984. "Database Relations with Null Values." *Journal of Computer and System Sciences* 28(1):142–166.

Zerubavel, Eviatar. 1985. *The Seven Day Circle.* New York: The Free Press. ISBN 0-029-34680-0.

INDEX

ABOUT THE AUTHOR

Joe is an independent consultant based in Atlanta, GA. He is the author of *SQL for Smarties* (1995), *SQL Puzzles and Answers* (1997), and *Data and Databases* (1999) from Morgan Kaufmann Publishers and *Instant SQL Programming* (1997) from Wrox Press. He is a noted consultant, lecturer, teacher, and columnist for *Intelligent Enterprise* and former columnist for *DBMS* and *Database Programming & Design*. He was a member of the ANSI X3H2 Database Standards Committee from 1987 to 1997 and helped write the ANSI/ISO SQL-89 and SQL-92 standards. He is well-known for his dependable help on the DBMS CompuServe Forum and for his use of entertaining anecdotes and war stories to provide real-world insights into SQL programming problems and solutions.